2650

EXPLORING INDIVIDUAL MODERNITY

EXPLORING INDIVIDUAL MODERNITY

ALEX INKELES

*With Contributions by David H. Smith,
Karen A. Miller, Amar K. Singh,
Vern L. Bengston, and James J. Dowd*

COLUMBIA UNIVERSITY PRESS
NEW YORK   1983

Library of Congress Cataloging in Publication Data

Inkeles, Alex, 1920–
Exploring individual modernity.

Bibliography: p.
Includes index.
1. Underdeveloped areas—Social conditions.
2. Civilization, Modern—1950-   . 3. Sociology—
Methodology.   4. Social surveys.   I. Title.
HN980.I545   1983   303.4'4   82-19758
ISBN 0-231-05442-4

Columbia University Press
New York   Guildford, Surrey

Clothbound editions of Columbia University Press books are Smyth-
sewn and printed on permanent and durable acid-free paper.

Contents

List of Charts

List of Tables

Preface

Although this book is, in a sense, a sequel to *Becoming Modern* (1974), it is designed to stand alone as a self-contained report of the findings of the Harvard-Stanford Project on Social and Cultural Aspects of Modernization. The specific role assigned to this volume will, however, be better understood if it is seen in relation to that earlier publication.

The Modernization Project focused on two different models of the modern man. One, called the analytic model, assumed there was a coherent psychosocial syndrome of characteristics which defined individual modernity, including qualities such as a sense of efficacy, openness to new experience, and an interest in planning. The syndrome was summed up in a general measure which we called the OM scale. The theory behind this model, the construction of the scale, and the explanation of the social forces which produced modernity as measured by OM were the more or less exclusive focus of our attention in *Becoming Modern*.

Given its specific focus, *Becoming Modern* did not report our findings concerning many other features of individual modernity which we had grouped in a second model which we called the "topical" model. This approach to individual modernity was more frankly eclectic. Without assuming we would find a consistent syndrome of the sort measured by the OM scale, we explored what was true of the more modern man in developing countries as he approached several different realms of daily social action. These included, among others, local and national politics, decisions about birth control and problems of old age, and personal adjustment in the face of rapid social change. In effect, the topical model concentrated not so much on the personality of the modern man as on his social roles as a member of an ethnic community, the citizen of a nation, the husband and father in a family, and so on.

The special role of this volume is, then, to complete our portrait of the modern man and of the forces which shape him in developing countries by bringing together our explorations of the important dimensions of individual modernity not dealt with in *Becoming Modern*. These studies were previously scattered through a considerable number of different scholarly journals, symposia, and collections, so that only by substantial and determined effort could one have assembled all the pieces. And even then, the pattern of concerns which linked the discrete elements would not have been so readily apparent as we hope they will be in the framework we have provided in this book. I hope, thereby, substantially to augment and enrich the description of the modern man presented in our earlier report.

As the initial results of this research became known, and especially after the publication of *Becoming Modern*, a substantial debate developed concerning the theory of individual modernity, the problems involved in its measurement, and the implications of our approach for an understanding of contemporary and future social change in developing and advanced countries. Our participation in this debate provided an opportunity to deepen, extend, and more fully elaborate the analysis of individual modernity which we had earlier formulated. These amplifications and clarifications of our theoretical orientation and our methodological practice have been included in this volume as a context or frame within which we present the more detailed and concrete studies of discrete aspects of individual modernity.

Finally, to permit this volume to stand alone, I have added materials from several sources which provide a general description of the Modernization Project sufficient to permit readers not familiar with our previous report to orient themselves adequately as to the design and execution of the larger research project of which these explorations constituted an integral part. These elements, as well as all the others previously published, have been edited to facilitate their integration into the structure of this book. In particular, I excised repeated descriptions of the design of the research and the composition of our samples, which would have been obviously redundant. In addition, where appropriate, new introductory and transitional materials have been added. However, so far as the basic data and fundamental conclusions from them are concerned, they have not been altered, except for obvious numerical errors, from the exact form in which they were originally presented.

Numerous individuals and organizations assisted the Modernization Project in various ways intellectual, financial, and administrative, and we acknowledged our debt to a great many of them in our introduction to *Becoming Modern*. Given the continuity of our effort, all of them should be credited for support of this volume as well. In addition, I here express appreciation to some who were not mentioned before, or whose roles in preparing this book were particularly important. Gloria Parks, my administrative assistant, orchestrated work on the manuscript with great good will and liberal contributions of her own time; Priscilla Hopkins generously volunteered the skill and time necessary to edit the first half of the book at a period when the demands of her own doctoral dissertation were quite compelling; and Holly Wunder and Paulette Truman completed that job, as well as preparing the bibliography, so quietly and efficiently that one might easily have failed to realize the intelligence and competence which their contributions reflected. Anna Boberg and Annette Stiger showed patience and good will in dealing with the often frustrating demands of the new technology built into the word processor on which they typed the manuscript. Marie-Jeanne Juilland, Larry Meyer, and Bernadette Inkeles gave valuable assistance in the last stages of the book's preparation.

These services, and many others which made it possible to develop this book, were financed by the Hoover Institution on War, Revolution, and Peace, thanks to the generous and unstinting support of my work by its Director, Dr. W. Glenn Campbell. In addition, at various stages of working on parts of the manuscript I enjoyed the support or facilities of the Van Leer Jerusalem Foundation; the Royal Institute for International Affairs in London; the Institute for Advanced Study at Princeton; the Dorothy Danforth Compton Fellowship; the John Simon Guggenheim Memorial Foundation; and the United States Educational Foundation (Fulbright) in Greece. The encouragement and wise counsel of Charles Webel at Columbia University Press were critical in motivating and sustaining the effort required to complete the book.

Since much of the material in this book is adapted from papers published elsewhere, I am indebted to the original publishers, identified by a footnote at the beginning of each chapter, for permission to utilize material under their respective copyrights. Finally, I express my gratitude to my collaborators, listed on the title page, who co-authored one or more of the original papers on which this book draws. The specific sections to which they contributed are also identified in the footnote introducing each chapter.

INTRODUCTION

CHAPTER 1

Understanding and Misunderstanding Individual Modernity

One can get rather good agreement as to what should be noted on a simple checklist of the important changes in human existence over the last several hundred years: Most everyone's list would include the emergence and florescence of the nation-state; the vast expansion of industry; the mechanization of agriculture; the prominence of science; the spread of bureaucracy; the diffusion of education; the growth of cities; and so on. Although we can get agreement as to the discrete items on the list, every attempt to offer a *general* characterization of all these changes is greeted by a barrage of challenges. Even more dissension is generated by every proposed *explanation* of these phenomena. Marx was surely telling us something terribly important when he urged us to concentrate on the mode of production and the resultant class relations. Nevertheless, Weber has convinced many that the ethic of social action embedded in religious and other transcendent world views impinges significantly on economic behavior. And Sorokin is not readily faulted in his assertion that we have witnessed the displacement of an ideational supercultural system by one of the sensate type. While the debate over these conceptions continued, the phenomena these grand theories confronted have persisted, and many of the trends they identified have deepened and accelerated.

In approaching this process of global change, our generation of sociologists had a number of obvious options. One was to take up one of the grand schemes which were part of our heritage and to apply it to newly emerging phenomena. Another alternative was to emulate one's precursors by devising and promulgating new overarching systems, as Talcott

Adapted from Alex Inkeles, "Understanding and Misunderstanding Individual Modernity," in Lewis A. Coser and Otto N. Larsen, eds., *The Uses of Controversy in Sociology* (New York: The Free Press, 1976), pp. 103-30.

Parsons did with his "pattern variables." We found neither course suitable. The grand schemes of the past seemed too much like actual or potential orthodoxies, and in an era committed to the end of ideologies, one eschewed orthodoxies. Moreover, critical analysis and more systematic research made us aware of how limited were the perspectives, implicit or explicit, adopted by both the classic models and the newer general systems.

A new spirit was abroad in the sixties which was more eclectic, less ideological, more interdisciplinary. The lead was taken by economists in the study of what they called development or growth. Relying heavily on factor analysis, they sought to identify the common socioeconomic characteristics of the "advanced" countries, and to discover the common paths, if any, that had led to economic growth. Political scientists concentrated their attention on the development of the nation state. Anthropologists looked at the process as one of acculturation and community development. Population experts studied the demographic transition. Psychologists delineated personality characteristics they assumed to be critical in fostering entrepreneurial behavior or measured the psychic adjustment of the individual exposed to rapid change.[1]

Each discipline was, of course, studying but one aspect of a larger process of social change which was widely diffused and deeply penetrating. For a decade or so during the fifties, economists played the primary role in research in this field and their concept, "economic development," served as the rubric under which other aspects of the problem were subsumed. But as other disciplines turned their attention to the issues, and other dimensions of social life came under scrutiny, there was an obvious need for a more general term which would better reflect the wide range of institutions under study and the diverse disciplinary perspectives being brought to bear. Throughout the sixties the term "modernization" gained increasing currency and came to be widely accepted as the general designation for the process of common interest for numerous social scientists.[2] Society and institutions were then regularly characterized as more or less modern, and a polarity delineated between "modern" and "traditional" systems and their components.[3]

The total body of research on modernization is organized around a series of discrete foci of analysis. Most of the work is concerned with the institutional level. The investigators ask what are the institutional forms characteristic of more developed nations, or they interrelate the degree of change in one realm, say industry, with that in another, such as education.[4] A minority, however, have concerned themselves with the place of the *individual* in the process of modernization. They study the characteristics of individuals in relation to the properties of institutions and societies. Among those focusing on such system-person relations, several different lines of work may be discerned. One set of studies concerns itself with the process of psychosocial change and adaptation in individuals as they come increasingly into contact with modern institutions and participate in the socioeconomic and political roles characteristic of more modern societies.

A number of sociologists and social psychologists have addressed themselves to this process, and they have generated a substantial body of empirical research.[5] Although some of this work is richly informative, many basic issues continue unresolved. Indeed, the study of individual modernity in its relation to social change has generated more than its share of misunderstandings as to what researchers are trying to do, what they have found out, and what their findings mean. We hope we may reduce this misunderstanding by setting down our answers to some ten questions which are frequently asked about research on individual modernity.[6]

1. *Why Study the Individual? Doesn't the Nature of the Social System Determine the Characteristics of the Individuals in It?*

Whether one studies individuals or institutions and social systems is partly a matter of sheer taste. For some, social change means more or less exclusively institutional and system change. Either they have no interest in the individual, or they feel that some other discipline should concern itself with the personal aspect of the change process. To take this stand is to adopt a narrow definition of the proper scope of sociology, and one at variance with some of the major tendencies of the sociological tradition. But as a matter of taste the position simply cannot be argued. All one can say is that others feel that the study of individuals is obviously important in its own right, and should be dealt with by sociologists.

One has, however, gone beyond matters of taste when one asserts that it is, after all, the social system which determines the nature of the individual. That is a testable proposition. Moreover, we may concede the general proposition, which obviously must in some degree be true, without at all concluding the discussion. Much more interesting than the general statement is its specification. We want to know what aspects of the social system change which individuals, in which respects, at which speed, and under what conditions?

If, in fact, the social system simply and totally determined the charactertistics of the individuals in it, we should be able to state those characteristics with precision solely on the basis of knowing the nature of the social system and the position of the person in it. But, as many a social scientist has discovered to his chagrin, he can perform this feat very imperfectly if he can perform it at all.[7] The basic starting point of research on individual modernity is that the relation of social structure and personal attributes is *problematic*. Whatever their other differences in emphasis, the common concern of the scholars who have done research on individual modernity has been to test empirically the widespread assumptions about the relations of social systems to the personal attributes of the individuals whose properties those systems presumably "determine." The special responsibility of the scholars involved has been to specify the concrete indicators of social structure and the exact personal attributes which should be measured; to measure those features in research designs which are relevant to theoretical concerns; and to interpret the findings with the objective of confirming, or disconfirming, revising, and extending the original theory.

Neither the general desire to test the theory that social structure determines personality, nor the urge to specify more precisely the scope of the theory's application, should be interpreted as a challenge to it, and even less as a rejection. On the contrary, in my experience virtually all those working within the framework sketched above believe that what we find in individuals does, in good part, reflect the nature of the social system they live in and their particular statuses within that system.[8] Moreover, commitment to studying the individual in the modernization process implies no automatic judgment as to either the primacy or the relative importance of the individual as against the system. In fact, the majority of those studying individual change actually see it as more caused by than causing institutional modernity, and in explaining the variance in levels of societal modernity they usually assign much greater weight to historical, economic, or political factors than to the impact of modern personalities.[9]

2. *Should Changes in "Objective" Status Characteristics or in "Subjective" Personality Attributes Be the Focus of Attention?*

If by a modern person is meant someone with a particular set of socioeconomic characteristics, such as "employment in industry rather than agriculture" or "urban rather than rural residence," then it follows that to assess how far individual modernity is determined by changes in the socioeconomic system (SES), one should indeed trace changes in the distribution of this type of socioeconomic attribute *in individuals* as correlated with prior *social system* changes. In some instances, such measurement may highlight issues of considerable importance.[10] In most cases, however, individual characteristics of the objective SES type only express in another form what we already know from the aggregate system level statistics.

An attractive alternative, therefore, is to define individual modernity exclusively in terms of psychosocial attributes—as values, orientations, opinions, and action propensities. This has the obvious advantage of eliminating the redundance and circularity built into many measures taken at the individual level. Thus, it is true by definition that if a nation has become "predominantly urban," then at least 50 percent of its citizens will be found to be "urban residents." But it is by no means true by definition that in a predominantly urban country, the majority of its citizens must be more efficacious or feel more alienated.

Building such presumed outcomes of the process of modernization into the definition of individual modernity precludes testing the most important proposition. Thus, in the otherwise illuminating research of Daniel Lerner, the definition and classification of individuals as "modern," "transitional," or "traditional" simultaneously took into account the individuals' social characteristics *and* their scores on a test of empathy. This made it impossible to tell with any precision whether and how far empathy, seen as a *subjective* outcome, had resulted from changed *objective* conditions such as exposure to education, urban residence, and mass media exposure, since these other variables were also built into the general index of individual modernity.[11] To facilitate testing the relation between the facts of social structure and the properties of individuals, a series of investigators have all defined the modern individual exclusively in psychosocial terms. This approach has been common to the work of Armer and Youtz (1971), Doob (1960), Dawson (1967), Galtung (1971), Guthrie (1970), Inkeles and Smith (1974) and most users of the OM scale, Kahl (1968) and those who use his modernization scale, Klineberg (1973), and Stephenson (1968).

Here, again, it needs to be emphasized that merely by focusing on attitudes, values, needs, and modes of acting we do not prejudice the question as to whether such qualities lead to, or are merely determined by, socioeconomic status. In fact, most of the research in this field starts with the assumption that it is status which determines personality rather than the reverse.[12]

3. *Which Psychosocial Characteristics Should Define an Individual as Modern?*

So long as we are still operating at the level of definition, the decision is, of course, a matter of preference. In deciding which psychosocial qualities of individuals should be the focus of one's attention, one may be guided by a theory, by one's special purpose in a particular research, by one's reading of the empirical evidence so far collected, or by observation, casual or systematic, of real people in natural settings. Durkheimian analysis might lead you to expect anomie; Marxian thinking might point to alienation; a Freudian perspective could suggest high levels of anxiety; and a Parsonian view would focus on qualities such as affective neutrality. Being interested in the role of mass communication in the modernization process, Lerner (1958) selected as the key personal quality the holding of opinions, while Rogers (1969), concerned about the productivity of peasants, emphasized the importance of innovativeness and the adoption of new technology in agriculture.

The Project on the Social and Cultural Aspects of Economic Development, initiated at Harvard and continued at Stanford University, set itself the task of explaining that process whereby people move from being traditional to becoming modern personalities, hence the title of our first book, *Becoming Modern*. We looked at six developing nations: Argentina, Chile, India, Israel, Nigeria, and East Pakistan (now Bangladesh). Our main objective was to attain greater understanding of a vitally important social process. But we entertained as well some hope that from this scientific understanding might come some increase in our ability to select wise and effective policies to guide national development.

In the Harvard-Stanford six-nation study we were guided by a particular theoretical perspective. In most general terms, the main purpose of the research was to test whether, where, and how far individuals come to incorporate as personal attributes qualities which are analogous to or derive from the organizational properties of the institutions and the roles in which these individuals are regularly and deeply involved. To give this model greater specificity we selected the factory as the embodiment of one major type of modern institution, so that our general question could be rephrased more concretely as follows: "What are some of the personal qualities which extended employment in a factory might inculcate in individuals who moved into such service after growing up in the typical agricultural village of one of the less developed countries?"[13]

From an analysis of factory characteristics such as the use of inanimate power, the extensive division of labor, the system for allocating working time, the technical hierarchy, and so on, we derived a set of qualities which we assumed would likely be "learned" and incorporated as personal attributes by men engaged in factory work. Among the qualities we expected under these conditions were: a sense of personal efficacy; openness to new experience; respect for science and technology; acceptance of the necessity for strict scheduling of time; and a positive orientation toward planning ahead. Each of these characteristics we then designated as components in our definition of the modern man conceived in psycho-social terms.

To this first set of personal qualities we added a second, derived on a different basis, following a "social demand" model. The roles which the citizen of a modern large-scale, industrial, urban social system is expected to play presumably require, or at least favor, his having certain personal attributes. In the political realm, for example, the modern polity, whether in a capitalist democracy or a socialist dictatorship of the proletariat, expects individuals to be participant citizens, that is, to take an interest in the news, to identify with the national system as against more local, parochial, or primordial ties, to be active in voting, campaigning, rallying, and so on. We applied the same mode of analysis to other institutions and the roles associated with them. For example, in the family realm we defined as more modern the insistence on selecting one's own spouse rather than accepting a wife chosen by one's parents or other "elders," the preference for small rather than large families, the willingness to practice birth control, and the actual limitation of family size as against the passive acceptance of "whatever number of children God might send."

The result of this series of analyses was a list of some twenty-four main themes, each delineating a dimension which we considered part of the larger set of qualities defining individual modernity. These themes are listed in chart 2-1 of chapter 2. Long as it was, the list was certainly not exhaustive. It reflected a definite theoretical position, which we believe it should have, since that permitted testing whether certain explicit expectations underlying the definition were sound.

A challenge often put to such a definition is that is excludes the possibility of testing other assumptions which, if granted, would place the matter under investigation in a different light. For example, it may be argued that our definition highlighted the "positive" qualities of the modern man, but failed to acknowledge how far he was also alienated, under psychic stress, and unfaithful to his obligations to kith and kin.

There are two responses possible to such a challenge. One can say, and quite properly, that it is not the obligation of a researcher to test someone else's theory. If others believe that men who are otherwise modern are likely also to be alienated, distressed, and unreliable, it is incumbent on them to test the assumption. There is, however, an alternative response, which we on the Harvard-Stanford project adopted: One can accept the challenge, and oneself test the externally given assumptions. Following this principle, we introduced into our interview measures of political participation, anomie, alienation, psychic adjustment, and readiness to fulfill conventional obligations to kith and kin. Many of the explorations of individual modernity described in this book deal with those measures. Thus, although we do not include those qualities in our formal definition of the modern man, our field work created the basis for testing not only our own assumptions, but also others not made by us.

In actual fact, the personal qualities defined as modern in many different researches show a remarkable degree of overlap. Variants on the themes of fatalism, empathy, efficacy, innovativeness, flexibility, achievement orientation, information, and active citizenship abound. Almost as frequently the students of individual modernity have felt it appropriate to measure stress, alienation, and anomie. This recurrence of certain themes may result merely from diffusion and imitation, perhaps suggesting some lack of imagination in those who entered the field later. The phenomenon could also have resulted from differential recruitment, that is, from the fact that only individuals following a particular theoretical perspective have entered on this field. But we prefer to interpret the observed convergence as indicating that there is a compelling theoretical case to be made for the relevance of the core elements built into most psychosocial definitions of individual modernity.

4. *Is Not the Idea of Individual Modernity Essentially a Western Conception? And If It Is, Isn't Its Exportation to the Less Developed Countries Just Another Form of Cultural Imperialism?*

To settle this question we must agree on some rule for saying what is "Western." The attributes by which we have defined individual modernity, such as a sense of efficacy and openness to new experience, are rather general human qualities which obviously can appear, and surely have done so in some degree, in many places and times. It follows that the syndrome certainly cannot be considered Western in the same sense as are Christianity or the Germanic languages. Nevertheless, in will be said that the cultural traditions of the West are, in general, comparatively more congenial to, or more likely to foster, the qualities we identify as modern. To this contention one might respond by noting that the Dark Ages were hardly eras in which the traits delineating individual modernity were favored or widely distributed in Europe. Indeed, from the ninth to the twelfth century the qualities of individual modernity were probably much more common in those parts of the world dominated by Islam.

Nevertheless, in the twentieth century the qualities we have identified were most favored and most widely diffused in the populations of Europe or of European origin. And, in the last fifty or seventy-five years, many individuals in other parts of the world have come to be more like those we call psychologically modern. Some may, therefore, insist that such individuals have become "Westernized," or, at least, more *like* Westerners. We prefer to think of them as having become more modern, because we find it more appropriate to think of the qualities which make up the modernity syndrome as not being the distinctive property of any single cultural tradition. Rather, those characteristics seem to us to represent a general model expressing one form of the human potential, a form which comes more to prominence in certain historical times under certain types of social conditions. Nevertheless, if some prefer to call ours a Western model, little is to be gained by spilling a great deal of ink over the issue. It seems much less important to settle whether individual modernity is Western or not, than it is to decide what consequences follow from its spread.

If the new institutions being widely adopted by developing countries, such as the factory, the school, the modern hospital, and the mass media, are thought of as Western; and if the habits, attitudes, values, and behaviors which are built into the social roles associated with these institutions are also defined as Western; then some sort of psychological Westernization may be a practical necessity for any country which seeks to modernize its institutions. New institutions remain at best empty shells, and at worst become graveyards of national resources, if they cannot be staffed by people who have the requisite personal qualities to fill effectively the role demands necessary to the operation of those institutions. Each nation and each people should be free to make the choice either to import the set of institutions which are generally considered to be modern, to live as they have always lived, to borrow some other pattern, or to invent wholly new institutional arrangements of their own. Each path will make its own distinctive demands on the psychology of the population. But if a people choose modern schools, mass production, mass communication, science-based technology, and scientific management, then the personal qualities we have called modern will be sorely needed, whether considered a Western import or not. Moreover, they will be needed whether the new society is socialist or capitalist, and if communist, whether the system follows either the Stalinist or the Maoist model. Imperialism can export Coca-Cola, blue jeans, Hollywood movies, and capital intensive production, but it cannot export individual modernity. Individual modernity may develop as a response to prior colonial action, but, being built into the psyches of the people, it must of necessity be a native product, home-grown, no matter how foreign was the origin of the seed.

5. *Does Definition Make It Real? What Is the Empirical Status of the Concept of Individual Modernity?*

There is a long-standing tradition in sociology and social psychology of inventing types of men—the most famous of the recent models being David Riesman's typology of inner-, other-, and self-directed men.[14] Although such types of men were only theoretical constructs, the custom in sociology, at least in the past, has been to accept them as if they were real. Little or no systematic effort went into testing whether these types could in fact be found in nature, and if they existed, to ascertain the frequency of their distribution in different societies and social strata. By contrast, the hypothetical construct of the modern man has been extensively tested empirically. Indeed, it has probably been as widely and systematically tested in field studies as any other comparable conception of a "type" of man.[15]

There are two main methods for testing the realism of a conception about human types. Each approach is identified with a school of scale construction, one known as the external criterion method, the other the coherence method.

The coherence method addresses itself directly to the issue of whether or not the personal qualities delineated in the conceptual model of a given researcher really constitute a "type," rather than being a mere assemblage of discrete and unrelated characteristics. In measuring coherence one takes no necessary position as to the frequency with which the type appears, nor, necessarily, with regard to where in the social structure that type may be found. Initially, therefore, the validity of a type delineated by the coherence method is necessarily limited to theoretical or face validity. The coherence test may be applied to what is conceived of as a single, discrete quality, say the sense of personal efficacy, or to a set of such qualities, as in testing a multidimensional model of "the modern man" of the sort described in chapter 2.

The criterion method for testing the soundness of a conception rests, as its name suggests, on one or more criteria external to the qualities being studied. In the case of individual modernity, the criteria which suggest themselves as obviously relevant are the objective social status characteristics associated with modern institutions and modern societies.[16] Thus, to show whether it is sound to define individual modernity in terms of greater efficacy or more openness to new experience, one should demonstrate that these qualities are found more often among those with more formal schooling, or among industrial workers as against farmers, or among urban as against rural residents, selecting the particular criteria used in accord with either some theory or common expectation. The criterion method, clearly, is valuable for establishing the validity of the elements of a definition. But it tells us nothing, directly, about the existence of a "type of man," that is, of a *set* of qualities which cohere and form an identifiable syndrome.

The criterion and coherence approaches, although quite discrete methods, are not mutually exclusive. Once a syndrome has been shown to exist, one may still seek to validate it against known criteria. And once a set of qualities has been identified by the criterion method, one can still test to see how well the qualities cohere and delineate a discrete "type."

Whether any given research finds a meaningful syndrome depends, of course, on a number of factors. If one's theory misleads one into attempting to put together things not joined in nature, no coherence will be found. What coheres in one population may not go together in another.[17] And what qualifies as coherent by one standard will be judged by another to be only a conglomeration of discrete elements.[18] Considering all the opportunities to go wrong, it is notable that a substantial number of studies, conducted relatively independently and applying to diverse populations, have found a syndrome of individual modernity meeting fairly rigorous standards of coherence based both on factor analysis and on tests of scale reliability.[19] This is true for the largest and most complex studies, as well as for many smaller-scale operations, and applies to both sexes and across a wide range of nations, occupations, educational levels, ethnic groups, and ages.[20]

A comparable range of studies may be noted which have tested the internal coherence not of a multidimensional syndrome but rather of one of the subthemes which the more global measures treat as components of the more complex whole. Empathy, the sense of efficacy, the need for achievement, and fatalism are among the concepts which have been put to the test.[21] There are clear-cut theoretical and empirical justifications for insisting on such more limited measures as one's unit of analysis. It is nevertheless noteworthy, in the perspective of our discussion of coherence, that the level of reliability attained by these more restricted measures proves generally to be no higher than that of the multidimensional measures, indicating there has been little loss of coherence paid as the price for emphasizing the multidimensional syndrome.[22]

The criterion method also has its vicissitudes. There is, for example, no general agreement as to whether the criterion should be some group having "known" status characteristics, such as higher education or wealth, or whether another familiar scale, presumed to measure the same qualities as one's new scale, can serve as a criterion. Moreover, those who insist that validity can only be established by showing that one's scale (or a single question) discriminates among "known groups" must face inherent difficulties in deciding which groups are appropriate candidates to serve as criteria, and how fully a scale must discriminate between groups before it is considered a truly valid instrument.

Despite all these pitfalls, it is again gratifying to note that both the large-scale and the more limited researches yield numerous instances of the criterion validity of both the subcomponents and the summary scales of individual modernity. For example, across five villages in Columbia, both modern and traditional, Rogers (1969) found those with low empathy scores were slow to adopt new agricultural practices, whereas those high in empathy tended to be among the innovators who adopted many new practices early on. Moving up to the level of the more general syndrome of individual modernity, Armer and Youtz (1971) found among youth in Kano, Nigeria, that only 37 percent of those with no education scored "high" on their modernity measure, but among those with some secondary schooling the percentage jumped to 84. In six developing countries we found that among those with least exposure to modern institutions, as few as 2 percent scored as modern, whereas among those in the upper decile of exposure to modern experiences, as many as 90 percent showed modern attitudes and values.[23] Again, comparable results are available from numerous other studies, large and small, by different investigators proceeding relatively independently.

There is, then, massive evidence for the existence of a syndrome of individual modernity, tested both by the method of coherence and by the criterion method. In *Becoming Modern* we described this syndrome as follows:

> The modern man's character, as it emerges from our study, may be summed up under four major headings.[24] He is an informed participant citizen; he has a marked sense of personal efficacy; he is highly independent and autonomous in his relations to traditional sources of influence especially when he is making basic decisions about how to conduct his personal affairs; and he is ready for new experiences and ideas, that is, he is relatively open-minded and cognitively flexible.
>
> Although these are the principal components, they by no means exhaust the list of qualities which cohere as part of the modernity syndrome. The modern man is also different in his approach to time, to personal and social planning, to the rights of persons dependent on or subordinate to him, and to the use of formal rules as a basis for running things. In other words, psychological modernity emerges a quite complex, multifaceted, and multidimensional syndrome. (Inkeles and Smith 1974, pp. 290–1)

Working independently from a related but distinctive perspective, Everett Rogers summed up the opposite pole of the modernity dimension, with specific reference to the "subculture of peasants," as including: "(1) mutual distrust in interpersonal relations; (2) perceived limited good; (3) dependence on and hostility toward government authority; (4) familism; (5) lack of innovativeness; (6) fatalism; (7) limited aspiration; (8) lack of deferred gratification; (9) limited view of the world; (10) low empathy" (1969, p. 25).

We assume that there are some populations in which the modernity syndrome would not be found, that some elements of the syndrome would combine differently in some populations than in others, and that some measures of modernity would not discriminate among at least certain criterion groups. But to acknowledge all this is rather like affirming that in human affairs nothing is certain beyond death and taxes, and not even taxes are certain. What is so notable about the qualities of individual modernity, as tested by both the coherence and the criterion method, is how pervasive are the confirmations that the original definitions are, in fact, matched by what one may observe in real people. Third-grade children in Brasilia, high school students in Puerto Rico, peasant farmers in Nigeria, street hawkers in Bangladesh, and industrial workers in Chile all manifest the syndrome (Holsinger 1973; Cunningham 1972; Inkeles and Smith 1974). One may use it to discriminate between those with more or less education in Mexico, and between those who do and do not listen to news broadcasts in Colombia (Kahl 1968; Rogers 1969). It distinguishes within sets of the young and the old, within white and black communities in the United States, among males and females, and within all religious and ethnic groups in Chile, Argentina, India, Bangladesh, Nigeria, and Israel (Klineberg 1973; Suzman 1973a; and chapters 7 and 8).

While it is clear that the concept of individual modernity has very general utility, we yet cannot assert it to be universal in its applicability. It may be that in China or Cuba the same qualities would not cohere, nor be associated with the same criteria in the same way. It seems quite possible that in those countries qualities not elsewhere observed to be part of the syndrome, such as self-effacement, collectivism, or subordination of individual choice to group goals, would figure centrally in the syndrome, whereas that has not been the case in populations so far tested. But it does seem highly likely that even in China and Cuba, qualities such as the sense of efficacy, openness to new experiences, and commitment to planning will go together, and will be associated with distinctive external criteria, just as in most of the populations so far studied. Some of the evidence supporting that assumption is presented in chapter 14.

6. *What Makes People Modern?*

At least five major theoretical perspectives may be distinguished among the answers which are regularly given to the question. Some of these positions are supported by evidence in great depth. Others have been the object of very little systematic research. The available evidence also varies in character, ranging from the most systematic field studies, through historical illustration, to the purely anecdotal.

MODERNITY AS AN INNATE TENDENCY

No one seems vigorously to argue explicitly that modernity is an innate tendency, but the idea comes up repeatedly in efforts to explain why it is that people coming from the same background, and even having the same subsequent exposures to modern institutions, nevertheless vary so greatly in how modern they have become.

Given the specifically social content of individual modernity, it is obvious that in a strict sense no one is born modern. People can be modern only by *becoming* modern, through either maturation, or socialization, or both. Nevertheless, if qualities such as intelligence, dominance and assertiveness, activeness, curiosity, or flexibility are in part innate dispositions, then they could influence individual modernity as it is measured.[25] Some of that influence could be direct, since some modernity tests, in part, measure the very qualities mentioned above. But the main effects would, presumably, be indirect, leading those innately more curious or dominant either to search out modernizing experiences, or to be better "learners" in situations having the intrinsic ability to "teach" lessons in modernity.

I know of no research which has gone forward from systematic measures of early personality to later measures of "individual modernity," although existing panel studies of individual development could be used for this purpose. Working back from the current modernity of individuals to their early traits is an attractive alternative, although the procedure is subject to imposing methodological obstacles.[26] In any event, there is very little evidence, if any, bearing on the issue.

MODERNITY AS A PRODUCT OF EARLY FAMILY MILIEU

Those who stress this explanation accept learning as the cause of modernity, but assume that the learning occurs mainly early in life, as a result of distinctive family constellations, and that the resultant qualities remain more or less fixed in the person for life.

To assume that differences in the home environment are what account for differences in individual modernity is, in effect, to state a special case of a much more general model. There is no obvious reason to expect greater success in predicting modernity from knowledge of the home environment than there has been in predicitng other personality outcomes on that basis. My reading of the evidence suggests that families are more successful in endowing offspring with socioeconomic status characteristics than they are in transmitting to them a set of predetermined personality characteristics. Nevertheless, there is substantial evidence of the transmission of personality from generation to generation at levels of statistical association that are far from trivial. And we must acknowledge the important studies which rest on the assumption that the decisive factor in determining the modernity of individuals, now adults, was the special character of the early experience provided by parents and families.

Everett Hagen (1962) argues vigorously for the influence of the home environment in shaping the innovative personality, although his data are essentially anecdotal and his conclusions not based on the direct study of living individuals. The work of McClelland (1961) and his associates provided more systematic evidence on the familial antecedents of high need achievement. A pattern of significant correlation between the modernity scores of parents and those of their children has been found by Cunningham (1972) in Puerto Rico, Holsinger (1973) in Brazil, Klineberg (1973) in Tunisia, and Pandey (1971) in India. Pandey, moreover, shows the outcome to result from the different approaches parents took to socialization in regard to achievement, authority, and human concerns. All this suggests some significant direct transmission of modernity from home to child.[27] But the evidence is, unfortunately, not consistent.[28] Moreover, in the Harvard-Stanford six-nation study, a measure of home-school background—based on perceptions of the behavior of parents and teachers in such matters as keeping promises and respecting one's feelings—proved only a weak and inconsistent predictor of individual modernity, especially once other factors were controlled.[29] In sum, it seems that the home environment, while significant, may be a less important factor than many had assumed it to be.

MODERNITY AS AN EXPRESSION OF SHARED GROUP CULTURE

Each of us is the carrier of at least one culture, and those who come from complex societies may embody elements of more than one distinct cultural tradition. Cultures are differentiated by the values they inculcate, the behaviors they encourage, and the skills they transmit. It follows that some cultures might much more emphasize the qualities which are considered modern. Individuals from those cultures would then be more modern, at least insofar as they had been successfully socialized into their respective cultures.

Weber's analysis of the Protestant ethic is the prototype for this mode of analysis. Hagen's (1962) characterization of the Antioquenos of Colombia, and other groups, is a variant on the theme. McClelland's (1961) research provides more systematic evidence across a large number of societies. However, he based his characterization of each culture on an analysis of children's readers. Since he did not compare samples of individuals from each society, he left us with considerable doubt as to the validity of his ratings. LeVine's (1966) comparison of the Yoruba and the Ibo overcame this difficulty although without very compelling results. In the Harvard-Standford six-nation study we found the men from some countries, notably Argentina and Israel, much more modern than those from other countries, especially East Pakistan (now Bangladesh). Since the samples differed greatly in education and income, the differences might have been attributed mainly to "wealth" rather than to culture. But the differences persisted, even if somewhat muted, when we compared groups from different countries selected to be alike on such characteristics as education and occupation. In one typical matching, for example, only 8 percent of those from East Pakistan scored as modern, whereas 30 percent of the otherwise comparable Argentinians did so.[30] Chapter 8 explains how we made these comparisons of individual modernity across countries. Chapter 7 is also relevant for its comparisons of cultural subgroups within the same country.

Now that we have strictly comparable measures of modernity which can be used cross-nationally, this mode of analysis can be extended to other countries. Pending a more systematic survey, we may tentatively conclude that some national populations do indeed seem much more modern than others. Moreover, since such differences persist after matching for education and occupation, we must grant the assumption that such differences may stem from distinctive cultural systems shared by particular populations.

DIFFUSION-IMITATION-DEPENDENCY THEORIES

If the set of institutions defined as modern, and the sentiments and behaviors associated with them, are seen as a distinctive cultural product of "the West," then modernization may readily be interpreted as only a special case of the general process of cultural diffusion. Certainly, the systems of industrial production, of scientific management, and of mass communication originated in and diffused from the West, and a good case can be made that many other institutions making up the set we usually call modern had a similar origin.[31]

It is relatively easy to imagine how one can transplant a complete factory, or even a university. But what of the attitudes, values, skills, and patterns of interpersonal relations which are typically associated with these institutions at their Western point of origin? Behaviors can, of course, be imitated, and attitudes simulated. But most attitudes and behaviors must be more nearly authentic, or else their inappropriateness and ineffectiveness rapidly becomes painfully apparent. And the basic, deeper-lying personal dispositions and psychic tendencies, such as cognitive flexibility or field independence, seem by their very nature not subject to imitation, but rather come about only through slow development after long learning.

The extent to which the modern attitudes, values, and behaviors found outside the West got there mainly because of diffusion, is intrinsically difficult to test with any precision. Where certain social classes in developing countries come directly in contact with the international bearers of this new culture, the case for imitation can easily be made. For other classes lacking this direct contact, one can claim that the mass media, especially the movies and television, have likely had considerable impact in diffusing superficial forms of adherence to some Western model. This is essentially the logic followed in dependency theory, which stresses the extent to which the power of the advanced (colonial) system drives out the indigenous culture patterns and replaces them wholesale with foreign models. But to explain the deeper changes in personal dispositions which we observe in factory workers who are located in provincial areas and do not have foreigners present as models, would seem to require adopting a rather different theoretical perspecitve, based on the concept of social learning.

SOCIAL LEARNING THEORY

Following the leads Marx provided when he declared that one's relationship to the mode of production shapes one's consciousness, we may expect individuals to learn to be modern by incorporating within themselves principles which are embedded in the organizational practices of the institutions in which they live and work.

This general perspective, first presented in the paper "Industrial Man" (Inkeles 1960), influenced the research design adopted by Joseph Kahl (1968) for *The Measurement of Modernism*, and was given a more explicit test in the Harvard-Stanford six-nation study reported in *Becoming*

Modern by Inkeles and Smith (1974). As the theory predicted, work in factories, in modern bureaucratic organizations, and in agricultural cooperatives all produced significant and substantial increases in the sense of personal efficacy, in openness to new experience, and in the approval of science and technology. Similar changes, even more marked for any given year of exposure, were brought about by attending school. Yet neither the school nor the bureaucracy rely heavily on the use of the sort of machinery typically found in factories. We were stimulated, therefore, to conclude that school and factory produce the same result because they both expose individuals to certain common principles of organization, procedures for assigning power and prestige, modes for allocating rewards and punishment, and approaches to the management of time. Individual modernity then becomes a quality learned by the incorporation into the self-system of certain qualities characteristic of particular institutional environments.

It seems likely that the five approaches described above would together account for most of the variance in individual modernity, if we could but find some way to represent them all in a single study. Moreover, we are convinced that of the five, the social learning theory would account for by far the greater proportion of the variance explained. Indeed, in our opinion, the point is already established by the evidence presented in *Becoming Modern*. Nevertheless, it remains true that a definitive test of this assumption has not been made. And it is also true that we have far to go in understanding precisely which features of schools and factories make them effective teachers of modernity, and how such features achieve their results.

7. What Consequences Does Modernization Have for the Individual's Psychic Adjustment? Can Modernization Only Be Gained at the Cost of Psychic Stress?

To answer this question we must get agreement on what we mean by adjustment, and how we shall measure it. Moreover, interpretation of any results obtained not only should take into account how the individuals we study feel now, but also should consider their adjustment prior to their exposure to modern institutions.

A great many anthropological field reports, along with other types of observation, provide extensive evidence of the extremely deleterious personal consequences regularly accompanying the impingement of powerful European nations on the peoples of relatively small, insular cultures not having the benefit of advanced technologies. Although there are clearly important exceptions, such as the Manus described by Margaret Mead, this type of contact seems to produce a high frequency of deculturation, personal disorganization, alcoholism or other forms of addiction, lassitude, depression, anxiety, hyperaggressivity, and evidence of stress.[32]

By contrast, individuals from nonmodern societies with their own high culture, especially if they are part of a more or less autonomous nation-state, seem to fare quite differently as a result of their contact with the institutions introduced by the modernization process. In our six-nation study we found that, in general, there were no consistent differences in the psychic adjustment of those who were more exposed to factory work, urban living, or the mass media. The evidence to support this conclusion is presented in detail in chapter 12. We do not interpret these findings as meaning such exposure was intrinsically tonic. Rather, we suggest that the pursuit of agriculture in the typical traditional village was much less gratifying an experience than many Western intellectuals imagined it to be. Consequently, in relative terms, the urbanized, industrially employed ex-migrant tends to be no worse off psychically than his cousin who stayed on the farm.

We believe that our findings accord well with the results of other systematic researches of the impact of modernization on individual adjustment, but the picture is complex, and no definite conclusion can hope to win general adherence at this time.[33].

8. *What Does Becoming Modern Do to the Individual's Politics? Is Alienation an Inevitable Accompaniment of Modernization? And Is Individual Modernity Antithetical to Political Radicalism?*

One senses that the New Left sees the concept of modernization as a rival doctrine to the Marxist laws of capitalist development, or as some kind of new opiate of the masses which will distract them from the struggle to build socialism.[34] In such an atmosphere it is extremely difficult to develop a dispassionate discussion of the implications which becoming modern has for an individual's political role. Nevertheless, the issue is fundamental, and one must take an initial position, however tentative.

One fact seems unmistakable, indeed it seems to come as close to being a law as anything to be observed in social science. As individuals move up the scale of individual modernity, whether judged by objective status characteristics or by psychological attributes, they regularly become more informed, active, participant citizens. With exceptional regularity, increasing individual modernity is associated with voting, joining public organizations and participating in public actions, interacting with politicians and public figures, taking an interest in political news, and keeping up with political events. Although they were not oriented to testing a theory of individual modernity, Almond and Verba (1963) provided fundamental comparative evidence relating these dimensions of political participation to increasing education. That the same patterns of response were to be found in developing countries, and that they constituted a syndrome of participant citizenship, is established in chapter 11.

As far as moving to the left or the right on the political spectrum is concerned, it seems reasonable to assume that the concomitant of becoming modern, at least for most people in most developing countries, should be a move to the left. This would seem to follow from the fact that, as many studies have shown, more modern individuals are more desirous of change, more open to new experience, less fatalistic, and less in awe of authority and received tradition.

Of the six nations in the Harvard-Stanford modernity study, it was only in Argentina and Chile that our local advisors agreed to our intention to ask questions which tested radicalism and conservatism. As we shall see in chapter 11, in both countries the more modern men were more "radical," in that they much more favored an immediate and profound transformation of the basic institutions of their respective societies. The point is not well documented elsewhere, but we read the existing evidence as in general agreement with our results (Nelson 1969; Cornelius 1975).

Since political and economic change is generally slow, and political systems often unresponsive, it might seem to follow that change-oriented modern individuals would be more alienated. But the firmness of this association should, presumably, depend on the larger political and social context. Thus, in societies in which the government was especially responsive, or was bringing about rapid social change, the more modern men might well be *less* alienated.

There is less evidence on this issue than one might like. Two studies in the United States, one in inner city Chicago (Armer and Schnaiberg (1972), the other in the suburbs of Boston (Suzman 1973a), found modernity to be strongly associated with lack of alienation and nonanomic feelings. In our six-nation study we found the same thing to be true only of East Pakistan and Chile, and then less sharply so. In Nigeria, by contrast, the more modern were more anomic and more alienated. The other countries showed other patterns still, and we were forced to conclude, as explained more fully in chapter 11, that

> The participant citizen is not also consistently nonanomic, nonhostile, and satisfied with the performance of his government. Rather, we must say, "it depends" on the country—and no doubt on the segment of the population being studied.

Clearly, we need to do much more research before any firm conclusions can be drawn. But it seems likely that participant citizenship will be consistent in being almost everywhere strongly associated with individual modernity, whereas alienation and anomie will behave inconsistently, sometimes being associated with modernity and sometimes not, depending on the national and community context.[35]

9. What Are the Consequences for Kith and Kin of a Person's Becoming Modern? Does Individual Modernity Automatically Lead to Defaulting on Traditional Interpersonal Obligations?

There is a widespread impression that modernity, whatever the advantages it may bring to individuals, is always bought at high cost to the local community because it leads people to default on their traditional obligations, most notably those owed to kith and kin. This assumption is strengthened by the common tendency of both theoretical discussion and empirical research to establish a polarity between the modern and the traditional, thus encouraging the presumption that supporting most modern modes necessarily implies rejecting all traditional ones.[36]

Such direct conflict is probably inevitable in some realms. For example, one cannot, without contradiction, favor relaxed and informal scheduling, while simultaneously insisting that individuals be at the school or the factory by a fixed hour. And if, in a given culture, "respect for elders" means explicitly accepting their choice of one's occupation or spouse, then modern individuals will quite consistently be found failing in this virtue. Such direct confrontation of principle, and such inherent incompatibility of different acts are, however, much less common than is often assumed. While effective participation in modern institutions fosters some selected psychic dispositions, it does not determine, or even have implications for action in, *all* particulars of *all* realms of life. Indeed, so long as the minimum imperatives of the industrial-bureaucratic system of production and administration are met, the individual's behavior in other realms may vary widely without serious conflict with the norms of modernity as we have defined and tested them.

In fact, individual modernity is found, and apparently lives compatibly, alongside of many orientations and behaviors which some analysts consider to be part of traditionalism. This point has been an important element in the general theory of modernization as presented by Eisenstadt (1973) and Gusfield (1967), and suffuses the Rudolphs' (1967) analysis of modernization in India. Unfortunately, the force of the argument depends on creating a straw man. In common practice, most measures of modernity give individuals a summary score based on numerous questions. Since most people get a middling score, and almost no one gets a "perfect" score, it follows that even those classified as "modern" by this means must be holding many attitudes which are theoretically defined as "traditional." When, therefore, critics point so vigorously to nominally "modern" individuals whom they know to also engage in certain "traditional" practices, they are only restating in words what every scale of modernity has already repeatedly expressed in numbers.

The realm of religious commitment and observance provides an important illustration. Numerous conceptions of modernization assume, by definition, that the modern spirit is antithetical to religion, and that becoming modern means giving up one's religious tradition. However, even a moment's reflection on this proposition brings to mind evidence so glaringly in contradiction to this expectation as to immediately call into question the soundness of the underlying theory. Consider, for example, the United States, which by almost any measure is one of the most modern nations in the world, yet which also has one of the highest rates of church membership and one of the highest levels of regular church attendance.

So far as concerns obligations to kith and kin, we found in our six-nation study that becoming modern was not at all consistently associated with the rejection of, or defaulting on, traditional obligations. Indeed, very often those who had left the village to take up industrial work in town were more willing than their country cousins to give financial aid to a relative in dire need. They also were equally ready to give respect to the aged, on the simple ground that age deserved respect. And they were, in general, not less exacting in carrying out the basic practices required by their tradition.[37] Some of the relevant findings are presented in chapter 13.

Since our modernity or OM (Overall Modernity) scale was based on the internal coherence of the responses to it, most questions touching on religious practice and respect for the aged failed to qualify for the scale, a point fully discussed in *Becoming Modern*. It must be acknowledged, however, that in some other researches on individual modernity using more arbitrary criteria for deciding the content of their scales, such questions have been treated as part of the definition of individual modernity, generally with deleterious effects on the scale's reliability. More information concerning the content and derivation of one form of our OM scale is presented in chapter 4.

Further research will be required to assess whether the seemingly peaceful coexistence of the modern and traditional is characteristic only of the early stages of modernization. We are of the opinion that it may be found at later stages as well. But to specify which forms of coexistence are possible, and in what contexts, will require much additional research over a wider range of situations and in a diversity of settings.

10. *What Are the Consequences of Individual Modernity for One's Society? Does Individual Change of This Sort Do Anything to Bring About Social Change, or to Improve the Lot of the Rest of the People?*

We have come full circle, returning to our first issue, but now viewing it in a different perspective. Because we committed ourselves to studying how individuals change as a result of living in modernizing societies or of coming into contact with modern institutions, we are often charged with presuming that individual change must precede societal change, or that personal change is more important than system change. No misunderstanding of the work on individual modernity is more pervasive nor more serious in its ability to misrepresent the actual views of most of those engaged in research on this topic.

Just as the impact of institutions on individuals must be taken as problematic, so should the impact of individual properties on the social system be recognized as a matter for study. Merely to put a question is in no way to prejudge the answer. Moreover, confusion is inevitable if discussions are couched in extremely general terms rather than by specifying precisely what types and degree of social change are in question.

No doubt a systematic search can turn up some quotation from some work which will demonstrate that at least some people have made extreme and implausible claims for the ability of psychological properties to shape social forces. But if one focuses more on the main thrust of the argument made by the corps of scholars who have been studying individual modernity, one finds common a more modest, indeed a highly qualified, set of claims. Specifying more precisely the different levels of system change, the prevalent positions may be characterized as follows:

A. Basic structural transformations of a radical or revolutionary kind, involving the social system as a whole, are rather uniformly acknowledged to be very little determined, if at all, by the psychological properties of a national character or by the modal personality of significant subordinate strata. In the case of the political revolutions such as those of Russia, China, or Cuba, it is obvious that the transformation of society rested not on the diffusion of new personality patterns but on a sudden rupture of power. But even in the case of the more gradual transformations, as in the successive industrialization of England, France, and Germany, it seems clear that institutional change did not need to wait on prior personal transformations.

B. Nevertheless, we are not in a position to deny that under conditions of equal opportunity, peoples with a distinctive "national character" may manifest a differential propensity to adopt new institutions, and may enjoy very different rates of success in getting those institutions "to work" effectively. The Japanese are the obvious case in point. Stalin's effort to create "the new Soviet man" may serve to highlight the sense of frustration national leaders can feel when they are mounting massive efforts of social change but find, to their chagrin, that the human material they have to work with seems not suited to their purpose.[38]

Only now that we have the technical means to measure the average level of individual modernity in national populations are we in a position to achieve a more objective assessment of the relative contribution of the psychological characteristics of a people to the overall modernization of their society. Measures of such qualities could be weighed, along with other factors in the standard matrix of measures, to predict how the properties of nations in an earlier period predict their standing at later points in time. This is basically what McClelland tried to do in *The Achieving Society*, but his method of measuring the personal qualities of the populations concerned was so indirect as to leave a residue of profound doubt as to the reliability and validity of his conclusions.[39]

C. Certain religious, ethnic, or other cultural subgroups seem to play a distinctive role in the modernization process by generating in their members qualities which attract them to, and make them especially effective in, certain roles, notably that of entrepreneur.

Weber's stunning analysis of the Protestant ethic, McClelland's study of family patterns generating high need for achievement, Hagen's case studies of innovative personalities, all start with this assumption. They also present extensive documentation which they see as proving their thesis. But it seems more accurate to say that theirs are essentially case studies which merely *illustrate* the thesis without establishing its general validity. Later, more extensive studies with large samples of entrepreneurs seem not to turn up much evidence that the incumbents of this role came from distinctive family milieus.

D. The case for the social consequences of individual modernity rests mainly on evidence showing that becoming more modern leads individuals to undertake new transformative social roles within their societies and in their more immediate social networks.

Individuals who attain psychological modernity, especially in less developed societies where that character is not yet the predominant norm, adopt different social roles than do their less modern countrymen. They are more active in voluntary organizations and participate more in politics;

they practice birth control more regularly and have fewer children as a result; they are quicker to adopt innovative practices in agriculture and are more productive as workers in industry; they keep their children longer in school and encourage them to take up more technical occupations; and, in general, they press more actively for social change. This catalog of behavioral differences could be considerably extended. And although such differences cannot be guaranteed to appear in all groups and in all settings, they are well documented in a strikingly large number of groups and places.[40]

Such behavior may be viewed as merely a more effective means of coping that is of advantage to the modern individual and his dependents, but is no particular boon to society at large. But when it is cumulated across large numbers of individuals, such modern behavior may also become a collective input essential to the overall success of any program of national development. And this may be true even in those cases in which a revolutionary transformation of the ownership of the means of production has already been accomplished.

As we will see in chapter 14, in Communist China the national leaders are constantly urging the local community not to become dependent on grandiose national plans, nor to seek constantly for help from the central authorities, but instead to cultivate and practice self-reliance in all things. The soundness of this advice is evidently well grasped in numerous other countries by people who have not had the benefit of Mao's teaching, but who have come to the same conclusion in the process of becoming modern. In our six-nation study we asked the question: "Which is more important for the future of your country?" There followed four alternatives:

The hard work of the people.
Good planning on the part of the government.
God's help.
Good luck.

It will be no surprise that the more traditional selected the last two alternatives, the more modern the first two. But of the first two, the most frequent first choice of the more modern men was not the government plan but rather "the hard work of the people." Was this choice merely a manifestation of individual self-interest, or did it express some fundamental collective wisdom?

PART ONE

THEORY AND METHOD

CHAPTER 2

A Model of the
Modern Man

The main purpose of this chapter is to describe the conception of the modern man which guided the research of the Harvard project. We emphasize here the part of the general scheme which we called the topical model, since most of the material reported in this book relates to that model. But first, we should briefly inform those new to the project, and refresh the memory of those familiar with it from earlier reports, as to the main features of our research design.

THE DESIGN OF THE RESEARCH

We started with the assumption that no one is born modern, but rather that people become so through their own particular life experience. More specifically, our theory emphasized the contribution of man's work experience to making him modern. We believed that employment in complex, rationalized, technocratic, and even bureaucratic organizations has particular capabilities to change men so that they move from the more traditional to the more modern pole in their attitudes, values, and behavior. Among such institutions, we gave prime emphasis to the factory as a school in modernity, for the reasons set forth in chapter 3.

We also thought that urban living and contact with the mass media should have comparable effects. While emphasizing such modes of experience as more characteristic of the modern world, we did not neglect to

Originally published as Alex Inkeles, "A Model of the Modern Man: Theoretical and Methodological Issues," in Nancy Hammond, ed., *Social Science and the New Societies: Problems in Cross-Cultural Research and Theory Building* (East Lansing: Social Science Research Bureau, Michigan State University, 1973), pp. 59–92.

study education, which earlier research had shown to be a powerful predictor of individual modernity, as well as other personal attributes such as age, religion, ethnic membership, and rural origin.

These and several dozen other variables that our theory, or other theories, identified as plausible explanations for individual modernity were taken into account in the design of our research. Interviewers trained by our project staff questioned almost 6,000 men from six developing countries: Argentina, Chile, India, Israel, Nigeria, and East Pakistan (now Bangladesh). The interview was extensive, up to four hours long. Our samples were highly purposive, each including subgroups of cultivators, migrants from the countryside newly arrived in the city, urban workers earning their living outside large-scale productive enterprises, and workers in industry. The industrial workers were the largest group in each country, some 600 to 700, whereas the other subgroups were to be 100 each. The selection of cases was on the basis of the respondent meeting certain common characteristics as to sex (all male), age (18–32), education (usually 0–8 years), religion, ethnicity, rural or urban origin, residence, and, of course, the occupational characteristics already mentioned. The initial interviews were conducted during 1963 and 1964. Subsamples of 100 each were reinterviewed during 1968 and 1969 in India, Israel, and Bangladesh. Our experiences in mounting this research under diverse field conditions and adapting it to the special circumstances of our six countries is described in *Becoming Modern*.[1]

Since we were not making generalizations to the total national populations, we gave greater emphasis to keeping the subsamples like each other in all respects except occupation, rather than selecting them to be representative of any "parent" population. Our strategy, then, was to treat the research in each country as essentially a replication of our basic design, on the assumption that any relationship that held true in six such different countries would be a powerful connection indeed.

The ultimate meaningfulness of our sample design rested on our ability to construct a reliable, cross-national measure of individual modernity. We do not claim to have invented the idea of the modern man. The concept was already there when we began our work, even though its content was vague. Inventing "types" of men has, after all, always been a fundamental preoccupation of sociologists. Yet it has been the rare instance, indeed, in which any systematic attempt has been made to measure whether there are real people in the world who, in their own persons, actually incorporate the qualities identified by these ideal types. We were determined to break with this tradition, and firmly committed ourselves to testing how far the set of qualities by which we defined the modern man actually cohered as a psychosocial syndrome in real men.

The characteristic mark of the modern man has two parts: one internal, the other external; one dealing with his environment, the other with his attitudes, values, and feelings. The change in the external condition of modern man is well known and widely documented, and it need not detain us long. It may be summarized by reference to a series of key terms: urbanization, education, mass communication, industrialization, politicization. The particular focus of our interest, however, was in the psychological characteristics that might distinguish the more modern from the traditional man. This model of the modern man, briefly described in chapter 1, is more fully developed below.

To convert our conception of the modern man into a tool useful for research, we created a long and fairly complex interview schedule yielding answers each of which could be scored to indicate whether a respondent was more inclined to the modern or the traditional pole. On numerous issues, using a separate subset of questions to reflect each topic, we explored all of the themes we had built into our own conception of the modern man as well as themes that other theorists had identified as relevant to judging individual modernity. The complete questionnaire has been published in *Becoming Modern*, but the most important questions are also reproduced in this volume in abbreviated form in table 4-1 of chapter 4.

One of the major challenges facing us was to discover whether these discrete elements held together in a more or less coherent syndrome that one could sensibly speak of as designating a "modern man," or whether they would prove to be a mere congeries of discrete and unrelated traits, each of which characterized some modern men and not others.

In fact, it proved possible to develop composite scales to measure individual modernity in general. These scales have considerable face validity, meet quite rigorous standards of test reliability, and can be effectively applied cross-culturally. We called them OM scales to reflect their status as our overall measures of modernity. In one group of people after another differentiated by occupation, religion, ethnicity, educational level, and country of origin, the same set of qualities went together. We therefore felt quite confident in affirming the empirical reality of the psychosocial syndrome our theory had originally identified.[2]

Since the modernity scale enabled us to distribute men validly and reliably along a dimension of individual modernity, we were in a position to ask the next basic question: Why did particular individuals fall at one or the other end of the continuum, in other words, what makes men modern?

The answer to that question is pursued in chapter 5. To be in a position to appreciate and critically evaluate those results, however, the reader should be more thoroughly briefed on our conception of the modern man, our theory of the social influences which made him so, and our method for studying both his character and the forces impinging on him. We therefore elaborate our conception of the modern man, especially as it relates to our concerns in this book, in the remainder of this second chapter, and in chapter 3 we explain our theory as to how men are made modern.

CONCEPTUAL MODEL OF INDIVIDUAL MODERNITY

The great danger of any definition of the "modern" is that some more powerful group may arbitrarily impose its own traditional *values* on a less powerful group as if it were bestowing the same benefit it confers when it offers a railroad network, a television station, a well-equipped field hospital, or any one of a dozen other so-called miracles of modern technology. Do we not do something peculiar and distorting if we make the American businessman's grey flannel suit more modern than the Indian civil servant's high-necked coat or for that matter his *dhoti*? Isn't it potentially misleading, as well as arbitrary, to treat monogamy as more modern than polygamy? Indeed, are we not presuming a great deal when we consider an Arab chieftain more modern merely because he replaces his camel with a Cadillac or even a private jet plane? The tendency to equate the modern with foreign technology does not prevail only in the West. As we shall see in chapter 6, in the Indian state of Bihar a man is considered more modern if he believes that food cooked over charcoal tastes better than food cooked over dried cow dung cakes, and insists that factory cloth feels better on the skin than homespun cloth. He might be right on both counts, but should we consider him more modern merely because he uses charcoal and factory-spun cloth?

The issues are subtle, complicated, and difficult, and they could occupy us a long time, but if we pursued them all we would never get on to telling how we attempted to resolve the problem in our research. Indeed, one could argue that the position one really takes on these issues is manifested most clearly not in what one says about them, but rather in the precise way in which one designs his measures of modernity.

In our questionnaire-guided interview, we touched on the thirty-odd themes listed in chart 2-1 at the end of this chapter. Each theme which we considered to be discrete and important was assigned a pair of code letters, such as EF for efficacy, and all questions we thought of as bearing on that theme carried the code letters and a number, as in EF-2 which asked: "Does

CHART 2-1

Main Themes and Areas of the Questionnaire, by Key Letter and Model

Analytical Model		Topical Model		Behavioral Model	
Aspirations, occupa-tional and educa-tional	(AS)	Active public participation	(AC)	Political activity	(AC)
Calculability	(CA)	Citizenship	(CI)	Family behavior	(BD and WR)
Change orientation	(CH)	Consumption attitudes	(CO)	Consumption behavior	(CO)
Dignity	(DI)	Family size restrictions	(FS)	Information test	(IN)
Efficacy	(EF)	Identification with nation	(ID)	Media information test	(MM)
Growth of opinion	(GO)	Kinship obliga-tions	(KO)	Opposites word test	(OT)
Information	(IN)	Mass Media	(MM)	Psychosomatic test	(PT)
New Experience	(NE)	Religion	(RE)	Sentence completion test	(ST)
Optimism	(OP)	Psychosomatics and adjustment	(PT)	Interviewer's ratings	
Particularism	(PA)	Work Commitment	(WC)	Supervisor's ratings	
Planning	(PL)	Women's rights	(WR)	Factory records	
Time	(TI)				
Technical skill and distributive justice	(TS)				

the prevention of accidents on the job depend mainly on luck or mainly on being careful?" All of the major themes were examined and tested to assess their relevance for our general research objectives. Some of the themes to which we assigned distinctive status we now view more as merely subthemes. Other themes, which we earlier did not distinguish with the stamp of a key phrase and code letters, emerged either in our field experience or in the course of our analysis as important and worthy of the status we had assigned to other subjects. Several of those subthemes which we later came to think of as more discrete are listed in chart 4-1 of chapter 4. We take some pride, however, in the fact that no theme was used in our study unless a substantial theory linked it to modernization.

The thirty-odd themes we explored are not a random list. They have a definite structure, a structure derived from the main research objectives of our project. They reflect the interests and ideas of the staff members who joined in this cooperative venture and the theories advanced by leading students of the modernization process. Although each theme could reasonably be explored in its own right, we originally conceived of some of them as holding together in a syndrome, or complex, of attitudes and values that for us constituted the core concept of modernity and the central focus of our research. This subset, or syndrome, of themes constitutes our *analytical model* of individual modernity. The study of that model was the main concern of the first book on our project under the title *Becoming Modern*.

We were aware, however, that our analytical model did not touch on all the themes that students of modernization have pointed to as major concomitants or effects of the modernization process. Many of those ideas were supported by some evidence but warranted further testing, others were virtually untested by empirical field research, and still others we believed were wrong and we thought to prove them so. This second set of themes was selected on a more eclectic basis than were the elements of the analytical model. We did not view them as tied together in a distinctive pattern or syndrome. Each might stand or fall alone without affecting the validity of any other. We refer to them as the *topical themes* on modernization. The research reported in this volume deals mainly with the subjects encompassed by that topical model.

Both the analytical model and the topical themes dealt mainly with attitudes and values. We were cognizant of the possibility that a man might think and speak in the modern vein but still *act* in a more traditional way. It could be argued that the ultimate test of the modernization process lies not in its ability to teach a man how to give "modern" answers on a questionnaire, but rather in its ability to produce men who in their everyday lives perform like modern men. We could not assume that the connection between *thinking* modern and *acting* modern was automatic and perfect. Indeed, we had good reason to suppose that it might be tenuous and uncertain. We resolved, therefore, to collect materials that would permit us to judge the modernity of men by their actions rather than their words. This test of individual modernity we called our *behavioral measures*.

Let us now turn to a brief exposition of the theory and the content of each of these three approaches to modernization—the analytical model, the topical themes, and the behavioral measures—as they were actually elaborated in our research.

THE ANALYTICAL MODEL

Readiness for new experience and *openness to innovation and change* constitute the first elements in our definition of the modern man. We believe that the traditional man is less disposed to accept new ideas, new ways of feeling and acting. We are speaking, therefore, of something that is itself a state of mind, a psychological disposition, an inner readiness, rather than of the specific techniques or skills a group may possess because of the level of technology it has attained. Thus, in our sense, a man may be more modern in spirit, even though he works with a wooden plough, than someone who already drives a tractor. The readiness for new experience and ways of doing things, furthermore, may take a variety of different forms and appear in different contexts—in the willingness to adopt a new drug or sanitation method, to accept a new seed or adopt a different fertilizer, to ride on a new means of transportation or turn to a new source of information, to approve a new form of wedding ceremony or new type of schooling for young people. Individuals and groups may, of course, show more readiness for the new in one area of life than another, but we can also conceive of the readiness to accept innovations as a pervasive, general characteristic that makes itself felt across a wide variety of human situations. And we consider those who have this readiness to be more modern.

The realm of the *growth of opinion* represents the second in our complex of themes. This area is itself divisible into a number of subthemes or scale areas. We define a man as more modern if he has a *disposition to form or hold opinions* over a large number of the problems and issues that arise not only in his immediate environment but also outside it. The more traditional man, we believe, takes an interest in fewer situations and events, mainly those that touch him immediately and intimately, and, even when he holds opinions on more distant matters, he is more circumspect in expressing such opinions.

We also consider a man to be more modern if his orientation to the opinion realm is more differentiated and democratic. Here, we mean that he shows more *awareness of the diversity of attitude and opinion around him*, rather than closing himself off in the belief that everyone thinks alike and indeed thinks just as he does. In our conception, a modern man is able to acknowledge differences of opinion; he has no need rigidly to deny differences out of the fear that they will upset his own view of the world. He is also less likely to approach opinion in a strictly autocratic or hierarchical way. He does not automatically accept the ideas of those above him in the power hierarchy or reject the opinions of those whose status is markedly lower than his. In other words, *he puts a positive value on variations in opinion*. Intimately related to our study of opinion but conceived as a separate dimension were our measures of *information*. We consider that being modern means not merely having opinions but being more energetic in acquiring facts and information on which to base those opinions.

Time: We view a man as more modern if he is oriented to the present or the future rather than to the past. We consider him more modern if he accepts fixed hours, that is to say, schedules, as something sensible and appropriate, or possibly even desirable, as against the men who think that fixed hours are something either bad or perhaps a necessity but unfortunately also a pity. We also define a man as more modern if he is punctual, regular, and orderly in organizing his affairs.

Efficacy is a fourth theme, one that is especially important in our conception of the modern man. The modern individual believes that, to a substantial degree, man can learn to dominate his environment in order to advance his own purposes and goals, rather than being dominated entirely by that environment. The sense of efficacy is, of course, not limited to feelings concerning man's potential mastery over nature. It includes, as well, the belief that one can effectively do something if officials are proposing what one considers to be a bad law, that care will help prevent accidents, that human nature can be changed, and that men can arrange their affairs so that even nations can live in peace. His sense of efficacy, then, expresses the modern man's confidence in his ability, alone and in concert with other men, to organize his life to master the challenges it presents at the personal, the interpersonal, and communal, the national, and the international levels.

Planning is a theme closely related to efficacy, but we initially conceived of it as important in its own right. We consider a man more modern if he is oriented toward planning and organizing affairs and believes in planning as an approach both to public affairs and to his own personal life.

Calculability (or *trust*). By our definition, the modern man is one who has confidence that his world is calculable, that other people and institutions around him can be relied upon to fulfill or meet their obligations and responsibilities. He is more prepared to trust a stranger than is the traditional man. He does not agree that everything is determined either by fate or by the whims and particular qualities and characters of men. In other words, he believes in a reasonably lawful world under human control. This, therefore, is a theme we might also expect to find closely related to the sense of efficacy.

Distributive justice, especially with regard to technical skill, provides the seventh theme in our set. One of the central principles of modern organization is that reward should be proportionate to skill and measured contribution to the purposes of the organization. The belief that rewards should be according to rule rather than whim and that the structure of rewards should, insofar as possible, be in accord with skill and relative contribution are what we call the sense of distributive justice. As thus formulated, the principle has its most obvious application to work in organizations such as factories or office bureaucracies. When applied to other roles such as that of a customer dealing with a merchant, or a citizen dealing with an official, the principle is often referred to as the principle of *universalistic*, as against *particularistic*, treatment.

Aspirations, education, and the new learning. We defined the more modern man has having an interest in and placing higher value on formal education and schooling in skills such as reading and writing and arithmetic. He feels that modern learning and even science are not intrusions into a sacred realm, which should be left a mystery or approached only through religion, but rather that science and technology will benefit mankind by providing solutions to pressing human problems. We measured attitudes in this realm by asking how much schooling a man should try to get for his son if costs were no obstacle, whether schools should teach more morality and religion or more practical skills, and what the father prefers for his son's future occupation.

Awareness of, and respect for, the *dignity* of others is a quality many people feel has been lost in the modern world. If we wanted to make a judgment as to whether this quality was, in fact, more deeply instilled and more widely distributed in traditional societies, a great deal would clearly depend on which traditional society we used as a standard of comparison. Many intellectuals are firmly convinced that *all* men enjoyed greater personal dignity, even if they consumed fewer goods, when they lived in the pre-industrial, pre-urban age. We are not persuaded that this dictim is true. Indeed, we expected that the modern man not only would be more protective of the dignity of weaker and subordinate persons in the work setting, but would extend the principle to other relationships and thus would manifest such behavior in his treatment of all those inferior in status and power, such as women and children.

THE TOPICAL MODEL

The analytical model of the modern man was derived primarily from a theoretical consideration of the requirements of factory life. The components were selected because they were assumed to cohere as a psychological syndrome. While not arbitrary, such a conception is clearly limited and highly selective. Scholars studying the modernization process as it involves the individual often point to quite a few other problems as central issues. Some of these factors are identified as preconditions of modernization; that is, the assumption is made that, unless these issues can be resolved, a society's successful attainment of modernization will remain highly problematic. Others are identified as the accompaniments or consequences of modernization, the price, in a sense, that people pay for obtaining the benefits, such as they are, of entering the modern world. Each problem has its own sponsors, as it were, men who have particularly devoted their energies to its explication and investigation. In some instances their argument rests on a good deal of evidence; in others it is merely an assertion of opinion, however plausible.

Some of these problems were of special interest to one or more members of our research team, and to satisfy their interest we undertook to study them. Others, less interesting to us, still seemed issues of recognized importance sufficient to impose on us an obligation to include them in our research. We would thus provide further information, from *new* settings, that could be brought to bear on the standard issues of modernization research. Some of these problems had previously been studied in relative isolation, whereas our research provided an opportunity to relate them one to the other. There was finally a third set of issues about which we felt that either popular thought or expert opinion was in error, and we took the opportunity to see if evidence would support or disprove the opinion. Because each of these problems was treated by itself, and because the set as a whole was not derived from any common conception, we called the set our "topical model" of modernization. Whereas the first volume reporting the results of our research focused more or less exclusively on the analytical model as summed up in the OM scale, this current volume is devoted predominantly to exploring aspects of individual modernity encompassed in the topical model. The topical model covered about ten major areas several of which were further divided into major subthemes. The majority are discussed in some detail in subsequent chapters, whose numbers we shall indicate as we review the several elements of the model.

KINSHIP AND FAMILY

With the possible exception of religion, no institution of society is more often depicted as either an obstacle to or a victim of modernization than is the extended structure of kinship. Wilbert Moore (1951, p. 79) sums up the prevailing opinion when he says: "In general, the traditional kinship structure provides a barrier to industrial development, since it encourages reliance of the individual upon its security rather than upon his own devices." The image of the structure of family ties as a *victim* of the modernization process is well presented in M. B. Deshmukh's report on the migrant communities in Delhi, where Deshmukh (1956) observed, "The absence of social belonging, the pressure of poverty, and the evil effects of the urban environment made . . . the family bonds, regarded to be so sacred in the villages, . . . of absolutely no importance" in the migrant colonies.

After reviewing the question we concluded that there was certainly some truth to the frequent assertion that increasing urbanism and industrialism did tend to diminish the vigor of extended kinship relations. Examples of societies that emphasize extended kinship ties would be those with a strong clan system, as in China, or those in which life is organized around a kin-based compound community or multi-generational, extended family such as the famous *zadruga* of Yugoslavia, in which all the brothers, their wives, and their children occupied a common household, worked common land, and shared more or less equally in the benefits of their cooperative economy. We had little reason to doubt that when urbanism increased the physical distance between kin, and industrial employment decreased their economic dependence, the strength of kinship ties as manifested in common residence, frequent visiting, and mutual help in work would decline. A series of our questions inquiring about residence, visiting patterns, mutual help, and the like was designed to test whether these assumptions were true.

While ready to follow popular assumptions up to a point, we also came to the rather radical conclusion that in some ways industrial employment might actually *strengthen* family ties.[3] We felt that many of the common assertions about the family and modernization were much too sweeping and general, that they overlooked the difference between the extended and the immediate family, and that they failed to discriminate between degrees and types of kinship relatedness. It could well be, for example, that, while the experience of modernization weakened *extended* family ties, it would strengthen those to a man's family of *procreation* and would lead him to cling less to his mother and cleave more to his wife.[4] Again, it could be that, while a man might give less attention to his more extended kinship ties after moving to the city, the increased stability and improved well-being that characterize his life as an industrial worker would lead him to accept more fully some of his kinship obligations, at least as compared with his less secure and more impoverished brother still earning his living as a peasant in the village. We tested these relationships with a set of questions on kinship obligations, such as:

> Suppose a young man works in a factory. He has barely managed to save a very small amount of money. Now his relative (selected appropriately for each country, such as a distant cousin) comes to him and tells him he needs money badly since he has no work at all. How much obligation do you think the factory worker has to share his savings with this relative?

Our effort to weave this question and others into a scale of "family modernism" is described in chapter 9.

"WOMEN'S RIGHTS"

Intimately related to the changing pattern of family relations, but broader than it, is the question of the status of women in society. Most of the traditional societies and communities of the world are, if not strictly patriarchal, at least vigorously male-dominated. The extreme example, perhaps, is found in the Hebrew religion, in which a man may each day say a prayer of thanks to God for not having made him a woman.[5] We predicted that the liberating influence of the forces making for modernization would act on men's attitudes and incline them to accord to women status and rights more nearly equal to those enjoyed by men. We tested the men's orientation through questions on a woman's right to work and to receive equal pay, to hold public office, and freely to choose her marriage partner. Factors which are associated with the readiness to grant women equal rights, and our effort to develop a scale of family modernism, are treated in chapter 9.

BIRTH CONTROL

Few points about the contemporary world have been better documented than the fact that in many underdeveloped countries population is increasing so rapidly as to equal and sometimes exceed the rate at which the supply of food and other necessities increases. Despite an annual growth rate of some three percent per year in per capita gross national product, some of these countries are either standing still or even falling constantly behind in the standard of welfare they provide for the population and in the general development of their economy. One solution obvious to almost everyone is to reduce the number of children born to the average family. Although birth control depends in great measure on scientific technology and on particular practices guided by that technology, even the most spectacular advances in science, such as the new contraceptive pills, cannot have the desired effect except as they may be supported by the motive to use them and by patterns of interpersonal relations that make that motivation effective. To assess attitudes in this area, therefore, we inquired into our respondents' ideas of the ideal number of children and into their readiness to restrict that number under various conditions. These issues are analyzed in detail in chapter 10.

RELIGION

Religion ranks with the extended family as the institution most often identified as both an obstacle to economic development and a victim of the same process. The classic case of resistance is that of the Asian religions, and many studies going back to Max Weber's pointed to such religions as major obstacles to modernization because they are the bulwark of traditionalism and a repository of beliefs and values incompatible with modern science, technology, and the idea of progress. (See Singer 1966a.)

Many students of the subject argue rather vigorously that the individual's adherence both to the fundamental doctrine of his traditional religion and to the religious ritual and practice it requires of him will be inevitably undermined by urban living, industrial experience, and scientific education. Thus, speaking about western Africa, Dr. Geoffrey Parrinder (1953) notes: "It is sometimes said that Africans are incurably religious. . . . But the ancient religious beliefs cannot stand the strain of modern urban and industrial life. . . . They have been attacked by what someone has called 'the acids of modernity.'"

Systematic evidence for this proposition is, however, much less ample than one might imagine. We thought it appropriate, therefore, to attempt to ascertain the facts by asking a series of questions designed to measure religiosity and secularism, and we inquired into such matters as the role of God in causing and curing sickness and accidents, and the contribution of a holy man, as against a great industrialist, to the welfare of his people. We also took note of the regularity with which our subjects prayed or otherwise fulfilled the formal ritualistic proscriptions of their religion.

We were prepared to find that the influences assumed to make for attitudinal modernity in general would also lead to greater secularism, that is, rising education, urbanism, and industrial experience would all lead to greater secularism, more faith in science and similar remedies, and less reliance on religion. Yet we also made the less conventional assumption that the fulfillment of religious obligations in *practice*, especially in ritual, might actually increase as peasants shifted from their life as farmers in the village to workers in urban industry. As with the fulfillment of kinship obligations, we reasoned that the poor, harassed peasant would often lack the funds to pay for special religious services and would have neither time nor energy to undertake many of his ritualistic obligations, especially as the lack of local facilities might increase the trouble to which he must go in order to do so. We concluded, therefore, that, in the city, with religious facilities often more numerous and easily accessible, and with income steadier and more substantial, the industrial worker might find it less a burden to pay for the services his religion might require.

THE AGED

The special role of the aged is intimately linked to the strength of the family and the vigor of religion in most traditional settings. The respect, indeed the veneration, shown for the aged is often considered one of the most distinctive marks, as well as one of the outstanding virtues, of the traditional society. It is widely believed that two of the most common, indeed almost inevitable, concomitants of industrialization, urbanization, and modernization in general, are an eroding of the respect for the aged and the fostering of a youth culture in which old age is viewed not as a venerable state to which one looks forward, but rather as a dreadful condition to be approached with reluctance, even horror.

On this issue of age, as on the family and religion issues, we were not inclined to follow automatically the dominant opinion. It seemed clear that the structural changes accompanying modernization must certainly undercut the special position of the aged. In an era of technological revolutions, for example, it would be hard for the village elder relying on his long personal experience to preserve his authority indefinitely in competition with the agricultural expert relying on the latest scientific advances. As young people come to earn their own living in factories and shops without dependence on their father's land or animals, it seems inevitable that the father's authority over them should be lessened. The mass media and other models of new and competing styles of life should, in turn, make it difficult for the elders authoritatively to enforce the old norms and ways of doing things.

Yet we also felt that many analysts had perhaps exaggerated the corrosive effects of industrialism on the treatment of the aged. Nothing in urban living *per se* requires a person to show disrespect for the aged, and nothing in industrial experience explicitly teaches a man to abandon the aged. Many old men and women in the villages have been abandoned by their children because the children lacked the means to support them. Steadier wages and generally more stable conditions of life for those gainfully employed in industry could well enable those who enjoyed these benefits to be more exacting in their fulfillment of obligations to old people. And they might well be as respectful of the aged as their more traditional counterparts farming in the villages. These ideas are tested against our data in chapter 13.

POLITICS

Political modernization has been cited by many scholars as an indispensable condition of the modernization of economy and society.[6] To characterize the citizen of a modern polity the word "participant" is often used, as is the word "mobilized." There is an expectation that the citizen of a modern polity will take an active interest not only in those matters that touch his immediate life, but also in the larger issues facing his community. His allegiance is supposed to extend beyond his family and friends to the state and the nation and its leaders. He is expected to join political parties, to support candidates, and to vote in elections.

Our study was not designed to answer the question of whether or not a society could modernize its economy and still manage with a traditional political system. Nor is it appropriate for testing how far modern political institutions can operate effectively unless the citizens are also "participant" and "mobilized." But we were in a position to say how far men who were otherwise modern in their attitudes and values would also be modern in their orientation to politics. And the design of our study gave us an unusual opportunity to understand the social forces that generate in men those qualities the sociological studies of politics have identified as necessary or desirable in the citizens of a modern polity. We therefore added a large number of questions, in some countries as many as fifty, that permitted us to assess the politically specific and politically related attitudes of the subjects of our research. We included questions on political participation, attitudes toward politicians and the political process, evaluations of the effectiveness of the government, and levels of political knowledge and information. The analysis of those questions is presented in chapter 11.

INFORMATION MEDIA

Just as the wearing of a watch is often the first dramatic sign of a man's commitment to the modern world, the acquisition of a radio may be the act that really incorporates him into the world. In his study of modernization in the Middle East, Daniel Lerner (1958) treats the way in which people accept the mass media as one of the key elements in his classification of them as traditional, transitional, or modern. Indeed, he holds that "no modern society functions efficiently without a developed system of mass communication." The model of modernization, he claims:

> exhibits certain components and sequences whose relevance is global. Everywhere, rising literacy has tended to increase media exposure; increasing media exposure has "gone with" wider economic participation (per capita income) and

political participation (voting). . . . That. . . same basic model reappears in virtually all modernizing societies on all continents of the world. (p. 46)

Because other students of modernization, such as Ithiel Pool and Karl Deutsch, give heavy emphasis to mass communications as one of the key issues in the modernization process, we felt obliged to include it as one of the themes in the topical model. Our working assumption was that a modern man would more often expose himself to the media of mass communication—newspaper, radio, movies, and, where available, television. We considered it much more problematic that he would thereby shun the more traditional sources of information and advice such as village elders, traditional political leaders, or religious functionaries. Experience in research on communications behavior suggested that those who were very active in establishing contact with some sources of information tended to be outstanding in the frequency of their contact with *all* sources, modern and traditional. We were quite strongly convinced, however, that, when it came to *evaluating* the different sources of information, the more modern men would have greater confidence in and rely most heavily on the newer mass media, whereas the less modern would rely more on the more traditional sources. Indeed, we expected that the most traditional would look on the new-fangled mass media, such as the movies, as possibly dangerous and harmful to the morals of the young.

As our analysis progressed we found that interest in the news seemed very much part of the modernity syndrome. Moreover, we decided to treat exposure to the mass media as an independent variable. On both grounds, therefore, the subject qualified for treatment in our first report, and a separate chapter was devoted to it in *Becoming Modern*. Consequently, we shall not treat it separately in this volume. Interested readers may, however, discover from chapter 4 how attitudes toward the news entered into the modernity syndrome, while in chapter 5 they will find an assessment of the relative contribution which exposure to the mass media made to shaping individual modernity.

CONSUMPTION

His role as consumer is one of the most problematic aspects of the life of a citizen in a developing country. On the one hand, we hear repeatedly that economic development is impossible unless the great bulk of the population enters the money economy and begins to demand and buy modern items of mass consumption. Otherwise, the argument runs, the market for goods is too small to support national industries that can operate profitably, the circulation of money is too weak to satisfy the requirements of a modern monetary system, the base of the tax system is too narrow, and so on. On the other hand, we so often encounter the phenomenon of an alleged runaway inflation, presumably created by an uncontrolled demand for consumer goods that far outstrips the capacity to produce and, much more serious, far exceeds the growth in wealth and productivity. The result is that national outlays exceed national income by excessive amounts. To the extent that these outlays are for consumption rather than for investment in future production, deficit financing and mounting inflation follow each other in a vicious circle, economic stability is undermined, further investment is hindered, and economic stagnation or even retrogression must follow.

Economists can perhaps suggest some ways of resolving the apparent contradiction between these two models of development. For our part, we found ourselves reluctant to decide whether we should consider as more modern the man who believes mainly in savings or the man who believes that one should spend his newly acquired income in obtaining beds, sewing machines, radios, bicycles, or whatever are, for his country, the most desired and reasonably accessible of the new goods of modern mass production. In the end, we came down on the side of spending. We predicted that the less modern man would be guided by his tradition and encouraged by his circumstance to consider frugality a virtue and the chasing after goods a frivolous and perhaps even slightly immoral preoccupation. By contrast, we expected the stimulus of the city and work in industry to persuade men that there was a plenitude of goods in the world for all to have. We also anticipated that his firmer financial position plus, perhaps, easier access to credit would stimulate the urban worker to affirm the rightness of a consumption ethic. Through various questions we solicited information about the goods a man owned and would like to own, and we sought his views on frugality and liberal spending.

As in the case of attitudes towards the news, attitudes about consumption proved an integral part of the modernity syndrome and so will not be treated separately here. It may be noted by looking at the items marked CO in table 4-1 of chapter 4 that the more modern men had a strong interest in acquiring the more modern type of electrical goods. They inclined, albeit mildly, towards the view that extra effort to increase one's income is worth the trouble, but they did not agree that a man's happiness is assured by acquiring material possessions.

SOCIAL STRATIFICATION

Traditional societies are generally defined as having closed class systems, and in the extreme case as possessed of a rigid caste structure. Mobility is minimal, men are born into the positions in which they will die, and sons succeed their fathers generation after generation. Status and prestige are assigned mainly on the basis of long-established, hereditary, family connections. Authority is feared and respected, often held in awe, and treated with an elaborate show of submission and deference. In an open modern society all of these features of stratification are supposed to be quite different. Along with the changed social structure, attitudes and values about stratification are expected to change significantly. Prestige comes to be assigned more on the basis of education and technical skill, and the belief that mobility is possible for one's self and especially for one's children becomes widespread. The move to industrial labor or white collar work is perceived by most who experience it as an improvement of their social standing. They come to feel more a part of society, citizens on an equal footing with others in the national polity. To test how far such patterns of change were being experienced in the countries we studied, and to assess the relationship of changed attitudes about stratification and social classes of modernizing influences and to modern attitudes, we asked a series of questions dealing with the attitudes and experiences relating to social class and to social mobility. Those which involved interclass and intergroup hostility are treated as a subscale in chapter 11.

PSYCHIC ADJUSTMENT

No belief is more widespread among critics of industrialization than the conviction that industrialization disrupts basic social ties, breaks down social controls, and therefore produces a train of personal disorientation, confusion, and uncertainty, which ultimately leads to misery and even mental breakdown among those who are "uprooted" from the farm and "herded" into the great industrial cities.

We could not accept the assumptions that underlie this statement. It was our impression that in many traditional villages the strains of making a living, indeed of merely staying alive, were often enormous, as they certainly are in many parts of India and Pakistan, and for the hired hands who do most of the agricultural work on the large and nearly feudal Chilean hacienda, or *fundo*, as they call it. A fresh reading of many field studies and literary accounts of village life revealed jealousies, betrayal, exploitation, conflict, and hatred, which we could hardly see as being conducive to good adjustment and sound mental health. By contrast, we noted that the shift to industrial work often seemed to guarantee more income and greater security. Opportunities for self-expression and advancement, and increments of status and prestige, often accompanied the move to the cities, and we felt that they would actually lead to greater mental health among industrial workers, even in the often chaotic setting of many developing countries. We gained confidence in this rather radical position from the evidence of numerous studies on the relationship of mental health to occupation and status in the more advanced countries. These studies rather consistently showed an inverse relationship between mental illness and status in society, as well as status within industrial organizations. In other words, those higher in skill and income generally had better mental health.

There seemed good reason to evaluate the move from farm to city work, and the move from new worker to experienced worker, as improvements in status. It was reasonable, therefore, to assume that in developing countries the experienced worker well integrated into the industrial system might be *better* adjusted than one still on the farm. This proposition could be entertained without denying the possibility that those newly arrived in the city, having lost the security of the place they knew well but not yet having found a secure place in the industrial order, might indeed manifest a high degree of psychic malaise.

To test these ideas we needed measures of personal adjustment. We therefore asked several fairly simple questions, about satisfaction with one's job, social status, and opportunities, like those that had served well as indicators of adjustment in studies of industrial social-psychology. We relied mainly, however, on a simple test of psychic adjustment, known as the Psychosomatic Symptoms Test, which had proven itself remarkably useful, in culturally diverse situations, as a quick and simple diagnostic assessment of individual mental health. The content of the Test, the creation of the scale based on it, and the summary of the result of using it are given in chapter 12.

THE BEHAVIORAL MODEL

Sociology is often charged with being too abstract, divorced from the concrete reality of social life. Even when he leaves his study to go into the field, the sociologist almost invariably puts an instrument—his question-naire—between himself and the direct observation of people in social action. Insofar as the sociologist wishes to study large numbers of individuals he does not have many alternatives. And many people are too quick to dismiss as unimportant those changes in men that are limited to changes in attitude. We are not persuaded of the justice of this point. What men do is much influenced by the climate of opinion in which they find themselves. If a man, especially a young man, hears all around him an opinion conducive to modern behavior he is likely to act in accord with his impulses in that direction even if the elders are expressing only *opinion* and are not themselves personally acting in a modern way. Yet we were aware that a questionnaire need not restrict itself to questions concerning *attitudes.* The questionnaire may also be used to elicit information concerning the behavior of the man who answers it. We were acutely aware of the possibility that many of our subjects might espouse, might even have sincerely adopted, modern attitudes and opinions, while they still continued to act in their usual traditional way in the course of their daily human relations. We wished, therefore, to obtain as much information as we could about the actual behavior of our subjects. The materials we gathered for that purpose we called "behavioral measures," and, taken together, they constitute the third, or "behavioral," model of individual modernity.

The self-reported behavioral measures were those on which the subject rated himself, in effect, by stating that he did or did not do certain things. For example, he was asked to indicate whether he had voted, to report how many times a week he attended religious services, read a newspaper or listened to the radio, and whether and how often he talked with his wife about politics, his job, and raising the children. Such self-reported behavior is, of course, subject to many distortions. A man may not remember very well but give you one or another answer according to the impression he wishes to create. The same risks are run in acquiring into opinions, however, and we could not, therefore, accept the possibility of distortion as sufficient to rule out self-reported behavior as evidence relevant to our judgment of a man's modernity.

Nevertheless, we were sufficiently impressed by the potential limitations of measures of self-reported behavior to supplement them with such *objectively* ascertained measures as we could reasonably mobilize. Some of these measures were built into our interview procedure, and this device permitted us to rate all of our subjects. For example, to test how far a man might accurately be reporting that he read the newspaper or listened to the radio every day, we asked everyone to name several newspapers and radio programs, and we also tested them on the extent of their knowledge of political leaders who figured prominently in the news. We must acknowledge that a man might well really listen to the radio and not be able to tell us the names of any programs, but quite apart from judging his truthfulness we learn something important about him when we make this discovery.

The results of our work with the behavioral model of individual modernity are briefly summarized in chapter 5.

SUMMARY

The three models of individual modernization—the analytic, topical, and behavioral—guided our thinking as our research took shape, and their mark is therefore clearly visible in the content of our questions and the general design of our questionnaire. The distinctions emphasized by the three models were useful in assuring reasonable thoroughness in the selection of themes within each area, yet they prevented us from taking too narrow a view of the process of modernization. The distinctions among the models viewed as dependent variables permitted us to be much more precise in deciding which influences to study among those generally assumed to generate modernity.

Indeed, this seems an appropriate point to draw together the various elements discussed in the preceding pages, and we therefore present in chart 2-1 the complete list of the major subjects pursued in our questionnaire. Each is identified by its code letters, and is grouped under the model or models to which we felt it was most relevant. This meant that some themes were listed as part of more than one model. There was, furthermore, nothing about this arrangement which would prevent us from combining elements from all three models in a general syndrome of individual modernity such as the OM scale. Nevertheless, the three models served as a convenient organizing principle within which to encompass the considerable diversity of the various themes and areas we explored in our research.

CHAPTER 3

Forces Producing Individual
Modernity: A Theory
of Effects

Having described the characteristics of the modern man, we must now
specify the forces that produce such a man, attempting to answer the
question: What settings, and which experiences within them, most rapidly
and effectively bring a population to develop those attitudes, values, needs,
and ways of doing things that we presume better fit people for life in a
modern society? Just as modernity seems to be defined not by any one
characteristic but by a complex of traits, so we assumed that no one social
force but a whole complex of influences contribute to the transition from
the traditional to the modern man. The complete list of those factors, given
at the end of this chapter, constitutes our set of what are conventionally
called "independent variables." That means, of course, that in our scheme
we treated them as cause rather than caused. But we cannot leave it at that.

We are under some obligation to explain how and why these influences
worked. This then requires that we have a theory of effects, an explication
of the *process* whereby exposure to modernizing institutions and situations

In this chapter we have combined elements from several different papers, and added some
new connective tissue. The theory of educational effects is taken from Alex Inkeles, "The
School as a Context for Modernization," *International Journal of Comparative Sociology* 14
(1973): 196–78. The section on the factory as a school in modernity appeared originally as part
of Alex Inkeles, "The Role of Occupational Experience," in Cole S. Brembeck and T. J.
Thompson, eds., *New Strategies for Education Development* (Lexington, Mass.: D. C. Heath,
1973), pp. 87–99. The summary and conclusion section is freely adapted from Alex Inkeles,
"Social Structure and Individual Change: Evidence from Modernity Research," in Godwin
C. Chu, Syed A. Rahim, and D. Lawrence Kincaid, eds., *Communications for Group
Transformation in Development*, Communication Monograph No. 2 (Honolulu: East-West
Communication Institute, East-West Center, 1976), pp. 73–91.

produces qualities of the sort we recognize as *individual* modernity. Of the many independent variables we studied, however, we must here limit ourselves to sketching the presumed mode of influence of only those few we consider most important or most interesting. We hope that by following our model our readers may be able, for themselves, to fill in the picture for those variables with whose mode of influence we do not deal.

THE THEORY OF EDUCATIONAL EFFECTS

When we described our work in progress to various audiences, our expectation concerning the prominent role education would play generally aroused the least resistance. Almost everyone accepted the idea that education should modernize, but virtually no one asked why it should have that effect. Yet, what everyone took for granted was not at all obvious on the grounds of logic.

Had our modernity scale tested people on subjects constituting part of the typical school curriculum, that fact might have provided an obvious explanation for a high correlation of education and modernity. Yet the content of OM and of the school curriculum overlapped only with regard to measures of verbal fluency and the information questions which tapped knowledge of geography, public figures, and consumer goods. Moreover, by using OM-1 we could control the possible influence of such questions, because that form of the modernity scale tested attitudes and values only.[1] Nevertheless, OM-1 *also* showed a very strong relationship to education with a median correlation of .36, a figure significant beyond the .001 level, and one which held that level of significance under partial correlation. It was clear, therefore, that one could not account for the higher OM scores of the better educated men on the grounds that the formal curriculum of the school *directly* prepared them for high performance on our test of modernity. Even when our measure of modernity excluded any test of information or verbal fluency, the fields in which the formal curriculum specializes, education still showed as a substantial independent cause of individual modernity.

Indeed, we know of no curriculum which provides significant *formal* instruction in how to join public organizations, to be open to new experience, to value birth control, or to develop a sense of personal efficacy, to name but a few of the themes measured on the OM scale. Since the men who received more education displayed these qualities in greater degree, there must have been a good deal of learning in the school *incidental* to the curriculum and to formal instruction in academic subjects. As children in school they not only learned geography and acquired skills in reading and arithmetic; they evidently had also learned new attitudes and values, and developed new dispositions to act, whose full significance would not be manifest until they were adults.

Of course, since we tested individuals only after they reached adulthood we cannot say for certain that the modernity to which education evidently contributed was already manifest in them at the time the better educated men left school. We assume that in good part it was, and have been confirmed in that assumption by evidence from other studies (Inkeles and Holsinger 1973; Bergthold and McClelland 1968). It is, however, not necessary to insist on the point. We are equally comfortable with the assumption that in many areas schooling merely laid the groundwork which made it possible for later life experience to give concrete content to a more general disposition established in childhood. This would seem the more likely sequence for something like the readiness to accept birth control methods, which surely was not dealt with in most schools, whether directly or indirectly.

MECHANISMS OF LEARNING

But what are the mechanisms by which the school inculcates the attitudes and values, teaches the psychosocial dispositions, and trains in the behavior we define as modern? We believe that the answer lies mainly in the distinctive nature of the school as a social organization, something which has little to do with the curriculum as such. In our view, the school is not only a place for teaching; it is, inevitably, a setting for the more general socialization of the child. The school modernizes through a number of processes other than formal instruction in academic subjects. These include: *reward and punishment, modeling, exemplification*, and *generalization*.

These learning processes are not unique to the school. They occur in other formal organizations, and also in informal settings such as the family or the play group. However, the special nature of any organization gives distinctive form and content to the socialization process which goes on within it. We may illustrate the point by considering several of the OM themes individually. Since our purpose here is not to present an exhaustive analysis, but rather to illustrate an approach, we shall discuss at most two of the modernity themes only with reference to one or at most two of the socialization processes in the school. This should *not* be taken to mean that there is *a simple one-to-one correspondence between any one theme and any one process*. On the contrary, we believe that any one feature of the school as a social system may influence the child's development with regard to several themes relevant to the definition of individual modernity. Moreover, several socialization processes may be involved in the acquisition of any one of the attitudes, values, and modes of behaving relevant to defining individual modernity.

Consider first the acquisition of a sense of efficacy, which is one of the central elements in the personal profile of the modern man. In the acquisition of this feeling, *generalization* plays a substantial role. Generalization occurs when an individual enjoys so satisfying an experience in one specific relationship or performance that he is led to believe that he can attain comparable success in other contexts. Having mastered one or more specific skills, he comes to believe in his general capacity to acquire skills; having solved some problems, he may come to have confidence in his ability to solve others.

Before coming to school, children have already enjoyed mastering certain fundamental skills, notably walking and talking, feeding oneself, and sphincter control. If school did not intervene, however, there would usually be a lull until adolescence provided them new opportunities for mastery in hunting or farming, sex, or combat. For those who attend school, this interim can be filled with important new opportunities for mastery, learning to read, to write, and to figure being the most fundamental and perhaps the most rewarding. Each of these skills opens up new opportunities for increasingly competent behavior. The child who learns to read his school books later finds himself able to read directions and instructions and to follow events in the newspaper. The boy who learns his arithmetic can later assume more complex responsibilities on the farm or in the factory. By extension and diffusion, or what we have called generalization, a heightened general sense of personal efficacy results.

What the child learns in school about planning illustrates the process of *exemplification*. By exemplification we refer to the process whereby the individual incorporates into himself not a personal model but *an impersonal rule or general practice* characteristic of the social organization or institution as such.

School starts and stops at fixed times each day. Within the school day there generally is a regular sequence for ordering activities: singing, reading, writing, drawing, all have their scheduled and usually invariant time. Teachers generally work according to a plan, a pattern they are rather rigorously taught at normal school. The pupils may have no direct knowledge of the plan, but its influence palpably pervades the course of their work through school day and school year. Thus, principles directly embedded in the daily routine of the school teach the virtue of planning ahead and the importance of maintaining a regular schedule. The principle of planning may, of course, also be inculcated more directly through *reward and punishment*, as when pupils are punished for being late, marked down for not getting their papers in on time, and held after school for infractions of the rules. Moreover, application of the principle need not be limited to the context of the school, but may later be diffused to other settings.

By *modeling* we mean the child's incorporation into his own role repertoire of the ways of behaving, feeling, and thinking which he observes in significant and powerful *persons* in his milieu. It is the imitation of a person, as against the incorporation of a rule of organization, which distinguishes modeling from exemplification. In the school the most notable model is, of course, the teacher.

Modeling may be seen at work in various ways. When a teacher listens attentively to, and takes seriously, the suggestions of the children, he serves as a model of sensitivity to the feelings of subordinates and of openness to new ideas. If he is careful to keep his personal preferences from influencing grading, and gives marks in accord with objective performance, the teacher serves as a model of "universalism" or distributive justice. For such modeling to occur it is not necessary that the individual child be directly reinforced by rewards for his behavior, as in getting praised for having new ideas or helping younger children. Modeling is presumed to work because the greater visibility and influence of the teacher leads to incorporation of the behavior he manifests, even when he is mainly interacting with persons other than the learner. It is a process more like imprinting or introjection.

LIMITS ON EFFECTIVE LEARNING

The modernizing outcomes sketched above are not necessarily produced in every classroom. They represent developments which can, and often do, occur, but which are by no means inevitable. Some teachers make fun of children, humiliate and even beat them. This hardly serves as a model of respect for the dignity and feelings of subordinates and people weaker than you are. Teachers may have favorites for whom they show every preference, not only in personal matters, but also by overlooking errors on presumably objective tests in arithmetic and spelling. Such behavior will hardly inculcate faith in distributive justice. Similarly, a teacher who gives substantial evidence of being superstitious, who shows his anxiety about witches and the evil eye, cannot make a very convincing case for the relevance of science to daily life. One who is rigid, cumpulsive, and doctrinaire is not likely to stimulate openness to new ideas, and so on.

Just as the teacher may lack the qualities making him an appropriate model of modernity, so may the school fail to exemplify the organizational principles we identify with the modern mode. The flow of work in the classroom may be chaotic, the school day subject to constant disruption, the annual schedule erratic, and the very continuance of the school uncertain. Such a school will not effectively exemplify the virtues of planning and will provide little training in developing fixed schedules. Moreover, either the conditions of the pupil's life outside, or the nature of the school itself, may lead his school experience to be one of continuous frustration, failure, and rejection. In so far as this pupil generalizes from his school experience, therefore, it will hardly be by way of feeling more efficacious or more open to new experience.

To acknowledge, as we have, that there are deficient schools and teachers, even to allow that they may be extremely common in developing countries, does not fundamentally challenge our theory. Emphasizing the common shortcomings of the school and the teacher makes us aware of how much more effective school *might* be, but it does not follow that the school, imperfect as it may be, is without any effect in inculcating individual modernity. As we shall see in detail in chapters 4 and 5, our data show unambiguously that the schools in each of our six developing countries, flawed as they undoubtedly were, clearly had a substantial effect on the pupils exposed to their influence. Their pupils did learn. Furthermore, they learned more than reading, writing, and figuring. Our tests show that they also learned values, attitudes, and ways of behaving highly relevant to their personal development and to the future of their countries. Those who had been in school longer were not only better informed and verbally more fluent. They had a different sense of time, and a stronger sense of personal and social efficacy; participated more actively in communal affairs; were more open to new ideas, new experiences, and new people; interacted differently with others, and showed more concern for subordinates and minorities. They valued science more, accepted change more readily, and were more prepared to limit the number of children they would have. In short, by virtue of having had more formal schooling, the personal character of each was decidedly more modern.[2]

THE FACTORY AS A SCHOOL IN MODERNITY

The effects of the school, we believe, do not reside mainly in its formal, explicit, self-conscious pedagogic activity; rather, they are inherent in the school as an *organization*. Its modernizing effects follow not from the school's curriculum, but rather from its informal, implicit, and often unconscious program for dealing with its young charges.[3] The properties of the rational organization as a hidden pursuader—or, as we prefer to put it, as a silent and unobserved teacher—become most apparent when we consider the role of occupational experience in shaping the modern man.

That the school might modernize was quite readily accepted by almost everyone. But our idea that work in factories should be a modernizing experience was met by skepticism or outright rejection from a surprisingly large number of persons to whom we initially described our project. Their reasons were by no means insubstantial.

First and foremost, they challenged the assumption that basic changes in personality could occur with any regularity in individuals who had already reached maturity. The OM scale, our overall measure of modernization, measures some patterns of response which lie at the core of the personality. These include the sense of personal efficacy, cognitive openness, trust, orientation to time, and modes of relating to social "inferiors." Modern psychology considers these attributes as "basic" in the sense that they are assumed to be laid down in childhood and adolescence, and thereafter to be stable or relatively unchanging, certainly much more so than are mere opinions. Consequently our critics were led to express the same view as Professor Bloom (1964, p. 218) when, in his famous review of research on *Stability and Change in Human Characteristics*, he concluded: "We are pessimistic about producing major changes in a [personal] characteristic after it has reached a high level of stability." Bloom had in mind mainly such attributes as intelligence or cognitive capacity, but a large segment of the community of personality psychologists takes essentially the same pessimistic view of the prospects for bringing about significant change in basic characteristics of personality after the age of sixteen or eighteen.

The second reason our critics advanced was doubt that the factory provided a sufficiently powerful environment to bring about changes in basic value orientations and need dispositions. Some psychologists hold that there are almost no circumstances under which really basic traits of personality laid down in early childhood can be altered substantially in adulthood. Most would, however, agree with Bloom that under extreme environmental conditions—such as are prevalent in concentration camps, prisons, or "brainwashing" sessions—"one may encounter considerable deterioration in characteristics which are ordinarily quite stable." This concession to the idea of adult change, however, is limited largely to instances of deterioration or retrogression; it does not apply to long-term positive transformations, that is, to growth and new development in adulthood. Those who assumed such extreme conditions to be necessary for bringing about transformations of fundamental personality characteristics in adulthood were, therefore, convinced the factory could not produce the sort of changes we anticipated.

The third line of attack was based on a challenge to our interpretation of the factory as a social organization. Our critics saw the factory in a quite different light. They agreed that even if the factory could bring about significant personality change in adulthood, the kind of change it produced would probably make men less rather than more like the project's model of a modern man.

They pointed out, for example, that factories are hierarchically organized, and argued that therefore one should not expect them to stimulate the sort of participant citizenship required by our model of the modern man. Since technical considerations must always be uppermost in making decisions in industry, they noted, there was little likelihood that the factory would train men to pay respectful attention to the opinions of subordinates and others less powerful or prestigious than they were. Our critics went on to point out that most factory workers are in a dependent and passive position. They perform routine repetitive functions, often dull and deadening, and do so mainly on the initiative of others. According to this view, workers are coerced and harried by the clock and the inexorable pace of the machine. Changes in the machinery or in the arrangement of their work are likely to require that they work harder, or faster, and may even threaten some of them with a layoff. Therefore, our critics claimed, factory work would encourage passivity and dependence, foster fear of and resistance to change, and stimulate a reaction against the domination of strict schedules and a preference for more spontaneously arranged work.

We challenged our critics' interpretation on all three counts. Of course, we did not rest our case on the mere assertion that our critics were wrong. There were sound reasons for doubting the validity of their assumptions.

THEORETICAL FOUNDATIONS

First we looked more closely at the assumption that the main features of individual personality are laid down in early childhood and adolescence and persist basically unchanged into adulthood. We were at once struck by how little systematic empirical evidence there was to support that assumption. Since the idea seems to accord so well with most people's practical experience, there has been little incentive to challenge or even test this theory, which has nevertheless become almost a dogma of the psychoanalytic age.[4]

Benjamin Bloom (1964) performed a great service by pulling together the research available on the stability of responses to a variety of psychological tests. These included the Kuder Personal Preference Record, which tests interests such as the mechanical and artistic; the Strong Vocational Interest Test; the Allport and Vernon Test of Values; the Thurstone Personality Scale, and others. One striking fact which emerged from Bloom's review was that virtually all of the available longitudinal studies on which so many of our conclusions about the stability of personal traits rested had been done with high school and college students. These researches, therefore, typically covered only two years or so of elapsed time, and in very few cases really extended very far into adulthood. Most, therefore, simply have no bearing on the question of how far basic attitudes, values, and dispositions are stable throughout adulthood. Even those few studies which covered a period of three or four years, however, indicated that a good deal of change may have taken place in that short interval, because the correlation of test scores over that span of time was generally only about 0.60 on tests such as the Allport-Vernon value scale, Plant's tests of ethnocentrism, and Thurstone's personality scale.

How much stability or change there will be depends, of course, on the area of personality one is testing. Apparently there have been very few, if any, truly longitudinal studies of features of personality which are strictly, or even remotely, comparable to those dealt with by the OM scale. Furthermore, how much personality change one observes in the given group will, in our opinion, depend greatly on how far the group's environment has been changing. It is noteworthy, therefore, that after reviewing the evidence with regard to the stability of adult characteristics Bloom concluded:

> Much of the stability we have reported in this work is really a reflection of environmental stability. That is, the stability of a characteristic for a group of individuals may, in fact, be explained by the constancy of their environments over time. (p. 223)

The essential feature of our modernization study, however, is its emphasis on the *change* in the social and physical environment which men experience as they shift from the more traditional settings of village, farm, and tribe to city residence, industrial employment, and national citizenship. We believed that in such circumstances the stability of personal characteristics commonly observed under conditions of social and cultural continuity must give way to a more rapid and profound rate of personal adaptation. We proceeded, then, on the assumption that the personality can continue to develop and grow well into adulthood, and that basic change, even in fundamental characteristics such as the sense of efficacy, was more than merely possible. Rather, we assumed it to be highly likely, at least when men lived under social conditions conducive to personal transformation, such as those prevailing in the sectors of developing countries experiencing the process of modernization.

Our second challenge to our critics rested on the belief that basic personal change can be stimulated by experience in settings less extreme or stark than prisons and concentration camps. While taking this position, we were not unaware that on completion of his intensive review of stability and change in personal characteristics Professor Bloom had stated that "a central thesis of this work is that change in many human characteristics becomes more and more difficult as the characteristics become more fully developed," with the consequence that "to produce a given amount of change . . . requires more and more powerful environments and increased amounts of effort and attention as the characteristic becomes stabilized" (pp. 229-30). In our view, the factory qualified as such a "powerful environment," one which should be able to impinge upon individuals with sufficiently concentrated force to bring about changes in core features of personality.

We noted, first, that contact between the individual and the factory system was not fleeting or irregular. To work in a factory means to expose oneself to its regimen for at least eight hours a day, five to six days a week, and continuously, week in and week out, over a period of years.

Second, we believe this involvement with the factory is serious and engaging for the participants. Work is one of the most important elements in most men's lives. Moreover, in developing countries, jobs with the pay and steadiness of industrial employment are rare. That alone makes factory work particularly desirable. In addition, such employment often confers prestige. Most men in industry in these countries are, therefore, not merely sojourners casually passing time in the plant.

Third, and most important in conferring on the factory the quality of a "powerful environment," are certain features of its activity and organization. Technical constraints, the objective standard of productivity, and strict requirements of profitability all act to give the factory a firm and relatively invariant character. It does not so much adapt to men as it requires that they adapt to it.

The essential logic of machinery and mechanical processes must be rigorously observed, else the machine, or its attendant, or both, must break. It requires only a few instances in which hair, or a flowing gown, or fingers get caught in the machine, to impress the point indelibly on all who come in contact with it. This same sharpness of outline tends to be manifested in the organization of the factory. Departments, shops, even individual machines are distinctly set off and clearly demarcated. Division of labor is generally precisely and rigorously maintained. Hierarchies of authority and technical skill give a definite structure to interpersonal relations. Standards of performance tend to be objective and precise. And the system of rewards and punishments is highly relevant to all the participants, unambiguous, powerful, and by and large objectively calculated.

These characteristics of the factory that make it a "powerful environment" point to the basis for the third challenge we addressed to our critics, namely, that the factory's effect would make men more rather than less modern.

In our view, the organization of the factory and its mode of functioning embodied a series of fundamental principles to which men from a traditional background would respond favorably. We anticipated that rather than respond with confusion or react defensively, traditional men would be open to the lessons the factory had to teach, incorporating and adopting as their own standard the norms embedded in modern factory organization. This learning, we believed, would come about through the same processes of socialization identified by us above as the basis for learning modern attitudes and values in the school—modeling, generalization, exemplification, and reward and punishment. These processes can be observed at work across the whole range of the main themes which defined our analytic model of the modern man, but it should suffice to illustrate the point with reference to a select few.

EFFICACY

By the very nature of the forces at work in it, the factory exemplifies efficacy, since in it is concentrated the power to convert obdurate materials into new shapes and forms far transcending the capacity of the unaided individual to do so. In the factory the worker sees large pieces of metal or mounds of ore given new shape: coal and coke become steel, bauxite powder becomes aluminum, thick bars of steel are twisted and bent, small globs of plastic are molded to complex, intricate, and even beautiful contours—sometimes with little more visible human effort than pushing buttons or moving levers. The total working of the factory affirms man's capacity, through organization and the harnessing of mechanical power, to transform nature to suit man's needs. One worker we spoke to in Nigeria expressed the basic idea for us perfectly when, in reply to our questions about how his work left him feeling, he said: "Sometimes like nine feet tall with arms a yard wide. Here in the factory I alone with my machine can twist any way I want a piece of steel all the men in my home village together could not begin to bend at all."

The factory provides models of efficacy in the person of the engineer, the technician, and the more highly skilled workers such as tool and die makers. These men have the professional responsibility to solve problems, to develop new combinations of elements, to convert ideas on blueprints into concrete mechanical reality. In bringing their technical training and experience to bear on the production problems of the factory, they should provide regular, sometimes daily, personal models of efficacious behavior.

The system of reward and punishment in the factory should also serve to reinforce the lesson in efficacy it offers. The inducement to greater personal efficacy is probably most immediate in a piecework system, although the learning it induces may quickly be extinguished if management's response be continuously to raise the quotas. Nevertheless, efficacious behavior in the plant may be, and often is, stimulated by direct reward, such as bonuses, reclassification to higher skill categories and promotion to more responsible work.

Readiness for innovation and openness to systematic change, the struggle to keep costs down to competitive levels, and the constant pressure to keep up with the demands of the market, oblige factories to be outstanding among large-scale institutions in the introduction of new machinery, techniques, and administrative arrangements. We recognize that the main responsibility for effecting such changes usually lies with management, and with its associated engineering and technical personnel. We assumed, therefore, that in stimulating men toward openness to new experience and readiness to accept change, the factory would work mainly through the process of modeling.

Insofar as the factory as an institution is generally receptive to innovation, readily adopting new techniques for processing material, new machinery, and new personnel policies, it should also encourage openness to new experience by exemplification. Managerially sponsored innovation may, of course, mean harder, faster, or more dangerous work for the employee. In most reasonably modern factories, however, technical innovations are more likely to lead to safer, less strenuous, and more evenly paced work. Technical innovation may also result in higher individual productivity and elevated skill ratings. Although there is, again, no guarantee that these gains will be fed back to the workers in the form of increased earnings, in many instances the technological innovations of management do redound to the interest of the workers. Insofar as their experience was thus positive, we expected workers to generalize the lessons of the factory to other situations in which openness to new experience and readiness for change are called for.

By bringing together a much wider variety of men than one commonly finds in the village, the factory offers the worker an encounter not only with new ways of doing mechanical things, but with new people whose thinking and customs may be quite different from his own. Since the factory is a culturally neutral ground, since it presents a firm structure which it applies more or less equally to all its members as a guide to their interaction, and since it holds up certain common standards of evaluation such as objective skill and productivity, much of the uncertainty that usually surrounds contact with strangely different people may be eliminated or at least be made more bearable in the context of the factory. A more secure basis is thereby provided for exploring new customs and for discovering common interests and propensities, which are otherwise typically masked by the more salient dissimilarities with which people from different cultures initially confront each other. In the context of the factory, the cost of exploring new ways is low, and the rewards may be quite gratifying. Such success in opening up relations with people who are culturally rather different from oneself may, furthermore, be generalized into a lessened fear of strangers and a heightened confidence in one's ability to understand foreign people and ways.

PLANNING AND TIME

To attain its goal of maximizing productivity the factory must emphasize planning. The principle of planning is exemplified in the very layout of the factory, designed to permit the most rational movement of goods from their point of entry as raw material to their exit as finished product; in the flow of the work, as the product is subjected to one process after another in the technically prescribed succession; and in the coordination which insures that despite extensive division of labor, the required tools and materials will be available at the appropriate place and at the right time.

The management of time is intimately related to planning. Industrial production requires precise scheduling in bringing together the diverse elements entering into the production process. This requirement is most evident with the assembly line, since it rigorously imposes the necessity that everyone start and stop at the same time, that each process be allocated a precise amount of time, and that each step be completed as scheduled. According to the socialization principle of exemplification, men working in factories should come to internalize a concern for orderly advanced planning and precise scheduling. This learning should be facilitated by the system of factory reward and punishment since persistent lateness brings reprimands and may lead to discharge, and bonuses are often paid for completing important jobs on or ahead of schedule.

RESPECT FOR SUBORDINATES

The predominance of rules and formal procedures in the factory should teach respect for the rights of subordinates and of other individuals of inferior standing in the hierarchy of status. Of course there are still factories run by cruel and vicious bosses, and even in the best run plant a particular foreman or other supervisor may be able to hound and even persecute a man. By and large, however, the norm of treatment in the factory emphasizes relatively just, humane, respectful treatment of subordinates, at least compared to what goes on in many other settings in underdeveloped countries.

Factories are generally owned by public corporations. This may make them places in which authority is cold and distant, but their public character generally also insures that the extremity of personal, vengeful treatment by harsh bosses is much less manifested in them than in other types of work situations. Generally the factory is dominated by men of relatively higher education, in whom a more civilized standard of personal conduct is likely to have been inculcated than will be commonly found among absentee landowners or their overseers. Industrial managers and engineers are likely to look for their "ego tonic" outside, in the larger community, rather than seeking it vicariously through abusing the dignity of their subordinates in the plant. In addition, the trade union, generally totally absent in the countryside but quite common in urban industry, serves as an additional important source of restraint to insure that the men in the plant are treated with respect in accord with objective rules for decent supervision.

The interdependence of men in the complex production process of the factory requires that there be a substantial flow of information up as well as down the status hierarchy. Inexperienced engineers and foremen quickly learn, often to their dismay, that their own success is heavily dependent on the cooperation and goodwill of their subordinates. The men in most immediate contact with machines and materials see and know things which are vital to the fulfillment of the factory's production goals. To be effective, therefore, supervisors cannot merely tell the men what to do; they must also pay attention to what the men tell them about how things are going.

In general, then, by modeling and exemplification, men working in factories should have an opportunity to learn lessons in showing consideration for subordinates and in respecting the feelings of those weaker or of lesser status than themselves. To the extent that their views are listened to and given some weight in the decision-making process, they should also be learning to see the value of diversity of opinion as opposed to unanimity.

All of the other themes built into our analytical model of the modern man should also, in some degree, be reflected in a man's work experience in an industrial establishment. Belief in the calculability of the world and the people in it should be encouraged by the regularity of work and pay in the factory, by the fulfillment of its imperatives for close coordination in the division of labor, and by the model of responsible norm-oriented behavior usually presented by the engineering and technical personnel. A preference for universalism over particularism might well be fostered by the factory organization's embodiment of bureaucratic principles of governance through impartial rules, and its conformity to technical and normative standards. A rejection of fatalism and its replacement by optimism and active striving should be fostered by several attributes of the factory, including the steadiness and relative security of industrial work, its mastery over materials, and its evident ability to exercise some substantial control over natural forces.

Of course we are completely aware that none of the effects we anticipated is a necessary concomitant of industrial employment. Our description of the factory was cast in what Weber called "ideal-typical" form, in order to highlight the theoretical basis for our expectations. In doing so, we meant neither to assert that the factory was unique, nor to deny that in many, perhaps most, concrete instances it might fail to live up to its potential.

These then were among the main reasons we selected work in factories as the special focus of our attention in seeking to assess the effects of occupational experience in reshaping individuals according to the model of the modern man. Just as we viewed the school as communicating lessons beyond reading and arithmetic, so we thought of the factory as training men in more than the minimal lessons of technology and the skills necessary to industrial production. We conceived of the factory as an organization serving as a general school in attitudes, values, and ways of behaving which are more adaptive for life in a modern society. We reasoned that work in a factory should increase a man's sense of efficacy, make him less fearful of innovation, and impress on him the value of education as a general qualification for competence and advancement. Furthermore, we assumed that in subtle ways work in a factory might even deepen a man's mastery of arithmetic and broaden his knowledge of geography without the benefit of the formal lessons usually presented in the classroom. Indeed, the slogan for our project became, "The factory can be a school—a school for modernization."

SUMMARY AND CONCLUSIONS

The factory and the school share certain characteristics which should, in our view, make them effective in inculcating modern qualities in individuals exposed to their influence.

First, both qualify as strong environments, by which we mean having a clear formal structure which is relatively unambiguous to the participants who occupy positions within it, and which is relatively unyielding about adapting itself to the special requirements of different individuals.

Second, contact between the individual and these strong institutions is of relatively long duration. It is spread over months or years, and each day continues for six or even eight hours or more.

Third, these settings are entered voluntarily, and are seen by the participants as offering relatively fair terms of exchange by providing substantial returns not only to the organization but to the individual participant in it. This condition is important for distinguishing a sojourn in prison from one in a school or factory.

Fourth, the impact of the school and the factory is assumed to rest, in part, on the contrast between these settings and those previously experienced by the individual. Thus, the family may also be a strong institution based on relatively noncoercive participation of long duration, yet leaving it to attend school may produce a substantial effect on the child because the principles on which the school operates present so marked a contrast to those on which family relations are based. Similarly, traditional village agriculture presents a system of very definite character, but one which contrasts sharply with the salient features of the factory as a productive enterprise.

What is perhaps most salient about a factory is probably its great concentration of inanimate power. It is therefore tempting to look to that fact in explaining its modernizing potential. But if schools also modernize, the presence of machinery cannot be an indispensable ingredient. Many schools operate with a very simple technology limited to a teacher equipped with only a blackboard, pencil and paper, and perhaps some books. It seems more likely that the common effect of school and factory stems from common organizational features such as planning and rationalized allocation of assignments; technical division of labor; reward according to competence, skill, and performance; specificity of function; competence-based hierarchies of authority; respect for learning and science; and commitment to treatment according to objective rules. Such organizational features could also explain why we found certain forms of cooperative farming also had a substantial modernizing effect.

Yet our search cannot end at this point because we have both good reason and considerable evidence for believing that exposure to the mass media also modernizes. Such exposure clearly is quite different from participation in the sort of organizational setting represented by a school, a factory, or a cooperative farm. The role of the mass media in communicating information is obvious, and one can readily imagine the case for its ability to shape cognitive patterns likely to qualify as modern. It is less obvious why such exposure should increase one's sense of efficacy. Perhaps having detailed knowledge of important events is ego-enhancing. And empathic identification with the public figures who make the news may induce a sense of one's own potential for mastery on at least a modest scale. Intriguing as these ideas may be, we must acknowledge that much remains to be done at both the theoretical and empirical level to flesh out the theory of effects and thus explain the process whereby individuals become more modern.

Each of the measures we introduced as explanatory variables in our research invites the same sort of analysis. The set included the following main variables:

1. *Formal Education:* self-report, in years, excluding correspondence schools, night schools, short-term trade schools, and the like.

2. *Parental Status:* self-report of father's education, in years, excluding special schooling as in own formal education; father's occupational prestige level was substituted in Israel, where nonresponse was great.

3. *Quality of urban experience:* project rating or ranking based on the distance of present residence and/or place of work from urban centers, and the judged degree of cosmopolitanism of the urban center relative to other urban centers.[5]

4. *Living Standard:* self-report of number of consumer goods stated as possessed out of a list of five items presented.

5. *Mass media exposure:* self-report, combination of stated frequency of exposure per week to radio and to newspapers; TV was substituted for radio exposure in Argentina, since the former showed a closer relationship to newspaper exposure.

6. *Occupational type:* self-report leading to a five-category rank order as follows—rural cultivator, urban new factory worker (less than 6 months of total experience), urban nonindustrial worker, middle experienced factory

worker, highly experienced factory worker. This ordering was based on both theoretical and empirical considerations.

For our analysis of the factory workers alone, we shall use three variables in place of occupational type. Two of these variables related to the amount and quality of factory experience an individual had been exposed to, and one relates to urban experience.

7. *Individual factory work experience:* self-report, composite of total months of factory experience, number of different factories worked in, and skill level of specific job—as rated by project staff from the job description given by the respondent.

8. *Modernity of present factory:* part self-report, part objective data from records, part rating by project staff; composite of size of factory work force, project rating of factory modernity, and number of fringe benefits perceived by respondent as being offered in the factory.

9. *Urban vs. rural origin:* self-report, dichotomy representing our sampling distinction between (a) men raised in rural areas (under 2,000 population) for at least 12 of their first 15 years, and (b) men raised in urban areas (over 20,000 population) for at least 12 of their first 15 years; available as an adequate variable only in Argentina, Chile, and Nigeria, owing to nature of sampling.

PART TWO

RESULTS OF
THE FIRST PHASE

CHAPTER 4

Creating and Validating
the Modernity Scale

Although *Becoming Modern* explains in detail why we were interested in developing a summary indicator of individual modernity and how we constructed the measure we called the OM scale, we nevertheless felt it would be inappropriate to pass over that topic completely in this volume. The OM scale played so central a role in our research that one cannot adequately orient oneself to other aspects of the project without some understanding of that measure. In addition, however, there are some aspects of our effort to measure individual modernity which were not dealt with systematically in our first volume. It seems appropriate to present them now.

The analysis in *Becoming Modern* is based almost exclusively on what we called the "long forms" of the modernity scale, by which we meant that the scale utilized the full range of questions included in our questionnaire. Although that suited our purpose very well, other researchers could not invest the hours of questioning required for this purpose. To meet an obvious need we tried to develop a distillation of our longer questionnaire which would permit a much quicker identification of individuals as modern or traditional. The result of that effort was a "short form" of the OM scale. It is that scale, rather than the full-length version utilized by us in *Becoming Modern*, which has been used by most subsequent researchers influenced by our effort. That fact alone would justify reproducing here the description of the short form. In addition, however, the article on the short form was the first publication in which we presented any of the empirical

This chapter is adapted from David H. Smith and Alex Inkeles, "The OM Scale: A Comparative Socio-Psychological Measure of Individual Modernity," *Sociometry* 29(1966): 353–77.

evidence our project generated, and it has become the *locus classicus* for citation purposes. It thus became a strong candidate for inclusion in this volume.

DEVELOPING A SHORT FORM OF THE OM SCALE

The concept of modernity has emerged as one of the central themes in social analysis, not only among sociologists, but also in the work of economists, historians, and political scientists. In the next decades it seems destined to assume an even more prominent place in the thinking of behavioral scientists. The term may refer to two quite different objects. As used to describe a society, "modern" generally means a national state characterized by a complex of traits including urbanization, high levels of education, industrialization, extensive mechanization, high rates of social mobility, and the like. When applied to individuals, it refers to a set of attitudes, values, and ways of feeling and acting, presumably of the sort either generated by or required for effective participation in a modern society. In this report we deal only with *individual* modernity, that is, with a sociopsychological rather than an exclusively sociological problem.

As is true of some important concepts, individual modernity is more often defined than measured. On the occasions when it is measured, it is generally done on an *ad hoc* basis, separately by each team going into the field. This consumes much energy for a task which may be incidental to the main interest of the various projects. The venture is, furthermore, inherently fraught with much risk of failure. Even when the effort is successful, the lack of comparability of one's new measure with the measures of modernity used in other studies greatly reduces its contribution to cumulative social science knowledge.

As a byproduct of our large-scale comparative study of modernization in six developing countries we believe we have been able to devise a brief, reliable, valid, and cross-culturally useful measure of the relative standing of individuals on a scale of modernity. We feel this scale not only has potential for use in research, but could serve in developing countries as a practical personnel screening device to aid in the selection of individuals for training or employment, or for selecting communities which might, or should, be prime targets for community development programs. We here present the scale we have devised, and explain very briefly the research operations by which we arrived at it.

After reviewing the literature and defining our own theoretical position we identified some thirty topics, themes, areas, or issues which seemed relevant to a definition of modernity. The complete list is given in chart

4-1, which will be recognized as listing many of the themes first cited in chart 2-1 and described in chapter 2. What is new here is the breakdown of many of those major themes into subthemes, as in the case of *efficacy* (EF) which, for present purposes, has been divided into three subthemes.

Basically, we assumed that modernity would emerge as a complex but coherent set of psychic dispositions manifested in *general* qualities such as a sense of efficacy, readiness for new experience, and interest in planning, linked in turn to certain dispositions to act in *institutional relations*—as in being an active citizen, valuing science, maintaining one's autonomy in kinship matters, and accepting birth control. As indicated above, we assumed these personal qualities would be the end product of certain early and late socialization experiences such as education, urban experience, and work in modern organizations such as the factory.

To measure each of these themes we devised a long series of questionnaire-interview items, largely of the fixed-alternative type, but including a number of open-ended questions. More than 60 of the questions are presented, albeit in highly abbreviated form, in table 4-1, with code designations which permit them to be related to the themes described in charts 2-1 and 4-1. Some of these items we borrowed from prior or concurrent studies of modernization, but the majority we created ourselves.[1] By avoiding an agree-disagree format, we attempted to develop an instrument that would not be susceptible to the effects of automatic acquiescence. We also strove to offset the tendency of some to give the socially desirable answer by presenting item alternatives of balanced attractiveness.

After careful pretesting of our initial pool of items over a two-year period, first in Puerto Rico and then in three of the field stations, our original interview with sixteen hours of questions was boiled down to a more manageable, though still quite lengthy, four hours of average interviewing time. The principal bases of selection used for deriving the final set of items were: (a) that an item measure a theoretically important aspect of one or more of our themes; (b) that every theme be measured by at least two items; (c) that none of the themes be measured by more items than the complexity and importance of the theme demanded; (d) that the question deal with general human situations, understandable in other cultures and accessible to men of little or no formal education; (e) that the item be readily translatable into languages other than English without substantially changing its meaning or intent; and (f) that the pretest results show the item had elicited a good range or distribution of responses in each of the countries in which it was tested.

CHART 4-1

Major Themes Explored in Defining Psychosocial Modernity

Project Code	Descriptive Title of Theme	Project Code	Descriptive Title of Theme
AC	Political Activism	GO(2)	Growth of Opinion Valuation
AG	Role of Aged	ID	Political Identification
AS(1)[a]	Educational Aspirations	KO(1)	Extended Kinship Obligations
AS(2)	Occupational Aspirations	KO(2)	Kinship Obligation to Parental Authority
CA(1)	Calculability of People's Dependability	MM	Mass Media Valuation
CA(2)	Calculability of People's Honesty	NE(1)	Openness to New Experience—Places
CH	Change Perception and Valuation	NE(2)	Openness to New Experience—People
CI	Citizens Political Reference Groups	PA	Particularism-Universalism
CO(1)	Consumption Aspirations	PL	Planning Valuation
CO(2)	Consumer Values	RE(1)	Religious Causality
DI	Dignity Valuation	RE(2)	Religious-Secular Orientation
EF(1)	General Efficacy	SC	Social Class Attitudes
EF(2)	Efficacy and Opportunity in Life Chances	TI	Time (Punctuality) Valuation
EF(3)	Efficacy of Science and Medicine	TS	Technical Skill Valuation
FS(1)	Family Size—Attitudes	WR(1)	Women's Rights
FS(2)	Family Size—Birth Control	WR(2)	Co-ed Work and School
GO(1)	Growth of Opinion Awareness	IN	Information Eliciting Questions
		b	Behavioral Measures

[a] Some of the larger and more complex theme areas identified by a single code have been broken into two or more subthemes for this analysis. To indicate this, the code letters are followed by a number in parentheses to identify which subtheme it is.

[b] All but the last two codes (information and behavior) refer to attitude areas. There was no single code designation for behavioral measures. In addition, a question falling mainly in one of the attitudinal realms might be coded not for attitudinal content, but as a behavior item.

The same pool of items used to derive some more selective measure may yield quite a different set of items depending partly on the procedure used to extract the final set, and partly on the nature of the samples to which the questions were presented. The samples we studied were chosen to answer certain analytic questions of concern to the larger project. They were, therefore, highly selective, rather than representative or random. Yet they were, we believe, sufficiently diverse to insure that the final distillate of our procedures for screening items from the larger pool cannot be assumed to be mainly, or even very largely, shaped by the peculiar or distinctive characteristics of our sample. We have samples from six different countries, which are all in the classification of "underdeveloped," but range from those with predominantly European culture, such as Argentina and Israel, through Chile, to the relatively "exotic" cultures of India, Pakistan, and Nigeria. Any scale which works with samples from such a range of countries must be general indeed.

So far as the samples within each country are concerned, while not covering the full range of variation, they do deal with representatives from a large proportion of the main population groups in each. Our samples are focused on the common man in a range of settings—the peasants (or cultivators, to use a less value-laden term) represent the traditional, base-line culture in the several societies. The urban nonindustrial workers represent men who either migrated to the city from the countryside, or who were born in the city but who have *not* been exposed to factory work or any other large bureaucratic work setting. The industrial workers were selected purposively from a variety of modern and traditional factories to include one-third to one-half as many new (less than 6 months experience) as experienced (3 years or more) factory men. The industrial worker and urban nonindustrial worker samples include men of urban and rural origin who have recently been exposed to both the city and the factory as modernizing social influences. Because we were working mainly with the common man, the educational range in our samples was limited, running in most cases from illiteracy to 6 or 8 years of schooling. In each country, however, we added a special sample of highly educated workers, and this increased the range to 12 or even 14 years of schooling.[2]

Because we were studying modernization as a *process*, we conducted our research in developing countries, rather than in fully developed, industrialized nations. To avoid the danger of false generalizations based on the special cultural or social structural attributes of a single country, we decided to collect samples from several quite different developing countries. We do not claim our samples are *representative* of any of these countries,

TABLE 4-1—*Continued*

Code Number	Abbreviated Version of Questions[a] (Italic Alternative Indicates Modern End of Scale)	Six Country Average Item to Scale Pearsonian r in Form[b]						
		Long[c]	Short 1	Short 2	Short 3	Short 4	Short 5	Short 6
EF-3	Man's position in life depends on: fate always to *own effort always*	.344	.386	.368	.368	.362	—	—
EF-4	Can able, smart, industrious, ambitious boy succeed against fate: *completely*/partly/no	.234	.266	—	—	—	—	—
EF-8	Do you prefer job with *many*/few/no responsibilities	.294	.335	—	.332	—	—	—
EF-11	Which is most important for future of country: *work*/gov't planning/God/luck	.373	.434	.425	.420	.428	.483	.456
EF-13	Will man someday understand nature: *fully*/never can	.286	.319	—	—	—	—	—
EF-14	If man explores nature's secrets (by science) is it: *good*/bad (ungodly)	.335	.388	.378	.363	.378	.467	.417
FS-1	What is ideal number of children for man like yourself: *low* to high number	.218	—	.280	.281	.296	—	—
FS-3	Limiting size of family is: *necessary*/wrong	.315	.370	.318	.321	.325	.394	.347
FS-4	Is harmless pill contraceptive for wife: *good*/bad	.263	.338	—	—	—	—	—
FS-5	Should people take government advice on family size: *yes*/no	.213	.278	—	—	—	—	—
GO-2	What are biggest problems facing your country: few to *many* problems	d	—	—	—	—	—	.356
GO-4	Are the opinions of other people different from yours: *many*/few/none	.090	—	.157	—	.152	—	—
GO-5	Who should speak for family: husband only/both/*wife too*	.187	—	.233	—	—	—	—
GO-6	Should one pay more attention to opinion of: *people*/both equally/leaders only	.140	—	—	.222	.222	—	—
ID-1	Do you consider yourself primarily citizen of: *nation*/region/state/city	.279	.323	.339	—	.342	—	—

IN-6 or 7	Where is Washington (or Moscow): *correct*/incorrect	d	—	—	—	—	—	.559
KO-1	Should man feel closer to: *wife*/other family member (e.g., mother, father, brother)	.152	—	.206	.207	.222	—	—
KO-2	Should man choose job preferred by: *himself*/parents	.242	.282	—	.225	.305	—	—
MM-5	How often do you get news from newspapers: *daily*/often/rarely/never	d	—	—	—	—	—	.520
MM-6	What sources do you trust most for world news: *mass media*/non-mass media	.236	.261	—	.267	—	—	—
MM-10	What news interests you most: *world*/nation/village/sports/religion	.294	.350	.350	.340	.356	.440	.399
NE-1	If you could improve standard living 100% would you: *be willing to move*/prefer not	.152	—	.206	—	—	—	—
NE-2	Want to know stranger with different customs, speech or religion: *well*/prefer not	.255	.309	—	.293	—	—	—
NE-3	In meeting people do you prefer: *to meet new people*/see familiar ones	.272	.310	—	.318	—	—	—
NE-4	Could you understand thinking of men of different religion: *yes*/no	.284	.353	—	.379	—	—	—
NE-5	Could you understand thinking of man from distant country: *yes*/no	.278	.352	.350	.372	.351	.424	.404
NE-7	Would you prefer rural/*urban life*	.150	—	—	.216	.203	—	—
PL-4	Do you prefer to plan affairs in advance: *mostly*/sometimes/never	.244	.262	.249	—	.234	—	—
RE-8	Who do you admire most: monk/*both*/factory owner	.250	.303	.262	—	—	—	—
RE-9	Who has done more for his country: monk/*both*/factory owner	.231	.290	—	—	—	—	—
RE-10	Which has best lived up to his religion: monk/*both*/factory owner	.200	—	—	—	.232	—	—
RE-11	Most important in caring for sick person: prayer/*both*/medical care	.305	.359	—	.327	—	—	—

TABLE 4-1—Continued

Code Number	Abbreviated Version of Questions[a] (Italic Alternative Indicates Modern End of Scale)	Six Country Average Item to Scale Pearsonian r in Form[b]						
		Long[c]	Short 1	Short 2	Short 3	Short 4	Short 5	Short 6
RE-12	Can man be good without religion: *yes*/no	.260	.326	.328	.342	.331	.436	.390
RE-14	A man should give to the poor because of: fear of God/*generosity*	.266	.298	—	—	—	—	—
TI-5	After how many minutes would you consider pal late for date: *few* to many minutes	.205	—	.278	.281	.284	—	—
TS-12	Best way to increase factory output: more workers/*more training for workers*	.204	—	.247	.245	.239	—	—
WC-2	Kind of work you would prefer: low to *high status*	.173	—	—	.296	—	—	—
WR-7	If women do same work as men pay should be: *same*/less/much less	.216	.250	.288	—	.291	—	—
WR-9	If family has both boy & girl children prefer next child: boy/girl/*either*	.105	—	—	.159	—	—	—
WR-11	Choose spouse to suit: parents always to *self always*	.244	.286	.304	.307	—	—	—
WR-13	Worry about illicit relations if men and women work together: lot/little/*none*	.163	—	.205	—	.214	—	—

[a]In this compressed form of the original question is often necessarily poorly represented. The exact text of each question should be consulted in Inkeles and Smith (1974).

[b]In each column, the figures entered give the correlation of the abbreviated question on the left to the modernity scale form identified at the head of the column *averaged* for six countries. A blank cell in any column indicates that the question was not included in the given scale form.

[c]The Long Form included 119 attitudinal items, but for lack of space we have given here the correlation of the item to the Long Form scale only for the 64 items which also appeared in one of the Short Forms 1–6.

[d]Four items were not included in the Long Form. A fuller explanation is given in notes 29 and 30 of chapter 4.

[e]Initially the project coded *material possessions* as the modern answer. It entered the Long Form with that coding, and produced a negative correlation with overall modernity. In the two short forms in which the question was used, *other things* was treated as the modern answer.

especially in the case of Pakistan, India, and Nigeria, where all of our respondents were drawn from relatively homogeneous cultural-linguistic subareas, rather than from the nation as a whole.[3] But for purposes of deriving a *measure* of modernity the requirement of representativeness is clearly not critical. Our objective was to devise a measure which has *general applicability*. Diversity was therefore more important than representativeness, and we feel that a measure based on samples as diverse as are ours, both within and across countries, meets this objective very well. We believe the measures we devised will work well in almost any developing country, and probably in more advanced countries as well.[4] Although the instrument is designed with the common man in mind, it can, with some upward adjustment in the scale of alternatives, be easily adapted for use with highly educated men.[5]

Our four-hour interview went through extensive translation, retranslation, and pretesting in each country. When finally ready, it was administered by native language interviewers, usually social workers or college students whose social origins were the same as those of the interviewees. The samples included the following numbers of young men between the ages of 18 and 32: Argentina, 817; Chile, 931; India, 1,300; Israel, 739; Nigeria, 721; and Pakistan, 1,001. In each case the total was made up of approximately 15 percent urban nonindustrial workers, and 70 percent urban industrial workers.

As a result of these procedures we were left with the data for some 5,500 men in six countries responding to 159 different interview items measuring attitudes, information, and behavior conceived to be relevant to our theoretical conception of modernity.[6] There were many other items in the interview, but the large majority of these dealt with background data, or else were only nominal (nonordered) codes for open-ended items. In addition, there were some items excluded on theoretical or methodological grounds from the pool of 159 items: for example, items in the test of psychosomatic symptoms were excluded because theory and past results made us believe their relation to psychological modernity was complex or even unclear. Several work commitment and work satisfaction items, home and school experience items, and work experience items were excluded because we wished to use them as intervening and independent variables in our analysis, rather than as dependent variables.[7] Of the 159 questions which remained, 119 we consider to be measures of attitudes, values, and opinions, 17 measures of self-reported behavior, and 23 tests of information or verbal fluency. Our attention will here be given mainly to the attitudinal items, although we shall also make some use here of the behavioral and informational items.

There are many possible types of analysis one could perform on this large and complex set of attitudinal items, but two principal analytic approaches merit our consideration. The first, followed in this chapter, seeks to create a general summary index score that represents the degree to which a man possesses the attitudes measured by these items. Insofar as the set of items measures "psychological modernity," this summary index may be called a measure of Overall Modernity ("OM"). The second general analytic approach treats these items as defining a multidimensional property space and analyzes the results for each individual in terms of profiles of many different characteristics, rather than in terms of a single summary score. One way to construct these more complex profiles is first to establish a set of distinctive specialized scales, and then to describe an individual in terms of the pattern of scale scores which characterizes him. Although this approach has many virtues, it is clearly not compatible with the objective we set for ourselves here—to develop a *brief* and *easily scored*, simple measure of overall individual modernity.[8]

Given that we have chosen here to develop a summary modernity score, rather than to develop a detailed modernity profile, there are still two different analytic approaches we might follow, and several methodological varieties within each of these. The two broad approaches are the *item analysis* and the *criterion group* method. Rather than follow one exclusively, we chose to use both approaches, including subvarieties, and then to compose the results in a highly compact final distillate. In this way, we hope to avoid some of the arbitrariness that is so often manifested when new scales are proposed. Both the item analysis and the criterion group methods for deriving the short scale of individual modernity rest on the fundamental assumption that the larger pool of items from which they are derived is adequate to support the operations which lead to the short scale. But what is an adequate basis?

Our test of adequacy is purely theoretical. If our conception of modernity is profoundly different from the reader's, then whatever the procedures we use, the final product will not be accepted. To help make the case for our approach to individual modernity, note the following points: (1) our conception of modernity rests on thoroughly elaborated theory as to the qualities which modern settings are likely to generate, as well as consideration of personal attributes which are likely to best adapt a man to life in such institutional settings; (2) we checked this conception against numerous theoretical and empirical studies of modernization, and found that almost without exception, our basic themes were also commonly cited by other students of the problem; (3) in the interest of the broadest testing of ideas we incorporated many themes which were not central to our original conception, but which had been cited with sufficient frequency in the literature to warrant inclusion in the set we studied. We believe, therefore, that our list of themes is quite comprehensive, certainly as much, and probably more so, than any other which has been used up to this time in any substantial research in modernity.[9]

A second test of adequacy is empirical. One way of assuring that our set of items does indeed measure modernity is to examine the relation of the individual scale scores to social indices which are generally acknowledged to be associated with modernity. Each person in our samples was assigned a summary modernity score based on his answers to the entire set of 119 attitudinal questions, by procedures described in the next paragraph. The individual scores were then correlated with social factors presumed to be associated with modernity. These independent variables did indeed correlate significantly and substantially with the overall modernization score.[10] We were therefore quite certain that this was a set of items which seemed definitely to reflect empirically what theory indicated it should measure, namely the amount of modernizing influences to which a man had been subjected.

Mention of this *summary attitudinal* measure of modernization provides an opportunity to review certain decisions concerning our procedure which are relevant to almost everything that follows. The 119 items used were, as we noted, those which, in our judgment, measured attitudes *and* could be unambiguously scored as having a "modern" vs. "traditional" answer. To avoid making too many judgments, however, we arbitrarily, and sometimes forcefully, drew in every item which was not a background, intervening variable, or psychological test item. In the analysis presented here we largely restrict ourselves to the *attitudinal* items available in all six countries.

Although trichotomies might have been more effective for correlational analysis, some of the field directors used mainly two-step, fixed-alternative answers to questions. Accepting dichotomies made it possible to follow the same procedure in all countries. Because of the inherent variability of the response pattern in any country, however, we were obliged to make some divisions which may not seem logical. For example, if 90 percent of the sample combined said either that education was "good," or "very good," then the 45 percent saying it was only "good" (but not "very good") might be classified on the traditional side along with the 10 percent who said it was "no good." Draconian as these procedures might seem, a case can be made for their logic on the grounds that we are judging not the *absolute* but the *relative* attitudinal modernity of an individual as compared to his peers and compatriots. In the end, then, the set of alternative answers to each question was dichotomized into a modern and a traditional pole as close to the median as possible.

The dichotomization of the answers to the questions was done separately for each country. This meant that the summary scale score could be used to compare individuals from within the same country, but could not be used to compare individuals from different countries. To compare individuals across countries required that we construct a scale in which all questions were dichotomized in exactly the same way in all countries. Despite the many thorny theoretical and methodological issues such a procedure raised, we did eventually follow it, with the results reported in chapter 8.

Once the responses to a question were dichotomized, one part of the dichotomy was classified as the "modern" answer, the other as the "traditional." The classification was arrived at by Inkeles and Smith in accord with the general theory guiding the project. They consulted but were not bound by the opinion of those of the field directors who were in Cambridge and could be consulted at the time the classification was developed. In case of disagreement, the opinion of David Smith, who had prime responsibility for this operation, generally prevailed. Inevitably, we made some mistakes, as indicated by the fact that some items had negative correlations with the summary score. Only 5 percent of the items were thus incorrectly rated, whereas if chance alone had operated, 50 percent would have shown such minus correlations. See footnote 13 for further details.

Traditional answers were scored 1, modern 2, so that the minimum score was in effect 1.00 and the maximum 2.00, a result given us forthwith by a basic computer operation which averaged the answers a man gave to all 119 questions. [11] The result we call the Long Form of the overall modernity score (OM).[12] Since it is based on the largest appropriate pool of attitudinal items, we consider it one of our most reliable measures of an individual's attitudinal modernity.[13] Yet the fact that an individual had to answer 119 questions to be rated made it clearly desirable that we use our data and experience to derive for others some short forms for measuring individual modernity.

DERIVATION OF SHORT FORM VIA ITEM ANALYSIS METHOD

The derivation of short forms via the item analysis method rests on a simple principle. Using the OM long form score based on all items as a standard, we ask what subset from the larger pool has the strongest relation to the overall score.[14] But since everything depends first on having the complete long form and a measure of the relation of each item to the total score, let us turn to consider that set of relationships.

We may note, first, that the long form proved to have much the same characteristics in all the countries in mean (about 1.54), in median (1.55), in range (about 1.20 to 1.80) and in standard deviation (about .07). Since the items were the same in each country, and the procedure used to derive the scores was also identical, this result is no surprise. A standard procedure for interpreting the internal consistency and coherence of a scale such as OM uses the Spearman-Brown formula.[15] Calculations reported in table 4-3 show that for each of our countries the long form OM scale has test reliability coefficients of .73 or higher. Considering that the long form OM measures so complex and multidimensional a concept as individual modernity, the similarity from country to country of the reliability levels, and of the item to test correlations on which they are based, is quite notable. Many widely used scales devised to measure one single attitude or trait do not do much better, and for a scale measuring a multifaceted personal property the long form OM achieves a level of internal consistency which is quite respectable indeed.[16]

There is, then, substantial reason to conclude that the Long Form OM scales for each country are internally consistent and coherent to a significant and substantial degree. We take this to be evidence that there is an underlying dimension of psychological modernity pervading our set of 119 attitude items.[17] This heightens the justification for using the items in the OM long form, and particularly their relation to the summary score, as a basis for deriving a short form of the scale.

Having established the character and quality of the long form OM, we may now return to the procedures for deriving the short forms.

Our first method was maximally empirical, that is, it required and allowed us minimal opportunity to exercise our judgment to influence which particular items entered into the short form. For each country separately, we simply listed the 50 items with the highest correlations of item to long-form-OM-score. Any item which appeared on top in four countries out of six was automatically judged to have survived the competition. Thirty-eight items met this stringent test, and taken together they constitute our OM Short Form 1.[18] The items which compose the scale may be identified by the entry of an item-to-scale correlation coefficient in the cells of the second column of table 4-2, headed "Short 1."[19] The fact that there is so much overlap among the top 50 items in our six countries

TABLE 4-2

Average Item-to-Scale Correlations and Scale Reliabilities for Seven Scales
of Modernity (OM), by Country and Scale

Country	Long	Short 1	Short 2	Short 3	Short 4	Short 5	Short 6
Pakistan: Mean r	.167	.299	.250	.251	.237	.391	.361
Reliability		.767	.774	.685	.685	.653	.622	.660
India: Mean r	.235	.372	.334	.323	.314	.466	.438
Reliability		.873	.852	.808	.792	.784	.736	.769
Nigeria: Mean r	.151	.279	.244	.254	.228	.403	.394
Reliability		.732	.759	.678	.702	.697	.659	.719
Chile: Mean r	.158	.291	.268	.261	.265	.422	.411
Reliability		.754	.779	.721	.713	.713	.685	.741
Argentina: Mean r	.165	.290	.272	.287	.284	.436	.415
Reliability		.767	.776	.724	.752	.744	.701	.744
Israel: Mean r	.170	.297	.266	.265	.252	.428	.395
Reliability		.779	.782	.709	.719	.688	.691	.719

indicates a great deal of underlying similarity in the meaning of psychological modernity across our samples.

While Short Form 1 has the virtue of being untouched by human hands, at least beyond the decisions involved in selecting the initial item pool, it has the defects of all scales derived purely empirically. In the larger pool some areas may be represented by more items than others. In addition, some one or two closely related sets of items may cohere so well, and relate so strongly to the larger scale, as to crowd out items representing many other subscale areas. The victorious set of items may then represent a coherent scale, but one which no longer so well represents the universe—in this case, modernity—which the scale was originally designed to measure. That has happened, to some extent, with Short Form 1. The questionnaire contains more items testing efficacy (EF) than any other area, and they generally cohere quite well as a set. We must, therefore, take note that of the 38 items in Short Form 1, there are 8, or more than 20 percent, from the efficacy area alone. All 4 questionnaire items which test *openness to new experience* with people (NE 2-5) made it. When to these are added the items on birth control (FS 3-5), and similar items, it seems that the Short Form 1 is heavily weighted towards what Parsons calls "instrumental activism." If one insists that the modernity measure give weight to other themes as well, Short Form 1 will not serve. It taps too few of the dimensions, and is too dominated by a few others.

To represent other areas more fully we imposed an additional qualification for the selection of items. We selected from within each of our theoretically defined major attitudinal themes, as listed in Chart 4-1, the single item which best represented the theme in all countries. For each theme, only one item was selected.[20] No matter how low the item-to-total-score correlations were on a particular theme, we nevertheless selected one question from the area. And no matter how high the item-to-scale correlations were, no more than one item was selected for any one of our 33 themes. When two items were equally good candidates from the area (in terms of item-to-scale correlations), preference was given to what we judged to be the more general and theoretically more relevant item. This derivation procedure, therefore, combined both subjective and objective item-selection criteria in what we felt was a reasonable compromise. Its end product was a coherent 33-item scale of psychological modernity that included representatives from all of our theoretically defined attitudinal themes.

This scale, which we designate OM Short Form 2, is internally consistent in all six countries by a variety of tests presented in table 4-2. The average item-to-scale correlations of Short Form 2 are somewhat lower than for Form 1, because of the selection procedure which required the inclusion of some items with relatively low correlations with the Long Form. Nevertheless, the average item-to-scale correlations of OM Short Form 2 for each country are quite a bit greater than the corresponding average correlations for the OM Long Form, even though their *test reliability coeffiecients* are quite similar. The reason for this is that the increase in the average item-to-scale correlation in Short Form 2 is offset by a large decrease in the number of items it contains when compared to the Long Form OM.

On balance, Short Form 2 will probably be the most generally useful and cross-culturally applicable, purely attitudinal, measure of psychological modernity that we can suggest on the basis of our theory as it is disciplined by our data. It strikes a balance between the undue length of the long form and the undue brevity of other short forms of OM yet to be described, and between the purely theoretical and the more or less purely empirical mode of derivation, such as we used for Short Form 1. The overall picture that Short Form 2 gives of the modern man may be obtained at a glance by reading off the questions identified by the entry of an item-to-scale correlation figure in the cells of the third column in Table 4-1. Each of these 33 items should be considered as *representatives* of their respective theme or subtheme areas, rather than as absolutes in any sense. For each there are one or more "back-up" items which might have been selected, in some cases, were the countries in our sample different.

The OM Short Forms 1 and 2 share 19 items, and it is therefore not

TABLE 4-3

Intercorrelations of Modernity Scales, by Scale and Country

Form	Country	Short Form 1	Short Form 2	Short Form 3	Short Form 4	Short Form 5	Short Form 6
Long	Pakistan	.861	.805	.789	.786	.619	.626
Form OM	India	.910	.903	.886	.880	.790	.813
	Nigeria	.836	.811	.804	.775	.635	.617
	Chile	.837	.837	.797	.803	.699	.686
	Argentina	.832	.814	.813	.796	.638	.651
	Israel	.863	.832	.803	.784	.650	.648
Short	Pakistan	—	.806	.827	.775	.739	.722
Form 1	India	—	.898	.896	.875	.859	.852
	Nigeria	—	.808	.837	.762	.776	.747
	Chile	—	.836	.841	.824	.822	.790
	Argentina	—	.839	.869	.834	.791	.783
	Israel	—	.839	.861	.789	.776	.765
Short	Pakistan	—	—	.773	.859	.706	.701
Form 2	India	—	—	.880	.914	.847	.855
	Nigeria	—	—	.791	.867	.769	.736
	Chile	—	—	.805	.894	.795	.755
	Argentina	—	—	.825	.891	.778	.763
	Israel	—	—	.817	.874	.763	.736
Short	Pakistan	—	—	—	.813	.700	.705
Form 3	India	—	—	—	.899	.847	.857
	Nigeria	—	—	—	.835	.760	.743
	Chile	—	—	—	.851	.808	.786
	Argentina	—	—	—	.874	.806	.801
	Israel	—	—	—	.849	.784	.764
Short	Pakistan	—	—	—	—	.703	.685
Form 4	India	—	—	—	—	.842	.842
	Nigeria	—	—	—	—	.756	.725
	Chile	—	—	—	—	.808	.779
	Argentina	—	—	—	—	.806	.796
	Israel	—	—	—	—	.774	.738
Short	Pakistan	—	—	—	—	—	.892
Form 5	India	—	—	—	—	—	.940
	Nigeria	—	—	—	—	—	.908
	Chile	—	—	—	—	—	.917
	Argentina	—	—	—	—	—	.923
	Israel	—	—	—	—	—	.913

surprising, as indicated in table 4-3, that they correlate .80 and above in all six countries. Both are highly related to the Long Form (correlation of .80 or above), and in much the same way in each country. Because Short Form 2 is just about as good a representative of the Long Form as is Short Form 1, and since it also has the other virtues we have indicated, expecially theoretical breadth, we would prefer it in competition with Short Form 1.

THE CRITERION GROUP METHOD OF OM SCALE DERIVATION

The principal alternative to coherence methods of deriving a reduced scale for rating overall psychological modernity is the criterion group method. This involves selecting items from the larger pool of 119 attitudinal modernity items on the basis of their power in differentiating known criterion groups. This method has the defect of precluding unbiased subsequent analysis of the relationships of independent variables to the resulting reduced version of OM. Once OM is derived by this method, then only in a new and separate sample can one freely analyze the relationships of these independent variables to the reduced OM scale. But anyone else's sample other than our own six is, for this purpose, a "new and separate" sample, so in developing this form we aid others while little hindering our own analysis work because for our purposes we could use any of the other forms of the OM scale not derived by the criterion method.

We could have randomly split our own samples into two halves, and then have derived a criterion group short form OM using one half and cross-validating it on the other random half in each country. We could also have used our countries in two sets of three, the second set testing the reliability of the first. The method we used is even more stringent, since, in effect, each of the countries is a reliability check for the others in devising the criterion-based short forms. But this does have the effect of precluding the use of those short forms in our own later analysis relating modernity to the independent variables. It was for this reason, among others, that in the analyses of our own Project data we made it a practice to use only those versions of the OM scale which were derived theoretically. The criterion-based scales presented here were developed exclusively as a contribution to the profession for use on samples other than those we had collected.

In a review of the literature we had identified education, urban experience, and occupation (especially industrial experience) as three of the most powerful influences determining individual modernity. In our study these were measured by years of formal education; urban vs. rural origin, and years of urban residence since age 15 for those of rural origin; and years of factory work, for factory workers only. Our criterion group procedure therefore was to determine, for each of the 119 Long Form OM items, the correlation with each of these three independent variables treating the two urbanization measures combined as one variable.[21] For this purpose we used not dichotomies, as in the item-analysis or "coherence" derivation, but rather the raw, uncorrected data. Since this method did not require prejudging which end of the answer continuum was modern or traditional, the criterion group approach allowed the very few items which earlier suffered from our having misjudged their direction in the item analysis now to enter freely into competition for high standing as indicators of individual modernity.

In each country, for the same basic set of 119 attitudinal items, we computed the Pearsonian correlation of the item with each of the three independent variables in turn. Then we selected in each country the top 50 items in terms of the average of their correlations with the three criterion variables—education, urban experience, and industrial work experience. Finally, the six lists of 50 were compared, and all items noted which appeared on the list of at least four countries. There were 34 items which survived this additional test. Taken together they constitute Short Form 3.[22]

Short Form 3 is our first *criterion group derived* scale. Its content may be discerned by reading the list of items with entries in the column headed "Form 3" in table 4-2. Since Form 3 is arrived at almost entirely by objectively defined operations (as was Form 1), it will appeal to those who prefer a scale in which the scalemaker is kept, by his procedures, from suiting the items to his conscious or unconscious propensities. As a criterion group derived scale, of course, it gains its validity not from the theoretical integrity conferred by an independent concept of modernity, but rather from its empirical or predictive relation to categories of people assumed to be modern. It gives heavy weight, as did Short Form 1, to the single area of Efficacy,[23] but this may be compensated for by very broad representation of other themes. Twenty-four areas are represented, only 9 less than the maximum possible number of 33 themes.[24] Short Form 3, therefore, has much to recommend it.

Finally, we derived a Short Form 4 by again, as in Short Form 2, placing the "theme constraint" on item selection, but now using the criterion group method. That is, we selected one item from each of the 33 theme areas to best represent that theme in terms of its average correlation with the three criterion variables. The questions constituting the resultant 33-item scale may be identified by the column entries under "Form 4" in table 4-2.[25] In all six countries Form 4 correlates well with Form 3, at .81 or above, and with the Long Form OM, at .77 or better. Note that there are 22 items in common between Short Form 3 and 4. Again, on the grounds that it is more theoretically based, we recommend Short Form 4 over Short Form 3 for those who prefer a criterion group derived scale rather than an item analysis derived scale.

A MINIMUM SCALE OF ATTITUDINAL MODERNITY

Even a 33-item scale limited to measuring attitudes may be too long for the purpose of many potential users. For them we can recommend a scale which gets down to the bare minimum.

Again there are many paths one might follow in pursuit of that end. The formula we chose was a composite procedure designed simultaneously to satisfy a number of requirements. First, we felt objective procedures should serve as a screen, to permit only those items with a truly outstanding record to be in the competition. To that end we selected any item which appeared on all four short forms discussed above. This gave us a pool of 12 items. Second, we reviewed this list to discard items which could not be coded more or less automatically in the field directly by the interviewer. Finally, we reviewed the content of each item, to identify those which seemed to overlap most—either in the area they dealt with (such as religion), the relationship they concerned (such as teacher-pupil), or the psychological quality they reflected (such as efficacy). Using these standards we worked toward a final list of not more than 10 items which we designate Short Form 5.[26].

Since this brief attitudinal modernity scale is the final distillate of our successive efforts, and we hope it will be widely used, we present in chart 4-1 the exact wording of the questions, both for their theoretical interest and as an encouragement to further use. We have also prepared a set of coding instructions, and a set of comparably tested alternatives for items which might prove especially sensitive or would pose coding problems too severe for the given field conditions of many investigations.[27]

Since our items are complex in content it becomes almost impossible to develop even a short scale in which each question involves absolutely no similarity in any attribute to some other item. We feel, however, that this scale maximizes the range of material covered within the limits of size and the objective criteria we have established. In terms of area or topic covered, it includes religion, strangers, change, mass media, birth control, education, the family, science, and government. The particular relationships the questions treat are almost as diverse, including man and God, native and foreigner, self and information media, man and wife, boy and school, man and knowledge, citizen and government, and official and public office. The

CHART 4-2

Minimum Scale of Individual Modernity: Short Forms 5 and 6

A. Purely Attitudinal Items (Form 5)

AC-6   Have you ever (thought over much) gotten so highly concerned (involved) regarding some public issue (such as . . .) that you really wanted to do something about it?

              1. Frequently   2. Few times   3. Never

AS-1   If schooling is freely available (if there were no kinds of obstacles) how much schooling (reading and writing) do you think children (the son) of people like yourself should have?

CH-3   Two twelve-year-old boys took time out from their work in the corn (rice) fields. They were trying to figure out a way to grow the same amount of corn (rice) with fewer hours of work.

              1. The father of one boy said: "That is a good thing to think about. Tell me your thoughts about how we should change our ways of growing corn (rice)."

              2. The father of the other boy said: "The way to grow corn (rice) is the way we have always done it. Talk about change will waste time but not help!"

       Which father said the wiser words?

CI-13   What should most qualify a man to hold high office?

              1. Coming from (right, distinguished, or high) family background

              2. Devotion to the old and (revered) time-honored ways

              3. Being the most popular among the people

              4. High education and special knowledge

EF-11, 12   Which is most important for the future of (this country)?

              1. The hard work of the people

              2. Good planning on the part of the government

              3. God's help

              4. Good luck

EF-14   Learned men (scholars, scientists) in the universities are studying such things as what determines whether a baby is a boy or girl and how it is that a seed turns into a plant.

       Do you think that these investigations (studies) are:

              1. all very good (beneficial)   2. all somewhat good (beneficial)

              3. all somewhat harmful   4. all very harmful

FS-3   1. Some people say that it is necessary for a man and his wife to limit the number of children to be born so they can take better care of those they do have (already have).

              2. Others say that it is wrong for a man and wife purposely (voluntarily) to limit the number of children to be born.

       Which of these opinions do you agree with more?

CHART 4-2—*Continued*

MM-10-12	Which one of these (following) kinds of news interests you most? 1. World events (happenings in other countries) 2. The nation 3. Your home town (or village) 4. Sports 5. Religious (or tribal, cultural) events (ceremonies) or festivals
NE-5	If you were to meet a person who lives in another country a long way off (thousands of kilometers away), could you understand his way of thinking? 1. Yes 2. No
RE-12	Do you think a man can be truly good without having any religion at all? 1. Yes 2. No

B. Behavior-Information Items (added to above=Form 6)

AC-1, 2	Do you belong to any organization (associations, clubs), such as, for example, social clubs, unions, church organizations, political groups, or other groups? If "Yes," what are the names of all the organizations you belong to? (Scored for number of organizations)
GO-2	Would you tell me what are the biggest problems you see facing (your country)? (Scored for number of problems or words in answer)
IN-6 or 7	Where is (in what country is the city of) Washington/Moscow? (Scored correct or incorrect)
MM-5	How often do you (usually) get news and information from newspapers? 1. Everyday 2. Few times a week 3. Occasionally (rarely) 4. Never

Note: Words in parenthesis are alternative phrasing for aid in translation. In every case the items should be adapted to make sense in the particular culture. See chart 4-1 for parallel attitude items and codes. Detailed coding instructions and item alternatives are given in Appendix B of Inkeles and Smith (1974).

particular qualities or personal attributes dealt with include openness to new people, acceptance of new ideas and practices, trust, aspirations, efficacy, and civic mindedness or political activism. Even if it seems immodest to say so, we do not see how one could do better within the limits we imposed.

Since it is so highly selective, Form 5 has lower correlations with the Long Form OM, but it still represents it reasonably well as reflected (in table 4-3) in correlation between .62 and .80. Despite the diversity of material represented, the scale shows quite high average item-to-scale correlations in table 4-2, although this is in part due to the limited number of questions used. Perhaps more important, despite the great diversity of content represented by the questions, the scale continues to have reliabilities close to .7, falling to .62 only in East Pakistan, as may be seen in table 4-3.

INFORMATION AND BEHAVIORAL ITEMS IN THE
MEASURE OF MODERNITY

In the analysis presented above we focused exclusively on the 119 items we considered attitudinal. We thereby excluded from consideration 23 items which test our respondent's ability to produce various types of information, and 17 items in which he describes his behavior rather than attitudes. We thought it wise to keep these apart from the attitude questions for several reasons. For one thing, the sheer amount of information a person possessed might reflect not so much his interest in the world around him as his basic intelligence. We saw no reason to classify a man as modern simply because he was smart. For another, we knew from experience that the information items, although numerous, correlated very highly with one another. Allowed to enter a pool of items used to derive an OM scale, therefore, they might well crowd out other items and overweight the end product in the direction of this one area. So far as the behavioral items are concerned, the case is similar but with reversed emphasis. We had little independent experience in working with them, but we assumed that because of their experimental character and diverse content they might not correlate well with each other, nor be able to survive in a completely open competition with a large set of powerful attitudinal items. Yet we felt that a strong case could be made for considering what a man actually does, or at least says he does, as important an indicator of modernity as what he feels or believes. We wished, therefore, to give these behavioral items a special analysis shelter, much like that given an infant industry by means of protective tariffs or tax relief.

Since a definite theoretical case could be made for the relation of both information levels and behavior to individual modernity, and since the answers to the relevant questions could unambiguously be scored as having a modern and traditional direction, we decided to broaden further the base of our most distilled attitudinal scale, Short Form 5, by adding two items from the information set and two from the behavioral set. This final summary measure, including all of Short Form 5 and four informational-behavioral items, we designate Short Form 6.[28]

In deciding which information and behavior items to use, we followed the same basic procedure already familiar as the "item-analysis method" for deriving short forms from the long form. Items were screened first by item analysis for their ability to "work" simultaneously in 5 or 6 of the six countries.[29] From this set we selected those which gave us the widest theme representation, and which promised to be simple to code in the field, if necessary.

In the information area, questions requiring the respondent to identify correctly a public figure of world prominence, such as Kennedy or Nehru, or a national leader of the respondent's own country, proved very effective, as did questions about important distant places such as Washington or Moscow. These questions were consistently among those with the strongest item-to-overall-scale correlations we observed. For example, the item-to-Long-Form-OM correlation for the question on Nehru ranged from .46 in Pakistan to .65 in India.[30] Since the information questions were numerous, this seemed to justify our earlier having segregated them in computing the attitudinal OM. But we now also felt the case was clear for adding at least one such information-soliciting item to the final short form of the modernity scale. A second and distinct type of information-soliciting item was that which asked the respondent to give his opinions freely on some topic, to name a series of things he wanted to own, to name some books or newspapers he had read, and so forth. Of these "verbal fluency" items, the all-around best item to emerge asked the respondent to name what he considered to be the main problems facing his country. When coded for the number of problems cited, without probing by the interviewer, this item shows excellent results both by the item analysis and by the criterion group method.

The situation of the behavioral items is somewhat different. As we expected, the fact that they dealt with behavior—even though reported by the respondent rather than being observed by us[31]—meant that they related less strongly to the total pool of items than did the attitude questions on the very same topic. For example, the question AC-4, which asked whether the respondent had ever *actually* written to or otherwise actively contacted a public official, had much lower correlation with the overall OM score than did the item AC-6, which asked only whether he had ever felt so concerned with a public issue that he merely *wanted* to do something about it.

Two different behavior items, however, emerged quite unambiguously in all countries as strongly related to both the subset of behavioral items and the larger pool of attitudinal items. The first item (AC-1,2) asked whether the individual belonged to any voluntary organizations, and if so, how many. It thus tested in part the degree of active, or realized, interest in public and community affairs, although our denotative definition of voluntary organizations permitted social clubs and the like to be counted here also. In addition, we found the question on how often a man read, or was exposed to, a newspaper to be a very powerful indicator in all countries. We therefore included it as the second behavioral item.

When the informational and behavioral attitudinal items are added, in the second part of chart 4-2, to the attitudinal items previously selected to make up Form 5, the result is a 14-item scale we designate Form 6,[32] which gives a broad base for judging individual modernity. The proportional weight of attitudinal vs. informational *and* behavioral measures in Form 6 is, of course, quite arbitrary, and we make no special theoretical case for it. We can see how some might insist on giving equal weight to all three types of questions—attitudinal, informational, and behavioral. Further experience with these measures will help reach a decision on empirical grounds, although the ultimate balance anyone establishes will be in large degree a matter of personal preference. For now we offer Form 6 as a highly serviceable start toward devising the "ultimate" brief measure of individual modernity. This is no ordinary stopgap we offer, since it has the virtue of having questions which have run an exceptional gauntlet of tests by both the item and criterion method of selection in six countries. It is broadly based and catholic in conception to weigh not only attitudes but also behavior and information levels. It represents the Long Form OM even better than did Form 5, as may be seen from the correlation coefficients in table 5-1. In reliability, Form 6 is also superior, as indicated in table 4-3, going below .7 only in East Pakistan.

SUMMARY ON SCALE CREATION

With the presentation of Short Form 6 in chart 4-2, we complete our formal assignment to devise a theoretically broad, empirically tight, administratively simple measure of individual modernity which has been widely tested cross-nationally and can be used with little or no adaptation under all field conditions, in either research or practical work, which requires one to judge the modernity of individuals or groups in developing countries. To take account of personal preferences, theoretical and methodological, for one or another type of scale, and in response to the fact that some will have time and energy to use longer, but others only shorter tests, we have not restricted ourselves to developing only one scale. We have, rather, presented several, indeed a battery, of measures of psychological modernity. We sought to give a full and frank account of our method, so that others may check, or even seek to replicate, our efforts, and so that the intellectual and technical ground on which the end product rests will be reasonably clear.

Of course there are many alternatives to the paths we took which we know of and could not mention, and no doubt there are others we never imagined. Certainly even within the broad course we followed, there were by-paths we pursued but could not describe, and there were detours and short-cuts as well as pitfalls of which we may not even be aware. Our continuing analysis experience, and the critical discussion of our work by others, will presumably bring all that out. We limit ourselves here to stating our opinion that the final product of most efforts broadly similar to ours in conception would be unlikely to yield results really fundamentally different from the scales presented. Certainly the set of themes and topical areas could be somewhat different, but only within modest limits. Many an item could perhaps be substituted for one we recommend, but this would not make a structural change. Different subsamples of the national populations should be studied, and another set of countries might certainly make a difference in the outcome, but we doubt the differences would be profound. Only experience will tell.

We cannot leave the subject, however, without noting that from some points of view the derivation of a short scale to test modernity, however practically useful, is of only limited importance compared to some of the things we may note only in passing. To us the most fundamental of these observations lies in the evidence we find of the transcultural nature of the human psyche. We consider it notable in the highest degree that a pool of some 119 attitude questions and some 40 related informational and behavioral items should show such extraordinarily similar structure in six such diverse countries—and even more than that number of cultural groups.[33] If we had started with the same theory and the same pool of items, but then discovered we were obliged to create a separate and *different or distinctive* scale of modernity for each of the six countries, the result might still be interesting, but would not be compelling. To find, instead, that in all six countries basically the same set of items both cohere psychologically and relate to external criterion variables in a strictly comparable fashion is, we believe, a finding of the first importance. It strongly suggests that men everywhere have the same structural mechanisms underlying their socio-psychic functioning, despite the enormous variability of the culture content which they embody.[34] In chapter 5, in which we analyze the forces which make man modern, we shall find additional evidence which argues for the psychic unity of mankind in the sense in which we use that term.

CHAPTER 5

Results of the First
Phase: A Summary

Having described our objectives, theory, instruments, and procedures, we come to the critical point of reporting what we found out in the first phase of our research. We had available two separate summaries of our findings, one published some six years before the other. It might seem obvious that the latest should be selected for inclusion in this volume. But a fresh reading of these reports made it apparent that something of value would be lost if only the latest was reproduced. Indeed, we ran this risk whichever paper might be used, because there were some critical facts reported, and important points made, in each which were not included in the other. We considered, even attempted, to blend the two into a single unified summary, but our best efforts did not do justice to the character of either original. Therefore, we decided to include both, presenting them in the sequence and form in which they were originally published, with some deletions and interpolations. Such redundancy as this may subject our readers to what we hope is justified by the importance of the points which have been repeated.

FOUR CENTRAL ISSUES

To present our results within the rigorous limits of space and time currently allotted for scholarly communications requires imposing a

The first section of this chapter, under the heading "Four Main Issues," was originally published as part of Alex Inkeles, "Making Men Modern: On the Causes and Consequences of Individual Change in Six Developing Countries," *American Journal of Sociology* 75 (1969): 208-25. The second section, under the heading "Explaining How Men Became Modern" is taken from Alex Inkeles, "Becoming Modern: Individual Change in Six Developing Countries," *Ethos* 3 (1975): 323-42.

telegraphic style and forgoing the presentation of detailed evidence to support our arguments.[1] Each of our conclusions will address itself to one of the main issues to which our research was directed. These issues were raised in similar form earlier in this volume, especially in chapter 1. Now we present a summary of the evidence by which our research sought to answer the questions raised.

1. *How Far Is There an Empirically Identifiable Modern Man, and What Are His Outstanding Characteristics?*

Many social scientists have a conception of the modern man, but few have submitted this conception to an empirical test to ascertain whether this type really exists in nature and to determine how often he appears on the scene. Important exceptions may be found in the work of Kahl (1968), Dawson (1967), and Doob (1967). We too have our model of the modern man, a complex one including three components which we refer to as the analytic, the topical, and the behavioral models, all of which, we assumed, might well tap one general underlying common dimension of individual modernity.

We believe our evidence, presented in some detail in Inkeles and Smith (1974) shows unmistakably that there is a set of personal qualities which reliably cohere as a syndrome, and which identify a type of man who may validly be described as fitting a reasonable theoretical conception of the modern man. Central to this syndrome are: (1) openness to new experience, both with people and with new ways of doing things such as attempting to control births; (2) the assertion of increasing independence from the authority of traditional figures, such as parents and priests, and a shift of allegiance to leaders of government, public affairs, trade unions, cooperatives, and the like; (3) belief in the efficacy of science and medicine, and a general abandonment of passivity and fatalism in the face of life's difficulties; and (4) ambition for oneself and one's children to achieve high occupational and educational goals. Men who manifest these characteristics (5) like people to be on time and show an interest in carefully planning their affairs in advance. It is also part of this syndrome (6) to show strong interest and take an active part in civic and community affairs and local politics; and (7) to strive energetically to keep up with the news, and within this effort to prefer news of national and international import over items dealing with sports, religion, or purely local affairs.

This syndrome of modernity coheres empirically to meet the generally accepted standards for scale construction with reliabilities ranging from .75 to .87 in the six countries.[2] Looking at the range of items which enters into the scale, one can see that it has a compelling face validity. In addition, the empirical outcome accords well with our original theoretical model and, indeed, with those of numerous other students of the problem. Evidently the modern man is not just a construct in the mind of sociological theorists. He exists and he can be identified with fair reliability within any population which can take our test.

To discover that there are indeed men in the world who fit our model of a modern man is comforting, but perhaps not startling. After all, we can probably somewhere find an example of almost any kind of man one might care to delineate. It is important to emphasize, therefore, that men manifesting the syndrome of attitudes, values, and ways of acting we have designated "modern" are not freaks. They are not even rare. On the contrary, there are very substantial numbers of them in all six of the countries we have studied.[3]

Furthermore, we consider it to be of the utmost significance that the qualities which serve empirically to define a modern man do not differ substantially from occupation to occupation or, more critically, from culture to culture. In constructing our standard scales of modernity we utilized a pool of 119 attitude items.[4] In each country these items were then ranked according to the size of the item-to-scale correlation, and the subset of items having the highest correlations was then selected as defining the modern man for the given country. Using this "coherence" method to construct the national modernity scales, we might have found a totally different set of items defining the syndrome of modernity in each of our six national samples. Indeed, if we used only the twenty items ranking highest in the item-to-scale correlations for each country, we could theoretically have come out with six totally different syndromes, one for each country, no one overlapping in the least with any other. The actual outcome of the analysis was totally different. The probability that even one item would come out in the top fifty in all six countries is approximately five in a thousand. We actually had ten items which were in the top fifty in all six countries, sixteen more in the top fifty in five countries, thirteen more which were in this set in four of the six countries. The probability that the same thirty-nine items would by chance be in the top fifty in four of the six countries is so infinitesimal as to make our results notable indeed.

This means that what defines man as modern in one country also effectively defines him as modern in another. It argues for the actual psychic unity of mankind in a structural sense, and the potential psychic unity of mankind in the factual sense. In speaking of the unity of mankind in terms of psychic structure, we mean that the nature of the human personality, its inner "rules" of organization, is evidently basically similar everywhere. That is, the association of the elements or components of personality do not—and we think in substantial degree *cannot*—vary randomly, or even relatively freely. There is evidently a system of inner, or what might be called structural, constraints in the organization of the human personality which increases the probability that those individuals— whatever their culture—who have certain personality traits will also more likely have others which "go with" some particular basic personality system. So far as the future is concerned, moreover, we believe that this structural unity provides the essential basis for the greater factual psychic unity of mankind. Such a factual unity, not merely of structure but of *content*, can be attained insofar as the forces which tend to shape men in syndromes such as that defining the modern man become more widely and uniformly diffused throughout the world. This point requires that we consider the second issue to which our research addressed itself.

2. *What Are the Influences Which Make a Man Modern? Can Any Significant Changes Be Brought About in Men Who Are Already Past the Formative Early Years and Have Already Reached Adulthood As Relatively Traditional Men?*

Education has often been identified as perhaps the most important of the influences moving men away from traditionalism toward modernity in developing countries. Our evidence does not challenge this well-established conclusion. Both in zero-order correlations[5] and in the more complex multivariate regression analysis, the amount of formal schooling a man has had emerges as the single most powerful variable in determining his score on our measures. On the average, for every additional year a man spent in school he gains somewhere between two and three additional points on a scale of modernity scored from zero to 100.

Our modernity test is not mainly a test of what is usually learned in school, such as geography or arithmetic, but is rather a test of attitudes and values touching on basic aspects of a man's orientation to nature, to time, to fate, to politics, to women, and to God. If attending school brings about such substantial changes in these fundamental personal orientations, the school must be teaching a good deal more than is apparent in its syllabus on reading, writing, arithmetic, and even geography. The school is evidently also an important training ground for inculcating values. It teaches ways of orienting oneself toward others, and of conducting oneself, which could have important bearing on the performance of one's adult roles in the structure of modern society.[6]

We selected work in factories as the special focus of our attention in seeking to assess the effects of occupational experience in reshaping individuals according to the model of the modern man. Just as we view the school as communicating lessons beyond reading and arithmetic, so we thought of the factory as training men in more than the minimal lessons of technology and the skills necessary to industrial production. We conceived of the factory as an organization serving as a general school in attitudes, values, and ways of behaving which are more adaptive for life in a modern society. We reasoned that work in a factory should increase a man's sense of efficacy, make him less fearful of innovation, and impress on him the value of education as a general qualification for competence and advancement. Furthermore, we assumed that in subtle ways work in a factory might even deepen a man's mastery of arithmetic and broaden his knowledge of geography without the benefit of the formal lessons usually presented in the classroom. Indeed, the slogan for our project became, "The factory can be a school—a school for modernization."

Although our most sanguine hopes for the educational effects of the factory were not wholly fulfilled, the nature of a man's occupational experience did emerge as one of the strongest of the many types of variables we tested and is a quite respectable competitor to education in explaining a person's modernity. The correlation between time spent in factories and individual modernization scores on OM-3 was generally about .20.[7] With the effects of education controlled, the factory workers generally scored eight to ten points higher on the modernization scale than did the cultivators.[8] There is little reason to interpret this difference as due to selection effects since separate controls show that new workers are not self- or preselected from the village on grounds of already being "modern" in personality or attitude. Nevertheless, we can apply a really stringent test by making our comparisons exclusively within the industrial labor force, pitting men with few years of industrial experience against those with many, for example, five or more. When this is done, factory experience continues to show a substantial impact on individual modernization, the gain generally being about one point per year on the overall measure of modernization (OM).

It is notable that even when we restrict ourselves to tests of verbal fluency and to tests of geographical and political information, the more experienced workers show comparable advantages over the less experienced. To choose but one of many available examples, in Chile among men of rural origin and low education (one to five years)—and therefore suffering a double disadvantage in background—the proportion who could correctly locate Moscow as being the Soviet Russian capital rose from a mere 8 percent among the newly recruited industrial workers to 39 percent among those with middle experience and to 52 percent among the men who had eight years or more in the factory. Even among those with the double advantages of higher education (six to seven years) and urban origin, the proportion correctly identifying Moscow decidedly rose along with increasing industrial experience, the percentages being 68, 81, and 92 for the three levels of industrial experience, respectively. Summary evidence from all six countries is presented in table 5-1. It should be clear from these data that the factory is serving as a school even in those subjects generally considered the exclusive preserve of the classroom.[9]

To cite these modernizing effects of the factory is not to minimize the greater absolute impact of schooling. Using a gross occupational categorization which pits cultivators against industrial workers, we find that the classroom still leads the workshop as a school of modernization in the ratio of 3:2. Using the stricter test which utilizes factory workers only, grouped by length of industrial experience, it turns out that every additional year in school produces three times as much increment in one's modernization score as does a year in the factory, that is, the ratio goes to 3:1. The school seems clearly to be the more efficient training ground for individual modernization. Nevertheless, we should keep in mind that the school has the pupil full time, and it produces no incidental byproducts other than its pupils. By contrast, the main business of the factory is to manufacture goods, and the changes it brings about in men—not insubstantial, as we have seen—are produced at virtually zero marginal cost. The personality changes in men stimulated by the factory are therefore a kind of windfall profit to a society undergoing the modernization process. Indeed, on this basis we may quite legitimately reverse the thrust of the argument, no longer asking why the school does so much better than the factory, but rather demanding to know why the school, with its full-time control over the pupil's formal learning, does not perform a lot *better* than it does relative to the factory.

Our experience with the factory enables us to answer a secondary question posed for this section. Since men generally enter the factory as more or less matured adults, the effects observed to follow upon work in it clearly are late socialization effects. Our results suggested that substantial changes can be made in a man's personality or character, at least in the sense of attitudes, values, and basic orientations, long after what are usually considered the most important formative years. The experience of factory work is, of course, not the only form which this late socialization takes. It

TABLE 5-1

Percentage of Industrial Workers Among Low[a] Educated Giving Correct Answers on Information Tests
(by Country and Months of Factory Experience)

Question	Argentina		Chile		India		Israel		Nigeria		East Pakistan	
	3	90	2	96	2	72	3	84	3	48	1	48
Identify electrical apparatus[b]	37	63	33	62	44	76	80	88	91	91	50	70
Identify movie camera	60	69	6	8	29	51	84	88	68	70	9	37
Cite 3 or more city problems	5	18	15	32	0	1	24	25	30	22	52	52
Identify international leader[c]	26	67	47	85	1	31	80	81	11	17	2	26
Identify local leader	33	51	27	81	15	52	67	92	70	78	52	79
Identify Moscow	36	60	17	67	1	16	86	86	11	17	2	2
Name 3 or more newspapers[d]	12	21	81	92	6	28	75	61	81	91	20	44
Approximate N cases	40	70	90	130	75	130	25	100	60	25	65	120

[a] Data for high education groups on these seven questions in each country provide an additional 42 tests of which 33 were in accord with the conclusion that men with more factory experience score higher on information tests, 7 were inconclusive, and 2 contradictory.

[b] In Pakistan, India, and Nigeria a picture of a radio was shown; in Argentina, Chile, and Israel, a picture of a tape recorder was used instead.

[c] Respondents were asked to identify Lyndon Johnson in Chile, Argentina, and Israel; John F. Kennedy in Pakistan and India; Charles de Gaulle in Nigeria.

[d] In Argentina, "name books" was substituted for "name newspapers."

may come in the form of travel or migration, by exposure to the media of mass communication, or through later life in the city for men who grew up in the countryside.[10]

Our assumptions about these later life influences were not readily accepted by all. In the theories of personality most dominant in our time it is generally assumed that the basic attributes of personality are laid down in the early period of development. If this assumption were correct, there would be little hope of changing people from traditional into modern men, psychologically speaking, once they had reached adulthood. Instead, efforts to increase the proportion of modern men would have to be focused mainly on the family and early schooling.

We assumed, however, that men could be changed in quite fundamental ways *after* they reached adulthood, and that no man need therefore remain traditional in outlook and personality merely because he had been raised in a traditional setting. Putting these ideas to an empirical test, we measured how much variance in OM scores was accounted for by the set of *early socialization variables*—notably father's education, own education, ethnicity, and urban or rural origin—as compared to the explanatory power of a set of *late socialization influences*, including occupation, standard of living, mass media exposure, and age.[11]

We may observe (from table 5-2) that the late socialization experiences stake out a very respectable place for themselves in the competition to account for the observed variance in individual modernization scores. In five countries the set of late socialization variables explained as much or more of the variance in modernization scores as did the combined early socialization variables, each set explaining between one-fourth and one-third of the variance. Even in India, where early experiences appear far more powerful, it was nevertheless true that, in absolute terms, the late experiences are still doing very well.[12] All in all, we take this to be impressive evidence for the possibility of bringing about substantial and

TABLE 5-2

Variance in Scores of Individual Modernity (OM-3) Accounted for by Early and Late Socialization Influences in Six Developing Countries (%)

Variable	Argentina	Chile	India	Israel	Nigeria	Pakistan
Early socialization ...	28.8	26.0	52.4	22.1	23.0	22.2
Late socialization	31.6	34.4	31.4	22.4	28.2	28.3

extensive changes in the postadolescent personality as a result of socialization in adult roles. These results indicate that under the right circumstances
any man may become modern after he has passed his adolescence. And,
since the forces that can make men modern after the formative years seem to
be embedded in the institutions that developing countries are most eager to
adopt, the prospect is substantial that over time more and more of the men
in those countries will develop the attitudes, values, and behavior patterns
we have identified as defining the modern man.

3. *Are There Any Behavioral Consequences Arising from the Attitudinal Modernization of the Individual? Do Modern Men Act Differently
from the Traditional Man?*

Many people who hear of our research into individual modernization
respond to it by acknowledging that we may have discovered what the
modern man *says*, but they are more interested in knowing what he *does*.
This view overlooks the fact that taking a stand on a value question is also
an action, and one which is often a very significant one for the respondent.
For example, it was an act of substantial civic courage for a young man in a
traditional village to tell our interviewer he would be more inclined to
follow the local co-op leader than the village elders, or that he considered
himself more a Nigerian than a Yoruba. Our critics' comment also tends
implicitly to underestimate the importance of a climate of expressed
opinion as an influence on the action of others. And it probably assumes
too arbitrarily that men use speech mainly to mislead rather than to express
their true intentions. Nevertheless, the question is a legitimate one, and we
addressed ourselves to it in our research.

We have the definite impression that the men we delineate as modern not
only *talk* differently, they *act* differently. To explore this relationship we
constructed a scale of modernization based exclusively on attitudinal
questions, rigorously excluding those dealing with action rather than
belief or feeling.[13] This measure of attitudinal modernity we then related to
the behavioral measures in our survey. In all six countries we found action
intimately related to attitude. At any given educational level, the man who
was rated as modern on the attitudinal measure was also more likely to have
joined voluntary organizations, to receive news from newspapers every day,
to have talked to or written to an official about some public issue, and to
have discussed politics with his wife. In many cases the proportion who
claimed to have taken those actions was twice and even three times greater
among those at the top, as compared with those at the bottom, of the scale of
attitudinal modernity. Table 5-3 presents the relevant evidence. We should
note, furthermore, that the items included in table 5-3 are illustrative of a

TABLE 5-3

Percentage of High Educated[a] Engaging in Various Forms of Modern Behavior
(by Country and Modernity Score[b])

Form of Behavior	Argentina		Chile		India		Israel		Nigeria		East Pakistan	
	Low[b]	High	Low	High	Low	High	Low	High	Low	High	Low	High
Joined 2 or more organizations	26	48	50	61	32	31	2	6	86	97	0	6
Voted often	54	54	44	57	60	65	76	86	:	..	:	..
Talked politics with wife	40	57	29	61	74	80	46	72	50	65	65	83
Contacted official about public issue	2	9	4	17	20	26	17	27	11	21	5	15
Read newspapers daily	40	77	31	53	32	61	36	81	63	84	35	42
High on geographic information scale	44	78	23	60	20	51	29	75	7	48	9	53
High on political information scale	22	56	18	37	22	65	36	72	20	48	7	39
High on consumer information scale	10	21	7	39	67	94	29	53	84	89	23	52
High on opposites test	50	76	36	63	59	86	31	57	59	71	47	78
Approximate N cases[c]	50	150	60	160	55	115	40	110	60	120	45	125

[a] In each country the total sample was divided at the median into a "high" and "low" educated group. The average number of years of education for the high group was: Argentina: 7.6; Chile: 6.6; India: 10.2; Israel: 8.6; Nigeria: 8.5; and Pakistan: 4.8.

[b] The range of Overall Modernity Scores was split into "low"—bottom 25%, "middle"—middle 50%, and "high"—top 25% for each country's entire sample. Modernity scores are highly correlated with education. Since in this table only the high educated are represented, more men fall into the category of those with high as against low modernity scores.

[c] N's are approximate due to the disqualification of part of the sample on certain questions, e.g., those legally under age could not be expected to "vote often."

larger group of about thirty individual questions, and a dozen scales, selected on theoretical grounds as appropriate tests of the relations between expressed attitudes and reported behavior. The items used for illustration were not arbitrarily selected as the only ones supporting our assumptions.[14]

The particular behaviors we cited above are all "self-reported." The question inevitably arises as to whether then we are not merely testing attitudinal consistency—or merely consistency in response—rather than any strict correspondence between modernity of *attitude* and modernity of *behavior*. The answer is partly given by considering the relation of attitudinal modernity to our several tests of information. These questions did not deal with "mere" attitudes, but obliged the respondent to prove objectively whether he really knew something. Quite consistently the men who were more modern on the attitude measures validated their status as modern men by more often correctly identifying a movie camera, naming the office held by Nehru, and locating the city of Moscow. Men with the same education but with unequal modernity scores performed very differently on these tests, with those more modern in attitude scoring high on the tests of information two or more times as often as those classified as traditional in attitude. The details are summarized in the lower part of table 5-3, which presents summary scale results.

We conducted a further and more exact check on the extent to which self-reported behavior is fact rather than fantasy, by comparing what men claimed to do with objective tests of their actual performance. For example, we asked everyone whether or not he could read. Individuals certainly might have been tempted to exaggerate their qualifications. But later in the interview we administered a simple literacy test, asking our respondents to read a few lines from local newspaper stories we had graded for difficulty. In most settings, less than 1 percent of the men who had claimed they could read failed the literacy test. They proved objectively to have been accurately and honestly reporting their reading ability. Similarly, men who claimed to use the mass media regularly were—as they should have been—better able correctly to identify individuals and places figuring prominently in world news. In Nigeria, for example, among experienced workers of low education, the proportion who could correctly identify de Gaulle as the president of the French Republic was 57 percent among those who claimed to pay only modest attention to the mass media, 83 percent among those who asserted they listened or read more often, and 93 percent among those who claimed to read a newspaper or listen to the radio almost every day. Many additional examples which test the internal consistency of attitude and behavior are summarized in table 5-4.[15] Clearly, the men who claim to have the attributes we score as modern give a better account of themselves on objective tests of performance. We may conclude not only that modern is as modern does, but also that modern *does* as modern *speaks.*

4. *Is the Consequence of the Individual Modernization Inevitably Personal Disorganization, and Psychic Strain; or Can Men Go Through This Process of Rapid Sociocultural Change Without Deleterious Consequences?*

Few ideas have been more popular among the social philosophers of the nineteenth and twentieth centuries than the belief that industrialization is a kind of plague which disrupts social organization, destroys cultural cohesion, and uniformly produces personal demoralization and even disintegration. Much the same idea has been expressed by many anthropologists who fear—and often have witnessed—the destruction of indigenous cultures under the massive impact of their contact with the colossus represented by the European-based colonial empires. But neither the establishment of European industry in the nineteenth century, nor the culture crisis of small preliterate peoples overwhelmed by the tidal wave of colonial expansion may be adequate models for understanding the personal effects of industrialization and urbanization in developing nations.

To test the impact on personal adjustment resulting from contact with modernizing influences in our six developing countries, we administered the Psychosomatic Symptoms Test as part of our regular questionnaire. This test is widely acknowledged to be the best available instrument for cross-cultural assessment of psychic stress.[16] Using groups carefully matched on all other variables, we successively tested the effect of education, migration from the countryside to the city, factory employment, urban residence, and contact with the mass media as these modernizing experiences might affect scores on the Psychosomatic Symptoms Test. No one of these presumably deleterious influences consistently produced statistically significant evidence of psychic stress as judged by the test. Those who moved to the city as against those who continued in the village, those with many years as compared to those with few years of experience in the factory, those with much contact with the mass media as against those with little exposure to radio, newspaper, and movies, show about the same number of psychosomatic symptoms.

In each of six countries, we tested fourteen different matched groups, comparing those who migrated with those who did not, men with more

TABLE 5-4

Percent[a] among Low Educated[b] Whose Performance on a Test of Behavior Accords with Their Oral Claim
(by Claim and Country)

Objective Behavior (%) and Claim	Argentina	Chile	India	Israel	Nigeria	East Pakistan
Naming 3 newspapers among those who claim to read papers:						
Rarely/Never	c	73[d] (356)	13 (582)	68 (28)	59 (71)	c
Daily		98 (85)	60 (63)	90 (119)	85 (152)	
Correctly identifying international leader among those claiming mainly interested in:						
Other news	43 (299)	59 (414)	8 (668)	79 (216)	7 (276)	4 (459)
World news	73 (30)	76 (29)	12 (26)	84 (68)	8 (73)	10 (10)
Correctly identifying international leader who claim on total information media exposure they are:						

Low	14 (51)	45 (196)	1 (71)	73 (45)	4 (78)	0 (85)
High	79 (29)	79 (76)	18 (11)	84 (38)	17 (18)	10 (40)
Correctly identifying Washington who claim on total information media exposure they are:						
Low	14 (51)	43 (196)	3 (71)	64 (44)	3 (78)	2 (85)
High	72 (29)	70 (76)	7 (28)	90 (38)	28 (18)	3 (40)
Who can read at least a little among those who claim they:						
Can read	c	c	99 (408)	99 (266)	99 (346)	74 (80)

[a] Percentages are a proportion of the cells' base N who manifested a given behavior. These cell Ns represent all those of low education who made the indicated behavioral claim, e.g., claimed to read a newspaper daily.

[b] The average number of years of education by country was Argentina: 4.5; Chile: 3.7; India. 1.0; Israel: 5.1; Nigeria: 6.2; and Pakistan: .2.

[c] Data unavailable for country.

[d] Includes "a few times a week" in "rarely or never" category.

years in the factory with those with fewer, etc. Because some of these matches did not apply in certain countries, we were left with seventy-four more or less independent tests of the proposition that being more exposed to the experiences identified with the process of modernization produces more psychosomatic symptoms. Disregarding the size of the difference and considering only the sign of the correlation between exposure to modernization and psychosomatic symptoms as positive or negative, it turns out that in thirty-four instances the results are in accord with the theory that modernization is psychologically upsetting, but in forty other matches the results are opposed to the theory. Very few of the differences in either direction, furthermore, were statistically significant. Indeed, the frequency of such statistically significant correlations was about what you would expect by chance. Of these significant differences, furthermore, only two supported the hypothesis while two contradicted it. This again suggests that only chance is at work here. The evidence supporting this conclusion is given in detail in chapter 12. Here we limit ourselves to the conclusion that the theory which identifies contact with modernizing institutions and geographical and social mobility as certainly deleterious to pyschic adjustment is not supported by the evidence. Indeed, it is cast in serious doubt. Whatever is producing the symptoms—and the test does everywhere yield a wide range of scores—it is something other than differential contact with the sources of modernization which is responsible.

Life does exact its toll. Those who have been long in the city and in industry but who have failed to rise in skill and earnings are somewhat more distressed. But this outcome can hardly be charged to the deleterious effects of contact with the modern world. Perhaps if we had studied the unemployed who came to the city with high hopes but failed to find work, we might have found them to have more psychosomatic symptoms. If we were faced with this finding, however, it would still be questionable whether the observed condition should be attributed to the effects of modernization. The fault would seem to lie equally in the inability of traditional agriculture to provide men with economic sustenance sufficient to hold them on the land.

We conclude, then, that modernizing institutions, per se, do not lead to greater psychic stress. We leave open the question whether the process of societal modernization in general increases social disorganization and then increases psychic tension for those experiencing such disorganization. But we are quite ready to affirm that extensive contact with the institutions introduced by modernization—such as the school, the city, the factory, and the mass media—is not in itself conducive to greater psychic stress.

MACRO VS. MICROSTRUCTURAL INFLUENCES

Men change their societies. But the new social structures they have devised may in turn shape the men who live within the new social order. The idea that social structures influence the personal qualities of those who participate in them is, of course, as old as social science and may be found in the writings of the earliest social philosophers. Its most dramatic expression, relevant to us, was in the work of Marx, who enunciated the principle that men's consciousness is merely a reflection of their relation to the system of ownership of the means of production. The rigidity of Marx's determinism, and the counterdetermination of many people to preserve an image of man's spiritual independence and of the personal autonomy and integrity of the individual, generated profound resistance to these ideas. The idea that ownership or nonownership of the means of production determines consciousness is today not very compelling. To focus on ownership, however, is to concentrate on the impact of macrostructural forces in shaping men's attitudes and values at the expense of studying the significance of microstructural factors. Yet it may be that these microstructural features, such as are embedded in the locale and the nature of work, are prime sources of influences on men's attitudes and behavior.

In reviewing the results of our research on modernization, one must be struck by the exceptional regularity with which variables such as education, factory experience, and urbanism maintain the absolute and relative strength of their impact on individual modernization despite the great variation in the culture of the men undergoing the experience and in the levels of development characterizing the countries in which they live. This is not to deny the ability of the macrostructural elements of the social order to exert a determining influence on men's life condition and their response to it. But such macrostructural forces can account for only one part of the variance in individual social behavior, a part whose relative weight we have not yet measured with the required precision. When we attain that precision we may find some confirmation of popular theories, but we are also certain to discover some of them to be contradicted by the data—just as we have in our study of microstructual factors. The resolution of the competition between these two theoretical perspectives cannot be attained by rhetoric. It requires systematic measurement and the confrontation of facts, however far they are marshalled in the service of ideas. The facts we have gathered leave us in no doubt that microstructural forces have great power to shape attitudes, values, and behavior in regular ways at standard or constant rates within a wide variety of macrostructural settings.

EXPLAINING HOW MEN BECAME MODERN

Just as we had adopted a rather catholic position in considering a wide range of potential elements that might delineate the modern man, so we considered a large number of forces as possible determinants of individual modernity. Many of these were, however, only alternate ways of measuring the same thing, and we were able to reduce the explanatory variables to a basic set of some eight to ten major dimensions. These dimensions included: education, work experience, contact with the mass media, consumer goods possessed, father's education, urbanism of residence, skill level, length of urban residence, the modernity of one's factory, and the modernity of one's home and school background.[17] In the remainder of this chapter we relate these variables to the more sensitive OM-500 as our measure of overall modernity.

By using a composite measure summarizing each individual's total exposure to the entire set of presumed modernizing experiences and institutions, it proved possible to sort out our samples with great precision. Of the men with minimum contact with modernizing institutions, only about 2 percent achieved scores on our attitude and value test which qualified them as modern men. Each step up the ladder of exposure to modern institutions brought a regular increase, so that by the time we reached those with the most extensive contact 76 percent scored as modern. The results are summarized in table 5-5.

Taken together this limited set of independent variables produced multiple correlations with the individual modernity scores of .56 to .79, depending on the country. This meant that we were explaining between 32 and 62 percent of the variance in modernity scores, with the median for the six countries at 47 percent.[18] This performance compares quite favorably with results obtained in the more developed countries in studies using comparable measures of complex personal attributes. Indeed, we can more fully account for what makes a man modern in Chile or India than our political scientists can account for what makes him liberal or conservative in the United States.[19]

In addition to observing the effect of the explanatory variables grouped as early and late socialization influences, we naturally wanted to know how the separate variables performed independently, in their own right. The answers could be obtained in a global way by considering the zero order correlations of OM scores with the standard explanatory variables, as in table 5-6.

In all six countries, education emerged as unmistakably the most powerful force. Indeed, judged by the number of points on the OM scale a

TABLE 5-5

Percent Modern on the OM Scale with Increasing Exposure to Modern Institutions (by Exposure Decile and Country)

Exposure Decile[a]	Argentina	Chile	East Pakistan	India	Israel	Nigeria
1	0.0	2.2	8.3	0.9	11.0	1.3
2	4.9	6.1	15.6	5.2	21.1	4.8
3	18.7	4.9	26.3	8.6	26.4	12.7
4	28.6	20.9	28.2	17.0	28.4	9.7
5	31.8	23.4	29.0	24.8	27.7	34.2
6	38.0	36.4	38.5	40.7	43.1	47.8
7	32.7	49.1	36.3	52.1	30.6	40.0
8	51.0	43.8	44.5	52.6	38.0	50.6
9	65.9	62.9	53.1	66.7	46.7	66.7
10	73.8	78.6	71.4	80.3	56.4	80.6

[a] Those in decile 1 were rural resident farmers with the least education, least contact with the mass media, and least urban experience. The more contact with the factory, the city, the media, and the school, the higher the decile position of the respondent.

man gained for each additional year of schooling, education was generally two or even three times as powerful as any other single input. In this, our conclusions are not new but rather confirm findings in several other studies of modernity.

The distinctive emphasis of our project, however, lay in its concern for the potential impact of occupational experience, and particularly of work in modern large-scale productive enterprises such as the factory. Although each year in a factory yielded only one-third to one-half the increase in points on the modernity scale which an additional year in school could bring, the variable of factory experience was generally second in importance after education. Moreover, the association between work in a factory and individual modernity did not result from factories having selected only modern men to be their workers. Retesting the same individuals after a lapse of four years, we found that every year they had continued working in a factory had contributed to making them more modern. No such change was found in men who, over the same span of time, had continued working in agriculture.

Exposure to the mass media generally showed itself to be more or less equal to occupational experience as a force making men modern. By contrast, some of the institutions most commonly associated with the process of modernization failed to substantiate their claim to standing as important schools for modernity. Most notable of these was the city, whose

TABLE 5-6

Correlations of Ten Independent Variables
With Individual Modernity Scores (OM-500), by Country

	Argentina	Chile	East Pakistan	India	Israel	Nigeria
1. Formal education	.60***	.51***	.41***	.71***	.44***	.52***
2. Months factory experience	.24***	.36***	.26***	.11**	.26***	.29***
3. Objective skill	.34***	.25***	.24***	.33***	.23***	.23***
4. Mass media	.43***	.46***	.36***	.55***	.42***	.43***
5. Factory benefits	.09*	.13***	.10**	.25***	.17***	.28***
6. Years urban since age 15	.35***	.37***	.20***	−.02	n.a.	.22**
7. Urbanism of residence	.45***	n.a.	.11**	.25***	−.01	.36***
8. Home-school modernity	.11**	.22***	.01	.26***	.01	.02
9. Father's education	.33***	.33***	.21***	.42***	.02	.17***
10. Consumer goods	.44***	.35***	.35***	.38***	.17***	.42***
*N*s for rows 1, 4, 7, 8, 9, 10	817	929	943	1198	739	721
*N*s for rows 2, 3, 5	663	715	654	700	544	520
*N*s for row 6	239	305	654	700	0	184

Significance levels are as follows:
* = at .05 level; ** = at .01 level; *** = at .001 level or better.

failure to qualify was not corrected by taking into account either the size or the relative cosmopolitanism of different urban centers. As we will see in detail in chapter 7, ethnic origin and religion also proved to be relatively unimportant variables, at least once the educational and occupational differences usually characterizing such groups were brought under control. We were struck, and rather surprised, to find that the relative modernity of the school a man attended, and of the factory he worked in, at least so far as we were able to measure that quality, also played a very small role in determining a man's modernity when compared to the sheer duration of his exposure to those institutions.

These conclusions are of necessity stated here in very general terms, and do not reflect the many variations we observed when the forces at work were studied in greater depth. These more complex patterns were manifested in many ways, one of which is reflected in the contrasting direct and indirect effects of the explanatory variables as described in table 5-7.

TABLE 5-7

Total, Direct and Indirect Effects of Main Independent
Variables on OM-500: Median for Six Countries

Independent variables	Six Country Median Effects for:					
	All subjects			Factory workers only		
	Total[a]	Direct[b]	Indirect[c]	Total[a]	Direct[b]	Indirect[c]
Rural-urban origin[d]	—	—	—	.28	.10	.18
Ethnicity-religion	.19	.09	.10	.23	.09	.14
Father's education	.27	.05	.22	.22	.03	.19
Education-literacy	.52	.37	.15	.55	.37	.18
Occupational experience[e]	.41	.16	.25	.30	.12	.18
Mass media exposure	.45	.18	.27	.40	.16	.24
Living standard	.39	.10	.29	.33	.08	.25
Urbanism	.19	.04	.15	.02	.04	−.02
Life cycle stage	.03	.04	−.01	.06	.01	.05
Nature of present factory	—	—	—	.10	.06	.04

[a] Total effects are the zero-order Pearsonian correlation coefficients.

[b] Direct effects are the Beta weights (path coefficients).

[c] Indirect effect equals total effect minus direct effect.

[d] Rural-urban origin was measured only in Argentina, Chile, and Nigeria.

[e] In total sample this variable measures occupational type; in the worker sample it is a complex measure of factory experience.

We discovered that factory experience had a much greater impact on men of rural background and of little education than it did on men of urban origin who had had more education. Indeed, in explaining the modernity scores of the less educated men of rural origin, we found that their occupational experience could be of equal, or even greater, importance than was the amount of schooling they had received.[20] This was partly because such men entered the factory with lower scores to begin with, so that they were not yet near the "ceiling," and hence had more room to develop as modern men under the tutelage of the factory. We also assume the factory effect was greater for men of rural origin because for them the factory was their first extensive contact with modern organizational principles and the large-scale inanimate use of power. In other words, with those men the factory could and did produce a more powerful "demonstration effect."

While we were persuaded by our data that the factory was certainly a school in modernity, other results indicated that the factory is probably not the only form of occupational experience with that potential. Thus, some types of urban nonindustrial employment also seemed to be at least a modest stimulant to modernity, a fact that we attributed to the contact with a diversified public and to relative autonomy in arranging one's own work. In addition, men pursuing traditional occupations, such as those of porter, but doing so in the context of large-scale bureaucratic organizations, also become somewhat more modern, presumably because the organizational context exerted some influence, even if the job itself did not.

We were most struck, however, by the dramatic changes in the level of individual modernity which were manifested by the peasant farmers who came under the special influence of the Comilla cooperative movement in what was formerly East Pakistan. Holding other factors constant, every year in a factory in East Pakistan was worth only about 1 point on the OM scale; every year in school produced a gain of about 1.5 points; whereas each year of exposure to the co-op movement even as a nonmember netted approximately 1.7 points, and every year spent in the co-op as a member yielded a gain of 4 points or more per year. Since the cooperatives did not rely very heavily on new machinery to raise the productivity of the farmers, the exceptional impact of agricultural cooperation in Comilla must be accounted for by reference to other influences. We assume the success of the Comilla co-ops came, in part, from the models of behavior which the cooperative instructors provided, and in part from the new principles of social organization and interpersonal relations which the cooperatives exemplified.

In summary, then, we may say that at the point at which he left school, half the story of a man's eventual modernity score had been told. But this was true only "on the average." Actually, for many men the story really ended at that point. The score they had attained at the time they left school was basically the same one they were going to record when our project staff eventually came by to test them. Others would add a few points over the years. Still others, however, were to have later life experiences that would raise by many points the OM scores they had had at the time they left school. This increase was frequently as much as 50 percent, and in some cases was almost 100 percent, of the score these men had had on leaving the village. This outcome depended largely on the interaction between the stage at which the men left school, and the nature and extent of their later contact with modernizing institutions. Of these later experiences, the two that were critical were the occupations they entered and the extent of their contact with the media of mass communication.

Rural men who stayed in the countryside to farm as their fathers had were most likely to be frozen at the level of modernity that had characterized them when they left school. Few things in the nature of their work stimulated them to new ways of looking at things, to a heightened sense of personal efficacy, or to any of the other changes that would have made them more modern.

The greatest change in individual modernity was experienced by the men who left the countryside and associated agricultural pursuits to take up work in industry. As a result of this set of experiences, men of rural origin with modest education, say with three years of schooling or less, often moved almost completely to the opposite end of the continuum of individual modernity from that occupied by their former neighbors who continued agricultural pursuits in their natal villages. Indeed, such migrants often benefited enough from the combined stimulus of factory work and mass media contact to attain a modernity score the equal of that of men who had twice as much education as the migrants, but had remained in their traditional villages to work as farmers.

SOME FURTHER ISSUES

There remain a few issues related to measuring the process of individual modernization not raised before, to which we now should turn. They are again put in the form of simple questions, to which we will essay brief answers.

5. *Is the Process of Modernization Continuous and Lifelong, or Is There a Definite Plateau That People Reach, After Which They No Longer Continue Becoming Ever More Modern?*

Our experience with the OM scale suggests that the process of individual modernization can continue, if not indefinitely at least for a very long time, without any obvious limit being reached. This was most clear for education, where, at least up to the twelfth year of school, each year of contact produced pretty much the same increment in OM scores as the year before. The growth curve for modernity rose on the chart in virtually a straight line in every country, without any visible dip in the latter years.

Examination of the "curve of growth" in modernity for men at different stages of industrial seniority indicates that there, too, the process of modernization is relatively continuous over time. During a span of at least twelve years in the factory, which was generally the maximum seniority of men in our samples, workers continued to become more modern, year by year, the longer they continued in industrial employment. We cannot be sure that becoming modern is a "lifelong" process, because our samples cut off at age 35. Up to that age, however, a man in the right institutional setting can experience a continuous process of movement up the modernity scale.

6. *Granted That Change Toward Modernity Is Continuous So Long as Men Remain Under the Influence of Modernizing Institutions. What Happens to Those Who Lose That Contact? Is Modernity Irreversible, or Will Such Men Return to the More Traditional Mold?*

That is unfortunately a question we cannot answer on the basis of any substantial empirical evidence. We can only say, therefore, that we believe that becoming modern represents a fairly basic change in personality, and such changes generally tend to be relatively enduring. How long they endure will, of course, depend on various circumstances, including how persistent the given individual is in preserving his character, how deeply rooted were the modern attitudes and values he had adopted, how much his subsequent experience reinforces his newly acquired traits, and how strong are the countervailing environmental forces working to move him in different directions.

For example, we assume men who leave industry to start their own small shops will probably be among the most modern and, furthermore, that their subsequent experience in entrepreneurial activity will itself further conduce to increasing individual modernization. By contrast, a man who leaves the urban industrial setting to resume both peasant agriculture and the whole set of his traditional role obligations, would likely become less modern under the influence of such life conditions.

7. *Considering That the Modernization Process Seems to Work So Consistently in So Many Different Cultural Settings, Is There Then No Choice? Must Everyone Become Modern, and to the Same Degree?*

Our image of man's nature is not that of a sponge soaking up everything with which it comes in contact. In our view individual change toward modernization is a process of *interaction* between the individual and his social setting. Quite contrary to the conception of men as putty passively taking on whatever shape their environment imposes on them, we see the process of individual modernization as one requiring a basic personal engagement between the individual and his milieu. In this engagement the individual must first selectively perceive the lessons the environment has to teach, and then must willingly undertake to learn them, before any personal change can come about.

If the qualities of industrial organization are truly alien to a man, he will not incorporate them. And even if the environment is benign and the individual ready to learn, the process will not work if the environment itself is confusing and the messages it conveys are unclear or even contradictory.

All in all, then, we see little reason to fear that the modernization process threatens to impose on us a deadly, passive, totalitarian uniformity, especially if one keeps in mind that among the most outstanding characteristics of the modern man are his openness to new experience and his readiness for change. Indeed, as we shall see in chapter 11, at least in the kind of developing countries we studied, the more modern men were also the more radical, in the sense that they much more frequently asserted the need for immediate and total transformation of the existing socioeconomic system.

8. *Since a Whole Set of Institutions, Including the School, the Factory, and the Mass Media, All Operated to Make Our Men Modern, the Question Arises: Must a Nation Be Able to Bring All These Forces to Bear, and Do So Simultaneously, to Stimulate the Development of Individual Modernity?*

The issue is a sore one, since the key problem of many underdeveloped countries lies precisely in their lack of schools, factories, and media of mass communication. Our experience suggests that it is not necessary that all, or even most, of the more effective agencies be available and working simultaneously to bring about individual modernity. On the contrary, any one modernizing institution seems to be able to operate independently. Moreover, contact with any one modernizing institution evidently can be more or less readily substituted for contact with any other, making allowance for the fact that some institutions are more effective than others. Indeed, the evidence from the Comilla cooperative experiment indicates that even in quite isolated villages new forms of social organization can be highly effective in making men modern without the aid of machinery or electronic communication. The means for bringing about greater individual modernization are, therefore, potentially within the reach of even the least advantaged nations and communities.

9. *Does the Concept of Individual Modernity and the Measurement of It Through the OM Scale Apply Only to Men, or Are the Concept and the Measure Relevant to Understanding the Characteristics and the Situation of Women As Well?*

Our project studied only men solely because of practical considerations arising from the limits on our budget and the concentration of men in the industrial jobs in which we were especially interested. We are firmly convinced that the overwhelming majority of the psychosocial indicators we used to identify the modern man would also discriminate effectively among women. And we are quite certain that the same forces that make men modern—such as education, work in complex organizations, and mass media exposure—also serve to make women more modern. Of course, some adjustments in the content and scoring of the OM scale might be necessary to make it maximally effective in distinguishing modern from more traditional women, and some influences might play a different role in shaping the modernity of women rather than men. Nevertheless, we believe the pattern that will eventually emerge for women will be broadly similar to what we observed for men. We are given confidence in this assumption by some preliminary evidence already available.[21].

10. *Are the Individual Modernization Processes We Studied in Several Developing Countries Likely to Take Place Also in More Advanced Industrial and Postindustrial Societies?*

Our answer is "yes." Societal modernization is always a matter of degree. Even the most highly developed nations have more and less modern portions of their populations, according to differences in exposure to modernizing experiences. In the United States, we would expect the forces that make men modern to have their most dramatic impact on immigrants from less developed countries, on rural subsistence farmers who leave their farms and on "dropouts" who leave their schools to enter industry, and on members of disadvantaged minority groups. In general, however, we believe that the same qualities that are summed up in the OM scale would distinguish the more from the less modern individuals in the industrialized countries, and that the same forces that made individuals modern in our samples would emerge as important causes of modernity in the economically advanced countries.

11. *Is All This Purely an Academic Exercise? In Particular, Does It Have Any Practical Contribution to Make to National Development? Are Not Attitude and Value Changes Rather Ephemeral and Peripheral? Can We Offer Any Evidence That All This Has Much to Do with the Real Problem of Underdevelopment?*

In response, we affirm that our research has produced ample evidence that the attitude and value changes defining individual modernity are accompanied by changes in behavior precisely of the sort that give meaning to, and support, those changes in political and economic institutions that lead to the modernization of nations. As table 5-8 indicates, men more modern in attitude and value were much more likely to act or behave in more modern ways in their various social roles.

We were able to document most extensively the behavioral changes which accompany attitudinal modernization in the realm of political and civic action. The modern man more often than the traditional man took an interest in political affairs, he kept informed and could identify important

TABLE 5-8

Percent of Men High on Behavioral Modernity[a] *in Each Country,*
Who Are Low, Medium, or High on Attitudinal Modernity

Standing on attitudinal modernity[b]	Argentina	Chile	East Pakistan	India	Israel	Nigeria
Low	13	14	15	5	16	18
Medium	35	32	34	27	35	29
High	52	54	51	68	49	54
Total N high on behavioral modernity	100% (271)	100% (308)	100% (373)	100% (448)	100% (261)	101%[c] (286)

[a] Behavioral modernity is measured by a score on the summary (objective plus self-reported) behavior scale. Men in the upper third of the frequency distribution on this scale were considered "high" on behavioral modernity.

[b] Attitudinal modernity is measured by scores on OM-1, trichotomized as to the frequency distribution in each country.

[c] Percentages do not total 100 because of rounding.

political events and personalities, he often contacted governmental and political agencies, more often joined organizations, more often voted—and all these by large margins. As we shall see in detail in chapter 11, he was in every way a more active participant citizen of his society.

Beyond politics, the modern man showed himself to perform differently from the more traditional man in many realms of action having practical bearing on the process of societal modernization. The modern man is quicker to adopt technical innovation, and as we will see more fully in chapter 10, he is more ready to implement birth control measures. He urges his son to go as far as he can in school, and, if it pays better, encourages him to accept industrial work rather than to follow the more traditional penchant for office jobs; he informs himself about the goods produced in the modern section of the economy, and makes an effort to acquire them; and he permits his wife and daughter to leave the home for more active participation in economic life. In these and a host of other ways, the man who is more modern in attitude and value acts to support modern institutions and to facilitate the general modernization of society.

In saying this we are not espousing some form of naive psychological determinism. We are not unaware that a modern psychology cannot alone make a nation modern. We fully understand that to be modern a nation must have modern institutions, effective government, efficient production, and adequate social services. And we recognize full well that there may be structural obstacles to such development stemming not only from nature, but from social, political, and economic causes as well. Narrow class interests, colonial oppression, rapacious great powers, international cartels, domestic monopolies, archaic and corrupt governments, tribal antagonisms, and ethnic prejudices, to name but a few, are among the many "objective" forces that we know act to impede modernization.

Nevertheless, we believe a change in attitudes and values to be one of the most essential *preconditions* for substantial and effective functioning of those modern institutions that most of the "more practical" programs of development seek to establish. Our experience leads us to agree with many of the intellectual leaders of the third world who argue that, in part, underdevelopment is a state of mind.[22] It is admittedly difficult with currently available techniques and information to establish the case scientifically, but we are convinced that mental barriers and psychic factors are key obstacles to effective economic and social development in many countries.

PART THREE

ETHNIC AND
NATIONAL DIFFERENCES

CHAPTER 6

Indian Images of Modernity in Cross-Cultural Perspective

The Harvard project tested the attitudes and values of its samples by using a standardized questionnaire, which had essentially the same content everywhere. Inevitably this raised questions as to whether or not an alien conception was being imposed on people, not in accord with their local way of thinking about what was modern and traditional. To meet this challenge we sought, in the Indian phase of our project, to develop an entirely local, native, culture-specific measure of modernity to compare its content and correlations with that of the cross-cultural measure. To discover the popular images of modernity in Bihar, where we did our field work, we began by interviewing students—the most easily available and most exploited guinea pigs of socio-psychological research. We discovered that it was believed that a "modern" man preferred tap water to well water, and the toothbrush to the twig (*datwan*), the latter being the "traditional" preference. "Modernity" was believed to be associated with mill-made clothes as against the handwoven, with food cooked on a stove as against food cooked on the traditional hearth, with allopathic medicine as against the indigenous, and with disapproval of the dowry and of the wearing of ornaments by women. Furthermore, it was held by our local sources that a "modern" man will disapprove of the custom of having the wife serve her husband the best food while reserving for herself only the poorest; and that he will also believe that a *sadhu* (holy man) who brings out sweets from his

This chapter originally appeared as Alex Inkeles and Amar K. Singh, "A Cross-Cultural Measure of Modernity and Some Popular Indian Images," *Journal of General and Applied Psychology* 1 (1968):33–43, published at Ranchi and Patna, India. Although Professor Singh extended the project director the courtesy of placing his name first, it should be recognized that the junior author of this article was nevertheless its chief architect.

apparently empty-looking bag does it by cunning and trickery, rather than by the possession of supernatural powers. In addition, we were told that the modern man would not believe that fasts and promises made to gods help cure illness; and, finally, he will disapprove of the behavior of a school teacher who punishes the son of a poor farmer for not doing his homework, but does not punish the son of the *Zamindar* (landlord) for the same offense.

We were interested to find out if there existed any correlation and association between this purely local and popular image of modernity with the Harvard project's cross-cultural conception of it. To put it another way, would the people identified as modern by the cross-cultural scale because of their sense of efficacy or their punctuality be also recognized as modern by the local people according to their specifically Indian criteria, such as using the toothbrush rather than the *datwan*, drinking tap rather than well water, and disapproving of the dowry and the wearing of ornaments?

Following the leads provided by our student informants, our Indian field-team wrote a special set of questions to be included in the Indian questionnaire alongside the standard questions from the cross-cultural battery. We have divided the special Indian questions into two categories: (1) questions relating to uniquely Indian themes and (2) questions which relate to themes covered in the Harvard project's cross-cultural definition of modernity but interpreted in terms of local issues. Accordingly we made two separate Indian scales, to be called Indian Scale 1 and Indian Scale 2, and a combination of these two scales to be called Indian Scale 3.

The items which have gone into the Indian Scale 1 are shown in table 6-1, which also gives their correlations with the OM Scale. Table 6-2 gives the items in the Indian Scale 2, their counterpart Harvard project questions used in six countries, their inter-item correlations, and their correlations with the OM Scale.

The inter-scale correlations of the special Indian scales and the OM Scale are presented in table 6-3.

The following points may be observed in these tables:

(1) As may be seen in table 6-1, the special questions measuring unique Indian themes (Indian Scale 1) are correlated with the cross-cultural OM Scale at the .01 level, with the exception of the question concerning cooking, which seems to tap a different dimension. Indeed, although it is not immediately apparent from the numbers given in table 6-1, the special Indian attitude questions are almost as strongly related to the general cross-cultural OM Scale as they are to the separate Indian Scale 1.[1] This underlying similarity in the content of the two scales is also reflected in their substantial intercorrelation, noted below.

TABLE 6-1

Attitude Items in Indian Scale 1, Their Item-to-Scale Correlations, and Correlations with the Cross-Cultural OM Scale

Attitude Items	Correlation with Indian Scale 1	Correlation with OM Scale
Which do you like more:		
1. Well water or		
2. Tap water?	.59	.24
1. Washing your mouth with *datwan* (thin twig) or		
2. Toothbrush?	.47	.17
1. Food cooked in oven or		
2. Food cooked on stove?	.21	.03
1. Prevalence of dowry system or		
2. End of it?	.68	.41
1. Wearing of ornaments by women or		
2. Not wearing?	.69	.31

**Significant at .01 level or better.

(2) The special Indian questions in Indian Scale 2, measuring themes covered by the project in six countries, are also correlated at the .01 level or better with the questions used in all the countries. The four relevant correlations are given in column II of table 6-2. The question wording is given in column I of the table with, in each case, the special Indian question first and the standard cross-national question below it. It is worth noting that the correlations linking each special Indian question to one of the standard cross-national items are comparable in strength to those linking the standard items to each other. This again indicates that the special Indian questions tapped much the same dispositions as did the standard cross-national questions.

(3) The special Indian questions in the Indian Scale 2 are also correlated with the OM Scale at the .01 level. The figures are given in column III of table 6-2. As in the case of Indian Scale 1 it should be noted that if an adjustment were made for autocorrelation, the correlation to OM of the special Indian questions would be nearly as strong as the comparable correlation to OM of the standard cross-cultural questions. Again this suggests that the special Indian questions were tapping much the same

TABLE 6-2

Correlations of Questions in Indian Scale 2 with Comparable OM Scale
Questions, with the OM Scale, and with Indian Scale 2

I	II *Inter-item* *Correlation*	III *Correlation with* *OM Scale*	IV *Correlation with* *Indian Scale 2*
(A) Suppose a holy man came to you and showed you his bag which seemed empty. But he took out some sweets from it and gave them to you. Now tell how he did this. 1. By cunning and trick or 2. By supernatural powers of ghosts?	.12**	.26**	.58**
(B) A man's wife is seriously ill. He obtains the best possible medical care and also prays and worships fervently with a pure heart. She finally recovers. Which do you think was more important in her recovery? 1. Prayer or 2. Both or 3. Medicine?		.42**	
(A) What do you like: 1. Medicine from indigenous doctors and healers or 2. Western medicine?	.16**	.23**	.60**
(B) Suppose a farmer finds his paddy plants dying out, being infected with			

TABLE 6-2 (cont.)

I	II	III	IV
	Inter-item Correlation	*Correlation with OM Scale*	*Correlation with Indian Scale 2*
some disease, what should he do?			
1. Consult an experienced farmer of his village or one of the neighboring villages or		.47**	
2. Consult some agricultural officer in the block?			
(A) One day two students came to a village school without learning their lessons. One was the son of the landlord, the other of an ordinary farmer. The teacher did not say anything to the son of the landlord but punished the son of the farmer. Was his behavior:		.30**	.54**
1. Right, because after all there is a difference between a son of an important person and a son of an ordinary person or			
2. Wrong, because both should be treated in the same manner?	.15**		
(B) In your opinion, who should get most respect: A person. . .			

TABLE 6-2 (cont.)

I	II Inter-item Correlation	III Correlation with OM Scale	IV Correlation with Indian Scale 2
1. Born in a high family or 2. Having a high income or 3. Having high education?		.35**	
(A) 1. Some believe that the wife should cook better food for her husband than for herself. 2. But others believe that the wife should take exactly the same food as her husband takes. What is your own opinion?	.17**	.26**	.63**
(B) Suppose in a factory or office both men and women did exactly the same sort of work. What should then be true of the pay? 1. Women should get more 2. It should be equal 3. Men should get a little more 4. Men should get a lot more?		.44**	

**Significant at .01 level or better.
(A) designates wording for comparable special Indian question.
(B) designates question wording used cross-nationally.

TABLE 6-3

Interscale Correlations of Special Indian Scales and Harvard OM Scale

Scales	Indian Scale 2	Indian Scale 3 (1 + 2)	Harvard OM Scale
Indian Scale 1	.17**	.76**	.47**
Indian Scale 2		.77**	.43**
Indian Scale 3			.59**

**Significant at .01 level or better.

Note: All the attitude items in the scales were dichotomized at the nearest median point on the basis of the raw distribution of responses. (See D. H. Smith and Alex Inkeles 1966 and 1974.)

attitudes and underlying values as did the questions used in the six nation study.

(4) All the three special Indian scales are correlated with the six country OM Scale at the .01 level, as we see in table 6-3. The fact that the summary Indian scale correlates with the standard OM Scale at .59 is rather decisive evidence that the scales are measuring very similar qualities, especially considering that the reliability of the OM Scale itself was .77.

Though the correlations are significant at the .01 level, they are perhaps not the most satisfying way of examining such relationships. To look at the problem from yet another angle we decided to compare the high and low scorers on the OM Scale to see how far their responses on the special Indian questions might differ. For this purpose we divided our 1,300 cases into three groups on the basis of their scores on the OM Scale. An individual's score could range from 1.00 to 2.00, the latter being the "modern" end. The three groups we established were: "Low" Scorers (1–1.53), "Medium" Scorers (1.54–1.63), and "High" Scorers (1.64–2.00). The responses of these three groups against the special Indian questions are presented in table 6-4.

Table 6-4 expresses the relation of scores on the OM Scale and the answers to the special Indian questions in two ways. Reading across the top line of numbers opposite each question we discover the proportions who hold a given view among men at three levels of modernity. Thus, on the first line we discover that a preference for tap water is expressed by 40 percent of the most modern men, by only 26 percent of the less modern, and by a mere 16 percent of the least modern. These three percentages, computed on three distinct bases, do not total 100.

The second line of numbers opposite each question sorts all those who took a particular position on one of the special Indian questions into the three modernity levels measured by the OM Scale. Thus, on the second line

TABLE 6-4

Percent of "High," "Medium," and "Low" Scorers on Harvard's OM Scale Giving Modern Answer to Special Indian Questions

Attitude items I		"High" Scorers (N = 417) II	"Medium" Scorers (N = 459) III	"Low" Scorers (N = 459) IV	Chi square V
Prefer tap water against well water	1ᵃ.	40	26	16	58.73**
	2ᵃ. 47		34	19	100%=939
Prefer allopathic medicines against indigenous ones	1.	69	65	44	60.57**
	2. 38		39	24	100%=769
Prefer toothbrush against *datwan* (twig)	1.	14	12	3	29.33**
	2. 47		42	11	100%=126
Disapprove of dowry	1.	89	64	42	202.37**
	2. 45		35	20	100%=837
Disapprove of wearing of ornaments by women	1.	58	37	23	110.99**
	2. 49		33	18	100%=505
Believe that a boy who married the girl he loved will be happier in life	1.	51	36	21	79.75**
	2. 46		36	18	100%=465
Want wife to eat the same food as her husband	1.	93	87	72	72.42**
	2. 36		37	27	100%=1085
Disapprove the village school teacher who punishes only the son of an ordinary farmer	1.	98	98	83	103.97**
	2. 35		37	28	100%=1205
Believe that a *Sadhu* brings out sweets from an empty looking bag by trickery	1.	92	83	69	67.15**
	2.	37	36	27	100%=1084
Believe that promises and prayers to God do not help in averting personal crises	1.	28	12	5	163.42**
	2. 61		29	11	100%=191
Believe that only medicine can help an infertile woman to get children	1.	89	74	45	231.37**
	2. 42		38	20	100%=897
Prefer mill-made clothes to handwoven	1.	57	61	58	2.18
	2. 32		37	31	100%=762

**Indicates Chi square to test differences between high and low scorers is significant at .01 level or better.

ᵃ See text for key to reading line 1 versus line 2.

of the first box we see that 939 men preferred tap water to well water. Of these 939, 47.3 percent were high scorers on the OM Scale, 33.6 percent scored medium, and only 19 percent scored low, totalling 99.9 percent. These results again indicate that a man's response to the special Indian questions was a good predictor of his score on the OM Scale.

Comparably clear-cut patterns were manifested on most of the other questions. Thus, disapproving of the dowry fell off from 89 percent among men high on OM to only 42 percent amongst those low on OM. And of the 837 men who disapproved, 45 percent qualified as high scorers on OM while only 20 percent were low scorers.

The results shown in table 6-4 indicate a very strong association between the cross-cultural and popular Indian measures of modernity. Those who score "high" on the cross-cultural measure of modernity tend to select the "modern" alternatives in special Indian questions and vice versa. Thus a significantly larger proportion of "high" scorers on the cross-cultural measure of modernity, compared to the low scorers, prefer tap water to well water and the toothbrush over the twig; disapprove of dowry and ornaments; want the wife to eat the same food as her husband; believe a love marriage to be happier than an arranged marriage; disapprove of a village school teacher who gives preferential treatment to the son of the rich landlord against the son of a poor, ordinary farmer; are skeptical of the supernatural powers of a Sadhu; believe in the effectiveness of medicine over prayers in curing the barrenness of a woman; and do not derive any comfort from the belief that prayers and promises to God avert personal crises, such as a serious illness. Conversely, those who select the traditional alternatives on the special Indian questions are also the "low" scorers, on the cross-cultural scale of modernity. For example, out of 209 persons who want a wife to eat food inferior to that taken by her husband, 56 percent are "low" scorers against 15 percent "high" scorers. Eighty-two percent of those who support preferential treatment for the son of a rich landlord against the son of an ordinary farmer are "low" scorers, and only 8 percent are "high" scorers. Out of 240 persons who believe in the supernatural powers of a Sadhu, 52 percent are "low" and only 15 percent "high" scorers. Out of 314 persons who would rely on prayers for the cure of the infertility of a woman, 64 percent are "low" scorers, against 7 percent "high" scorers.

The differences between "high" and "low" scorers are significant at at least the .01 level, as tested by Chi-square, in all the special Indian questions except one. There is no difference between the high and low scorers so far as their preferences for mill-made and hand-woven clothes are concerned. This is not difficult to understand, though this had not struck us when we included this item. Mill-made clothes are cheaper and more durable than the hand-woven, and our respondents are farmers and factory workers with small incomes. Probably these economic considerations overrode any tendency the more modern farmers and industrial workers might have had to follow the preferences of the better-off students, from whom we had derived these popular images of modernity. But it is remarkable how true the students' images turned out to be in their application to wider and somewhat different social groups.

CHAPTER 7

Individual Modernity in Different Ethnic and Religious Groups

From the classic studies of Max Weber (1969) to the more nearly contemporary research of Everett Hagen (1962) comes a continuous line of research that identified certain religious and/or ethnic groups as manifesting special psychosocial traits, which, in turn, induced and helped the group's members to become entrepreneurs or otherwise to play a distinctive role in economic development.[1] The interpretation of some of the key cases has been vigorously challenged and as energetically defended in debates which may be followed in Samuelsson (1961) and Eisenstadt (1968). But whatever the merit of those challenges, the proponents of the Weber-Schumpeter type of theory must admit that they have so far mainly picked dramatic cases to illustrate the basic relationship in which they are interested. The *generality* of the theory across large numbers of cases has not been tested. The research reported here seeks to make such a test, at least with regard to one facet of the larger theory.

In Weber's work, and also in the later work of McClelland (1961) and Hagen, the critical link was that between the psychocultural characteristics of a set of individuals and their later performance as economic actors. In the research to be reported here we have no data, at least none really adequate, on the differential economic performance of the individuals selected as presumably embodying different psychocultural characteristics.[2] Rather, we focus mainly on an issue that may be defined as logically prior to that

This chapter was originally published as Alex Inkeles, "Individual Modernity in Different Ethnic and Religious Groups" in Leonore L. Adler, ed., *Issues in Cross-Cultural Research*, *Annals of the New York Academy of Sciences* 285 (1977): 539–64. The data analysis, on which the text reports, was done in collaboration with David H. Smith, who made a substantial contribution in the development of the approach adopted here.

with which Weber *et al.* were concerned. The question we ask is this: Is it generally true that sociocultural subgroups typically produce individuals with personality characteristics of the sort likely to lead them to perform quite differently once they enter the economic realm?

To represent the psychosocial side, we used our measure of individual modernity, the OM scale, because it delineates a set or syndrome of qualities similar to those emphasized in the work of Weber and McClelland. These qualities include a sense of personal efficacy, autonomy in dealing with authority, and openness to new experience. The ethnic and religious groups studied were drawn from all our six developing countries— Argentina, Chile, East Pakistan (now Bangladesh), Nigeria, India, and Israel. All comparisons were made on a within-country basis, and therefore on different sets of religions and ethnic groups as we moved from country to country. Thus, the Indian study compared so-called "tribal" and "non-tribal" groups, and within the tribal we distinguished "Hindu" from "Christian." In Israel, all were Jewish immigrants to that country, but they differed in having come from the Near East, North Africa, or Asia. And so on, as further explained below.

Our theoretical orientation and our actual experience had indicated that individual modernity was strongly influenced by the amount of education, the degree of mass-media exposure, and the amount of factory experience people had had. But in the phase of our project reported in this chapter, our concern is with the extent to which "culture," broadly conceived, contributed to individual modernity above and beyond the "objective" facts of education, occupation, or mass-media exposure. In this research specific cultural differences in values, child-rearing practices, interpersonal relations patterns, and the like were not explicitly measured, but rather were represented by the global characteristic of "religion" and/or "ethnic" membership. In a statistical perspective, this actually put the cultural variable in a stronger position, because it meant, in effect, that a lot of the inevitably unexplained variance in individual modernity scores might be assigned to the credit of the global "culture" measure.

Our basic method for testing the contribution of "culture," as measured by membership in an ethnic or religious group, was to create sets of individuals who were matched on all major characteristics, such as age, sex, and education, but still differed in culture-group membership. The matches were then used to test the association of individual modernity scores with membership in a given culture group, in order to yield a correlation coefficient. As a standard, one might keep in mind that when individuals were so matched in groups divided into the more and the less educated, the match correlations were consistent across six countries, and in the median case, the figure was .35, significant at better than .01. As will be seen, the case to be made for the importance of religious and ethnic differences in explaining individual modernity is much weaker and far less consistent. Changing the method of analysis to utilize a "dummy" variable to represent religion or ethnicity in a regression analysis somewhat improved the performance of ethnic-religious variables as predictors of individual modernity, but did not raise them to anything approaching the power of education, occupation, or the mass media in accounting for individual modernity.

RELIGION AND ETHNICITY AS DETERMINANTS OF MODERNITY

One of the most common forms of either advantage or handicap that men experience stems from their origin and membership in one or another ethnic and religious group. Not only may such ethnic membership place a person at a disadvantage by denying him legal rights and economic opportunities, but the traditional culture of his group may inculcate in him attitudes, values, and action tendencies that impede his ability to function effectively in the modern world.

It was clear, therefore, that in developing a general model to account for individual OM scores, we had to allow for the possibilty that a man's modernity might in good part stem from his membership in an ethnic or religious group whose culture patterns made its members decidedly more modern than other groups. Despite the many criticisms directed at them, Max Weber's classic thesis about the role of Protestantism in the rise of modern capitalism in Europe, and David McClelland's later research on "the need for achievement" as a force accounting for national economic development, had obvious implications for our work.[3] Consequently, we felt it incumbent on us to take careful note of the religious and ethnic characteristics of those who entered our samples.

As it turned out, there were indeed marked differences in the average modernity scores of the major ethnic and religious subgroups in our samples. For example, in Israel the percentage scoring in the upper third of the distribution on OM ranged from 16 percent among those Jews who had originated in Tunisia to 56 percent among those who came from Turkey. And in Nigeria only 26 percent of the Ekiti scored as modern, whereas 82 percent of the Ife so qualified.[4] Clearly, some ethnic and religious subgroups in our samples were decidedly more modern than others. But how far was this truly a *cultural difference*, and how far the product of differential opportunity? Since education and factory experience are highly effective in modernizing individuals, the men from certain ethnic and religious groups might have scored as they did mainly because they had had more contact with modernizing institutions. Indeed, we knew from government statistics that groups such as the lower-caste Hindus of India suffer marked disadvantages in education. Therefore, before we could conclude that cultural differences were an independent factor contributing to the standing of men as more modern or traditional, we had to control such factors as education, factory experience, urbanization, and contact with the mass media.

Some might argue that the act of "bringing under control" the influence of such variables as education and industrial experience is to beg the very question under investigation. In this view it is precisely through their differential readiness to stay in school, or move to town, or enter industry that tribal, religious, and ethnic groups express their cultural differences. Those who take this view will want to give particular weight to the straightforward zero-order correlations which we present, and will grant less validity to matching, partial correlations, and regression analysis. Others, however, will prefer a different analysis model.

One such alternative model assumes that the typical education or occupation of religious and ethnic groups is largely a result of their physical location, or of social forces external to any subgroup culture, such as a climate of prejudice and discrimination. In such cases, to obtain a fair picture of the residual contribution that group culture makes to individual modernity, one must adjust the individual scores to take into account the differences in the objective life chances common to a whole group.

A second alternative approach is to accept the assumption that cultural differences *per se* influence the pursuit of education or the choice of occupation, yet to insist on knowing whether or not there is any further residual effect of culture *after* differences in education and the like are taken into account.

These two alternative models might be tested either by a natural experiment or by a longitudinal study. Neither resource is available to us here. We must, therefore, fall back on other methods, meaning essentially statistical manipulations, in our effort to isolate the effects of some cultural residue which may exert its influence even after group differences in education, occupation, and the like have been taken into account. In this report we have relied mainly on two such statistical devices, one quite familiar, the other relatively little known.

Our less well-known method we call "matching." Matching is done by a special computer program which generates two (or more) sets of individuals differentiated on the match variable, but otherwise more or less exactly alike on other critical variables. Thus, to facilitate comparing Protestants and Catholics in Chile, the matching program pairs each Protestant to a Catholic who is like his "match" in education, occupation, age, mass-media exposure, residence, rural origin, and urban residence. The resultant matched groups permit us to examine the influence of any single variable while the other main variables are simultaneously controlled. Otherwise, the results we obtained in any comparison might reflect not so much the influence of the experience we intended to assess, but rather that of some other variable that happened, in our sample, to be closely associated with the one in which we are interested. Under the condition of matching, any differences we observe between two matched groups may be relatively unambiguously assumed to reflect the influence of the match variable, rather than being spuriously produced by one or more of the "uncontrolled" variables.

As a method of bringing "extraneous" variables under control, matching has the great advantage that one always knows concretely which people one is comparing, and one compares actual scores, not artificial scores generated by a process of statistical weighting. Nevertheless, we must acknowledge two attributes of matching that lead some to question its suitability.

First, the nature of the matching process may extract from the larger sample as representatives of the parent group those individuals who, in fact, are in the statistical sense most unrepresentative of that parent population. To match cultivators and industrial workers on education in a given country, for example, one may be obliged to rely on only those farmers with more than eight years of schooling, despite the fact that farmers with that much education are one in a hundred, and are special in other ways, such as owning much land. Perhaps even more important is the fact that the matching process inevitably greatly reduces the total number of cases with which the analysis is conducted. The smaller the N, the greater the size of the mean difference required to qualify at any given level of statistical significance.

To meet these objections, we sought a method that permitted working with the total sample, yet somehow approximated the flexibility and specificity of the matching method. The technique we hit on, well known in economic research, is called dummy variable analysis. For this purpose a set of nominal categories, as is the case with ethnic or religious groups, is organized as an ordinal variable by pitting everyone in one group against those in other groups, and assigning arbitrary values, such as 1 and 2 to those on either side of the line. By this method we could create a variable that would pit each Nigerian subgroup, such as Egba or Ekiti, successively against the others. Once such a variable is created, correlation coefficients indicating the strength of each dummy variable may be obtained. To control for the influence of other factors, one may resort either to partialing the correlation or to including it in a linear multiple regression analysis. Still other procedures might have been used, but our experience with these data leaves us quite confident that alternative methods would not have substantially altered the impression one is led to draw from these materials.[5]

ETHNICITY IN INDIA

We begin our exploration of ethnic and religion influence with our Indian sample because it included the most striking subgroup differences. We selected our Indian sample to include more-or-less equal numbers of four major groups: high-caste Hindus, low-caste Hindus, tribal Hindus, and tribal Christians.[6] The two caste groups require no special explanation, except perhaps for the observation that we made the distinction between "high" and "low" caste in accord with Indian law and on the basis of local expert opinion.[7] As to the tribal groups, they were part of what the Indian Constitution calls "the scheduled tribes,"[8] a term which probably needs a fuller explanation.

The State of Bihar, locus of our work in India, was home to 4.2 million members of the scheduled tribes, 94 percent of them concentrated in the Chotanagpur Division, which was the main center of our field work in the province. It was therefore particularly appropriate that in doing his sampling, Dr. Singh, our project field director for India, decided that about half of his 1,300 cases should be tribal, with strong representation in each of our standard occupational subsamples. On the recommendation of our local advisors, these so-called tribal men were further subdivided on grounds of religion, to separate those who had adopted Christianity from those who followed a Hinduized version of their tribal religion.[9]

Our local advisors considered these divisions to be culturally very meaningful. Yet we could not go directly to comparing their relative modernity without the risk of confusing cultural distinctiveness and social advantage. These groups were not merely culturally different; they also enjoyed very different opportunities in life. For example, the Bihar census for 1961 revealed that the percent literate among the higher-caste males was more than three times that for the lowest castes and twice the proportion prevailing among tribals.[10] Despite the narrow educational range over which we selected the cases, our sample subgroups also displayed marked differences in educational attainment, reflecting the sharp differentiation within the parent populations.[11] We therefore had great need of our matching procedure to permit us to compare any one of the four ethnic-religious groups with any other under such conditions that those compared would be almost exactly alike in education, occupation, and other important variables.

We looked first at a series of "two-way" matches, which pitted the groups against each other, one pair at a time. This method permitted us to obtain quite a large number of cases for each pair. The striking fact about the series of matches, as shown in table 7-1, was that all of them revealed only very modest differences between the pairs of ethnic-religious groups, so modest, indeed, that in no case was the difference statistically significant, despite the ample number of cases in almost all the matches. Even in those instances in which we had expected the greater contrast, for example, between high-caste Hindus and either tribal Christians or tribal Hindus, the high caste showed very little advantage over the others. We must

TABLE 7-1

Mean Modernity Scores and Correlations with Individual Modernity (OM) for Matched Indian Groups from Different Religious and Ethnic Backgrounds

Match No.	No. of Pairs in Match	Matching Groups Coded:		Correlation of Groups with OM[b]	Mean OM Scores	
		Group 1	Group 2		Group 1	Group 2
19	110	Tribal Hindu	Nontribal Hindu	.04[a]	48	49
19B	84	Low-caste Hindu	High-caste Hindu	.06	57	58
19C	95	Tribal Hindu	Low-caste Hindu	.06	47	48
19D	26	Tribal Hindu	High-caste Hindu	.07	55	56
18	104	Tribal Hindu	Tribal Christian	.07	52	54
18C	79	Low-caste Hindu	Tribal Christian	.08	53	54
18D	27	High-caste Hindu	Tribal Christian	−.03	57	57

[a]Positive correlation signs indicate that the group coded 2 had higher OM scores; negative correlations indicate the group coded 1 had higher scores. The correlation coefficients reflect the association of the codes 1 or 2 with the OM score of each individual in the match.

[b]Significance: Using a two-tailed *t* test, none of the correlations or mean differences were significant at the .05 level.

conclude that in our Indian sample neither religion, caste, nor ethnic group had any significant independent effect in determining men's modernity when the individuals compared were otherwise alike in the degree of their contact with modernizing institutions.

We should not be understood as asserting that these four groups, as one encounters them in all walks of life, are basically alike. We have already seen that they differ greatly in their life conditions, and we can affirm that because of those differences in life condition *on the average* they do differ in modernity. What we are suggesting, rather, is that individuals from these groups, however different they may be at the start, become increasingly more alike to the extent that they are equally exposed to the influence of modernizing institutions. The point may be dramatically illustrated by comparing the OM scores of representatives of the four Indian ethnic-religious groups in a simulation of a "before-and-after" experiment. This could be done by using sets of "four-way" matches, i.e., with each subset of men matched exactly to those in the other three sets.

First, consider the OM scores of men from the four groups under the condition that all are cultivators and have little schooling. At this stage of development, despite their being exactly matched on education, occupation, and several other variables, the four groups show marked differences in OM score, as indicated in the first line of table 7-2. Indeed, the gap of ten points separating the low-ranking tribal Christians and the top-ranking high-caste Hindus was significant at the .01 level, despite the small number of twenty cases involved in the match comparision. The tribal Hindu also fared badly in comparison with the high-caste Hindu. Ethnicity, caste, and religion evidently made quite a bit of difference in determining a man's modernity score when we tested the power of these identities in a group of cultivators with little education.

We next asked whether the differences persisted in the case of men more exposed to modernizing experiences. To get the answer we redid the matches, with each of the four ethnic-religious groups now represented by men drawn exclusively from among the better-educated factory workers. The situation these matches revealed was quite different, as may be seen in table 7-2. The gap separating the high caste Hindus from the tribal Christians shrank from ten points to two points, and the gap separating them from the tribal Hindus shrank from eight points to one. When the comparision is at the level of well-educated industrial workers, there are no longer statistically significant differences between the high-caste Hindus and either of the two tribal groups.

TABLE 7-2

Mean OM Scores for Matched Ethnic-Religious Groups at Different Educational-Occupational Levels In Bihar, India

Match Identification	No. of Individuals in Each Group	Educational-Occupational Level	Ethnic-Religious Groups			
			I Tribal Christian	II Tribal Hindu	III Low-caste Hindu	IV High-caste Hindu
19XC	20	Cultivators averaging 5 years schooling	45	47	51	55[a]
19X	19	Workers averaging 10 years schooling	61	62	62	63[a]

[a] Significance: Using a two-tailed *t* test, in Match 19XC differences in mean OM score were as follows: I vs. III .05, I vs. IV .01. In Match 19X none of the differences were significant.

We may conclude that in our Indian samples tribal, religious, and caste differences cease to have an independent effect on individual modernity scores once men have attained equality in the advantages provided by education, factory experience, and exposure to the mass media. Being born a high-caste Hindu evidently increased the man's changes of ending up among the more modern, but caste in itself did not confer a unique advantage secure against competition. Evidently the lowliest tribal member, Christain or Hindu, can be brought to almost the same level of modernity as any high-caste person merely by being given equal access to modernizing institutions.

RELIGION AND ETHNICITY IN NIGERIA

The "Yoruba people" are overwhelmingly predominant in the Western Region, to which we largely limited our work in Nigeria.[12] There is no sure way of defining a Yoruba, other than that he will acknowledge himself to be so when asked, and will be able to speak the "standard" Yoruba language. However, virtually all Yoruba-speaking people also identify themselves as members of one of the more-or-less distinctive tribes that share the Yoruba language. In some cases a man will actually respond to the question, "Are you a Yoruba?" by asserting, "No, I am Ijebu," even though as an Ijebu he will be speaking the Yoruba language. Moreover, the members of each tribe within the language family still know something of their separate history, and each tribe sees itself as descended from a particular tribal ancestor, even though a new ideology emphasizing the common descent of all the Yoruba has been gaining some currency.

Dr. Edward Ryan, field director for the Nigerian phase of our research, had hoped to keep his sample as homogeneous as possible in terms of tribal membership. Various available tribal groups were, therefore, considered ineligible on the grounds that they were not distinctly part of the Yoruba group, or in any event, did not contribute substantially to the industrial labor force.[13] Nevertheless, the necessity to broaden the base from which he drew his cases obliged Dr. Ryan to include in his sample a reasonable diversity of cultural backgrounds. Consequently, we could make at least two important distinctions within our Nigerian sample, one on grounds of religion, the other a tribal classification on the basis of "degree of Europeanization."

In Western Nigeria, and particularly among the groups we studied, the old tribal religions are no longer the basis on which men habitually identify themselves.[14] Among the men in our sample, 43 percent considered themselves Muslim, 57 percent Christian.[15] Despite the vigor with which most men affirmed their religious identity, some of our advisors doubted that such religious distinctions are culturally as fundamental in Nigeria as they often are elsewhere. Nevertheless, the issue seemed important enough to warrant the expenditure of effort required to develop a match.

The match putting the Christians and the Moslems in competition failed to show either group to have any significant advantage over the other. These results were confirmed by the regression analysis, which yielded partial correlations with OM so low as to indicate that once we controlled other variables, religion played an absolutely negligible role in predicting individual modernity in Nigeria.[16]

To assess the effect of subtribal differences in Nigeria provided a bit more complex. We had taken into our sample representatives of four main tribes: Ijebu, Egba, Ekiti-Ondo, and Ijesha. In addition, small numbers of other subtribes were included.[17] Over the last hundred years, some of these groups had evidently shown greater interest than others in adopting the institutions and practices brought to Nigeria in the colonial era. These differences did not, so far as we know, result mainly from the initiative of the colonial authorities or the differential application of their policies. Rather, they stemmed in good part from propensities rooted in the different tribal cultures. For example, the Egba and Ijebu were reputed to have shown interest in education much earlier than did other Yoruba groups. The Ijebu also were widely credited as being outstanding traders and as having been quicker than most to see the advantages their children might gain from professional training.[18]

These impressionistic observations were supported by objective census reports that revealed the differences between the groups to be often quite marked. The Egba, for example, were only about 8 percent of the population in the Western Region, but contributed 31 percent of its industrial labor force, whereas the Ondo were 21 percent of the population, but made up only 14 percent of those working in industry. As many as a third of the Egbado followed the native religion, whereas this was true for only 6 percent of the Ijebu and 11 percent of the Egba, who had much more uniformly become followers of either Islam or Christianity.[19]

Taking into consideration such evidence of tribal differences, Dr. Olatunde Oloko, our Nigerian collaborator, ranked the subtribal groups, placing at the top those "that had and still have the longest and most varied contacts with the agents of the European commerce, industry, education, administration, and religion." Dr. Oloko concluded that the Ijebu and the Egba shared the first rank, but should be maintained as separate groups. He recommended that all the others, in descending order on the scales— Ijeshas, Ondos, Ekitis, Ifes, and Egbados—could be grouped together as a set of tribes generally less exposed to outside contact.

We followed Dr. Oloko's ranking in constructing our ethnic matched groups in Nigeria, keeping the Egba and the Ijebu separate, and creating an "Other" category in which we placed all the remaining subtribes. By means of such a "three-way" match, the two leading groups could be compared with each other, and be paired in turn with the "others" in a separate comparison, all the while holding other relevant variables constant.[20]

It occasioned no great surprise that in their match the Ijebu and the Egba did not show significant differences in modernity.[21] These groups live in contiguous areas, they have similar histories, they both have the reputation of having been quick to take up the advantages offered by contact with the colonial administration, and their standing on an array of objective indicators of modernization led our Nigerian collaborator to rank them equally as most advanced.

It was more notable, however, that the group of "other" tribesmen, which had been collectively rated "low" in relative cultural modernity on the basis of both reputation and historical evidence, was not significantly more traditional when our match placed them in competition with either of the two more highly rated subtribes. If anything, the residual group came out ahead of the other two, although not at a statistically significant level.[22]

Since this outcome was so far contrary to the expectation established by our local expert, it seemed particularly important to check the findings by another method.

The "dummy variable" analysis tested seven combinations, each successively evaluated in the context of a regression analysis which, in effect, brought under control the same variables taken account of in the matching. The result confirmed the findings obtained by matching. Groups other than the Egbado, Egba, and Ijebu were the more modern, but none of the Beta weights were significant. No single subtribal group was at all distinctive, or even outstanding, in the modernity manifested by its members when the comparison rested on statistical procedures designed to take account of differences in life chances. Details are given in table 7-3.

In sum, the data seemed to warrant the conclusion that within the larger Yoruba-speaking Nigerian community, knowing a man's subtribe is of very little value in predicting his modernity, at least once account is taken of his education, occupation, and other "life chance" factors.

ETHNICITY IN ISRAEL

Israel is simultaneously one of the most homogeneous and heterogeneous nations in the world. The Hebrew population, to which our study was restricted, came from many different countries. In each period of its recent history Israel experienced new waves of immigration. Between 1948 and 1953 alone, some 375,000 entered Israel from North Africa, the Near East, and Asia Minor, greatly augmenting the 650,000 Jews who were there in 1948. These immigrants from Africa and Asia Minor were mainly Sephardic, as contrasted with the Ashkenazi, who made up the bulk of the population in the earlier waves of immigration, which had come predominantly from Europe. Collectively, the Mediterranean immigrants came to be called the "Oriental" Jews.

Their lack of educational attainment limited these Oriental Jews to positions in the rank and file of the working class. Indeed, as we studied the composition of the industrial labor force, it quickly became apparent that among those under the age of 32 the great majority were men who had come to Israel from Asia and Africa as young immigrants.[23] This seemed to us no great disadvantage, however, because it meant that the Israeli sample would be more broadly comparable to those from the other countries than

TABLE 7-3

Relation Between Individual Modernity and Dummy Variables for Religion-Ethnicity Expressed as Zero-order Correlations[a] *and Beta Weights*[b]

Argentina			India		
All others vs.			All others vs.	r	Beta
parent's birthplace	r	Beta	Tribal Hindu	−.28***	−.03
Both Argentina	−.27***	−.10**	Low-caste Hindu	−.16***	−.03
Both Italy	.04	−.01	Tribal Christian	.08**	−.02
Both Spain	.03	−.01	High-caste Hindu	.35***	.10
Argentina and Italy	.10**	.04			
Other Europeans	.14***	.06*	Israel		
Argentina and Spain	.17***	.07*	All others vs.		
			origin in	r	Beta
East Pakistan			Asia	−.02	−.03
All others vs.			North Africa	−.10**	.00
district	r	Beta	Near East	.12**	.02
Dacca	.02	−.08			
Comilla	−.08*	−.05	Nigeria		
Barisal	−.05	−.03	All others vs.		
Chittagong	.15***	.01	tribe	r	Beta
Mymensingh	−.12***	.02	Ijebu	−.03	−.04
Khulna	.07*	.03	Egba	−.06	−.04
Faridpur	−.00	.03	Egbado	−.02	−.00
Noakali	.07*	.06	Ondo	.08*	.05
			Ife	.08*	.05
			Ekiti	.02	.06
			Ijesha	.08*	.06

Note: Significance levels indicated as follows: * = .05, ** = .01, *** = .001. All others not significant. The significance of the Betas was established by the rule that a Beta should be twice the standard error to be treated as significant at .05.

[a] In the dummy variables "all others" were coded 1, the named group was coded 2. The zero-order correlation expresses the association between the variable so coded and individual modernity (OM) scores. Positive correlations indicate the named groups generally had higher OM scores, negative correlations indicate the named groups had lower scores than the "others."

[b] The Beta weights are from a linear regression of OM on eight variables. In addition to the ethnicity-religion dummy variable, the other variables in the regression were those listed in table 7-4.

would have been the case had the Israeli workers been predominantly of European origin and culture.

Because men of European origin were so scarce among the younger Israeli industrial workers, we restricted our sample to the Oriental Jews, and thus precluded a comparison of the relative modernity of the two groups. Those who were classified as Oriental, however, listed thirteen different nations as "country of origin." It was not feasible to pursue the influence of such origins for all these groups, especially since several had very few representatives. Yet there was no obvious and compelling principle to guide us in deciding how to combine the thirteen national origin groups into more manageable sets. We therefore followed our standard practice of taking the advice of our local collaborator.

Dr. Uzi Peled, who ran the project in Israel, recommended that we define three broad categories of origin: the Near East, North Africa, and Asia.[24] This division was not merely geographical, but also cultural. The Near East division, for example, brought together the Arab countries, and the North African division consisted mainly of men who had lived in an area that had experienced colonization and other cultural influences from France.

By our matching procedure we succeeded in locating three sets of men alike in education and other important respects, but different in their national origins. Essentially the same groupings were the basis for constructing dummy variables for use in a regression analysis, presented in table 7-3. Both methods yielded findings basically in accord with each other.

The group we designated as Asian, generally called "Eastern" Jews by the Israelis, was consistently the least modern, even when we adjusted their OM scores to account for group differences in education and other life chances. Those from the Near East were most consistently ahead in comparison with the other two. Those from North Africa fell in a middling position. We should note, however, that the observed correlations and Betas were generally not significant, and the absolute magnitudes, mostly below .10, very modest.[25] The conclusion seems warranted, therefore, that Israeli groups having different ethnic origins are not, on those grounds, reliably distinguishable as to the psychological modernity characterizing their representatives within our samples.

Our conclusion that the culture areas in which Israelis were born, and in which their forebears had lived for generations, played only a very modest role in determining the scores they eventually earned on our modernity scales, should be hedged round by a number of reservations. First, we must emphasize that our stated conclusion applied only within the limits of variation encompassed by our sample. We studied only Oriental Jews and searched for differences by country of origin within that realm alone. It might well be that had we compared Jews of European origin with those of Oriental background, we would have found evidence that one's region of geographical-cultural origin did play a more substantial role in accounting for the modernity of individuals.

Second, we must acknowledge that our way of grouping the national cohorts may have obscured differences by moving all three origin sets toward some arbitrary meaningless common denominator. As noted earlier, inspection of the average OM score for each origin group did reveal some high and some low-scoring national contingents within each set.[26] However, with thirteen countries of origin to deal with, we felt that a comparison pair by pair across the set of all possible pairs presented a task too complex for our resources and too methodologically risky, given the size of our samples.

Third, we must recognize that three-fourths of the men in our sample had spent ten or more years in Israel before we interviewed them. Half of them had been 14 or under when they had come to the country. Most spent some time in Israeli schools, virtually all had served a spell in the Israeli army, and all worked in Israeli factories and farms. This common experience could have exerted so powerful a homogenizing influence on our subjects, especially during their formative years, as to overshadow most cultural differences in relative modernization that might have been manifested in their parents' generation.

This last interpretation, which we favor, again underlines our main point. Men having different social origins will differ in their individual modernity only so long as their life situation, and especially their adult experience, exposes them to highly differentiated life conditions. If men of diverse social origins get the same amount of schooling, and then as adults work at similar jobs and are exposed to the same mass media, they may be expected to become increasingly alike in the degree of their modernity, despite the countervailing influence of the contrasting social milieux in which they had their personal origins.

RELIGION IN CHILE

Although Chile, like all of Latin America, has always been overwhelmingly Catholic, Protestantism has been well established there since the mid-nineteenth century. The early Chilean Protestantism had a decidedly middle- and upper-class character, and was identified with the more "established" churches brought to Chile by immigrants from Europe. In the last few decades, however, Chile has experienced the rapid spread of a different kind of Protestantism. The sources of influence have been the Pentecostal and Evangelican sects, among them the Iglesia Metodista Pentecostal and the Iglesia Evangelica Pentecosta. So rapid was their expansion that the number of Protestants doubled between 1940 and 1952. By 1960, 5.6 percent of the population was classified as Protestant, as against 1.4 percent in 1920. Of the total Protestant population, some 85 percent was by 1960 Pentecostal. The sects have recruited chiefly in the Chilean lower classes, and more particularly in the industrial working class. The main concentrations are in the industrialized areas, and the prime source of converts is believed to be among those newly migrated to the city.

Looking to the values that figure prominently in our project's conception of the modern man, the Chilean Pentecostals seemed likely to gain points for their reported tendency to grant equality to women, their emphasis on the independent conjugal family rather than the extended family, their concern with being frugal, and their strong aspirations for decent housing and some reasonable level of comfort through use of the gadgetry of modern living.

Against these tendencies we must, however, balance the fact that the Pentecostal Protestants in Chile evidently do not value education highly. Even though they consider simple literacy highly desirable, they are not noted for founding schools, and may even be characterized as anti-intellectual. Although they have a strong sense of group membership, they do not extend their concern to the rest of the community in which they live. For example, they are not inclined to join organizations other than their own church. Among them political activity is at best tolerated, and is often discouraged. The dominance of their lay preachers, and their fundamentalist emphasis on the infallibility of Scripture, introduce elements of authoritarianism into these groups, and a tendency toward dogmatic and sometimes rigid thinking. They are not necessarily open to new ideas or ways of doing things. Finally, their spiritualism is not very compatible with scientific explanations of natural events.

We were, of course, aware of the theories that assign the Protestants in Catholic countries a special role in the economic development of nations. In the light of what we had learned about the ideas and manners of the Chilean Pentecostals, however, it seemed to us unlikely that they would be markedly more modern than the Catholics.[27] But the issue could be settled only by the data.

Some 6 percent of our Chilean sample, fifty-seven men in all, acknowledged themselves to be Protestant.[28] By our matching procedures we were able to find thirty-four men among the Catholics who were otherwise almost exactly like thirty-four Protestants in education, age, occupation, income, and other characteristics.

Comparison of the Catholic and Protestant groups indicated that the Protestants were somewhat more modern men, even when we controlled for differences in background and experience other than religion. Protestants had an OM score of 54 against 53 for the Catholics. Expressed as a correlation between religion and modernity, the figure was .10. However, these differences failed to reach the .05 level of significance in a match with only thirty-four cases.[29]

Partial correlation analysis with the total sample led to the same conclusion. With other differences controlled by partialing, Catholics and Protestants were very much alike. The partial *r* was only .06, again favoring the Protestants, but not at a statistically significant level.[30] Thus, the theory that Protestant minorities may be expected to play a relatively more modernizing role in Catholic countries got no support from our Chilean sample.

RELIGION AND ETHNIC ORIGIN IN ARGENTINA

The pattern of settlement in Argentina has not been too different from that in the United States. In 1850 the country had not more than 1.5 million people. Massive waves of immigration between 1857 and 1937 brought some 6.5 million people, although this was balanced by an outflow of some 3 million who returned to their homelands or went elsewhere. Of the net immigration, 43.5 percent was Italian and 27 percent Spanish, the rest being distributed among much smaller groups from all over Europe. In Argentina, as in the United States, the official language was rapidly adopted by almost everyone. Assimilation in other respects was profound, and there emerged a new and distinctive cultural amalgam fairly uniformly spread across the country.

Under the circumstances, it did not seem especially urgent to attempt any division of our Argentinian sample according to ethnic origin. We assumed that for most people those origins came too far back in time, and had been followed by too much intermarriage, to be very meaningful. There were, however, enough individuals in the labor force who were more recent migrants from Italy and Spain to warrant establishing a special category of the "foreign born" in our Argentinian sample. There also were a small number of Protestants in our Argentinian sample, sufficient to support a match similar to the one made in Chile.

When the Catholics and Protestants in our sample were compared under matched conditions, the Protestants proved to be the more modern. The match correlation was .16, the OM score of the Catholics being 52 against 55 for the Protestants. Given the small N of eighteen cases in the match, however, the differences were not statistically significant. The partial correlation using the total sample did not challenge this finding.[31]

Turning next to the native vs. foreign-born distinction, we found that some forty-eight foreign-born had entered our Argentinian sample, all of them industrial workers. In matching, we found twenty-nine of the native-born who were in all important respects exactly like an opposite number among the foreign-born.

In making a comparison of these groups, we took no position as to which should be more modern. If Spain and Italy were considered more advanced countries than Argentina, the immigrants might turn in a superior performance. But we thought it would be difficult to make this case forcefully, especially for Spain, which is one of the least-developed countries of Europe. On the other hand, many social scientists, and not a few others, are firmly convinced that immigrants are self-selected to be more independent and open to new experience. If that were true, the immigrants could be expected to outperform the native-born on the OM scale. The native-born, however, had the advantage of greater familiarity with the language and the style in which the interview was conducted. So we made no prediction.

The outcome of the comparison of native and foreign-born gave neither group a significant edge over the other, but on the whole tended to favor the native-born. The OM score of the latter was 56, against 54 for the foreign-born. The correlation of the match on origin with the overall modernity score was .18, favoring the native-born, but not with statistical significance.[32] The partial-correlation procedure used with the larger group from which the matches were drawn also favored the native-born, but this advantage was far below any acceptable level of statistical significance.

Although the foreign-born/native-born distinction was not very productive, our local advisor felt there might be differences, within the set of native Argentinians, varying in accord with the national origins of their forebears, even though there was no obvious basis for asserting which groups should be in the lead. Therefore, we added an extensive dummy variable analysis to see if any combination of background was associated with noticeably more modernity among those having particular ethnic and religious origins. By this procedure we did indeed find three combinations that were associated with greater modernity at a statistically significant level, even when other major variables were controlled in a regression analysis. When they were placed in competition with all others, the groups that emerged as more modern were those with: one parent Argentinian, the other Spanish or Italian; or both parents from "other" parts of Europe. The details are given in table 7-3.

These differences were not predicted on the basis of any theory. They arose from a simple empirical exercise, and may be freely interpreted by one and all. We do note, however, that all of the observed differences are of very modest magnitude.

RELIGION AND REGION IN EAST PAKISTAN

Our East Pakistan sample was the most homogeneous, and therefore did not lend itself readily to further study of the role of ethnic and religious factors in accounting for individual modernity. We did make some effort to get a sample of Hindus still living in East Pakistan. They were a hard-pressed minority, however, and not easy to reach. Nevertheless, before we gave up searching for eligible Hindus we had interviewed twenty-eight men. Fortunately we succeeded in matching all but seven of these to Moslems who were like them in education, occupation, and other characteristics.

The correlation of the match with OM was .09, indicating the Moslems were slightly ahead. This was also reflected in the mean OM scores for the two matched groups, which were 55 for the Hindus and 57 for the Moslems. However, these differences were not statistically significant. They indicate some advantage for the Moslems, but hardly permit one to argue that religious background was a truly independent factor in determining individual modernity in East Bengal.

Since the Hindu-Moslem comparison rested on such a small number of cases, we were eager to find some related source of contrast within the Pakistan sample. Other than religion, the chief basis for such distinctions was a man's district of origin. Regional differences *within* a country are likely to be less fundamental than those between separate countries. Regional cleavages also generally mean less than religious or tribal divisions. Nevertheless, what we know of the contrast between the northern and southern regions in countries as different as the United States and Italy indicates that one can hardly rule out regional factors as a source of cultural influence on individual modernity.

The several districts of East Pakistan seemed to have a rather definite character. The men we interviewed were not only quick to identify themselves with their district of origin, but they also knew about and took an interest in that sort of information as it applied to people they worked with or met in other contexts. Moreover, each of the districts had a fairly well-defined image in the popular mind, a kind of collective reputation. For example, Schuman (1966b) found that men from Barisal were seen as aggressive and hot-tempered, whereas the image of men from Noakhli stressed their qualities as pious men who were nevertheless shrewd and concerned with money.

To assess the modernity of the men from the different districts of East Pakistan, we again relied on dummy variable analysis. In the regression analysis that tested the eight districts, none showed a statistically significant advantage over the others in the proportion of its men who scored as modern.[33] The results (table 7-3) do not argue for an important and distinctive contribution by the local cultures of different districts toward making men more modern.

SUMMARY

By matching we were able to test the effect of religion in five countries. Once our matching procedure equated men so that their education, occupation, and other salient characteristics were more or less identical, the residual differences in OM scores were generally two points or less, yielding correlations of .10 or less, none of which was statistically significant. This outcome could be challenged on the grounds that the matches were limited to only a few select cases. However, regression analysis using dummy variables and partial correlations, both drawing on the total sample, confirmed the match findings. Indeed, they gave a possibly starker picture. The Beta weights available for four comparisons in as many countries were in the very narrow range of .00 to .04, none of them significant, as may be seen in table 7-4. Across the range of groups we studied, religion decidedly failed to prove itself an important independent characteristic for identifying groups of individuals who were more modern than their countrymen from other denominations.

Ethnic and regional bases of cultural and social differentiation showed themselves somewhat more effective as distinctive indicators of modernity. For example, Argentinians whose parents were both native-born were significantly less modern than those whose parents had come from Europe.

TABLE 7-4

Beta Weights of a Set of Independent Variables as Predictors of Individual Modernity

Variables Entering Regression[c]	Beta Weights for Regression Including Variable for:								
	Religion[a]				Ethnicity[b]				
	Argentina	Chile	East Pakistan	Nigeria	Argentina	East Pakistan	India	Israel	Nigeria
Education	.39***	.34***	.30***	.23***	.39***	.30***	.50***	.34***	.22***
Mass-media exposure	.20***	.22***	.20***	.24***	.20***	.20***	.20***	.24***	.24***
Occupation	.17***	.21***	.16***	.11*	.17***	.17***	.12***	.16***	.11**
Living standard	.00	.11***	.16***	.13***	.00	.16***	.09***	.10**	.13***
Father's education	.07*	.08*	.01	.04	.08*	.01	.06*	.05	.04
Urbanity	.05	.06*	.05	.16***	.05	.05	.18***	.16***	.16***
Life-cycle stage	.10***	.09**	.04	-.01	.10***	.04	.00	.03	-.01
Religion/ethnicity	.03	.04	.03	-.00	.12***	.05	.04	.06	.10*
Zero-order correlation for ethnicity/religion	.03	.04	.07*	.08*	.30***	.13***	.43***	.17***	.10**
N =	817[d]	931	654	721	817	1001	1300	739	721

Note: Significance: * = .05, ** = .01, *** = .001.

[a] For the religion variables, the order of punching, by country, was : Argentina—(1) Catholic, (2) Protestant. Chile—(1) Catholic, (2) Protestant. East Pakistan—(1) Muslim, (2) Hindu, applying to factory workers only. Nigeria—(1) Muslim, (2) Christian.

[b] For the ethnicity variables, the order of punching, by country, was: Argentina—parents were (1) both Argentinian; (2) both Italian or Spanish; (3) Argentinian and Italian; (4) Argentinian and other, both other Latin American; (5) other European; (6) Argentinian and Spanish. East Pakistan—(1) Mymensingh, (2) Barisal, (3) Comilla, (4) Faridpur, (5) Noakali, (6) Khulna, (7) Chittagong, (8) Dacca. India—(1) Hindu low-caste or tribal non-Christian, (2) tribal Christian, (3) Hindu high-caste. Israel—(1) Iran, India, Afghanistan; (2) Morocco, Tunis, Algeria, Libya; (3) Syria, Lebanon, Egypt, Iraq, Yemen, Turkey. Nigeria—(1) Ijebu, (2) Egba, (3) Egbado, (4) Ekiti, (5) Ondo, (6) Ijesha, (7) Ife.

[c] For a description of each of the variables making up this set, see chapter 3.

[d] N's are approximate because of cases missing on some variables.

However, it was only in a few scattered comparisons that such differences were statistically significant, and in magnitude the association between ethnic status and modernity, as expressed by Beta weights, never was greater than .10 when the influence of other variables was controlled in a regression analysis. The details are given in table 7-3.

What then can we say to those who assume that the subcultures of religious and ethnic groups are fundamentally important in imbuing their members with qualities that will qualify them as more or less modern? Our results provide, at best, only very weak support for their assumption, and at worst may be interpreted as disproving the hypothesis. Since our findings rather challenge more sanguine estimates, we should both elaborate and clarify our position.

First, we acknowledge that our cases were certainly not selected with the purpose of *highlighting* the independent role of religious and ethnic factors as determinants of individual modernity. Admittedly, differences in district of origin in Pakistan are not ordinarily assumed to be very dramatic. It might well be that if in Israel we had compared Arabs and Jews, or in Nigeria had put the Ibo in competition with the Hausa, then the striking differences that the culturological perspective anticipates would have been evident in our data as well. Nevertheless, we feel that the contrasts between low-caste and high-caste Hindus in India, Hindu and Moslem in East Pakistan, and Catholic and Protestant in Chile would generally be accepted as being quite fundamental. The fact that they did not prove to be so does not deny that in other places and times comparable distinctions may have produced dramatic differences. Our findings do, however, cast serious doubt on the *generality* of the proposition that such differences are key factors in accounting for individual modernity.

Second, we recognize that our method of combining sets of ethnic groups under collective headings such as "Jews from North Africa" or "Yoruba tribes *other than* Egba and Ijebu" might cover up the distinctiveness of precisely that one group that could prove the point about the importance of ethnic and religious differences. In most cases, however, the matches did pit one discrete group against an "other." And while the dummy variables almost always used an "other" category as criterion, each separate group in turn got to pit its strength against that "other." Nevertheless, it is true that we did not test all possible pairs, and so may have missed the one case that might have produced an outstanding performance. But that one case would be like the proverbial swallow. Even in the event that such cases had happened, we would still feel constrained to state that those who insist that powerful effects on modernity are most everywhere associated with religion and ethnicity have exaggerated the distinctive contribution of such characteristics.

Third, we are aware that by applying multiple controls through matching, partialing, and regression, we may have been following an inappropriate model. What is distinctive about certain cultures may express itself most clearly in the differential propensity to obtain more schooling, more industrial work, or more exposure to the mass media. To control statistically for such propensities may, therefore, be to expunge the critical antecedent indicators of which the adult modernity score is only the final expression. From this point of view, a relevant test of whether subgroups differentially socialize their members to greater modernity would require us to test children before they go to school, or to follow a long-term longitudinal design, or perhaps to do a path analysis. In the absence of such data, the argument continues, one should give serious attention to the zero-order correlations.[34] Since we have no interest in sweeping this argument under the rug, we presented the relevant zero-order correlations in tables 7-3 and 7-4.

In the case of religion, there were no difficult measurement problems, because only two sets of individuals entered into each comparison. As may be seen in the first part of table 7-4, the religious differences are very modest in size, although in two of four cases they reached statistical significance.

The correct procedure to use in the case of multiple ethnic groups is problematic; but the dummy variables, as presented in table 7-3, seem to be appropriate measures. In this case a more diversified picture emerged. In Nigeria, two subtribes were noticeably more modern. In Argentina, those men whose parents had both been born in that country were decidedly more traditional, and in India, the high-caste Hindus were markedly more modern. Indeed, in the list in table 7-3, one can find up to a dozen groups whose sociocultural background seems to identify them as noticeably and, in the statistical sense, "significantly" more modern or traditional as judged by zero-order correlations. But whether this is a large or a small number of cases depends on one's expectation, which, in turn, rests on one's theoretical orientation and one's comparative experience. We know of no objective standard for making that judgment. We prefer, instead, to note that after obtaining these figures we are, in effect, "back in square one." After all, at the very outset of this chapter we showed that some groups in our sample clearly had a high proportion of modern men. The zero-order correlations merely restate that fact in a different form. The basic issue, however, is what meaning or weight to assign to zero-order correlations, especially in the context of the investigation here undertaken?

Our inclination is not to give them great weight for two reasons. Perhaps the most serious consideration is that our samples are not representative, and hence are not suited to intergroup comparison except insofar as some processes of standardization on key variables is undertaken. In addition, there is the fact that in applying statistical controls to the religious/ ethnicity variable, we are doing to that variable nothing more or less than we did to the measures of other social factors, such as education, occupation, and mass-media exposure when those variables were evaluated as part of the larger research program. This observation may serve as introduction to our fourth point, concerning the competition among variables.

As our fourth point, then, we note the importance of distinguishing between an analysis designed to identify particular groups that are distinctively modern, and one oriented toward assessing the relative importance of religion and ethnicity as variables entering into competition with other dimensions of social structure. For example, we can assess the importance of education by comparing the mean modernity score of high school graduates otherwise matched to primary school graduates. But we also can, and do, treat education as a continuous variable forming an ordinal scale on which we place all individuals according to the years each spent in school. In that form, the variable "education" yields correlations and can be entered into regressions to assess its contribution in competition with other variables as predictors of modernity. Ethnicity and religion are prototypically nominal variables, which leads to their being used more as we have used them here in the matching, in order to compare one completely discrete group with another. But if a set of ethnic groups is assigned values according to the presumed degree of modernity inherent in their respective cultures, the resultant ordinal scale can be used in operations just like those used with the measure of education.

On the basis of our dummy variable analysis, we arranged the ethnic and religious groups within each country on scales from least to most modern, and then, through a linear regression analysis, placed those scales in competition with measures such as education, mass-media exposure, and other important dimensions.[35] Under these conditions, the *relative* importance of some forms of religious/ethnic membership was enhanced, at least in some countries. The summary of the results is given in table 7-4.

In this new arrangement, no surprises are given us by the four available measures of religion. In the linear regression analysis, the Beta weights for religion are consistently the lowest in the set of eight. Moreover, the Beta weights are all well below .05 in magnitude, and none is statistically significant.

However, when the ethnicity measure was rearranged to give it as much influence as possible in its competition with other variables, it did not fare so badly. We do see here again the extent to which the ethnic groups that were outstanding in modernity depended for that advantage on their superior education and occupational placement. This is most dramatically illustrated in the case of India, where a strong zero-order correlation of .43 for the ethnicity variable was reduced to a trivial Beta weight of .04 in the regression. But this should be contrasted with the cases of Argentina and Nigeria, where the characteristic onslaught of the regression analysis nevertheless could neither reduce the Beta weights below .10 nor impugn their claim to be statistically significant.

Returning to the issue of the importance of ethnicity *relative* to other variables, we may note the following: overall, the ethnicity measure was substantially less important than education, mass-media exposure, or occupation in accounting for individual modernity, in competition with the set of seven other variables entering into the regression. The Beta weights for education, occupation, and mass-media exposure were always at least .10, and with one exception, significant at .01 or better. By contrast, three of the five Beta weights for ethnicity were below .10 in magnitude and were not statistically significant. This makes a less than compelling case for the variable. But on the positive side one should note that the ethnicity variable was regularly more important than either father's education or the age-life-cycle measure.[36]

CONCLUSION

In this research in six developing countries, we explored the role which the religious, ethnic, and regional origins and identity of workers and peasants played in determining to what extent they were "modern" or "traditional" men. Religion consistently failed to prove itself a significant indicator of modernity. Some ethnic and regional groups did, however, seem typically to turn out men who were appreciably more modern or traditional than were their countrymen from other sociocultural milieus.

Such differences could readily result from differential access to education, factory work, and mass-media exposure, which we know to be powerful forces in making men modern. We therefore needed to test whether there was a distinctive cultural residue effective in making men modern above and beyond the "objective" advantages granted to certain groups by virtue of local public policy, prejudice, or historical accident. An outstanding example of the operation of such factors was found in India, where the high-caste Hindus scored as much more modern than did either low-caste Hindus or tribal Christians, both objectively disadvantaged groups. When we controlled statistically for other factors such as education, however, the edge in modernity earlier displayed by certain groups was largely erased.

These results have important bearing on our assessment of the Weberian model of economic development. Our data in no way disprove the cases cited in research in that tradition. But our results do suggest that the cases often used to support the Weberian hypothesis were probably special cases. Our data indicate that, *in general*, religious and ethnic groups within the same country are not markedly differentiated on a dimension such as modernity, at least once one takes into account their differential access to education, factory work, and the mass media.

We must acknowledge, however, that the application of statistical controls, in effect equalizing the life chances of different groups, may obscure the basic process by which groups that actually *are* culturally distinctive manage to bring their members to a state of greater modernity. It may be precisely by keeping children in school, or directing them to industrial employment, that certain cultural groups express their greater modernity. The issue can probably be settled definitively only by carefully controlled longitudinal studies. As a substitute for that, path analysis was used in our research, and it did indicate that in some groups, at least, the path to the relative modernity of their members is in good part due to heavy reliance on schooling, which in turn leads to greater individual modernity.

Thus, we can see that some cultures and subcultures may produce a greater proportion of modern men because they more encourage their youngsters to follow life paths which, in turn, inculcate in them modern attitudes and values. From this fact one can move back into the cultural group to probe more deeply the qualities that lead them so to guide their young, and the processes that in turn generate those tendencies. Alternatively, one can, as we prefer to do, focus attention on the noncultural life chances that produce the observed individual modernity. In particular, we choose to stress the permeability of the barriers to individual modernity. Even where ethnic and religious traditions typically operate to produce men who are less modern, individual change is possible. Our analysis leads us to affirm that men from very traditional groups can become as modern as those from communities more modern in outlook if the men concerned can gain more contact with modernizing institutions. Given the right opportunity by their larger society, most men may become more modern.

CHAPTER 8

National Differences in Individual Modernity

In chapter 5 we reported that for our set of six developing countries we were able to "explain" a median of 47 percent of the variance in individual modernity scores by weighing the contribution of a series of eight variables, of which education, occupational experience, and mass media were most notable.[1] Since our basic design committed us to looking at the phenomenon one country at a time, we were of necessity precluded from utilizing national membership as one of the explanatory variables.[2] Yet the question of how far national (or indeed ethnic) groups vary in their relative modernity is one of the oldest and most basic of those raised in the standard works on economic development (see McClelland 1961; Lerner 1958; Hagen 1962). In this chapter we offer an answer to that question, at least as it applies to men from our set of six countries.

Our approach to this phase of our research was frankly exploratory rather than being oriented to the testing of an explicit hypothesis. Thus, we considered it quite possible that once we took account of the educational and occupational differences in our samples, the different national groups would be equal in modernity. On the other hand, if national character, religion, or some other cultural factor really were an important force in shaping individual modernity, then the national groups might vary considerably in their psychological modernity even after being matched on education. But there was no obvious principle which could guide us in

This chapter appeared originally as Alex Inkeles, "National Differences in Individual Modernity," in Richard F. Tommason, ed., *Comparative Studies in Sociology* (Greenwich, Conn.: JAI Press, 1978), pp. 47–72. Larry Meyer and Amnon Igra rendered creative research assistance in the preparation of this paper, which also benefited from a critical reading by the latter.

deciding in what order the countries would stand, and whether they would be widely spread out or bunched up in special ways. Another possibility was that some simple principle, such as the level of economic development measured by GNP per capita, would account for any underlying order which might emerge. But it was not clear how such a principle, if it operated, might interact with distinctive cultural factors.

Therefore, to prepare the ground for more effective systematic hypothesis testing, we set ourselves two more limited tasks. First, we took on the responsibility of working out the difficult methodological challenge of measuring the quality of individual modernity in such a way that a given score assigned to a person in one country would have exactly the same meaning when assigned to someone in another country. Second, using this new measure, we meant to discover the relative modernity of our six national samples after we had rendered them equivalent in average education, occupation, and so on. This done, we intended to study any pattern in the national rankings which might emerge, in order to draw out its implications for a theory as to the qualities of nations which make them more or less likely to produce psychologically modern citizens.

THE SAMPLE AND RESEARCH DESIGN

Although our sample design was well suited to some purposes, it was obviously not so appropriate for others. Normally, to compare nations, one would prefer that each country sample be strictly representative of its parent national population. Unfortunately, from this perspective the requirements of the larger project made a highly purposive sample more appropriate. Nevertheless, we believe the samples we did collect are not only relevant to our purpose here, but even have some special virtue in relation to our objective.

We pursued our national comparisons in order to assess the extent to which any given society produces a more or less distinctive human product whose personality and orientation to the world express some essence of his culture or some distinctive features of the characteristic institutions of his nation. However, other factors than national tradition were known to shape the very qualities we were studying. It was important, therefore, not to confuse the issue by attributing to the "national setting" what should be more accurately attributed to some force like individual education. Consequently, to discern what was the distinctive role of nationality in shaping the modernity of Argentinians and Nigerians, we were under obligation to consider only men who had had about the same amount of schooling and who pursued comparable occupations. Otherwise, we ran the risk of attributing to nationality what really should be attributed to formal education or to work experience. From this perspective, therefore, the fact that our samples had the same general "structure" in all countries, being more or less alike in average education, age, sex, and occupation, was an advantage. We did not, however, rest in that position. Rather we undertook, through matching and regression analysis, to bring under statistical control any remaining differences in the relative advantage or disadvantage any of our national samples might suffer in education, occupation, and the like. We hoped thus to isolate as far as possible the "pure" influence, if any, of the national setting as a factor shaping individual modernity.

CONSTRUCTING A STRICTLY COMPARABLE CROSS-NATIONAL SCALE OF INDIVIDUAL MODERNITY (IM)

Although the measures of individual modernity used in the main part of our study were all constructed by the same method and were highly comparable in content, they were nevertheless not identical from country to country. Indeed, the OM scale had been calibrated separately within each country.

In constructing the OM, as against the International Modernity (IM) scale used in this chapter, each item was dichotomized as close as possible to the midpoint of the distribution of answers *within* each country taken separately. Thus, on a question concerning the ideal family size, the "modern" answer could have been two or less in one country, and four or less in another. The summary of modernity, or "OM score," for each individual, therefore, told us how far above or below the average he was *as compared to his own countrymen only*. An OM score of 80 was a "high" or "modern" score in all countries, but there was no clear-cut way of saying what the man who got 80 in India would have gotten if he had been scored using the coding criteria utilized in Argentina or Israel. The procedure used to construct the OM scale was appropriate, indeed desirable and even necessary, to attain the goals set by our initial research design. In that design, we treated the research in each country as a separate replication of the basic study. Since we were mainly testing for the existence of an OM type syndrome in all six nations, and correlating that with a comparable set of independent variables, we wanted a scale which best discriminated *within* each national sample. By using variable cutting points, and eliminating some items which were obviously not understood in a particular country, we maximized certain objectives. Each country's scale had maximum reliability; we obtained scales with a normal distribution in each country; and scales in which all items were being given equal weight in the total scale. But calibrating the OM scale separately for each national group had the disadvantage of precluding systematic comparison of the OM score of an individual from any one country with that of someone from another country. To make possible such comparisons we had to construct a new scale which was exactly the same for all the countries, not only in content, but in the standard used to classify answers as modern or traditional. That scale, which we labeled IM, for International Modernity measure, must now be at least briefly described before we proceed with our analysis.

To suit our purpose we needed a scale which met the following requirements:

(a) It covered basically the same ground as did the OM scale, treating modernity as a complex multidimensional attitude, value, and behavior syndrome in which more or less equal weight was given dimensions such as: a sense of efficacy, openness to new experience, active participation as a citizen, and acceptance of birth control.

(b) It used only those questions which had been worded in more or less exactly the same way from one country to another, thus reducing the variability of the stimulus presented by the questions.[3] This similarity of question wording extended to the requirement that, for a given question, the number and form of the alternatives offered in a "closed alternative" type question were also identical from country to country.

(c) It scored the alternative answers to questions as "modern" or "traditional" on a strictly comparable basis from country to country. For example, in scoring the question about the ideal number of children, we would consider those who mentioned three or less to have given the modern answer in *all* countries.

(d) It weighed responses identically from country to country, and preferably by the method used in scoring OM, so that each individual's score would fall in the range from 0, indicating all his answers were "traditional," to 100, indicating all his answers were "modern."

(e) It yielded a scale having comparable reliability in all the countries, in no country falling below the level of .60.

Insofar as we could construct a scale meeting these requirements, we felt it would be reasonable to advance to the next stage of searching for, and attempting to explain similarities and differences in, the modernity of individuals representing different national groups. We recognized, of course, that there were a host of theoretical and methodological issues raised by any effort to score men from different cultures and societies on a single unified measure of a quality as complex as individual modernity. The discussion of these issues could easily take up all the space allotted us in this chapter, indeed, could easily fill a modest-sized volume.

CONSTRUCTING THE SCALE

Our first step in constructing the IM scale was to compile a list of all questons used in the six national versions of our OM questionnaire which had consistently demonstrated that they were part of the modernity syndrome and, in addition, had been asked in a more or less identical way in all six countries.[4] How many questions met this qualification depended, of course, on how strictly we applied the test of what was an "identical" wording. Although the six country field directors were committed to fairly strict adherence to the general form of the questionnaire, they were free to make adaptations to suit local conditions. This sometimes led to changes in wording, and to variations in the number or the form of the alternative answers from among which people were asked to make their choices. Using the strictest criterion we would count on 55 items asked in exactly the same way in all countries. By recoding some answers to make the items more comparable we could increase to 93 the number of questions appropriate for international scale construction.[5] Finally, if we relaxed our standard to include questions which were merely "more or less" comparable everywhere, we could bring the pool of items up to 125.[6]

In deciding which of these sets of items to use in which combinations we faced the usual kinds of trade-off. A longer scale might yield higher reliability, but at the possible cost of reduced comparability. A shorter and more selective scale promised maximum comparability, but was more prone to distortion if even a few questons were widely misunderstood in some countries. We could find no obvious rule dictating which set of advantages and disadvantages to prefer. We therefore compromised on the middle ground. Our candidate, used throughout the analysis in this paper, was our scale IM2A.

We selected IM2A because it had a very large number of items, 93 to be exact, yet excluded those which our staff thought to be of somewhat questionable comparability.[7] These qualities earned it a higher reliability than most other IM scales we constructed, its range across six countries going from K-R .59 to .80, with the median at .63.[8] In addition, IM2A, being rather long, could include questions representing all the subthemes which we had included in our theoretical conception of individual modernity and had found empirically to be part of the syndrome.[9] Moreover, the length of the scale made it less likely to be overresponsive to the influence of a single question or a subset of questions which, in a short scale, could have a disproportionate effect on the standing of one or another country.[10] IM2A had an observed range of 70 points, from a low score of 6 to high of 76, across the total set of men, and the scale had a standard deviation of 9.1 for the total sample of some 5,500 men.[11]

Given that the content of the scale for all countries was virtually identical, and the scoring scheme likewise; that the individual items used had all shown themselves part of the modernity syndrome when modernity scales had earlier been constructed separately within each country; and that the reliability and the standard deviation of the scale were basically alike within each country—we felt confident in accepting IM2A as an international measure of individual modernity suitable for the sort of analysis we anticipated making.

BASIC QUESTIONS AND BASELINE DATA

Accepting IM2A as a reasonable measure of individual modernity permitting meaningful cross-national comparisons put us in a position to answer the following questions:

1. Holding other things constant, are there significant differences in individual modernity manifested by sets of men from the six different countries in our study? In other words, how much of a bonus on his modernity score does a man somehow secure by virtue of his membership in a national group or his residence in a given country?

2. Insofar as such differences are manifested, what weight should we assign to "national" origin as against other factors, such as education and mass media exposure, as explanations of differences in individual modernity?

3. How far can we attribute the contextual effect of nationality to visible and "objective" factors such as greater national wealth and more widespread diffusion of the mass media, and how far to some ineluctable residue of advantage built into the "culture" which any person shares as a member of a given national community?

There are, of course, other interesting questions which might be put to these data. For example, it is intriguing to consider how far the men from each country earn their standing as modern men on the basis of a different profile of psychological characteristics, some countries producing people more modern in their independence from family control, others in their openness to new experience. We are obliged, however, to leave that issue for further research.

BASELINE DIFFERENCES

To establish our baseline we calculated the mean IM score for each national sample. The differences were notable. The Israelis and the Argentinians were as much as 13 points, almost 1.5 standard deviations, ahead of the men from East Pakistan, with Nigerians, Chileans, and Indians, respectively, occupying the middle ranks. The details are given in table 8-1, on the lines 1 and 3 for "Unadjusted Country Means."

The full significance of these differences in mean scores can probably be better appreciated by considering the proportion of each national sample qualifying as modern. To that end we arbitrarily classified as modern anyone whose IM score placed him in the upper third of the distribution for the total sample of almost 6,000 men. Using that criterion we found 57 percent of the Israelis and 51 percent of the Argentinians to be modern, while a mere 5 percent of the men from Bangladesh could so qualify. The other three countries were bunched on the middle ground, the percent modern in those samples being, respectively: Nigeria 34, India 33, and Chile 28.

TABLE 8-1

Six Country Mean Scores in Individual Modernity (IM2A):
Unadjusted and Adjusted

	Argentina	Chile	India	Israel	Nigeria	East Pakistan
	(A)	(C)	(I)	(S)	(N)	(P)
1. Unadjusted country means $F = 298$***	52.3	47.9	46.9	53.5	49.2	40.7
2. Adjusted means (controlling for 6 covariates)[a] $F = 75.5$***	50.1	47.3	48.5	50.7	47.2	44.5

| 3. Unadjusted means | 40 — P — 45 — I C N — 50 — A S — 55 |
| 4. Adjusted means[a] | 40 — P — 45 — NC I — AS — 50 — 55 |

***Significant at the .001 level.

[a] Note 20 of chapter 8 describes the covariates. For the procedures used to calculate the adjusted means and significance levels see Johnston (1972).

We felt, however, that it might be quite misleading to draw any conclusions from these mean scores because of differences we knew to exist in the composition of our several national samples. Our samples were broadly similar in occupational composition, as per our design, but despite our efforts they were sometimes unequal on other critical dimensions. For example, the median years of schooling in the East Pakistan group was only about two years, in the Chilean about six, and in the Nigerian it reached eight. Since the number of years of schooling a man had received had shown itself in all the countries to be the most powerful fact in explaining individual modernity, all comparisons of the national samples which did not control for this factor invited confusion as to whether any observed differences in modernity should be attributed to the education of the respondents rather than to their national environment and cultural heritage. There were less extreme but comparable disparities in the national patterns of mass media exposure, again an important variable in explaining individual modernity.[12]

PERSISTENCE OF NATIONAL DIFFERENCES

To answer the question as to whether individual modernity differs by country when other things are held constant, we utilized two relatively independent methods for adjusting the IM scores to take account of educational, occupational, and other sampling disparities.

THE "MATCH" ADJUSTMENT

First, we used the technique of matching. The match results presented in table 8-2 indicate some variation in the outcome, depending on which subgroup—such as worker or cultivator—is used as the basis for the match.[13] Nevertheless, table 8-2 also gives evidence of a clear-cut pattern,[14] about which we may observe the following:

1. Nationality does make a statistically significant difference in predicting a man's level of individual modernity, even when the men compared are matched to be more or less exactly alike on up to five other basic characteristics.

This is indicated by the F ratios, most of which were significant at the .001 level. Typically the spread between the highest and lowest scoring national groups was 5 or 6 points on the IM scale. This meant that an individual from the high performing country, compared to someone from a low scoring country, would have given modern answers to five or six more questions out of every hundred even though the two individuals were

TABLE 8-2

Mean Scores on IM2A for Various Matched Groups, by Country[a]

Matched Group	Match Number	Argentina	Chile	India	Israel	Nigeria	East Pakistan	F[d]	No. of Pairs in Match
Cultivators	C1	45.5	40.1	44.0	—	44.9	40.6	6.82***	53
	C2	—	—	46.4	53.7	—	—	14.8**	31
Urban nonindustrials	U1	—	—	—	52.8	48.4	—	7.31**	40
	U2	51.2	52.5	—	50.3	45.5	—	3.30*	17
	U3	—	—	41.6	—	—	38.8	1.42	15
Factory workers[b]	F1	55.3	52.4	—	55.6	52.0	—	6.73***	105
	F2	57.1	—	54.2	57.5	53.7	—	4.36**	50
All occupations[c]	A1	46.8	42.6	45.7	—	46.0	41.8	6.96***	80
	A2	52.4	48.7	—	—	49.3	—	20.3***	293
	A3	54.4	51.9	—	54.1	50.6	—	8.50***	145

[a] Empty cells indicate that that country was not included in a particular match. See note 14 of chapter 8 for details.

[b] Only workers with three or more years of industrial experience could enter Match F1; in F2 the additional restriction was placed that they be relatively better educated.

[c] All occupations includes cultivators, new workers, urban nonindustrial workers, and experienced workers in A1 and A2. In Match A3, however, cultivators were excluded.

[d] Significance is indicated as follows: * = .05, ** = .01, *** = .001.

otherwise identical in education, mass media exposure, and other characteristics.[15]

These contrasts may perhaps be more readily grasped if we express the differences in terms of the percent of each national group which qualified as "modern men." This designation, as noted above, was assigned to anyone whose score put him in the upper third of the overall distribution on the IM scale. A typical contrast was that shown in Match A-1 representing all occupational subgroups, in which the proportion who scored as modern rose from a low of 8 in East Pakistan to a high of 30 percent in India. Similarly, in Match F-2, restricted to the better educated industrial workers, the proportion qualifying as modern rose from a low of 58 to a high of 78 percent, as one moved from Nigeria to Argentina.[16]

2. Within the pattern of overall differentiation there appears to be a definite structure in the placement of the several countries. Indeed, we found a more or less invariant rank order regardless of the occupational or educational subgroups being compared.

The East Pakistan group was consistently the least modern. The Chilean, Nigerian, and Indian samples generally represented an intermediate position. These three, usually not statistically distinguishable from each other, were, nevertheless, generally significantly different from the people of Bangladesh.[17] Argentina fell substantially further along on the continuum, generally at a statistically significant level.[18] The Israelis were still a bit further on, but generally were not significantly different, statistically, from the Argentinians.[19]

REGRESSION BASED ADJUSTMENTS

Since every method achieves its advantages at the cost of developing peculiar weaknesses and distorting propensities, we used a second quite independent method to check the results obtained by matching. The B weights, i.e., the unstandardized regression coefficients, from a regression analysis based on the total of some 5,500 cases, were utilized to calculate an adjusted mean score for each national group. By this process we adjusted for differences in the observed characteristics of national subsamples on five important variables such as education.[20] The result, in effect, answers the following question: if a group from each of the six countries in turn was either "compensated" or "penalized" for being above or below average in education, mass media exposure and the like, what would its resultant IM score then look like? Clearly, if nationality made no difference, the resultant adjusted scores would all come out statistically indistinguishable from one another. The actual outcome was quite different.

It is immediately apparent from table 8-1 that adjusting the country means to take account of differences in the composition of the sample in the several countries had substantial consequences. As compared to the array of unadjusted means on line 1, the adjusted set, on line 2, reveals the gap separating the high from the low scoring groups to be substantially reduced. Moreover, the rank order of Chile, Nigeria, and India changed. At the same time, however, these shifts brought the data more into line with the basic patterns observed when we had used the matching process to adjust for differences in sample characteristics. As a result of the adjustments based on the regression, the gap separating the high and low scoring groups, being 5.6 IM points, fell into the same range as the gap shown in the typical match. The adjusted country means still yielded a highly significant F ratio, indicating nationality does make a real difference (see Johnston 1972 p. 196). The rank order previously observed in the matches was preserved, with Argentinians and Israelis indistinguishable from each other in the front rank. Nigerians, Chileans, and Indians, bunched in the middle, and the East Pakistanis trailing behind by a substantial margin.

THE RELATIVE IMPACT OF NATIONALITY IN COMPETITION WITH OTHER VARIABLES

We have established that taking nationality into consideration makes a significant difference. But how much of a difference? In particular, what portion of the variance does it account for? Is it as important as education or twice as important as occupation, in accounting for a man's modernity? To answer these questions, we again utilized two methods.

First, we performed a regression analysis in which nationality was entered as a variable along with six other standard explanatory variables our research has shown to be important predictors of modernity.[21] The results are presented in table 8-3.

As was the case in our within-country studies described in chapter 5, education had by far the most substantial Beta weight, at .34. The variable measuring nationality yielded a more modest Beta of .22. Nevertheless, it was actually larger than the .18 Beta for mass media, generally the second most powerful variable in our within-country analysis, and was considerably larger than the Beta for the variable measuring occupational experience in the modern sector of the economy. All in all, this outcome identified the "nation factor" as a major element in accounting for psychological modernity even in the context of powerful competing variables.[22]

TABLE 8-3

Regression on IM2A of Six Background Variables and Nationality[a]

	Beta	B	(Standard Error)
Country (nationality)	0.22	0.49	(0.03)
Years of education	0.34	0.95	(0.04)
Years of factory experience	0.13	0.28	(0.02)
Age	0.03	0.06	(0.03)
Mass media	0.18	0.94	(0.06)
Urban/rural origin	0.06	1.30	(0.22)
Consumer goods possessed	0.04	0.30	(0.08)
K		62.2	
$R^2 = 0.43$			

[a] See chapter 8, notes 21 and 22.

These results, while indicating that national membership was a consequential contributor to the modernity rating of individuals, left open the question of the extent to which nationality made a *unique* contribution. In order to get at that issue we looked at the stepwise increment to R^2 due to "country" when it was pitted against the composite influence of all the individual background variables. With six background variables already taken into account, putting "country" into the regression still added 4 percent to the variance explained. This distinctive contribution of country was very much less than that of the background variables. The unique variance explained by the background variables as a set was 22 percent, as indicated in table 8-4.

Actually, we were gratified by this outcome because our project, from its very inception, rested on the assumption that an individual's position in social structure, rather than his distinctive culture, would be the *prime* determinant of his psychological modernity. Nevertheless, the finding that the set of individual background factors, such as education and occupation, was much *more* important than the variable national-cultural milieux, should not be allowed to obscure the fact that the latter are nevertheless quite significant influences in their own right. To get additional perspective on this issue, and in addition to gain the advantage of being able to judge the extent of interaction effects in our data, we utilized a second method, namely an analysis of covariance. By using the analysis of covariance we were able to gain perspective on the meaning of moving up a step on the educational ladder, as compared to moving from one country to the next. We could do this by looking at the mean of the sample, on IM2A, in each education-country category. Table 8-5 presents the results.

TABLE 8-4

Partition of Explained Variance (R^2) *in IM2A into Unique and Joint Components, Due to Country and to Background Variables*

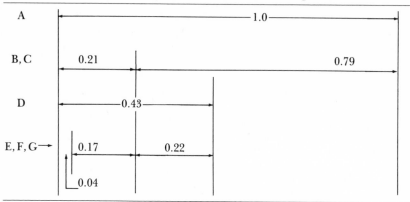

A: Total variance (standardized).
B: Between country variance.
C: Within country variance.
D: Variance explained by country and 6 background variables.
E: Variance unique to country.
F: Joint variance (country and 6 background variables).
G: Variance unique to background.

We again see substantial evidence for the importance of nationality as a determinant of individual modernity, even when the scores of the groups compared have been adjusted to equalize the effect of differences in education, mass media, and the like. Even in the narrow range of those with six to eight years of education, and with five additional covariates controlled, the East Pakistanis lagged 9 points behind the Israelis and

TABLE 8-5

Adjusted Means,[a] *with Interactions,*[b] *for IM2A by Education and Country*

Years of Education	Argentina	Chile	India	Israel	Nigeria	East Pakistan
0	—	—	43.2	—	—	40.5
1–5	48.4	45.0	46.2	48.4	46.9	41.4
6–8	51.1	48.6	48.7	52.4	48.5	43.4
9–15	54.0	50.5	53.8	54.9	51.7	—

[a] The covariates controlled in this regression were factory experience, mass media, age, urban/rural origin, and consumer goods possessed.
[b] The main effect of education yields an F of 401, significant at the .001 level. The main effect of country yields an F of 89, also significant at the .001 level. The interaction of education and country yields an F of only 2.3, significant at the .01 level.

almost 8 points behind the Argentinians, equivalent to almost a full standard deviation. The greatest gap in IM scores from the lowest to the highest *education group* within any country was about 10 points. But with men matched on education, the greatest gap between the most modern and the least modern *country* was of comparable magnitude. Although the main effect of education, over all, was much the larger, the main effect of country was quite substantial, an F of 89 significant well above .001.

It seems clear that merely by virtue of their nationality the men from certain countries received a substantial bonus toward their IM scores *above and beyond whatever they might have earned by virtue of their individual profile of education, factory experience, and the like*. A man from Argentina who had not gone to school at all apparently scored as modern as an East Pakistani who had completed more than eight years of schooling, and a Chilean with about seven years of schooling did only as well as an Israeli who had only been to school for three years. How can one account for such a powerful effect arising from the mere difference in a man's national citizenship?

EXPLAINING THE ADVANTAGE OF SOME COUNTRIES IN CONFERRING INDIVIDUAL MODERNITY

After extensive working and reworking of our data we found no way to escape the fact that the men from some countries consistently scored higher in individual modernity than those from other countries, even when the individuals compared were apparently alike in certain characteristics which had previously been shown to be the most powerful determinants of such scores. Since we could neither wish away, nor wash away, these facts, we would like to be able to explain them. At present juncture, however, we cannot offer a definitive conclusion. We can only point to a series of plausible alternatives, one or all of which may be the true explanation, and indicate our best estimate as to the probable contribution of each.

1. The first alternative runs as follows:

"All that these results show is that, after all, the modernity syndrome is really a specification of the Western man, hence the more Western a country the more its citizens get a bonus on the scale."

This raises a complicated issue much broader than its manifestation in this particular set of data. We hold that the modernity syndrome is not culture specific, and feel that our work has demonstrated its relevance in a variety of societies. To say that, however, is not to say that explanation number 1 is wrong. On the contrary, we always assumed that individual modernity, as we defined and measured it, would be more *prevalent* in Western countries while not being *exclusively* present there. We feel that being from a "Western" culture is neither a necessary nor a sufficient condition for being psychologically modern. Quite apart from any theoretical objections, the assumption that IM scores are adequately explained by some purported Western bias in the scale must face several important bits of contradictory evidence.

First, we note that our Chilean group, coming from a country as much "Western" as any other in our sample, nevertheless did not generally fall in with the presumably more Western Israelis and Argentinians, but rather stood closer to the very "un-Western" Nigerians and Indians. Second, we call attention to the sharp separation of the Indian from the East Pakistani groups, even though they were both certainly very much "non-Western."[23] And third, we need to reckon with the fact that the Israeli group was only nominally Western, being so only in the sense that Judaism is linked to Christianity, and thus to Western culture. Otherwise, those in our Israeli sample were almost exclusively "Oriental" Jews who, not many years before, had emigrated to Israel from countries such as Iran, Iraq, Syria, Turkey, Lebanon, and Egypt. Their values and living patterns quite often reflected strong Arab influence. The European Jews in Israel consider these people to be "Orientals," and often express the view that they are rather alien to, and not readily assimilated to, "European" culture. The fact that such Israelis scored high on the modernity scale cannot, therefore, be convincingly explained on the premise of their being so much more "Western."

2. The second alternative argues that:

"The trouble lies in assuming that the independent variables other than nationality really were controlled. For example, a man who had six years of school in East Pakistan may not have had an experience truly equivalent to six years of schooling in Argentina, even though the project scored them as equal in education."

This argument seems quite plausible. A "year" in school in Argentina could well mean attendance during 180 days, whereas the school in Bangladesh may have operated only during 90 days. The one school might have been staffed by well-trained teachers, equipped with books and paper and maintained at a comfortable temperature, while the other may well have lacked all these amenities. Under the circumstances, granting equal weight in both countries to the response "I completed six years of schooling," might certainly be misleading.

Although, as indicated, we find this argument appealing, it seems contradicted by one of our main findings. Our Indian and East Pakistanian samples included a substantial number of people who had never been to school. Yet, as may be seen from the first line in table 8-5, the illiterate group from India was considerably more modern than the strictly comparable set of men from East Pakistan. Differences in the quality of schooling can have had nothing to do with that outcome, since none of the men compared had been to school. There seems no escaping the conclusion, therefore, that something about a country or region other than the effectiveness of its schools can contribute to making its citizens more or less modern.

In addition, if school quality were a key factor, we should have found a powerful effect for the interaction of education and country in our analysis of covariance. Actually, the observed effect noted in table 8-5, while statistically significant, was modest compared to the separate main effects for education and country.

Admittedly, such statistical inferences leave something to be desired as a method for settling the issue. We acknowledge that a definitive resolution would require more direct measures of the actual quality of schools, newspapers, and other institutions in different countries. In the meantime we note that some studies in the West have failed to show that sheer length of the school year, or even the quality of the school, make very much difference in cognitive development (Husen 1972; Coleman 1966). It may be that those factors are not so important in the attitude-value realm either.

3. The third alternative explanation holds that:

"The observed differences are real, and reflect differences in culture and national character, which are distinct from and independent of level of national economic development."

Anthropologists, sociologists, and psychologists interested in group personality and in culture have often noted that certain groups have a distinctive ethos, a culturally defined systematic personality bent, or national character (Inkeles and Levinson 1969; Le Vine 1973). Indeed, from the time of Weber on, such tendencies have been of particular interest because of their presumed implications for economic growth and national development. In the past, efforts to compare the national character of different groups have been impeded by lack of a cross-culturally standardized measure of important personality dimensions. We see the IM scale as overcoming this difficulty in good part, and feel that IM scores may be interpreted as showing the relative standing of our respective national samples on this particular measure of group character.

While we acknowledge that our data present some surprises and some anomalies, we do not, on the face of it, see the results as patently contradicting common assumptions about where the six societies should have fallen on a scale measuring qualities such as those encompassed in the modernity syndrome. Even the departures from popular expectation may be explained on culturological grounds. For example, the Indian sample's advantage over the East Pakistani sample might be attributed to the differential effect of the Hindu and Islamic religions, or to the fact that half the Indian sample was "tribal." And Argentina's lead over Chile might be attributed to the greater diffusion of American Indian influence in the Chilean working class population.[24]

Certainly, in principle, we have no inclination to contradict the line of reasoning which seeks, in distinctive cultural properties or in national character, an explanation for the differences in modernity we observed. We can, however, readily anticipate the argument that our samples are not sufficiently representative of the respective parent populations to justify any such conclusion. Representing the full range of Indian and Nigerian groups might certainly alter the rankings those countries attained in our samples. But each of our samples certainly constituted a distinctive national group or subgroup, each different from the other even if not representative of any entire nation. Moreover, our statistical controls corrected for the possibility that any lack of representativeness was expressed mainly in unique advantages in education or occupation. Yet even after such controls were applied, the several national samples were significantly differentiated on our measure of modernity. It might well be, then, that each man's national or ethnic heritage had conferred on him a bonus, or a handicap, as the case might be, when he came to complete the interview leading to the assignment of his IM score.

4. The fourth alternative is to assume that:

"The differences are real, and they exemplify the impact on individual modernity of the general character of the social milieu in which each individual lived. Those who lived in more modern societies, with more opportunity for contact with modern institutions and objects, and more interaction with decidedly modern men, should have become more modern as a result. In other words we have observed true 'contextual' effects."

Of the explanations offered, this is the one we find most convincing.

Of the forces which make a man modern, we measured mainly the qualities one normally thinks of as individual properties, such as a man's education, occupation, or age. If, however, becoming modern is a process of socialization, and therefore depends, in part, on following role models, then individuals living in a more modern setting should become more modern merely by sharing a *generally* modern ambience. And one important factor in making a modern ambience may be the *average* level of modernity of the individuals who live in the environment. This line of reasoning seems most germane to our findings because the research reported in this paper utilized as its main indicator of a country's development the average modernity score of the men from that country. But basically the same sort of reasoning would apply if we used other more "objective" indicators of a nation's level of development such as its GNP, the extent of its newspaper and radio networks, or the average schooling of its population. Thus, a man surrounded by individuals with above average education might well acquire modern ideas by mere contact with his presumably more modern peers even if he himself had had little schooling. And whether or not he himself reads the newspaper, a man surrounded by people who do so every day will hear more about world news events just as part of the general conversation around him. Similarly, whether they work in a modern organization or not, individuals who live in an environment in which such organizations are widespread should more likely be aware of, and possibly incorporate in their own value scheme, the principles of rational order, and so on.

The most commonly used indicator of these types of objectively measured enrichment of national environments is GNP per capita. We therefore reran our regressions with each country represented in the variable for "nation" by its GNP per capita in the mid 60s, the era when our field work was done. The same six additional variables entered the regression as had been used earlier. This way of recording each nation's standing gave "country" somewhat less importance. Nevertheless, the Beta weight for the "nation" factor, at .16, was still highly significant statistically; it held third place, close behind mass media exposure, at .18; and it was well ahead of our own favorite, namely years of factory experience, which had a Beta weight of .10.[25]

In effect, then, each individual living in such an "enriched" environment thereby enjoys a bonus on the modernity scale over and above the points he earns from his own experience of schooling, mass media, and the like. If, in turn, the psychological modernity of a nation's citizens has the power to increase the efficiency of the economy, then the richer countries will enjoy a double advantage. In the first instance, the countries which are wealthier, or have otherwise developed a modern social system, will provide more of their citizens with more education, more newspapers, and more factory jobs. But *in addition*, the wealthier countries can evidently count on a "spill-over" or "trickle-down" effect. As a result, even their more disadvantaged citizens will be more modern than are comparably educated people from poorer or less developed countries. We may have uncovered here yet another reason why the gap between the have and the have not nations seems to grow ever wider.

PART FOUR

FAMILY AND KIN

CHAPTER 9

Construction and Validation of a Cross-National Scale of Family Modernism

As one part of the general effort to increase our understanding of the social psychology of modernization, our Project on Social and Cultural Aspects of Development undertook to develop and validate a scale of family modernism having cross-national applicability. This phase came after our successful experience in constructing the OM scale as a *general* measure of individual modernity, and such specific measures as the scale of participant citizenship to be described in chapter 11. In the construction of those scales we had found that our guiding theory had led us with a high degree of accuracy to identify the appropriate components of modernity in attitude, value, and behavior; that the resultant scales based on our theoretically derived questions cohered at a high level of reliability; that the content of both the overall scales and the subscales which emerged empirically was strikingly similar in all six countries we studied, and that the resultant scales had a strong and unambiguously consistent relation to independent explanatory variables such as education, occupational experience, and mass media exposure. In attempting to deal with the theme of family modernism, however, we found that on almost every count cited above we could not easily, and sometimes could not at all, duplicate the experience we had had with the scales previously constructed.

This chapter was originally published as Alex Inkeles and Karen A. Miller, "Construction and Validation of a Cross-National Scale of Family Modernism," *International Journal of Sociology of the Family* 4 (1974): 127–47. Credit is due here to Ana Marie Pinto, who assisted in the fieldwork in Chile, and, while a fellow of the Center for International Affairs at Harvard, developed the Overall Family Modernity Scale while working in collaboration with the senior author.

We did, in the end, succeed in constructing a series of scales of family modernism which were reasonably comparable cross-nationally, had modest reliability, and could be demonstrated as having significant validity. We feel those results to be useful in their own right, and they are therefore fully reported here. In addition, we feel that our experience highlights the fact that modernism in the family area is a more complex phenomenon than modernism in other realms, having both a culturally more specific and a situationally more variable structure which makes measurement more difficult, cross-national comparability harder to achieve, and validation much more problematic. We plan, therefore, to elaborate on the implications, both theoretical and empirical, of our experience which, we believe, has been shared by other investigators working in this realm.

THE EXPERIENCE OF OTHER RESEARCHERS

There is an enormous literature on the impact of industrialization on the family. Although the classic statement by Parsons (1943) relates industrialization to the nucleation of the family, numerous researchers have found that the relationship is really quite complex, with nucleation not at all consistently manifested (Sussman 1965), with ideals frequently not congruent with actual behavior (Goode 1963), and with attitudes toward different areas of family life not necessarily in accord with each other. Still, a general trend away from the authority of the elders and of the extended family, and toward egalitarianism in sex roles, has been noted repeatedly.

This trend is obviously a movement away from family traditionalism and toward family modernism, and may be expressed in *individual* as well as in structural terms. Yet attempts to construct scales of family modernism measuring the orientations of individuals have not been numerous. A search of the lengthy bibliography by Aldous and Hill (1967), for instance, yielded only two such references, both of which are also described in Shaw and Wright (1967). Levinson and Huffman (1955) constructed a traditional family ideology (TFI) scale which measured attitudes toward parent-child relationships, husband-wife roles, sex roles in general, and attitudes toward the family as an institution. When the scale was administered to United States college students and nurses, it yielded a split half reliability of .92. The scale's validity was indicated by its ability to discriminate among religious groups. The high reliability reported for this scale may have been due in large part to the homogeneity of the sample and its relatively high education. In any event, another attempt made by Bardis (1959) to measure attitudes toward the family as a social entity with a "familism scale" yielded a split half reliability of .79. In Bardis' study the subjects were also from the United States, but were of fairly heterogeneous backgrounds. As Shaw and Wright (1967) point out, lack of evidence of validity was a serious problem with this scale.

In contrast to the fairly high consistency of family attitudes found in the American studies, those undertaken in other nations have generally not found family modernism to be a highly coherent syndrome. For example, Camilleri (1967) cited six surveys in Tunisia measuring family attitudes of many social groups, taken between 1960 and 1965. These surveys showed that opinions about the family are diversely distributed according to the aspects of the family considered, and Camilleri concludes that one can see signs of considerable fluidity in modernization of attitudes toward the family. Marsh and O'Hara (1961) found most notable not the fact that Chinese students' attitudes were changing from traditional to modern, but rather the degree to which that change was highly uneven. Take, for example, two of the attitudes Marsh and O'Hara *assumed* to be highly related, namely, wanting to choose one's own marriage partner, and favoring having married couples live in residences separate from their parents. The *actual responses* correlated at about zero, as calculated by us from frequencies presented by Marsh and O'Hara.

The difficulty of getting highly consistent results in studies of family modernism in developing countries is further illustrated by Schnaiberg's (1970) experience in Turkey. Using 19 items to measure attitudes about sex roles in the nuclear family, he was able to develop a scale with the high K.R. (Kuder-Richardson reliability coefficient) of .83. But when, as part of the same research, Schnaiberg attempted to measure extended family ties, his seven-item scale yielded an unsatisfactory K.R. of only .34. The more successful outcome in the measurement of sex roles may have been due to the fairly narrow focus and apparent similarity among many of the items used in that scale; but the result may also reflect a lack of consistency as one moves from one area of family life to another. And since the sex roles scale has not, to our knowledge, been administered in another modernizing country, we cannot tell whether a similar consistency in attitudes and behaviors concerning sex roles would be manifested cross-nationally.

Indeed, cross-national comparisons of the consistency of family modernism are very rare. Kahl (1968) constructed a three-item scale measuring low integration with relatives in both Mexico and Brazil. The items had high factor loadings, but the scale was again narrow in scope. At the time we started constructing our scales we were still awaiting results of two more general comparative efforts at measuring family modernity: the nine-nation study directed by Marvin Sussman (Sussman and Brooks 1972), and a study of family modernism in Athens, Munich, and Helsinki directed by Constantina Safilios-Rothschild. (See Safilios-Rothschild 1970 for a theoretical discussion of family modernity.)

To our knowledge, then, this report represents the first time anyone has described an attempt to develop and test a broad, i.e., multidimentional, scale of family modernism applicable across a large number of countries. Our main objective, however, was not to achieve a "first." In the context of the larger Project on Sociocultural Aspects of Development, this report should be seen as part of our general effort to measure the psychosocial attributes of the modern man, in this case by focusing on his role as a participant in family and kinship networks. Our objective is to define the syndrome of family modernism, to measure its presence, and to discover its determinants.

THEORETICAL STANCE

We started with the assumption that individual modernity would not be limited to the economic or occupational realm, but rather was a multi-faceted, multidimensional phenomenon. The assumption was that there is a general psychosocial tendency or disposition which can and does manifest itself in a variety of roles relevant to a diversity of institutional settings and realms. To test that assumption we couched the questions presented by our questionnaire so that they covered a wide range of situations and settings, such as the factory and the farm, the school, the home, the street, the sports stadium, and the prayer meeting. On the whole our empirical materials confirmed the assumption.

In the final OM scale of individual modernity as it emerged from our data processing there were questions with high item-to-scale correlations touching on family planning, kinship obligations, women's rights, and child rearing. This indicated to us that attitudes and behavior in the family realm were clearly part of the general modernity syndrome, and encouraged us to believe that it should be possible to construct a focused and highly specific scale.

The components of the scale of family modernism were chosen when we constructed the general questionnaire used by our study. The material covered by our questionnaire was by main theme, of which there were some 26. These were further broken down into a total of 35 subscales.[1] Below we list the more important clusters which included questions we thought of as bearing on family matters, each illustrated by some representative questions. We also present some indication of our thinking about how these questions might relate to a measure of individual modernity.

Role of the aged (AG). One of the processes often noted as an accompaniment to modernization is the displacement of old people from positions of respect and authority in the family and in society as a whole. We asked a number of questions, measuring attitudes toward the role of the aged, such as whether young people should feel bound to obey old people, whether respect of young for old people is changing too rapidly, and whether a boy learns more wisdom from old people or from books. Questions about aging are treated in detail, as a separate area of interest, in chapter 13.

Aspiration (AS). It is widely assumed that a mark of the more traditional family is a son trained to follow in his father's footsteps; any other ambitions he might have, as for extra schooling, are put aside in the interest of sustaining the family economically. Our questions on this theme tested how far our respondents held to such traditional standards, rather than seeing the family as under particular obligation to encourage and support the more personal, individual, and autonomous aspirations of the child.

Independence from parents (KO). Many theorists have argued that the essence of a modern approach to family relations involves the increasing emphasis on the independence of the nuclear family from the authority of the previous generation. The questions in this set therefore asked whether a young man should pursue his *own* choice of job even if it were opposed by his parents, whether a man should feel closer to his wife or parents, and whether a married couple should live close to their parents.

Meeting kinship obligations (KO). One of the most commonly heard complaints about the modernization process is that it erodes the sense of obligation to kin, especially the obligation for economic help and mutual support. We had a set of questions, therefore, to explore how far a person, himself needy, should accept an obligation to support needy relatives.

Family planning (FS). Family planning has been identified as one of the greatest needs of developing countries, and the acceptance and practice of birth control as one of the most important indicators of the modern individual. We therefore asked a series of questions to ascertain what size family our interviewees considered ideal and to assess their attitudes toward, and actual practice of, family planning and birth control.

Women's rights (WR). The conventional model of the traditional man depicts him as denying women equal status and equal rights, as asserting his superiority and primacy in all manner of things, and as treating women as generally inferior beings who could be used accordingly. In particular, men cast in the traditional mold may be expected to restrict women's social and physical movement because they fear that women not guarded may have sexual contact with other men. Questions were included measuring these orientations.

Child rearing. If the family is to be an important element in helping to build a modern society, it seems reasonable to expect it to inculcate in children qualities which would help those children grow up, in sum, to be effective in modern social roles. Following this logic it may be argued that family modernism should reflect an aspiration to raise children who are efficacious, planful, and responsive to scheduling. Following this lead we asked a number of questions about the values one should attempt to inculcate in a young boy.

In addition to these main themes, our interview also touched on quite a few other dimensions which have been, here and there, considered relevant to assessing family modernism. Thus, we had questions on the strength of involvement with the conjugal family as against other loyalties and interests, on the preferences for children of one or the other sex, and so on through a number of additional themes.

For each theme and for each question there was a coherent theoretical position, and sometimes empirical evidence, indicating that it should be at least tentatively considered as part of a general effort to measure family modernism. Some questions were added because they touched on issues identified as important in the scientific literature, some because a member of the project staff or one of our national field directors had a particular interest in it, others because some leading authority in the field urged us to include it. This meant that not every theme, and certainly not every question, was assumed by the senior staff of the project to have a high probability of forming part of any syndrome of family modernism which might emerge. On the contrary, some very plausible propositions were seriously questioned by us.

For example, we were not at all certain that as men in developing countries increased their participation in the modern sector they would correspondingly decrease their readiness to help a relative in need. It seemed to us equally plausible that the more secure earnings of industrial as compared with agricultural workers might actually lead the former to equal or even greater readiness to help a kinsman in need. On the other hand, we must acknowledge that some of the outcomes we confidently expected were most vigorously disputed by some of our consultants either in the U.S. or in the developing countries in which we worked. For example, our assumption that the more modern man would be more involved with his immediate family, whereas the traditional man would have more interest in his work, contradicted the conception of modernity which a number of our consultants held.

Such differences of opinion could, of course, ultimately be resolved by the empirical evidence. Other issues in which there was a good deal of interest in some quarters could not, admittedly, be resolved by our data because we simply had not asked about them. We recognize the list of topics we did deal with was limited, and perhaps unfortunately selective. Interests in, and theoretical orientations and impressionistic hunches about, the family certainly vary. Nevertheless, we felt the range of topics we had covered was sufficiently broad, that most of the issues touched on by our questionnaire had clear-cut theoretical relevance, and that the material taken altogether provided a quite reasonable basis for asking the central questions which concern us in this report. Those questions are: (1) Is there a general syndrome of family modernism? (2) If such a syndrome can be found, has it the same, or at least highly comparable, content across nations and cultures? (3) Are the concomitants and "causes" of such a syndrome those which theory and previous empirical investigation have indicated they might be?

TESTING FOR THE FAMILY MODERNISM SYNDROME

First, using basically theoretical criteria, we constructed the "overall family modernity" scale; second, we broadened our pool of items and constructed a "maximum-K. R. scale," which was designed to yield the highest possible internal consistency in each country; and third, we took the best items from our second effort, and constructed strictly comparable scales labeled "Comparable Family Modernity" scales.

A FIRST ATTEMPT: AN "OVERALL FAMILY MODERNITY" SCALE

In studying individual modernity overall, and then in looking at participant citizenship, we had readily identified a general syndrome which tied together the separate questions and subscales which measured the more specific elements of the larger set. The existence of such a syndrome may be established either by obtaining a reasonably high scale reliability, or through a factor analysis, or more simply, by showing a substantial and statistically significant intercorrelation of the set of subscales assumed to make up the larger syndrome. On all these tests our first rather global efforts to demonstrate the existence of a general syndrome of family modernism failed to make the case unambiguously.

We proceeded as follows: first, we reviewed our questionnaire and identified 36 items the senior staff considered as tapping the dimension of family orientation and behavior. Second, we put these 36 items, dichotomized according to their empirical distribution in each country, into a single scale which we call "Overall Family Modernity" or "OFM." The number of items in the scale varies slightly by country because a few of the items were not asked in all countries. The highest Kuder-Richardson reliability quotient achieved by the resultant scale was .57 in India, and the median was a mere .32 for the other five countries, with a median over all six countries of .34. Considering that Shaw and Wright (1967) maintain that a twenty-item scale should have a coefficient of .75 if it is to qualify as having moderately good reliability, we must conclude that our overall family modernity scales were clearly far from showing adequate internal coherence.

The Shaw and Wright standard might of course be considered an unreasonable one to apply to our effort, because they set this standard for scales which had been cleaned up through the elimination of weak or contradictory items. By contrast, we had selected our 36 items on *a priori* theoretical grounds, and had included them all without screening to weed out those which did not relate well to the overall syndrome. Nevertheless, our approach in building the initial family scale was the same as that we had used in constructing the first general scale of modernity, or OM, as described in chapter 4, and also to build the scale measuring participant citizenship as described in chapter 11. On the very first try those two sets of items yielded much higher Spearman-Brown reliability coefficients, the median for OM-2 being .77 and for the politics scale .72. Thus our experience with the family scale was in marked contrast to our other efforts to construct modernity scales.

We were led thus to the preliminary conclusion that the realm of family relations is much more fractionated than other realms involved in modernization. In the family realm attitudes seem much more situation specific, and a man's position on any one dimension is a relatively weak indicator of his position on related issues. In the case of the family there seems to be no *general* logic, but rather a more or less distinctive *separate* logic for each culture.

This finding about the family area seemed to us a quite fundamental fact and we felt an obligation, therefore, to establish the point firmly and to illustrate it fully.

Take, for example, the theme of independence or autonomy from the control of parents. Our subscale in this area included three questions.[2] One,

KO-2, asked whether a man should choose the job he personally preferred or whether he should go along with his parents' choice even if that conflicted with his own perference. A second, WR-11, raised a similar issue, but this time with reference to choosing a spouse. The third, KO-5, elicited the respondent's preference for one or another living arrangement for married couples relative to the residence of the "in-laws." The alternatives ranged from living in the same house to living in different cities or towns.

The first two items, KO-2 and WR-11, were clearly related to each other in all six countries, with item-to-item correlations in all cases significant at the .001 level or above. By contrast, the question about locating the married couples' residence was not significantly correlated with the question on job choice in three countries, and was barely significant in the fourth (India), although the relationship was highly significant in the other two (Argentina and Chile). The outcome could also be expressed in different terms by reference to the factor loadings of these items on a summary scale of all family-related items. The question on job choice had a median loading of .25; that on choice of spouse .20; and that on choice of residence only .10.

This is an illustration of how attitudes which might well have been expected to go together did not do so regularly. Our experience is thus consistent with that of Marsh and O'Hara (1961) in Taiwan. This pattern may represent a rather fundamental cross-national regularity, i.e., that ideal residence patterns change less rapidly from traditional forms than do ideal job and mate choice. This explanation is especially tempting in view of the fact that in Argentina and Chile, two of the most modernized nations in our sample in which change may have gone farthest, residence preference *was* related to job and mate choice.

A second example of the variability in opinion structure in the family realm is provided by our scale to measure the extent of a man's readiness to participate with his wife in matters from which the traditional man often excludes women. Three of the questions asked a man whether he did, or if unmarried would consider, regularly entering into discussion with his wife about religion, work, and politics. The fourth question went somewhat afield, and asked the man whether he ever did, or would be willing to, help his wife with at least that part of the housework locally considered "heavy."

On the encouraging side, the three questions concerning discussion with wife were all significantly interrelated at levels which were statistically significant and which, in absolute terms, were comfortingly high. But participation with the wife by talking things over proved to have rather little to do with participation in doing housework. Nigeria was an exception. There all three of the relevant item-to-item correlations were significant. In two other cases it was only the question on politics which failed. Why, in Chile and India, a man willing to talk about work and religion with his wife will also consistently help her in the home, whereas one who talks politics with her will not, is beyond our powers of explanation. Going further we found that in Argentina and Pakistan only one form of discussion was related to helping in the home. Finally, in Israel home help proved to be totally unrelated to having discussions with one's wife.

The lack of consistency among attitudes toward different realms of family life may be illustrated further by considering the relations, or lack thereof, of the various subscales we developed to tap different dimensions of orientation to the family realm. In our initial attack on the problem we developed six such subscales, some of which have already been mentioned. The set included scales to measure attitudes toward independence from parents, readiness to support kinsmen, participation with the wife, family size preferences and family planning, women's rights, and mixing of the sexes in public places.

If there were a general family syndrome these subscales should have been consistently related to each other in a statistically significant degree. As table 9-1 indicates, only in India was this condition satisfied. There, all but one of the fourteen intercorrelations were statistically significant. Elsewhere, however, half or more of the intercorrelations of subscales failed to achieve significance at even the .05 level. Moreover, associations positive with one subscale were often negative with others in the set, even within the sample for a given country.

Again, this evidence may be taken as demonstrating, at least so far as our six-nation study is concerned, that the realm of family and kinship attitudes is not one in which attitudes follow a consistent cross-national pattern. There does not seem to be any clear-cut underlying dimension which ties together the discrete elements of this realm. One cannot, apparently, speak of a general tendency or a coherent syndrome of attitudes and values which express what is common to family modernism. Before drawing this conclusion firmly, however, we must examine some alternative explanations of the inconsistencies we found.

When individual items on scales fail to fall into a pattern according to expectation, the result may reasonably be assigned to measurement error. We are well aware that we must have suffered from a good deal of such error in investigating family attitudes and relations. Indeed, of all the aspects of individual modernity which we studied, the family realm was one in which

TABLE 9-1
Correlations Between Family Scales[a]

	1 I.P.	2 I.R.	3 P.W.	4 F.S.P.	5 W.R.	6 M.S.
Argentina						
1. Independence from parents	1.					
2. Independence from relatives	087*	1.				
3. Participation with wife	009	−093**	1.			
4. Family size planning	109**	031	−048	1.		
5. Women's rights	089*	−115**	036	070*	1.	
6. Mixing of sexes	001	−009	−055	049	159**	1.
Chile						
1. Independence from parents	1.					
2. Independence from relatives	108**	1.				
3. Participation with wife	−054	−199**	1.			
4. Family size planning	064*	031	−025	1.		
5. Women's rights	039	−070*	072*	−024	1.	
6. Mixing of sexes	−026	−046	−089**	021	017	1.
East Pakistan						
1. Independence from parents	1.					
2. Independence from relatives	−010	1.				
3. Participation with wife	−050	−023	1.			
4. Family size planning	068*	−002	021	1.		
5. Women's rights	039	−028	033	089	1.	
6. Mixing of sexes	−009	−009	−063*	047	221**	1.
India						
1. Independence from parents	1.					
2. Independence from relatives	120**	1.				
3. Participation with wife	065*	−055*	1.			
4. Family size planning	152**	−073**	014	1.		
5. Women's rights	102**	−088**	082**	281**	1.	
6. Mixing of sexes	087**	−090**	076**	124**	187**	1.
Israel						
1. Independence from parents	1.					
2. Independence from relatives	077*	1.				
3. Participation with wife	−060	069	1.			
4. Family size planning	162**	−006	−027	1.		
5. Women's rights	150**	−023	062	106**	1.	
6. Mixing of sexes	071	−031	018	045	122**	1.
Nigeria						
1. Independence from parents	1.					
2. Independence from relatives	146**	1.				
3. Participation with wife	−119**	−048	1.			
4. Family size planning	093*	137**	−005	1.		
5. Women's rights	004	026	017	−014	1.	
6. Mixing of sexes	064	113**	−091*	031	063	1.

*Significant at .05 level.

**Significant at .01 level or better.

[a] Correlations expressed in thousandths where decimal point is omitted.

we experienced the greatest difficulty in framing questions which were comparable from one country to the next, and in then translating the questions so that they corresponded with the original standard. The varied measurement techniques of other researchers yielded similar substantive inconsistencies, however, so we feel that it is unlikely that measurement error alone accounted for our results.

It might also be argued that our low internal consistencies were due to the measurement problems inherent in gathering data on *attitudes* rather than more "objective" data about the family. Yet our findings on the family were, as we have indicated, in sharp contrast to those obtained when we tried to create a comparable general scale of participant citizenship which also consisted mainly of attitudes. That scale combined different subscale elements such as those measuring identification with the polity, political activism, acceptance of the rules of orderly political processes, and political information, and all proved strongly interrelated with each other as shown in chapter 11.

Another possible explanation is that our sample was limited to *men* (for purposes of the larger study), and men may have less coherent ideas about family relationships than women. Unfortunately, we have no evidence to test this hypothesis, but we doubt that men would differ enough from women in coherence of family attitudes to account for the great discrepancy we found between family modernism and other types of modernism in our all-male samples.

It was a possibility, too, that other methodological approaches to scale construction might yield higher internal consistencies. In the sections below we report the results of several alternative methods of scale construction.

MAXIMIZING INTERNAL CONSISTENCY: THE "MAXIMUM-K.R. SCALE"

In assessing our experience as reported above, a friendly critic might well make two points: first, he might say we were probably too ambitious in trying to combine so great a diversity of material in one general scale. A smaller, more select set might have held together better. Second, he might say that we had been too rigid in insisting on the selection of items on *a priori* theoretical grounds. A more empirical approach might well bring out underlying relationships which our initial approach had entirely missed.

Following the implications of this criticism we went back to work on the task of constructing family modernism scales. First, we augmented the initial list of 36 questions which had been identified by our project staff as most relevant to family modernism. We also augmented the list by considering questions which had been asked in only two, or even only one, country. We thus ended up with an expanded pool of 54 items, as against the 36 we had used in our first stage. Second, we utilized a special new computer program to construct our scales. This program scanned the intercorrelation matrix and tested a large number of combinations until it came up with that assortment of items which maximized scale reliability while minimally sacrificing the length, and thus presumably the representativeness, of the resultant summary scale. The scales resulting from this procedure we refer to as "the maximum K.R. scales." The resultant had, on the average, 25 items in each country.

Following this procedure, we succeeded in improving the reliability of the family scales. Thus for India we achieved a comfortable K.R. coefficient of .76. In the other countries, however, the observed improvement still left a good deal to be desired, with three countries producing scales with a reliability of about .56 and two of about .47. Moreover, to achieve these levels of reliability we had paid the price of losing comparability, since a somewhat different assortment of items composed the scale in each country.

MAXIMIZING CROSS-NATIONAL COMPARABILITY: "COMPARABLE FAMILY MODERNISM" SCALES

At the level of reliability attained by our scales there is some doubt as to whether one is really justified in putting the items together to express an individual's position by a common scale score, or whether one would not be better advised to conduct further analysis either by item or by use of more limited subscales. However, we recognized an obligation to present to our colleagues the very best cross-national scales of general family modernism which we were able to extract from our data. And we had to acknowledge that the level of reliability for an attitude scale is a matter of taste, with some researchers feeling that for exploratory studies, and for group comparisons rather than individual diagnosis, a K.R. of about .50 may serve some substantial purpose.

In the light of these considerations we decided to pursue further our search for the maximally reliable cross-nationally applicable and valid scale of family modernism which we could devise.

Our first concern was to insure maximum cross-cultural comparability of question wording and response coding. Therefore, for this phase of the analysis we selected items which were as nearly comparable in wording as possible, and the responses were dichotomized as modern or traditional at the same point in all countries. Keeping these criteria constant, we then created two forms of the Comparable Family Modernism scale, a short one based on strict criteria and a longer one based on more relaxed criteria. "CFM 1" was composed of items which were:

1. asked in *all six* countries, thereby making six-nation comparisons possible, and

2. had qualified as part of the previously described "Maximum K.R. scale" in at least *five* of the six countries.

Eight items met the criteria for inclusion in CFM 1: attitudes toward family size and birth control (FS-1, 3); the individual's independence from his parents in making choices about basic life issues (KO-2) and (WR-11); whether the wife's as well as the husband's opinions are important (GO-5); the issue of equal pay for women (WR-7); acceptance of sexual integration on the job (WR-13); and the importance of family vs. education in determining the respect a man deserves (SC-2). The full text of each of these questions is reproduced in chart 9-1.

"CFM2" was composed of the eight questions in CFM1, plus some additional items which met the following criteria:

1. they had been asked in at least two countries, and

2. they qualified as part of the "maximum-K.R. scale" in at least two-thirds of the countries in which asked.

For CFM2, 21 items qualified in Israel, 20 in India, and 19 in Argentina, Chile, Nigeria, and East Pakistan. In addition to the CFM1 items already described, these included: attitudes toward medical means of contraception (FS-4); equality between husband and wife in responsibility for contraception (FS-6); allowing a boy to differ in ideas from his father (GO-50); the extent of duty of the young to obey the old (AG-50); the best living arrangement for married children and parents (KO-5); breaking an important rule for relatives or friends (KO-6); discussing politics with wife (WR-4); whether a girl should be allowed to work away from home (WR-6); voting for a woman (WR-8); sexual integration in schools (WR-14); whether irresponsibility and lateness should be excused in a boy (CA-11 and TI-17); whether a couple should take government advice on family size (FS-5); whether children mean more hands to work or more mouths to feed (FS-51).

The content of the scales clearly ranged over a broad spectrum of family issues, rather than being limited to only a few topical areas. As we expected, however, the internal consistency of the scales was modest. The K.R. coefficient of CFM1 ranged from .19 in Chile to .53 in India, with a median

CHART 9-1

Items Included in CFM-1: Comparable Family Modernism Scale
Full Wording and Response Categories

FS-1   What do you think is the best number of children for a man like you to have during your lifetime?

(Coded for number of children mentioned.)

FS-3   Some people say that it is necessary for a man and his wife to limit the number of children to be born so they can take better care of those they do have (already have). Others say that it is wrong for a man and wife purposely (voluntarily) to limit the number of children to be born. Which of these opinions do you agree with more?

KO-2   If a man must choose between a job which he likes or a job which his parents prefer for him, which should he choose?

The job he prefers/The job his parents prefer

WR-11 Should a girl's marriage partner be picked by herself or her parents?

If R says "Her parents" ask: Should she marry her parents' choice even if she does not like him?

Yes/No

If R says "Herself" ask: Should she marry him even if her parents do not approve?

Yes/No

GO-5   On most matters:
1. Do you think we ought to let the husband speak for his whole family, or
2. Should we be sure to get the wife's opinions also?

WR-7   Suppose in a factory, or office, both men and women did exactly the same sort of work, what should be the pay they receive?

It should be equal/Men should get a little more/Men should get quite a bit (lot) more.

WR-13 Suppose men and women work together in the same work shop (place). How much should one worry about (illicit) sexual contact (relations) between them?

Worry a lot/Worry a little/Worry not at all

SC-2   Which of the following in your eyes (view), should carry the most weight in determining the respect (prestige, honor) a man deserves?

Coming from a high or distinguished family background/Having much money/Having much schooling

TABLE 9-2

Number of Items in the Median Kuder-Richardson Reliability
Coefficient of Family Modernism Scales

Scale	No. of Items	Median[a] K. R. Coefficient
Overall Family Modernism (OFM)	34[b]	.34
Maximum—K.R.	25[b]	.57
Comparable Family Modernism		
CFM1	8	.27
CFM2	20[b]	.44

[a] Median across six countries.
[b] Average across six countries.

of .26. For CFM2, we improved to the extent of ranging from .31 in Chile to a healthy .69 in India, with a median of .44. This latter scale then represents our best effort at formulating a scale comparable across cultures.

Thus our attempt to improve our initial scale did bear fruit, but we must also acknowledge that the improvement—going from a median reliability of .34 in the case of OFM to .57 for the Maximum-K.R. scale—was quite modest in proportion to the degree of our effort. These low reliabilities certainly must be weighed seriously by anyone contemplating use of these scales. Indeed, the outcome forced us again to acknowledge how difficult it is to build a cross-nationally comparable multidimensional scale of family modernism. Nevertheless, we felt the scales we developed had sufficient virtue to be of interest to other students of the family, and so we undertook to test their validity.

VALIDATION OF THE SCALES

Whatever its intrinsic interest, the case for the utility of our proposed cross-national family modernism scales ultimately must rest on our demonstrating the scales to be valid. Of the available methods for establishing validity we selected the "criterion group" approach. This method requires one to locate groups whose known characteristics create a strong presumption that those characteristics will be systematically related to the quality measured by one's scale. To the extent that such a relationship can be empirically established, the scale is considered valid.

As our criteria for validation, we selected education, occupation, factory experience, urban origin, and exposure to the mass media. In addition we scored each man on a scale summarizing his exposure to all five presumably modernizing experiences. Very briefly, our reasoning was as follows:

Schooling has shown itself to be the single most important influence in making men modern in general. There was every reason, therefore, to assume it would also be important in the specific realm of family relations. We took into account the fact that boys and girls participate more equally in school than they do elsewhere within developing countries, and that girls could more readily show their general competence here than in more tradition-bound institutions. Such qualities of the school strengthened our confidence in education as a criterion of family modernism.

The occupation measure ranked men on a scale in which traditional rural agricultural employment was the baseline. Higher on the ladder we placed recent migrants, then urban nonindustrial workers, and finally experienced factory employees. Thus we placed our subjects on a continuum of exposure to modern work settings, although our most advanced group was not very high up the ladder. In any event, we assumed those in the more modern work settings should manifest more modern family orientations.

Factory experience was interpreted in the same light. The factory is one of the most modern of the institutions in traditional society. We assumed it should attract and hold the men more modern in family attitude, and perhaps also inculcate modern attitudes toward aspects of family life by the example it presents of modern values in operation.

Men raised in the countryside came from the milieu in which the traditional family is most firmly institutionalized. We assumed that later life experience in town, or in industry, might bring changes in such attitudes, but even allowing for that we expected those whose origins had been in the countryside to continue to hold more traditional family attitudes.

Mass media exposure is widely recognized both as an inculcator of modern attitudes and as an attraction to those already holding them. We expected that those more in contact with the radio, newspapers, and other forms of mass media would manifest more modern family orientations.

There is no generally accepted standard which specifies how strong the association between a criterion and a scale should be in order for the resulting correlation to qualify as validating the scale. We settled on two criteria. First, the correlation between the criterion and the scale should be statistically significant at the .01 level or better. Second, since large samples yield significant correlations even when in absolute size the correlations are extremely low, we required the minimum coefficient for establishing validity to be .10.

TABLE 9-3

Median Zero-order Correlations for Six Countries of Family Scales
with Independent Variables

	Scale			
	OFM	Max-K.R.	CFM1	CFM2
Independent Variable				
Education	.184	.277	.226	.231
Occupation	.122	.183	.176	.092
Factory Experience	.138	.160	.101	.134
Urban Origin[a]	.109	.216	.262	.244
Mass Media Exposure	.187	.225	.192	.199
Summary Modern Exposure Score[b]	.222	.275	.273	.213

[a] Median based on Argentina, Chile, and Nigeria only.
[b] Combined index of independent variables.

Table 9-3 shows that the empirical test we applied gave consistent evidence for arguing the validity of our family modernism scales. On all five dimensions—education, occupation, factory experience, urban/rural origin, and mass media exposure—and on the composite index labeled "Summary modern exposure score," the median correlation of the dimension was above .10 and statistically significant at the .01 level or better. The only exception was occupation with CFM2, i.e., only one out of the 22 correlations in table 9-3. Beyond this most basic fact, examination of the results invites some additional comment. Most important, we must acknowledge that the majority of the observed correlations are not robust. The median correlations across all countries ranged from about .09 to about .28, whereas the correlations in individual countries had a much wider range, from slightly negative to about .55. Therefore, the results, while establishing the validity of the scales, do not do so compellingly, at least by some standards.

Finally, in judging these results one should keep in mind that our samples represented only a relatively narrow range of the educational and occupational variation present in any national population. All of our respondents were in the working or "lower" classes, characteristically pursuing more routine jobs on the basis of limited education. Such groups generally share a fairly homogeneous culture pattern with regard to basic relationships such as those involved in family living. This would inevitably yield greatly attenuated correlations. We are quite confident, therefore, that the observed correlations would have been substantially higher if they had been obtained from samples covering a wider range of education and occupation, such as would ordinarily be used in a validation exercise. In any event, we feel that we have clearly established the family modernism scale as valid across national boundaries and cultural divisions.

CONCLUSION

From our experience and that of other researchers, we conclude that building a multidimensional scale of family modernism is a subtle, difficult, and problematic task. Our approach was to incorporate a broad range of themes relevant to the family area. We achieved reasonable validity even with scales of low internal consistency. This was basically true for all the various forms of the scale we constructed, scales having various lengths and variable degrees of cross-national comparability. But a scale exactly comparable across many nations is generally preferable to a scale not strictly comparable, and a short scale is preferable to a long one. Therefore, *all other things being equal*, we feel that our Comparable Family Modernism-1 scale will probably be of greatest utility to other researchers. We have, therefore, given the text of the questions in full in chart 9-1. That CFM scale has the virtue of ease of administration due to its brevity (eight items), and it has the strictest possible cross-national comparability. Its main disadvantage, of course, is its low internal consistency.

An alternative approach, which many national research teams may prefer, is to build a separate scale of family modernism for each country or sample. This sacrifices comparability, but that may be offset by the higher reliability which evidently can be obtained with this approach, at least judging from our own experience in constructing the "Maximum-K.R. scales." If we were asked by a colleague in a developing country for suggestions as to how to proceed in developing such a maximally reliable scale of family modernism our best advice would run about as follows:

1. Ask all of the questions described in chart 9-1. This is not meant to suggest that other questions selected from other studies or locally generated should not be included.

2. Where any given topic or theme would thus be represented by only one or two questions, add one or two, as the case may be, locally devised but cast in the same general mold as the questions from the larger pool. Beyond the 8 questions we used in the Comparable Family Modernism Scale CFM-1, the pool of family-related items used in constructing our other family scales included an additional thirty-one items.[3]

3. Be prepared to find that some questions which worked quite well in

our six countries do not relate to family modernism in your country, and may even contradict the evidence from other countries.

4. Rely on the redundancy of the questions asked to compensate for measurement error, drawing down from the larger set a balanced subset which gives maximum reliability while not being too dominated by the questions representing any one subdimension.

It may well be, however, that a broad, multidimensional scale of family modernism is not consistent with the reality of social change in this area. In that case the only sound practice would be to utilize only highly specific subscales, each measuring a narrowly delimited and precisely measured realm of attitude or behavior such as birth control or residential preference. Further research is needed to establish whether it is indeed true that the realm of family interaction really is so complex and locally variable, or whether family researchers have simply been failing to perceive the golden thread which binds it all together.

CHAPTER 10

Modernity and Acceptance of Family Limitation

The effect of modernization on population growth is of major concern to policymakers in the developing countries as well as of scientific interest. Empirically, a long-term inverse relationship between societal modernization and aggregate birth rates has been well documented (Weintraub 1962; Adelman 1963; Kirk & Srikantan 1969; Friedlander & Silver 1970; Kirk 1971a). However, troublesome complexities and even reversals within the broad outlines of this relationship have been observed (Heer 1966; Janowitz 1971). We cannot fully explain either the broad outlines or the detailed complexities of the relationship without taking into account how individual-level variables intervene between the two aggregate variables.

The relationship can be envisioned as a causal chain with seven links: (a) societal modernization; (b) individual experiences with modern institutions; (c) individual psychological modernity; (d) individual psychological acceptance of birth limitation; (e) individual use of birth limitation; (f) number of children born to an individual; (g) societal birth rates. This model is of course greatly simplified but is presented to serve the purposes of clarity. Note that a feedback relationship from (g) to (a) is not precluded. Other feedback relationships are also possible; for example, psychological modernity in individuals may cause those individuals to have experiences with modern institutions. However, we have shown empirically that modern institutional experiences increase psychological modernity regardless of any initial selection effect (See Inkeles and Smith 1974).

This chapter appeared as Karen A. Miller and Alex Inkeles, "Modernity and Acceptance of Family Limitation in Four Developing Countries," *Journal of Social Issues* 30 (1974): 167–88. The authors are indebted to Dudley Kirk for his critical comments on an earlier draft of this paper, and to Charles Wellander for editorial assistance.

In this chapter our main concern will be to explain the relationship of (b), (c), and (d), i.e., to test the model that individual experiences with modern institutions predict psychological modernity, which in turn predicts acceptance of birth limitation. We will examine the theoretical basis of this causal relationship, summarize relevant previous research, and present the results of new empirical analysis using data from the Project on Social and Cultural Aspects of Development.

We will also attempt to draw some conclusions regarding the relevance of modernity research to population policies. In order to do this, we must be concerned about the other links in the causal chain we have proposed, particularly (e) actual use of birth limitation methods; (f) the frequency of births to an individual; and (g) societal birth rate. We will therefore first briefly discuss the assumption that psychological acceptance of birth limitation is a causal factor influencing these variables.

PSYCHOLOGICAL ACCEPTANCE OF FAMILY LIMITATION AND NATALITY

The dependent variable of ultimate interest to those concerned with population growth is, of course, the excess of live births over deaths, with migration also a factor within any geographical unit. In this chapter we will be concerned with some of the variables affecting births. Davis and Blake (1956) list the variables affecting the three events which necessarily intervene between social structure and birth rates: sexual intercourse, conception, and parturition. Many of these intervening factors are physiological conditions not influenced by individual motivation, for example, fecundity or the ability successfully to carry a fetus.

To say that facts like fecundity are physiological is not to deny that social structural factors such as the availability of nutritious food and health care have independent effects on these physiological capacities. There are, however, other factors which involve voluntary actions more, such as the use of contraception. Obviously, these are also affected to some extent by social structural factors such as the quality of medical care and the availability and cost of effective means of contraception. However, it is precisely at this point—where the outcome depends in good part on the personal decisions of individuals and on their subsequent voluntary action—that psycho-social factors also become important. It is thus no surprise that acceptance of the *idea* that births can be controlled, and that it is proper to do so, have been commonly identified as variables affecting the actual use of contraceptives. However, there is considerable uncertainty as to the strength of the effect of psychological acceptance on actual use of contraception.

Fawcett (1971) criticizes the concept of "approval of family planning" as used in surveys of knowledge, attitudes, and practice of birth control in many nations (the knowledge, attitudes, and practice—KAP—surveys). Fawcett argues that an approval response may be due to such factors as interviewer bias, but that a disapproval response may be an indicator of genuine resistance to birth planning. The significance of expressed approval of birth control is also discussed by Stycos and Back (1964). They report that, in a Jamaican sample, only 27 percent of those who said they favored family planning were actually using birth control methods. Inkeles and Smith (1974) point out that the same study shows that of those not favorable to birth control a mere 8 percent practiced it. In a relative way, therefore, people's birth control attitudes were a good predictor of their behavior. Factors such as cost and availability of easy and effective means of birth control intervene between favorability toward, and actual use of, contraception. We feel, with Kirk (1971b), that psychological acceptance of birth control precedes effective practice of it.

Even granting a cause-effect relationship between psychological acceptance and use of contraception, some might still question the extent to which use of birth control actually reduces the frequency of births (Blake 1969). However, there is little argument that to the extent that there are still unwanted births occurring, effective birth control would reduce the frequency of births. And evidence is certainly not lacking to show that unwanted births are still a problem in both the developing and developed nations. For example, in the developing nations, average completed family size was regularly found to be consistently higher than stated ideal family size in the KAP surveys, indicating a need for birth control (Berelson 1966). In the more developed nations, ideal and actual family size were closer to congruence. Nevertheless, findings of the 1965 National Fertility Study in the U.S. (Ryder & Westoff 1963) indicate that, among the ever-pregnant who intended no more children, 32 percent had a pregnancy they did not intend, and of the rest, 62 percent had an intended pregnancy at an unintended time. Those percentages may even underestimate the true values (Bumpass & Westoff 1970). Even in the U.S., then, more effective birth control could help lower the frequency of births.

Even when birth control can prevent unwanted births and the unwanted timing of births, people may go on wanting and having large numbers of children. Berelson's (1966) survey of KAP findings indicates that ideal family size ranged from 2.4 in Hungary to 5.3 in urban Ghana, with no country reporting an average ideal family size at or below the replacement level of about 2.0. Nevertheless, it is possible that effective birth control use might actually lower ideal family size. According to the argument suggested by Kirk (1971c), ideal family size may operate in some cases more as a reflection than as a cause of the number of children a respondent actually has. In other words, people may psychologically match their ideal to an accomplished fact in order to achieve cognitive consistency. If Kirk's assumption is correct, we would find not merely the timing but also the frequency of births reduced considerably by effective birth control methods. Needless to say, other important factors, such as the number of alternative occupations available to women, have also been found to be of importance in reducing the frequency of births—see Rosen & Simmons (1971).

The assumption we make here is that psychological acceptance of purposeful family limitation, of specific effective methods such as the pill, and of governmentally organized programs expediting the use of such methods all have consequences for the practice of some form of birth control, which in turn lowers the birth rate. This assumption should certainly be subject to test, but in the absence of sufficient contrary evidence, we will take it as given for the present.

MODERN EXPERIENCE, MODERNITY, AND BIRTH CONTROL APPROVAL

We turn now to the core of our argument, which is that experiences with modern institutions affect psychological acceptance of birth limitation. The processes associated with structural or institutional modernization which are most often cited are mass education, urbanization, industrialization, and extension of the mass media. The greater proportion of modernization research has dealt with these processes on a societal level. In contrast, the starting point of research on individual modernity is the question of how these modernization processes affect individuals. All of these institutional changes provide a new basis for individual experiences in the school, the city, the factory, and with the mass media. As a nation develops, these experiences become available to, and in fact may be imposed upon, more and more people. The question posed by modernity research is this: What are the psychological and behavioral effects of these experiences on individuals?

The central hypothesis of the major bodies of research investigating individual modernity (Lerner 1958; Kahl 1968; Inkeles 1969a; Inkeles & Smith 1974) is that societal modernization produces changes in the ways people perceive, value, express, and act with respect to themselves, their interpersonal relationships, and the world around them. Different scholars have defined and labeled this individual outcome, which we refer to as modernity, somewhat differently, but the definitions generally encompass the same basic concepts. The results of the Harvard Project indicate that this distinctive personality pattern does indeed emerge in response to contact with modernizing institutions across the six cultures.

Given the relationship between social experiences on the one hand, and attitude and value patterns on the other, a series of questions relevant to acceptance of family limitation are potentially answerable by our research on individual modernity. First, to what extent do different experiences with modern institutions affect acceptance of birth control? Experiences such as the quantity and quality of education, urban residence, type of occupation, and amount of exposure to the mass media may have different effects on acceptance of birth control. A second question concerns the importance of overall psychological modernity as an intervening, and even independent, variable with respect to acceptance of birth limitation. The third involves the relative effects on the acceptance of birth control exerted by the distinct psychological subfactors within the overall modernity syndrome, such as subjective efficacy or attitudes toward women's rights.

PREVIOUS RESEARCH

An excellent review of the relatively small body of research relating modernization, individual modernity, and natality variables (i.e., number of children, acceptance and use of birth control, and ideal family size) is provided by Fawcett and Bornstein (1973). Accordingly, we limit ourselves here to brief mention of the results of relevant studies.

The KAP studies provide evidence relating modern background and experience variables to natality attitudes and behavior. These surveys, taken in about eighty countries, relate natality attitudes and behavior to background characteristics, such as education, occupation, rural or urban residence, and household composition (Berelson 1966; Population Council 1970). Although these studies have methodological limitations (Fawcett 1971), they are a rich source of data, and strongly support the general conclusion that, across widely diverse cultures, individuals with more modern background characteristics tend to accept birth control and have fewer children. Berelson (1966), in summarizing the results, noted that existing number of children, literacy and education, income, and urbanization were strong determinants of the number of children wanted.

Other studies of actual fertility in Latin America (Heer & Turner 1965;

Rosen & Simmons 1971) have found that industrialization appears to be more closely related to lowered fertility than does urbanization. With respect to occupational experience outside the urban/industrial sector, a study was made of the effects of agricultural cooperative participation on acceptance of family limitation (Schuman 1967; Inkeles & Smith 1974). The study used a special sample taken by the Harvard Project of the villages participating in the Pakistan Academy for Rural Development, Comilla District, experiment. Individual participation in the cooperative, in itself, was found to have no effect on acceptance of family limitation, although membership did have a striking effect on overall modernity. It should be noted, however, that family planning efforts, unlike other aspects of the cooperative movement, were aimed at the entire village where the cooperative was located, rather than being limited to members, and significant differences in acceptance of family limitation were found between villages with cooperatives and villages without. Evidently the occupational experience of cooperative membership had no effect independent of exposure to the intensive village-wide family planning programs.

There are relatively few studies which interrelate social background variables, a syndrome of overall psychological modernity, and natality variables. Since the analysis in this chapter tests a relationship of this pattern, it is particularly important to mention the findings of the few available studies. Kahl (1968) examined the relationship between modernism and fertility ideals as part of his larger study of modernism in Mexico and Brazil. His data show that those individuals rating higher on a general modern values scale stated lower ideal family size at all occupational levels except the high nonmanual. Clifford (1971) related socioeconomic status (SES), general modern-traditional value orientations, and natality values and behavior in a study using a sample of women in Kentucky. He found that socioeconomic status correlated negatively and significantly with number of children desired and expected, that modern value orientation correlated negatively and significantly with ideal number of children, and that other correlations were insignificant—including those of both SES and modern-traditional values with unplanned births.

In addition to the studies of the relationship of overall modernity and natality variables, others relate birth control to some of the many distinct factors which can be identified within the overall modernity syndrome. As Fawcett and Bornstein (1973) point out: "The kinds of values most frequently discussed in relation to fertility are those pertaining to family relationships and to religious systems." Back and Hass (1973), reviewing the literature on family relations and fertility control, found contradictory evidence for many of the hypotheses linking family structure and fertility, particularly within societies. One of the variables which does consistently relate positively to successful fertility control is marital communication, as found in Israel (Bachi and Matras 1964), in Peru (Stycos 1968), in Jamaica (Stycos and Back 1964), and in Puerto Rico (Hill, Stycos, & Back 1959). Another, more attitudinal variable in the family sphere which has been found to be related positively to ideal family size is integration with relatives (Kahl 1968). Attitudes toward women's rights were also found to be related to natality in Brazil (Rosen & Simmons 1971). Religion has, understandably, also been shown to be linked to natality and to similar variables; the strength of commitment to religion has been shown to exert this influence across religions and cultures (Stycos 1968; Westoff, Potter, & Sagi 1963; Yaukey 1961; Kirk 1966). Aspirations for upward mobility have also been hypothesized to be positively associated with birth control, although the results of research on this relationship are inconclusive (Duncan 1966; Westoff et al. 1963).

A distinction can be made between many of the relatively specific attitudes measured in numerous studies and certain underlying personality traits, i.e., general propensities which are relevant to a wide variety of situations and issues. Among the traits whose relationship to family size and related matters has been tested are: subjective efficacy, orientation toward time, and openness to change. Subjective efficacy may be broadly defined as the feeling or belief of an individual that he can affect what happens to him and that he has some control over his own fate. Orientation toward time is usually defined with reference to planning for the future and seeing time as a valued and useful commodity. Openness to change covers "a number of concepts, including empathy, freedom from tradition and dogma, willingness to innovate, readiness for new experiences, and change-proneness (Fawcett and Bornstein 1973)."

Williamson (1969; 1970) used the Harvard Project data to analyze the relationship of subjective efficacy to favorability to birth control and ideal family size. He found subjective efficacy to have no relationship with ideal family size (Williamson 1969); however, using the factory worker subsample, he discovered that subjective efficacy did have both independent and intervening effects, relative to eleven nonpsychological predictors, on favorability to birth control (Williamson 1970). Keller, Sims, Henry, and Crawford (1970) found that orientation toward time was associated with use of birth control. Finally, Yaukey (1961) found in a Lebanese sample that openness to change was inversely associated with number of children.

THE HARVARD PROJECT

We can establish several hypotheses which have received some support, either directly or through studies using independent or dependent variables related to those we are considering.

Hypothesis 1. Each of the following modern experience variables makes an independent contribution to explaining favorability to birth control: education-literacy, mass media exposure, living standard, urbanism of residence, and occupational experience (on a scale from cultivator to experienced factory worker).

Hypothesis 1A. Occupational experience makes a greater independent contribution to favorability to birth control than does urbanism of residence.

Hypothesis 2. The effects on favorability to birth control of the five modern experience variables listed above are much greater as indirect effects through the mediation of overall psychological modernity than they are as direct effects independent of such overall psychological modernity. If this is true, then it follows logically that overall psychological modernity has an effect on acceptance of birth control independent of the effects of modern experiences, and also that the independent effect of overall modernity on favorability to birth control is greater than that of modern experience.

Hypothesis 3. Of the sub-areas of overall psychological modernity, those dealing with religion, family, and sex role attitudes make the greatest independent contributions to explaining favorability to birth control.

SAMPLE AND MEASURES

We will use the Harvard Project data only from East Pakistan, India, Israel, and Nigeria. Data collected in Argentina and Chile presented special coding problems and will not be reported here. The dependent variable, acceptance of family limitation, was measured by three items in each country:

FS-3 (Identical wording all countries). With which of these opinions do you agree: (1) Some people think that it is necessary for a man and his wife to limit the number of children they have so that they can take better care of those they do have. (2) Others say that it is wrong for a man and wife ever to purposely limit the number of children they have.

FS-4 (India and Nigeria wording). A man has several children. He can bring them up well. If he gets more children, it would be inconvenient for him to bring them up. Suppose the doctor could give the wife a new kind of medicine which would prevent more children being conceived, but would not otherwise harm the wife or the man. In this case: (1) Would it be right for her to take such a medicine, or (2) Would it be wrong?

FS-4 (Israel and East Pakistan wording). A man and his wife have several children. This is as many as they can afford. They do not want any more. Suppose a doctor could give the wife a new kind of pill which would prevent more children being conceived, but would not bring any other changes in her. (1) Would it be right for her to take such a pill, or (2) Would it not be right?

FS-5 (Identical wording all countries). Answer (1) Yes or (2) No: Suppose the government advised the people to limit the size of their families and showed them how to do it. Should people then follow this advice?

For most of the analysis these three items were combined into a scale, composed of the mean response on the three items for each individual. The Kuder-Richardson coefficient of reliability of the scale was .83 in East Pakistan, .79 in India, .66 in Nigeria, and .48 in Israel. The coefficients in India and East Pakistan qualify as "good" according to the standard of .75 set by Shaw and Wright (1967), and the lower coefficients found in Israel and Nigeria should be kept in mind as limiting factors with respect to the strength of relationships found.

A major thrust of our Project was the creation of overall modernity (OM) scales to test to what extent the theoretical syndrome of psychological modernity does exist in the real world. A number of overall modernity scales were constructed using different criteria, and subjected to several tests of coherence. The scale used in this chapter was OM-500, which consists of 100 items, including five items for each of twenty themes in each country. The (Kuder-Richardson) coefficient of OM-500, as noted in chapter 4 above, was always at a level of .80 or better.[1]

From the pool of items hypothesized to be part of the syndrome of overall modernity, subscales using the criterion of face validity were formed to measure attitudes towards women's rights, the family, religious vs. secular orientation, social mobility, and science and medicine. Several other scales measure three underlying personality traits: subjective efficacy, orientation toward time, and openness to change. Kuder-Richardson coefficients for these scales by individual countries were generally quite low, ranging from .16 to .69 with a median of .35. Our policy has generally been to use only scales with reliability coefficients much higher than those of these subscales, but in view of the theoretical interest of these subscales it was decided to include them.

In addition to attitudinal measures, detailed questions were asked of each

respondent regarding his living standard and his background of experiences with the school, the factory, the city, and the mass media. Various
tests, such as a literacy test, were administered. Scales of small sets of these
independent variables, more fully described in chapter 4, were constructed,
measuring education-literacy; mass media (radio and newspaper) exposure; urbanism of residence, on a scale from village to major city;
modernity of occupational experience; and living standard, measured by
consumer goods owned. In addition to these separate short scales, scales of
combinations of these aspects of modern experience were constructed.

RESULTS

As a preliminary step in the analysis, we computed the zero-order correlations of the separate modern experience variables, and of the overall psychological modernity scale (adjusted for auto-correlation), with the acceptance of family limitation scale. These are presented in table 10-1. We
note that the median correlation of education-literacy with acceptance of
family limitation is the highest of the five background variables, and that
mass media, urbanism, occupation, and living standard have similar
coefficients. Most important, however, is the fact that all of the background
variables produce effects which, while statistically significant due to the
large number of cases used, are nevertheless of rather low magnitude, the
median *r* being only .12.

Considering that the forces of the modernizing institutions usually act in
concert, we also constructed a composite scale of all five of the variables
(labeled "modern experience" in table 10-1). This composite measure has a
more substantial median zero-order correlation of .20, but this is only
slightly higher than that for education alone. Finally, it is striking that the
overall psychological modernity scale has a considerably higher median
zero-order correlation of .33 with acceptance of birth control than do any of
the background variables, including the composite measure.

The observed relationship between the modern experience variables and
acceptance of birth control may be somewhat attenuated by the range of
variation in our sample. Occupation ranges from cultivators to experienced factory workers, with no representation of higher level occupations;
mass media exposure and living standard are limited to the lower ranges;
and education, though fairly broad in range, does not include college
graduates. Only urbanism of residence represents the full range possible
within each society. In considering all observed relationships, nevertheless,
it should be kept in mind that overall modernity would be expected to be
affected by a similar limitation in range, and hence we can be fairly safe in

TABLE 10-1

Zero-Order Correlations with Acceptance of Birth Control

	E. Pak.	India	Israel	Nigeria	Median
Education/literacy	.14	.38	.24	.09	.19
Mass media exposure	.07	.29	.13	.11	.12
Urbanism of residence	.00	.18	.15	.04	.10
Occupation	.12	.13	.11	.12	.12
Living standard	.13	.18	.06	.12	.13
Modern experience (scale of the above five variables)	.15	.35	.24	.14	.20
Overall modernity[a]	.32	.47	.34	.23	.33
(N)	(943)	(1198)	(739)	(721)	

[a] OM-500, adjusted for autocorrelation of birth control items.

accepting the *relative* effects of overall modernity vs. modern experiences on acceptance of birth control.

The results of a multiple regression of the separate modern experience variables with acceptance of family limitation as the dependent variable are presented in table 10-2; the regression is repeated in the lower half of the table, with the measure of overall psychological modernity added as a

TABLE 10-2

Predictors of Acceptance of Birth Control
(Beta Weights)

Modern Experience Variables	E. Pak.	India	Israel	Nigeria
Education/literacy	.12	.31	.23	.02
Mass media exposure	−.01	.08	.03	.06
Urbanism of residence	−.06	.09	.15	−.04
Occupation	.12	.01	.01	.08
Living standard	.04	.02	.02	.08
R^2	.04	.16	.08	.03
Modern Experience Variables and Overall Modernity				
Education/literacy	.02	.09	.11	−.05
Mass media exposure	−.07	.02	−.03	.01
Urbanism of residence	−.07	.08	.17	−.07
Occupation	.05	−.06	−.04	.03
Living standard	−.01	−.00	−.00	.04
Overall modernity[a]	.33	.39	.30	.24
R^2	.11	.23	.15	.06

[a] OM-500, adjusted for autocorrelation of birth control items.

predictor. It is notable that a rather low proportion of the variance in acceptance of family limitation is explained even when we take into account all the modern experience variables, but that including overall psychological modernity in the equation adds considerably to the R^2. Before overall modernity is included, education has a relatively consequential beta weight in East Pakistan, India, and Israel, even though mass media does poorly in all countries. When overall modernity is added, however, the beta coefficients of all the modern experience variables are weakened to the point of insignificance, except for education and urbanism of residence in Israel.

Our results clearly do not support Hypothesis 1, that each modern experience variable has an independent effect on favorability to birth control. Hypothesis 1A, that occupation is a better independent predictor of acceptance of family limitation than urbanism of residence, also appears to be unsupported by our data. Urbanism of residence in Israel is the strongest predictor of acceptance of family limitation of any of the modern experience variables in any country when overall modernity is entered into the regression equation, but the differentiation is unimportant because all of the experience variables turn in such poor performances in the regression.

At the same time, our results offer strong confirmation of Hypothesis 2—that the effects of modern experiences are indirect, operating *through* overall modernity rather than directly. In an effort to test more rigorously this emerging conclusion we combined the modern experience variables which had positive[2] beta weights in the regressions into composite modern experience scales, and then used these scales, along with the OM scale, in path analysis to test for the magnitude of the direct vs. the indirect effects of the modern experience scales on acceptance of family limitation. The path model, with coefficients estimated in each country, is presented in table 10-3.

The estimated path model indicates that direct effects of modern experience on acceptance of family limitation are much lower than indirect effects in three of the four country samples (India, Nigeria, and East Pakistan). The direct effects are near zero in two countries, whereas the indirect effects of modern experience are significantly positive in all four. In Israel, the causal pattern is somewhat different, in that the direct effect is greater than the indirect effect, with both being significantly positive.

These findings support Hypothesis 2. The effects of modern experience are stronger as they operate indirectly through OM, than they are as direct effects independent of individual modernity. In three country samples the

TABLE 10-3

A Path Model for Modern Experience (A), Overall Psychological Modernity (B), and Acceptance of Birth Control (C)

Path	E. Pak.	India	Israel	Nigeria
Total effect A on C (r_{AC})	.18	.38	.27	.15
Direct effect A on C $(\beta_{CA \cdot B})$	.01	.11	.20	.03
Direct effect A on B (r_{AB})	.53	.69	.31	.60
Direct effect B on C $(\beta_{CB \cdot A})$	.32	.39	.25	.21
Indirect effect A on C,				
through B $(r_{AB}\beta_{CB \cdot A})$	.17	.27	.08	.13

Note: Modern experience (A) is composed of the following background variables: East Pakistan: Education/literacy, occupation; India: Education/literacy, mass media, urbanism; Israel: Education/literacy, urbanism; Nigeria: Living standard, occupation, mass media.

hypothesis holds quite well. Only in Israel are the direct effects of modern experience greater than the indirect effects through OM.

It is evident that the overall syndrome of modernity has relatively important effects on acceptance of birth control. Hypothesis 3 proposes that family, sex role, and religious attitudes are the main components of overall modernity which have an effect on birth control acceptance. The modernity subscales measuring different attitudinal areas and underlying

TABLE 10-4

Individual Modernity Subscales Predicting Acceptance of Birth Control

Scale Content	Median K-R Coefficient	Beta Weights			
		E. Pak.	India	Israel	Nigeria
Independence of extended family	.39	.02	.02	.04	.08
Discussion with wife	.41	.02	−.01	−.01	.05
Women's rights	.29	.06	.08	.04	−.05
Secularism	.69	.15	.16	.09	.05
Educational aspirations	.13	−.05	.01	−.03	.03
Consumption aspirations	.49	.08	−.01	−.03	.05
Belief in science and medicine	.35	.14	.07	.12	.17
Subjective efficacy	.27	.02	.12	.02	.09
Planning	.26	−.04	−.06	−.02	.03
Time punctuality valuation	.16	−.01	.02	−.05	−.01
Change valuation	.20	.04	.05	.10	−.07
New experience with people valuation	.40	.07	.16	−.01	.01
R^2		.09	.15	.06	.07

personality traits assumed to be theoretically relevant to acceptance of birth control, along with their median Kuder-Richardson reliability coefficients and beta weights in a regression with birth control acceptance, are presented in table 10-4. The variables with the five highest ranking beta weights in each country are listed in table 10-5.

We note first that most of the relationships are very modest. The low magnitudes of the beta weights and the R^2 of the regressions are certainly due in part to the relatively low reliabilities of the scales. Nevertheless, interesting regularities in relative magnitude emerge.

The variables which most consistently rise above the rest in the strength of their relationship to favorability towards birth control are belief in science and medicine, and secular vs. religious orientation.[3] Both appear among the five highest ranked beta weights in all countries. The other scales show somewhat mixed results across countries. Indeed, planning and time punctuality valuation seem to be consistently unrelated to favorability to birth control.

The uneven associations of the scales measuring family attitudes with favorability to birth control should be noted, especially since we had hypothesized them to have strong relationships. Some of the family scales do have correlations in the top five in India, Israel, and Nigeria. The inconsistencies that exist are perhaps not too surprising in light of the conclusions of Back and Hass (1973) and Safilios-Rothschild (1970) that the content of family modernity is neither very coherent nor consistent across cultures. In addition, in our own work with family attitudes, as described in chapter 9, we have found that such attitudes seem to be less crystallized than attitudes toward some other major areas of life.

TABLE 10-5

Modernity Subscales: Highest Ranking Positive Beta Weights

Rank	E. Pakistan	India	Israel	Nigeria
1	Secularism	New experience	Science and medicine	Science and medicine
2	Science and medicine	Secularism	Change	Subjective efficacy
3	Consumption	Subjective efficacy	Secularism	Independence of family
4	New experience	Women's rights	Independence of family	Secularism/ consumption
5	Women's rights	Science and medicine	Women's rights	Secularism/ consumption

TABLE 10-6

Composite Modernity Subscales Predicting Acceptance of Birth Control
(Beta Weights)

	E. Pak.	India	Israel	Nigeria
Family/sex role	.07	.03	.06	.06
Aspirations	.04	.01	−.04	.07
Time	−.03	−.07	−.05	.03
New experience	.08	.17	.05	−.03
Technological mastery	.21	.19	.17	.16
Subjective efficacy	.01	.13	.02	.11
R^2	.08	.14	.05	.05

In order to allow maximum impact of the relevant modernity measures, we grouped the twelve subscales listed in table 10-4 into six broader composite scales in each country, measuring family/sex role attitudes, mobility aspirations, time orientation, attitudes toward new experience, valuation of science and technology (including medicine), and subjective efficacy. These six composite scales were entered in a regression equation with acceptance of family limitation as shown in table 10-6. It is clear that the measure of valuation of science, technology, and medicine (labeled "Technological Mastery") is the scale with the highest beta weight in all four countries. At a median of .18 the figure is certainly modest, yet the evidence indicates that this is the single most important element of the overall modernity syndrome in its impact on acceptance of birth control, and consistently so in four diverse cultures.

CONCLUSIONS AND IMPLICATIONS OF THE RESEARCH

We believe the analysis of our data leads to a basic conclusion with potentially far-reaching significance for research on population limitation. While experiences with modern institutions such as the school and the factory do have considerable impact on whether or not a man accepts the principle of limiting the number of his children, these experiences evidently produce their effect mainly through influence on the modernity of attitudes and values. In three out of the four country samples we examined, extended contact with modern institutions in itself had little or no direct influence on the acceptance of family limitation. In the fourth country the direct effect of institutional experience was still less than that exerted by psychological modernity. In short, our data indicate that structural change in institutions without intervening psychic change in individuals seems to have little or no effect on acceptance of birth limitation.

When psychological modernity is broken down into its major components, we find another regularity across countries which also seems fundamental. The attitudinal area which we labeled valuation of science and technology consistently made the greatest independent contribution, relative to the other components, in explaining acceptance of birth limitation. None of the other six components of modernity we examined showed any such cross-cultural regularity, nor did they consistently manifest comparably significant beta weights. The fact that overall modernity in general, and valuation of science and technology in particular, make such significant showings relative to the modern experience variables in predicting acceptance of family limitation, may have implications for policy, particularly in less developed countries wishing to decelerate their rate of population growth.

Because of the strong and consistent correlation of low birth rates and high levels of economic development, there has been a tendency among specialists in this area to make two basic assumptions. The first is that as the developing countries come increasingly to possess the institutions and life patterns which go with higher economic development their birth rates will, more or less automatically, come down. The second assumption, influenced in part by the general failure of information campaigns, is that attempts to achieve widespread acceptance of birth control must wait until the process of economic development is well advanced. More specifically, it is often assumed that the change process cannot be short-circuited by focusing attention on the social-psychological factors present in the general situation of action. It follows then, in this view, that the best and perhaps the only way to insure lower birth rates is to surge full speed ahead on the general front of economic development. Without in any way intending to come out against speedy economic development, we feel our data lead to different conclusions with regard to both assumptions.

First, we feel we should caution against the assumption that the mere fact of urbanization or industrialization will reduce birth rates. Our data indicate it will have the desired effect only if the process of institutional change is accompanied by changes in attitude and value. Moreover, we feel we should further caution against the assumption that all aspects of economic development are equally likely to produce the desired effects, thus permitting one to estimate progress on the basis of some single general indicator such as GNP per capita. On the contrary, our data indicate that higher living standards, as measured by the number of consumer goods possessed, have no independent effect within our sample range. Since better living standards are a common result of strictly economic development, one can argue on the basis of our data that the purely economic aspect of development is far from a sufficient guarantee that birth control will spread. By contrast, education seems to have a more substantial impact on psychological modernity, and through it on acceptance of family limitation, with some independent effect on the latter. Occupation and mass media exposure also have significant effects on modernity, although they have no effects independent of it on birth control acceptance. Insofar as one's objective is to influence birth control practices, these would seem to be the institutions offering the greatest leverage.

The second of our conclusions running counter to the policy suggestions commonly derived from research in this area is that there is a good case to be made for the reasonableness of policies designed to shape birth control practice by influencing relevant attitudes and values. We are well aware of the difficulties of influencing value dispositions and behavioral propensities by programs of direct communication. And we obviously do not mean to in any way ignore evidence from the Harvard Project showing that extensive contact with modern institutions is a powerful, perhaps the most powerful, means for shaping modern attitudes. Nevertheless, many nations simply cannot wait until they have great cities and large factories all over the land before beginning to enjoy the advantages of lower birth rates. They need more change in the relevant attitudes now.

At this point we think there may be some special implications arising from our finding that valuation of science, technology, and medicine is the component of attitudinal modernity which has the greatest impact in all four diverse cultures we sampled—East Pakistan, India, Israel, and Nigeria. If the causal model we have posited is correct, our results lead to the conclusion that this attitudinal area should be given particular attention in programs aimed at increasing favorability to the idea of family limitation. For example, through films, film strips, and illustrated literature, the point should be emphasized that man in general, and each individual in particular, can solve the problem of unwanted births just as man has conquered many diseases, increased food production, and invented machines which can do the work of many men. This approach can be integrated into the school curriculum. It would be even more effectively directed at adults at their work, and through health care services. After all, schools reach only a relatively small proportion of the population in developing countries. Birth control is of more immediate concern to the adult age group, and health care and work situations can provide concrete illustrations of man's achievements integrated into each individual's daily life experience. In rural areas, the value of science, technology, and medicine can be stressed in agricultural extension service programs, agricultural cooperative programs such as the Comilla experiment in East Pakistan, and rural health service programs. In urban areas, the idea can be incorporated into factory training programs, union meetings, and urban health clinics. In any of these settings, the idea of family limitation might be more effectively disseminated if it were linked to other scientific, technological, and medical achievements.

Our results have the further implication that even without any explicit reference to birth limitation, programs involving the application of science to human problems, as in food production and the extension of modern medical services, might well operate indirectly to increase acceptance of family limitation at the same time that they serve the direct aims of increasing human health and well-being. Since the latter are, after all, the most basic goals of national development, it is encouraging that serious population problems may be indirectly attacked at the same time as these larger goals are met.

PART FIVE

PARTICIPATION AND ADJUSTMENT

CHAPTER 11

Participant Citizenship in
Six Developing Countries

In this chapter we will endeavor to do the following: (1) test how far certain concepts dealing with individual orientations to politics, previously used in studies of relatively advanced European societies, are appropriate to populations in developing countries; (2) ascertain how far these separate dimensions of individual political orientation cohere as a syndrome, indicating the existence of a general underlying dimension of "participant citizenship"; (3) identify elements among common orientations to politics which cannot be incorporated in this general syndrome; and (4) assess the importance of certain social experiences or forces in inculcating the qualities of participant citizenship in individuals exposed to these influences. In our larger project we seek to assess the determinants of individual modernity, asking: What makes a man modern? In this chapter an answer to that question is essayed with reference to one component of our model of the modern man, namely his role as a participant citizen.

THE THEORY OF PARTICIPANT CITIZENSHIP

As we explained in chapter 2, our program of research on the social and cultural aspects of economic development was guided by two different, but not unrelated, models of the "modern" man. One, the "analytical" model, specified a set of relatively abstract qualities, such as "openness to new experience," which we assumed to cohere as a syndrome defining a particular personality type. The second model, called the "topical," focused on substantive issues such as religion, family planning, and

This chapter was originally published as Alex Inkeles, "Participant Citizenship in Six Developing Countries," *American Political Science Review* 63 (1969): 1120–41.

kinship obligations. With regard to each of these separate topics, we were faced with the challenge of specifying what complex of attitudes, values, and behavior patterns we would consider a "modern" orientation in the given realm.

In the case of politics, the temptation was great to define as modern those qualities presumably characterizing the participants in a democratic polity. To do this, however, was to open ourselves to the charge of being culture-bound, a stigma which students of comparative systems wish to avoid at all costs. Moreover, the historical record gave little reason to assume any inevitable, or even highly probable, association of economic development and a democratic polity. Admittedly, England was the unchallenged forerunner in the industrial revolution, and the United States has these many years been its overwhelmingly outstanding exemplar, and both are well known for their long tradition of democratic politics. But Japan modernized in the reign of an emperor who stood at the head of a state religion; Turkey made its great leap forward under a dictator who was rather like Russia's extraordinary modernizing Tsar Peter; the Soviet Union, and more recently China, undertook their modernization under the aegis of communist dictatorships, and Mexico, which many consider the outstanding example of development in Latin America, has made its progress under the tutelage of a one-party system while preserving little more than the external forms of competitive democracy. Clearly each of these states must have demanded quite different qualities in its citizens, yet a number of them have rather impressive records of performance as distinctly modern nations.

In the face of these facts, we can hardly insist that the qualities which most characterize the democratic man are necessarily the best, certainly not those which *exclusively* suit one for life in the political structure of a modern society, at least not so long as we acknowledge the modernity of Russia, Japan, and Germany.[1] Nevertheless, we should not overlook the possibility that the political systems of England, the United States, Soviet Russia, Communist China, Japan, and Mexico might all make certain common demands on citizens. If we could discover such common requirements to exist despite the enormous differences in the formal structure of these political systems, we surely would be entitled to speak of these qualitites as truly appropriate to the modern as opposed to the democratic citizen.

What modern polities otherwise as diverse as the U.S., the U.S.S.R., England, and Japan have in common is most easily grasped if we contrast them with the societies of Europe before the rise of the national state, or with great but uncentralized culture areas such as India before and in the early stages of British colonial rule, or with much of tribal Africa today. The contrast can perhaps best be summed up in the word *citizenship*.[2] Before the advent of the modern centralized state, the individual is a *member* of a family or tribe and he *belongs* to a community, but his identity as a person does not include his being a *citizen* of a nation. When, in such societies, there is a higher and even quite powerful central authority, some king or emperor, the individual may know himself as subject to the sovereign's control, but this subjugation is much like his bowing to the wind and waves. In such settings the common man does not believe that he can remotely influence the policy to which he is subjected, let alone make it.[3]

The modern nation-state, democratic or dictatorial, multi- or single-party, guaranteeing private property or exercising state control of wealth, requires and encourages its subjects to adopt a different relation to the government. First and foremost, it wants a man not merely to know his local community, his tribe and family, but to be aware of and to identify with that larger community which is the nation as a whole. It is, furthermore, expected that his new *awareness* will be linked to a shift in *allegiance*, from the local and peripheral to the national and central authority. A man must be prepared to follow not only his father and his tribal chief, but also, and even before these others, his country's prime minister or president.[4] The modern government does not value a passive citizen, but rather an active one. He is expected to participate in the process of running the country. Even in dictatorial and totalitarian systems, which drastically limit the citizen's ability to influence policy in actuality, the state nevertheless attempts to create the illusion that it expresses the common will, and urges almost everyone to take some part in political acts even though they may be fully staged and orchestrated by the supreme leader.

The modern state seeks to organize and, where necessary, to mobilize all its citizens to attain national goals of economic development, of civic improvement, of defense or expansion. This requires frequent communication between the government and the citizen, and he is expected to take an active *interest* in public affairs and keep *informed* about important events and decisions. Yet neither interest nor information alone can guarantee effective performance of the citizen role. The complexity of modern political life requires of the citizen some understanding of the larger processes of a system in which bureaucratic rule and impersonal criteria of judgment replace treatment based mainly on special personal qualities, on family ties, or friendship and connections.[5] The modern polity is suffused with that peculiar bureaucratic rationality which Weber identified as particularly outstanding in the economic behavior of modern man.

Thus, on theoretical grounds, we identify a set of related traits we may call "participant citizenship." The syndrome includes: freedom from traditional authority or, stated positively, identification with and allegiance to leaders and organizations transcending the parochial and primordial; interest in public affairs validated by keeping informed, and expressed through participation in civic action; and an orientation toward political and governmental processes which recognizes and accepts the necessity and desirability of a rational structure of rules and regulations. This syndrome is one any modern man might be expected to manifest, just as any modern polity is likely to desire, perhaps even require, that he possess it.

Those familiar with *The Civic Culture* will recognize these traits as very similar to those delineated by Almond and Verba (1963) as defining the model of a democratic citizen. According to them the citizen of a democratic polity is expected to take an interest in politics, engage in political discussion, participate by voting and other actions, have knowledge of politics, and express a general sense of competence to influence the government; in sum, to stress "activity, involvement, rationality." We quite agree that these are the qualities appropriate to, and expected in, the citizen of a democracy. But we hold that exactly the same qualities are appropriate to, and expected of, the citizen of a one-party dictatorship such as that found in the Soviet Union! The difference in what is expected of a citizen of a democracy as against one in an extremist or totalitarian regime lies not in the qualities designated above, but along quite different dimensions. We have elsewhere delineated the nondemocratic syndrome as including: "exaggerated faith in powerful leaders and insistence on absolute obedience to them; hatred of outsiders and deviates; excessive projection of guilt and hostility; suspicion and distrust of others; dogmatism and rigidity."[6] Any, indeed all, of these qualities which are common in the nondemocratic personality can quite easily be combined with any, or all, of the qualities which Almond and Verba defined as the characteristics of the democratic citizen. It seems, therefore, that Almond and Verba have labeled as specifically "democratic" something which is a more general requirement placed upon the citizen of a modern polity, whether democratic or otherwise.

By stressing those qualities which a Soviet, an American, a Japanese, or a British citizen should have in common, we inevitably gloss over differences which are enormously important if one is interested not so much in the forms of politics as in its content, not so much in action as in values. Voting is a political act equally encouraged in the Soviet Union and the United States, but we consider it to be a purely symbolic gesture in Russia, whereas we consider it an action of substantial consequence in America. A man may take an interest in politics and keep well informed, but he may nevertheless judge his government's action inadequate or even evil. Someone who joins a mob screaming for the head of the prime minister engages in a political act no less than one who dutifully salutes as he marches past the minister's grandstand in the independence day parade. We must then recognize the *evaluative* and *judgmental* element of the individual's confrontation with the state as a potentially independent component of his total political role. To be interested is not to approve. To act is not to acquiesce. A man's judgment of his governmental system may be as negative as his under-standing of it is complete. He may very much feel himself to be a good citizen, but be deeply offended by the behavior of others he considers either bad citizens or unworthy of citizenship altogether. We touch here on the familiar themes of radicalism, or rejection of the political system, and of apathy and alienation, or withdrawal from politics.

Although we may perhaps get ready assent to the hypothesis that the elements of participant citizenship constitute a syndrome of intimately related political orientations, the case for an underlying common di-mension is not so obvious when we enter the evaluative realm. Radical rejection of one's political system perhaps assumes hostility to those in power, but a man who joined a revolutionary party might feel quite benign toward most other groups working in the political arena. A person may feel that the particular politicians now in office are a bad lot who are not doing their job of serving the public interest, but he may nonetheless consider the governmental *system* under which he lives the very best there is, requiring not the slightest change in *basic* structure.

To some this line of argument will seem specious. In common experience, men who want revolutionary change in the structure of government also hate those identified with the system they want changed. Communists are generally hostile not only toward capitalists, but toward their competitor socialists as well. Those who suffer from profound anomie seem to express rather general hatred and those who hate usually want basic changes. Experience is here supported by systematic research, at least in the United States, which shows that alienation is a general syndrome. Those tainted by it reflect this basic orientation in all aspects of their political life. Such alienation, furthermore, is apparently strongly correlated with the holding of extremist views about the structure of the political system.[7] Alienation, hostility, and radicalism might, then, also be a syndrome of intimately linked modes of relating to the political order, so that someone markedly characterized by one trait in the set would be so on the others as well.

One may, indeed, take the even more extreme position of arguing that both participant citizenship and political benignity generally go together. A case can certainly be made for the idea that the complex functioning of a modern political system requires not only that citizens be active and interested, but also that they show tolerance for the other participants and have reasonable respect for those who are trying to run the government. Quite apart from what the political system may "require," one can argue persuasively on purely psychological grounds that a person who is informed, active, interested, and rational about politics is more likely to also be tolerant of politicians, to harbor friendly rather than hostile feelings towards other major groups in the society, and perhaps even to take a more positive view of the political system at large.

Faced by these competing theoretical positions, we adopted the narrower definition of the modern political man as the more or less official standard for our project. We were, on the whole, convinced that the same forces which act to make a man modern in other ways should also influence his attitudes toward political life and the style of his political participation. Nevertheless, we were not prepared to argue that political modernity is all of a piece. It seemed highly likely that active citizenship is indeed a cohesive syndrome of related characteristics. We were, however, less certain that alienation, resentment of the inadequacy of the polity to produce what is expected of it, and hostility to other groups in society, also form a separate cohesive syndrome. Forced to decide, however, we predicted this subset of measures would also cohere as a common factor. Even if there were a separate "resentment syndrome,"[8] however, we were not prepared to say whether it would be systematically related to the active participation syndrome. To the extent that participant citizenship and political benignity empirically went together we would be encountering in nature the embodiment of that set of qualities Almond and Verba (1963) used to describe the citizen of the democratic polity, who, they say, has:

> a sense of identity . . . in a political community in which one trusts and can cooperate politically with one's fellow citizens, and in which one's attachment to the political system is deep and effective. (p. 503)

The theoretical concerns, approached within the limits set by the nature of the larger study, helped to define the set of four tasks which we assigned ourselves in undertaking the empirical analysis of our data on citizenship attitudes and behavior.

EMPIRICAL TEST OF THE THEORY

The first step in our analysis was to ascertain how far the concepts which had been used extensively to measure political orientations in more developed countries were meaningful in the study of our samples of the common man in six underdeveloped nations. In designing our questionnaire we conceived of the political realm broadly, and included questions to assess attitudes toward citizenship obligations, identification with the nation-state, and the degree and forms of the individuals' participation in politics. We also included numerous questions to measure political information, to require people to evaluate the effectiveness of their government, to test the degree of their interest in politics, and to measure the amount of hostility they felt for other groups in the society. Altogether our core questionnaire included 33 items measuring attitudes and behavior relevant to politics, broadly conceived, which had been asked in more or less the same way in all six countries. Restricting ourselves to this set of core questions greatly facilitated cross-national comparisons.[9]

CONSTRUCTING THE SCALES

This core set of questions was grouped in what we conceived of as a set of scale areas, topics, or themes. The original design of the questionnaire suggested the broad outlines for this grouping, since the questions coded ID dealt with national identification; AC with "action in politics"; CI with citizenship; PA with "particularism," and so on. But we later adapted the arrangement in consideration of the theoretical issues raised above. The list of questions, each in necessarily abbreviated form, is presented in chart 11-1, grouped under the relevant scale headings. After the items were thus grouped on the basis of theory and "face validity," they were obliged to pass an empirical test of coherence. The resultant scales[10] were as follows:

Identification and allegiance: to test the individual's identification of himself as a political personage, as a citizen rather than someone limited to primordial ties, and to probe how far he would go in following national or modern, rather than purely local or parochial, leadership in case he received competing advice.

Interest in politics: to assess the extent of a man's interest in political rather than purely personal, familial, or parochial matters as judged by what he most follows in the news, is able to say about the problems facing his nation, and talks about with his wife.

CHART 11-1

Questions and Scales on Political Participation and Evaluation

Scale	Items Included		Possible Responses	
			Identity Primal	*Identity Political*
Allegiance[a]	CI-7	Whose advice would you more follow?	Church	Government
	CI-8	Whose advice would you more follow?	Friend	Political party
	CI-9	Whose advice would you more follow?	Father/Grandfather	Trade Union
			Low Interest	*High Interest*
Interest in Politics	MM-10, 11	Which news interests you most?	Sports/Religion	World/National/Local
	GO-2	What are your country's main problems?	Few problems	Many problems
	WR-4	Do you discuss politics with your wife?	Never	Often
			Uninformed	*Informed*
Political Information	IN-1	Who is Lyndon B. Johnson?[b]	Incorrect	Correct
	IN-2	Who is Nehru?	Incorrect	Correct
	IN-3	Who is . . . (national political figure)?	Incorrect	Correct
	IN-4	Who is . . . (national political figure)?	Incorrect	Correct
	IN-6	Where is Washington?[c]	Incorrect	Correct
	IN-7	Where is Moscow?	Incorrect	Correct
			Non-Participant	*Participant*
Participation in Civic Affairs[d]	AC-3	How many political organizations you belong to?	Few	Many
	AC-4	Ever written to government about public issues?	Never	Many times
	AC-6	Ever gotten concerned about a public issue?	Never	Many times
	CI-2	What would you do about an anti-local proposal?	Nothing	Take political action
			Traditional	*Rule Oriented*
Political Rationality	CI-13	What is important to occupy high public office?	Popularity/Family/Tradition	Education
	CI-14	Who should the government grant a petition to?	Friend/Needy person	Man with legal right

	EF-11	What's most important for your country's future?	Help of God/Luck	Gov't plan/People's work
Political Anomie[e]			*Anomic*	*Non-Anomic*
	CI-10	Do politicians pay attention to ordinary people?	No	Yes
	CI-11	Who are politicians interested in serving?	Themselves	The public
	CI-12	Do you trust politicians' speeches?	No	Yes
			Alienated	*Non-Alienated*
Evaluation of Government Effectiveness	CH-8	Are opportunities for poor man to improve his economic condition	Decreasing	Remaining the same/Increasing
	CH-9	Are opportunities for young man to get educated	Decreasing	Increasing
	CH-12	Is governmental consideration of the ordinary man's opinions[f]	Decreasing	Increasing
			Hostile	*Non-Hostile*
Group Hostility	CI-3	Do factory owners[g] do . . . ?	Harm	Good
	CI-4	Do unions[h] do . . . ?	Harm	Good
	CI-5	Do foreign capitalists[i] do . . . ?	Harm	Good

[a] For the National Identification and Allegiance scale, ID-2: "Would you sooner follow the advice of a local or national leader?" replaced CI-9 in Nigeria and CI-8 in India.

[b] In Pakistan and India, John F. Kennedy's name was substituted for Johnson's; in Nigeria, respondents were asked to identify Charles de Gaulle.

[c] In India, New York was used instead of Washington.

[d] In Argentina, AC-3 was omitted from the Participation scale.

[e] There is no Political Anomie scale for Pakistan.

[f] CH-12 for Argentina was slightly different: "Is political participation of the ordinary man decreasing or increasing?"

[g] Cultivators were asked if land owners did harm or good.

[h] In Pakistan and India, "businessmen" was substituted for "unions"; in Nigeria, the group used was "the Ibo people."

[i] In India and Pakistan, "government officers" was substituted for "foreign capitalists"; in Israel "extreme left parties" was used; and in Nigeria, the group used was the "Northern People's Congress."

Political information: to gauge the extent of a man's knowledge of international and national political figures, and his ability to identify major world capitals. We hoped thereby to see how far expressed interest is translated into effective knowledge.

Participation in civic affairs: to measure whether a man actually joins civic organizations, contacts government officials or politicians, and is prepared to take active measures to oppose a government regulation he considers unfair.

Political rationality: to use the term rational here may assume too much, especially since we mean its opposite to be not necessarily irrational, but rather "particularistic," i.e., action outside the pattern of the formal rules usually pertaining in a modern bureaucracy or polity. In any event, we included here the belief that a government should sooner grant a petition to the man with the *right* to it by law rather than to a man more needy or influential; that education more qualifies a man to hold public office than do illustrious origins or charismatic personality; and that the country would benefit more from a good government plan or hard work by the people than from prayer or good luck.

Political anomie: The concept of anomie has become one of the most widely used, and some would say abused, in contemporary political sociology. To add to the confusion, it is often used interchangeably with the equally popular concept of alienation.[11] As originally used by Durkheim, anomie applied mainly to the social order, indicating a general condition of normlessness or failure of individuals to agree on and to follow the rules of society. It has since been widely used to designate a condition of the individual, either as himself not knowing or following the rules, or as *feeling* that others are not complying. We use it in the latter sense, and restrict its application to the individual's *perception* of the extent to which politicians and government officials pay attention to the common man, serve the public rather than their own careers, and keep their campaign promises after the election. Those individuals who see the politicians as failing in these obligations we define as having feelings of political anomie. Those who perceived politicians and government officials as fulfilling their obligations we scored as non-anomic.

Evaluation of government effectiveness: we address ourselves here to judgments about how good a job the government is doing, what Almond and Verba would call the "output" side of government activity. We limited our study to judgments about the opportunities available to the common man, asking whether they were increasing or decreasing so far as concerned his chances to improve his economic condition, to get attention from the government, and to secure an education for his children. Our emphasis thus accords with that of Lloyd Fallers (1963), who argued that the politics characteristic of modern society tends toward egalitarianism.

We scored as nonalienated those who manifested high expectation of vigorous government intervention to increase the opportunities for individual improvement. Insofar as our respondents saw little evidence of change toward increasing opportunity, we classified them as critical of the government's effectiveness (or "alienated").

Group hostility: In their analysis of the civic culture, Almond and Verba point to social trust, a sense of identity with one's fellow citizens, and a feeling one can cooperate with them, as an essential ingredient for an effective democratic polity; and they note that quality may be especially lacking in the new nations.[12] Class antogonisms, or ethnic or racial cleavages are, of course, not unknown in highly developed and stable societies. Nevertheless, we may argue that a high level of personal antagonism against other groups is likely to disrupt the political process, and render difficult or even impossible the complex cooperation between the different segments of society required by the modern polity. A substantial amount of trust in the probity and goodwill of other groups is essential for the common undertaking of running a political system of the modern type. In the absence of such trust, solutions will likely be sought outside the regular channels of politics, often in ways disruptive or even destructive of the political system itself.

To measure the propensity to hostility we identified target groups such as industrialists, traders, trade-unions, the military, and various ethnic minorities, and asked our interviewees whether they considered these groups to be harmful, beneficial, or neither to the interests of our respondents. The tendency to see such groups as harmful we scored as indicating a high level of intergroup hostility. Such hostility might, in turn, be considered inimical to the effective performance of one's citizenship role in a modern polity.

On the whole, the questions we asked in the political realm seemed to be understood by our respondents as well as most others we asked, and created no special strain in the interview.[13] The eight scales we developed rest on well-grounded theory. Examination of the items on which they are based (see chart 11-1) indicates they have substantial face validity; and they pass a reasonably strict test with regard to coherence as scales.[14] Within the limits indicated by these statistical tests, we can say that concepts which had been fashioned for the study of political orientations in more developed countries provide a meaningful basis for measurement of the political attitudes, values, and action of the common man in underdeveloped countries.

THE PARTICIPANT SYNDROME

Insofar as the scales in our set have substantial theoretical face validity, and further meet a reasonable test of cohering empirically, they provide the means for answering our second major question: How far is it true that the set of attitudes and values which, on theoretical grounds, we identified as representing the model or ideal of the participant citizen, actually exists in nature as an empirically coherent syndrome? There were, of course, various methods we could have followed in seeking an answer to this question. We chose to approach it by considering the pattern of interrelations among the scales. Guided by the theoretical considerations stated at the beginning of this chapter, we decided to test first the existence of the syndrome of active citizenship, excluding those scales which we considered to be judgmental or evaluative—i.e., the scales of anomie, governmental effectiveness, and hostility. Proceeding in this way did not foreclose the option of adding these evaluative scales to the first set, assuming that set itself met the test of coherence as a general measure of participant citizenship.

To ascertain the existence of a general syndrome of participant citizenship we then explored the interrelations, country by country of five scales: those of allegiance, interest, information, civic participation, and rationality.[15] The relevant data are given in table 11-1. There is no absolute basis for judging the coherence of a set of scales, but we interpret the facts as clear evidence that the five separate scale areas are indeed strongly related, and indicate the existence of a general trait or syndrome of active citizenship. Certain of the scales do seem rather weakly related to the others in some countries, for example the allegiance scale in Chile, Argentina, and Nigeria. On the whole, however, there is evidence here of a strong set of interrelations.[16] In no case is the correlation sign negative, and this pattern is maintained in all six countries without even the approximation of an exception. The coherence of the entire set of scales is further attested to by their individually high correlations with a summary scale identified in table 11-1 as Active Citizenship.[17]

As theory indicated, there is clearly a general syndrome of individual psychopolitical traits whose coherence can be established empirically. The man who is informed about politics is also more likely to identify with the national state in competition with local leaders, to take an interest in political affairs, to participate actively in civic matters, and to support the use of more rational rules impersonally applied as a basis for running

TABLE 11-1

Intercorrelations[a] *of the Five Subscales of Active Citizenship, by Country*

| | | ARGENTINA (N = 820) | | | | |
CHILE (N = 930)	Allegiance	Interest	Information	Participation	Rationality	Active Citizenship
Allegiance	—	.08*	.12**	.05	.08*	.47**
Interest	.10**	—	.27**	.17**	.11**	.61**
Information	.05	.33**	—	.23**	.24**	.70**
Participation	.09**	.32**	.37**	—	.03	.52**
Rationality	.10**	.13**	.33**	.14**	—	.48**
Active citizenship	.47**	.62**	.70**	.59**	.56**	—

| | | INDIA (N = 1300) | | | | |
ISRAEL (N = 740)	Allegiance	Interest	Information	Participation	Rationality	Active Citizenship
Allegiance	—	.21**	.24**	.18**	.24**	.60**
Interest	.10*	—	.37**	.27**	.21**	.62**
Information	.13**	.27**	—	.19**	.39**	.75**
Participation	.15**	.28**	.25**	—	.15**	.53**
Rationality	.22**	.15**	.13**	.08*	—	.63**
Active citizenship	.59**	.61**	.61**	.58**	.56**	—

| | | NIGERIA (N = 720) | | | | |
EAST PAKISTAN (N = 1000)	Allegiance	Interest	Information	Participation	Rationality	Active Citizenship
Allegiance	—	.15**	.07*	.07*	.10**	.49**
Interest	.22**	—	.22**	.39**	.13**	.63**
Information	.15**	.29**	—	.27**	.27**	.64**
Participation	.13**	.22**	.36**	—	.11**	.60**
Rationality	.20**	.08**	.12**	.05	—	.55**
Active citizenship	.60**	.64**	.66**	.58**	.46**	—

[a] Correlations followed by * are significant at the .05 level; those followed by ** at the .01 level or better.

governmental affairs. This set of attributes is not only theoretically consistent, but now must be acknowledged to be empirically coherent as well. Such empirical coherence is generally expressed statistically by reference to a scale's "reliability." The reliability, country by country, of the summary scale based on the five subscales is quite respectable.[18] As a further check, we also constructed the summary scale using the individual questions, which had been used in the five subscales, as one undifferentiated pool of items. The resultant scale yielded even higher reliabilities.[19] All the evidence, therefore, supports the assertion that there definitely exists a general personal trait which may reasonably be called "active" or "participant citizenship."

THE JUDGMENTAL COMPONENT

Having established the less problematic fact that participant citizenship is an internally consistent congeries of attitudes and values, we may turn to our second question, and inquire how far the *evaluative* and *judgmental* component of political orientations is consistently related to the activist

TABLE 11-2

Correlations[a] *of Three Evaluation Scales to the Scale of Active Citizenship and Its Subscales*

	ARGENTINA (N = 820)				CHILE (N = 930)		
	Anomie	*Government Effectiveness*	*Group Hostility*		*Anomie*	*Government Effectiveness*	*Group Hostility*
Allegiance	−.02	.02	−.03	Allegiance	−.17**	−.02	.02
Interest	.01	.05	−.04	Interest	−.08*	.00	.04
Information	.05	−.01	−.05	Information	.00	−.02	−.02
Participation	−.01	−.06	−.02	Participation	−.06	.03	.05
Rationality	−.06	−.04	−.06	Rationality	−.05	−.08*	−.07*
Citizenship	−.01	−.01	−.08*	Citizenship	−.12**	−.03	.00
	INDIA (N = 1300)				ISRAEL (N = 740)		
	Anomie	*Government Effectiveness*	*Group Hostility*		*Anomie*	*Government Effectiveness*	*Group Hostility*
Allegiance	.07**	−.05	.06*	Allegiance	−.04	.03	−.04
Interest	.08**	−.10**	.05	Interest	−.02	−.03	−.02
Information	.26**	−.05	.19**	Information	.01	−.03	.08*
Participation	.03	−.08**	.02	Participation	−.07	.04	.04
Rationality	−.01	−.14**	.00	Rationality	.01	−.06	−.09*
Citizenship	.15**	−.13**	.11**	Citizenship	−.04	−.02	−.02
	NIGERIA (N = 720)				EAST PAKISTAN (N = 1000)		
	Anomie	*Government Effectiveness*	*Group Hostility*		*Anomie*	*Government Effectiveness*	*Group Hostility*
Allegiance	−.04	−.04	−.03	Allegiance	—	−.15**	−.03
Interest	.02	.06	.03	Interest	—	−.09**	−.08*
Information	.19**	.10**	−.01	Information	—	−.07*	−.08**
Participation	.08*	.08*	.07	Participation	—	−.08*	−.07*
Rationality	.03	−.03	−.04	Rationality	—	−.01	−.07*
Citizenship	.10**	.06	.01	Citizenship	—	−.14**	−.11**

[a] Correlations followed by * are significant at the .05 level; those followed by ** at the .01 level or better.

syndrome. The evidence in table 11-2 obliges us to give a negative answer. The participant citizen is not also consistently non-anomic, non-hostile, and satisfied with the performance of his government. Rather, we must say, "it depends" on the country—and no doubt on the segment of the population being studied as well.

In India, for example, the citizenship scale is negatively correlated with that indicating a critical judgment of the government's effectiveness, but positively correlated with hostile views of other groups and bad opinions about politicians. In other countries a particular evaluative scale will be positively associated with some of the subscales, and negatively with others. Most serious, the pattern of association between the summary citizenship index and the evaluative scales is not the same in all the countries. Only in East Pakistan does the observed pattern support the unitary conception of the modern political man. There, those who are active citizens are also consistently more benevolent toward other groups and more satisfied with the government's performance. In India and Nigeria, on the other hand, those who score high on participant citizenship are more often anomic and hostile, and in Nigeria they are dissatisfied with the government's performance as well. In general, however, there is no consistent pattern of relationship between the evaluative scales and the measures of active citizenship.[20] The pattern is unclear, and the associations weak. Only an analysis which took account of the special conditions in each country could do justice to this set of findings.

How one *judges* the political process not only clearly depends on one's psychological disposition, but is much influenced by the actual situation and policies of one's government. This conclusion is certainly not startling, and most may consider it obvious. It is nevertheless important to put the presumably obvious to an empirical test.[21] We must recognize, furthermore, that these facts have by no means been obvious to everyone. In discussion, of the polities of developing countries one often finds that strident demands, hostility toward the government, political strikes and other forms of unrest are cited as evidence of the lack of political "maturity" or the dearth of good citizenship in the new nations. These analyses run together what our study proves to be two quite distinct elements of the political orientation of those in developing countries. Good citizens are not necessarily happy, approving, or satisfied. In some countries the men who are informed, interested, and fully participant in the political process may also be alienated, anomic, and hostile. In some settings those manifesting such disgruntlement may be mainly expressing deep-seated personality tendencies, but in other lands they are making objective judgments perfectly consistent with their expectations as good citizens. Disgruntlement expressed in politics does not necessarily reflect a general personal tendency to anger and despair.

By contrast, it seems that the qualities of active citizenship are more general attributes, part of the individual personality, which will be manifested in much the same form regardless of the context of political action. Whether he disapproves or approves of what the government is doing, whether he feels friendly or hostile to other groups, the active citizen will keep informed, take an interest in public affairs, participate in public and civic organizations, and show preference for rational and orderly rules and regulations to govern political life. Participant citizenship is relatively "context-free," whereas the evaluative and judgmental orientations to politics cannot be understood outside of a specific setting. To understand them requires detailed contextual analysis, beyond the scope of this report.

Since the five nonevaluative scales are so consistently related to each other, we will pursue the analysis of the sources of influence not separately for each element in the syndrome, but rather by using the summary scale. This composite, which we call the "active citizenship" index, has the virtue of being much broader in conception, and a more reliable measure than the individual scales. Its use greatly reduces the complexity of pursuing an analysis of five different scales through six different countries each of which is represented by several different occupational groups. Instead, each individual can be characterized by a single score, and he receives it on a measure which shows the widest possible variation from individual to individual within each national sample.[22]

SOCIAL FACTORS FOSTERING ACTIVE CITIZENSHIP

In our larger study of modernization, we identified and measured almost 50 different social attributes of the individual, his social position, or his social setting which theory and/or earlier research had identified as likely to contribute to making a man more "modern." These ranged from characteristics acquired at birth, such as religion and ethnicity, through those developed in youth, such as education or village residence, to those relevant mainly to the adult, such as occupation or income. Since we thought of active citizenship as a component of the larger syndrome of individual modernity, there was every reason to relate the same set of independent variables used in studying the general syndrome to the scores individuals obtained on the index of participant citizenship.

The simplest way to test the relative strength of the different modernizing

TABLE 11-3

Correlations[a] of Active Citizenship Scale with Selected Independent
Variables in Six Countries

Independent Variables	Argentina	Chile	India	Israel	Nigeria	East Pakistan
Education						
Formal education	.46**	.42**	.69**	.37**	.42**	.42**
Opposites test	.46**	.48**	.50**	.44**	.23**	.44**
Mass Media						
Radio listening	.15**	.25**	.30**	.12**	.25**	.25**
Mass media exposure	.36**	.44**	.51**	.38**	.36**	.31**
Urbanism						
Years urban since 15	.29**	.33**	.06**	n.d.[b]	.26**	.15**
Urbanity of present residence	.29**	.13**	.17**	n.d.	.19**	.05
Work Experience						
Occupational subgroups	.37**	.39**	.27**	.12**	n.d.	.27**
Total time in factory	.23**	.32**	.19**	.20**	.24**	.22**
Objective skill (coder rated)	.23**	.25**	.29**	.20**	.13**	.17**
Number of factories worked in	.17**	.13**	.08*	.06	.08*	.14**
Factory Environment						
Factory modernity	.07*	−.06	n.d.	−.07	.07	.06
Factory size	.06	−.07*	.17**	−.02	.03	−.06
Factory benefits	.08*	−.05	.30**	.07	.23**	.09*
Standard of Living						
Consumer goods possessed	.30**	.30**	.38**	.19**	.35**	.29**
Income	.14**	.23**	.26**	.26**	.31**	.11**
Personal Qualities						
Age	.08*	.17**	.05	.12**	.19**	.09**
Perceived modernity of home-school	.05	.14**	.18**	−.09*	−.04	.05
Perceived modernity of factory	.02	.03	−.16**	.03	.09*	−.06
Self-rated skill level	.12**	.15**	n.d.	−.03	.13**	.29**
Approximate Number of Cases[c]	820	930	1300	740	720	1000

n.d. = no data

[a] Correlations followed by * are significant at the .05 level; those followed by ** at the .01 level or better.

[b] Variable "Years urban since 15" for Israel is blank because the whole sample was of urban origin and our procedure was to code "Years urban since 15" only for respondents of rural origin.

[c] N's given are approximate. Some of the correlation coefficients are based on sub-samples due to disqualification of parts of the sample on certain questions, e.g., "Years urban since 15" is coded only for respondents of rural origin.

influences is through the correlations between the index of active citizenship and the independent variables. The data for a variety of such variables are given in table 11-3. It is apparent that many factors have a substantial effect on the citizenship scale. Of our battery of independent variables, some 45 were applicable in at least five of the countries. Some half of these correlated with the citizenship index at the .01 level or above in four of the countries or more; sixteen had a perfect record, correlating at the .01 level or better in 5 of 5 or 6 of 6 tests. This is an impressive performance, both in general survey work and in our experience with other scales in this study.[23] It clearly establishes the index of participant citizenship as a highly sensitive measure having substantial cross-national relevance.

Formal education is clearly the most consistently powerful influence represented in table 11-3, never dropping below a coefficient of .37. Indeed, in India, in which there was the widest educational range of all the national samples, the correlation reaches the impressive level of .69. Other measures closely reflecting formal schooling, such as the opposites test, which serves as a kind of intelligence test, perform about as well as does the measure of education. Thus, our experience in these six developing countries is consistent with that of Almond and Verba (1963), who noted in their five-nation study that "among the demographic variables usually investigated—sex, place of residence, occupation, income, age, and so on— none compares with the educational variables in the extent to which it seems to determine political attitudes." (p. 379).

In our case, however, we must temper the absoluteness of Almond and Verba's statement, since a number of other variables compete quite well with education in their apparent power to influence political attitudes.[24] The most vigorous competition is offered by the measure of mass media exposure. Contact with the mass media is much related to education, especially in the case of newspaper reading, but the measure used in table 11-3 shows powerful connections for radio listening alone, which is not dependent on literacy. There is good reason to assume that extensive newspaper reading and radio listening would make a man better informed, more interested, and active in civic and political affairs. But in this case we have no way of demonstrating that the direction of influence is not the reverse, so that those with strong interest in civic affairs come more often to read newspapers and listen to the radio.

The argument of reverse influence cannot be applied so effectively, however, to urban experience, especially as measured by the years of city residence enjoyed by those who grew up in the country and came to the city after the age of 15. The greater intensity of political activity in urban areas, the increased accessibility of the individual to political influence, the heterogeneity of the groups represented in the cities and the obvious clash of their interests, all should contribute to stimulate political interest and civic involvement. Note that the effect of urban experiences seems very much less in East Pakistan and India than in the other countries. In Argentina, Nigeria, and Chile, those who came from the countryside entered major urban and truly metropolitan centers of large size such as Santiago, Buenos Aires, and Lagos. In India, by contrast, the "urban" centers included in our study, such as Ranchi, were in fact quite modest provincial towns. In East Pakistan the migrants came to the capital, Dacca; but it was, in fact, little more than a large provincial town as compared to a city like Calcutta. It would apear, then, that the degree to which an urban center is truly cosmopolitian can play a role in the extent of the influence it exerts in making men modern.[25]

Of special theoretical interest to our project was the influence of occupational experience as a modernizing force. We attached particular importance to the role of the factory as a kind of practical school in modern ways of thinking and arranging things. The correlation coefficients produced by the measure of occupational type—running from cultivator to highly experienced worker—and the more precise measure of total months of factory experienced, proved to be among the largest in each country.

The other attributes of the factory, however, did not produce a large or consistent effect. The size of the factory, for example, has been discussed both by Kerr and Lipset as making for discontent and worker radicalism; but it does not seem to play an important or consistent role in inducing active citizenship.[26] Factory product (not shown) also failed to exert influence. The rated modernity of the factory, to which our project assigned substantial importance, appears to play only a very modest role, and not a completely consistent one. This inconsistency is, however, less marked if we consider the worker's perception of his factory's modernity. Those factories which were reported by their workers to offer more benefits such as sick pay, lunch rooms, or family allowances were more consistently, and in Nigeria and India, quite noticeably, likely to produce workers with higher scores on the index of active citizenship. On the whole, then, we may assign to the qualities which make a factory modern some weight in citizenship training, while cautioning that this effect will not be manifested in all places. By contrast, the sheer amount of factory experience, of whatever kind, seems the more regular and powerful influence.

The findings in table 11-3 we least anticipated are those which indicate that individuals with a high standard of living are more likely to be active citizens. Evidently those who earn more, possess more goods, and live in better housing—this last not shown in the table—were decidedly more likely to keep informed and to participate more fully in civic affairs. It is often assumed that those most disadvantaged are likely to rush actively into the political arena, seeking there to gain some advantage to offset that denied them in economic competition. Our data give no support to that theory.[27] On the contrary, they suggest that a man will not have the inclination or extra energy to take an interest in public life and participate in civic activity until he attains a reasonably decent standard of living.[28] Good citizenship is, then, a kind of luxury which can be "afforded" only by those who have secured a standard of living above the minimum required for mere survival. Of course, active citizens are no luxury, but rather a necessity for running a modern polity and the society which relies on it. The implication is clear. To leave men in a condition of poverty so extreme that they are outside politics, in effect noncitizens, is to create an apathetic mass which is not integrated in society and cannot be mobilized for the purposes of national growth and development. Furthermore, such individuals, to the extent that they feel themselves not sharing in the process of running their country and without rights or responsibilities, may constitute an unstable and even explosive force acting outside of, or against, the political system rather than within the framework established for the ordinary resolution of political differences.

To be completely candid we must weigh against this conclusion the fact that in the two countries in which we had a measure of political radicalism, namely Chile and Argentina, the feeling that the society and the economy need a "total and immediate change" was more common precisely among the groups who were good citizens and had experienced the most extensive contact with modernizing influences such as the school, the factory, and the mass media. The correlation of scores on the participant citizenship scale with radicalism was .27 in Argentina and .25 in Chile. The percent scoring "high" on the radicalism scale in Argentina rose from 7 among those with 1–3 years of schooling to 39 for those with 8 years or more. In Chile, among those with less than 6 months of factory experience only 29 percent scored high on radicalism, whereas among those who had spent 10 years or more in factories the figure rose to 46 percent. Expressed as correlations, the association of radicalism and exposure to modernizing institutions in Argentina was, for education .25, factory experience .17, mass media .19. In Chile the correlations were, respectively, .16, .11, .18. All were significant at the .01 level or beyond.

The last set of variables in table 11-3 which requires our attention includes those which indicate the perceptual tendencies of the respondent—they reflect how he sees his world, and especially his place in it. These measures are important in enabling us to assess how far high scores on the citizenship index might be mainly a result of the tendency to take a rosy view of the world and the treatment one has received. Although there is evidence of some connection, it is not powerful, and is decidedly inconsistent. Since the citizenship scale requires passing an information test, it was unlikely that high scores could be obtained simply by "saying the right thing." Nevertheless, it is reassuring to find evidence that the active citizenship index apparently measures something more substantial than a mere "response propensity." Participant citizenship is not just talk.

THE FACTORY AND OTHER VARIABLES COMPARED

Many of the variables identified by the correlation coefficients as important in stimulating active citizenship are closely related to each other. This is true not only in obvious cases such as the two different measures of standard of living presented in table 11-3. An individual's standard of living in turn is dependent in good part on his skill level, and both skill and earnings increase with time in the factory. Variables such as total time in the factory and urban experience are also highly correlated, because most factories are in the cities, and people had to leave their villages and come to the city to obtain industrial employment.

To disentangle these influences, one must turn to some form of multivariate analysis, usually by applying "controls" to selected variables, while examining the effect of others. Table 11-4, taking Nigeria as representative, presents an array of such data with simultaneous controls for education, occupation, and rural origin. Education evidently maintains its influence, with one minor exception, within the occupational and origin groups. Factory experience also maintains its influence, but less systematically. The role of rural origin, however, becomes quite ambiguous when controls for education and factory experience are applied. By this tabular method, however, it is difficult to express the stability or instability of these influences through a simple composite metric. Furthermore, even when we control for as many as three variables, others in a battery as numerous as ours may be acting independently—but hidden from view—to give us a spurious impression of the power of any variable whose uncontaminated influence we wish to assess. One way to escalate the number of controls is by using "matched" groups of respondents. In each "match" one set of men is compared with another set chosen to be in all

TABLE 11-4

Percent in Nigeria Scoring "High"[a] *on Participant Citizenship Scale, by
Education, Occupation, Origin*

	Rural Origin Years Education		Urban Origin Years Education		
Occupation	1-7	8	1-7	8	9+
Cultivator	9	0	—	—	—
	(96)	(4)	(0)	(0)	(0)
New factory worker[b]	17	50	19	39	—
	(30)	(12)	(27)	(39)	(0)
Mid-experienced worker[b]	18	45	25	45	82
	(57)	(49)	(57)	(103)	(28)
High-experienced worker[b]	67	76	36	71	82
	(9)	(21)	(14)	(5)	(17)

Note: The figures in parentheses show the number of cases on which the percentage is computed.
[a] Respondents falling in the upper third of the distribution of scores on the participant citizenship scale are considered "high"; their actual scores, out of a possible 100, were 56 or better.
[b] New workers had less than 7 months experience; mid-experienced had 2 to 7 years; high-experienced had been workers 8 years or more.

respects like the first set except the match variable—on which they are chosen to be as different as possible. In the matches the critical variable is more precisely defined than is usual in the ordinary cross-tabulation procedure. More important, we gain in control because up to eight major variables were simultaneously controlled in the matching process.[29]

Table 11-5 presents the correlation which result when matched groups are considered in their relation to the active citizenship scale. In the first match the industrial workers are divided into those with more and less education. The next two matches test the effects of factory experience. The match between cultivators and experienced factory workers is, perhaps, the most appropriate to put in competition with the match on the extremes of education. The cultivator-worker match, however, could be influenced by selective recruitment, with politically more "modern" farmers disproportionately drawn to city employment.[30] We therefore offer a third match in which both groups are already factory workers, and are divided by having been either few or many years in industry.

It is unambiguously the case that, with most everything else important under "control," education still has a powerful residual effect on active citizenship. The high zero-order correlations between education and citizenship which we earlier observed clearly did not result mainly from the

TABLE 11-5

Correlations[a] of Selected Matches with Active Citizenship Scale, by Country

Line	Match Content[b]	Argentina	Chile	India	Israel	Nigeria	East Pakistan
(1)	Education:[c] low vs. high	.57**	.40**	.56**	.39**	.57**	.35**
		(10)	(21)	(52)	(35)	(20)	(50)
(2)	Cultivator vs. experienced worker	.34**	.40**	.30**	n.d.	.48**	.28**
		(63)	(63)	(69)		(21)	(176)
(3)	Factory experience: few years vs. many	.23**	.27**	.19*	.16	.06	.16
		(44)	(71)	(80)	(53)	(62)	(58)
(4)	Years urban: few vs. many	−.11	−.15	.06	n.d.	.08	.02
		(24)	(14)	(40)		(24)	(25)
(5)	Mass media: low vs. high exposure	.19**	.24**	.20**	.19**	.19*	.13*
		(143)	(147)	(94)	(97)	(90)	(124)
(6)	Cultivators vs. urban nonindustrials	n.d.	.49**	.11	−.18	.23*	.06
			(24)	(73)	(20)	(41)	(96)
(7)	Urban nonindustrials vs. experienced workers	−.12	−.16*	.16	.08	.11	.11
		(33)	(82)	(29)	(89)	(36)	(42)
(8)	Origin of workers: rural vs. urban	n.d.	.15	n.d.	n.d.	.16	.29
			(62)			(53)	(22)

n.d. = no data

[a] Correlations followed by * are significant at the .05 level; those followed by ** at the .01 level or better.

[b] The number of matched pairs on which each correlation coefficient is based is shown in the parentheses. For example, in Israel, the education match variable was created by giving 35 men with low education a score of 1 and assigning a score of 2 to 35 highly educated men of similar age, origin, skill and economic level and having the same amount of factory experience in factories of comparable size and modernity. This match variable was then correlated with the scores each man received on the participant citizenship scale. The resulting correlation coefficient, .392, is significant at the .01 level, indicating that active citizenship is in fact highly related to level of education.

[c] This match applies to factory workers only.

incidental intercorrelation of education with other factors. In all six countries the education match produces resoundingly high correlations, which, despite the small sample size, are consistently significant at the .01 level or better.

Matches 2 and 3 show that even with education and other powerful variables controlled, factory experience also still has a substantial independent residual effect. Certainly, the relationship is neither so strong, nor so consistent, as that observed in the education matches. Nevertheless, there can be no doubt that in our six developing countries the factory is, in significant degree, a school in citizenship, inculcating interest and active participation in the political process.

It is naturally tempting to take the difference in the size of the correlations for the education match as against the factory experience match as expressing the relative strength of the classroom versus the factory as "schools for politics." We must, however, urge extreme caution in comparing the relative size of these coefficients, since in a match the correlations are much affected by the size of the gap separating the high vs. low set.[31] To permit a less ambiguous comparison, we turn to another measure based on the matches but not relying on correlation coefficients. We may divide the *years* of experience in education or factory work separating high and low match groups by the number of *points* separating them on the scale of citizenship. The result indicates the number of points on the citizenship scale an individual gained, on average, for each year of additional schooling or factory work he experienced.[32]

In looking at the results, presented in table 11-6, it should be kept in mind that the citizenship scale was scored so that individuals could get anything from 0 to 100. Evidently each year of additional schooling, on the average, enables a man to earn approximately 2.5 more points towards a rating as a fully participant citizen. The impact of factory experience is much more modest, the gain being generally about 1.25 ponits per year. If the objective, therefore, is good citizenship, an investment in keeping people in school longer will apparently bring greater returns than an investment in having them employed longer in factories.

TABLE 11-6

Annual Loss or Gain in Points on Citizenship Scale, by Type of Life Experience

	Annual Point Gain Per Year		
	Education[a]	*Factory Work*[b]	*Urban Residence*[c]
Argentina	3.6	1.2	−0.7
Chile	2.0	1.6	−0.7
India	2.5	1.4	0.4
Israel	2.5	0.7	n.d.
Nigeria	3.5	1.5	0.6
Pakistan	2.2	1.2	0.1

n.d. = no data

[a] Calculated on the basis of average gain in two matches; project match #35, comparing low vs. high educated factory workers, and match #34 comparing low vs. high educated cultivators.

[b] Calculated on the basis of the average gain in two matches: #4, comparing cultivators with experienced factory workers, and either match #63, 64 or 65 comparing different years of factory experience.

[c] Calculated on the basis of match #12 using UNI's and factory workers grouped as having "many" or "few" years urban experience.

Nevertheless, it is striking that even with the effects of education and other variables rigorously controlled, the factory still has so definite, regular, and appreciable an effect. The factory evidently is a school for citizenship. It may work less efficiently, or more slowly, than does education, but it is effective in transforming attitudes, values, and behavior so as to make men more participant citizens. Since, in most cases, an adult's education is more or less terminal, the fact that factory work fosters the continued growth of citizenship values takes on added significance. It means that even in countries in which little formal education is attained by the average person, his schooling in citizenship can be continued informally through work in a factory. The marginal cost to society, furthermore, is nil. The entire gain in citizenship values, which would run 2 1/2 percent per year if we take 50 as a mean "starting point," is essentially a windfall profit.

There remains, however, the question raised earlier as to whether it is the factory or the town which is more truly the adult "school for citizenship." The matches permit us some resolution of the debate. First, how lasting are the effects of rural as against urban origin, at least for those who later leave the countryside and go on to industrial labor? We can answer the question for three countries. In each there is evidence of some long-term residual disability attached to rural origins, but in no case is the difference significant (line 8, table 11-5). "Urban experience after 15" does not seem to be any more powerful in its influence on citizenship. When industrial workers and urban but nonindustrial workers (UNIs) are matched on all major variables except years of urban residence, the correlations with the citizenship scale are consistently low, and fail to attain significance in any country (line 4, table 11-5). Furthermore, the two strongest associations are negative; that is, the score on the citizenship scale was ordinarily *less* for those with longer urban residence. The same impression is given by examining the points gained or lost on the scale per year of urban residence. The average change per year is very small where it is positive, and in Argentina and Chile the change is in the negative direction; that is, those longer in the city score lower on citizenship (column 3, table 11-6).

Under the circumstances, it is difficult to argue that it is the stimulation of urban life rather than his experience at work which makes the factory worker more fully a participant citizen. The seemingly substantial influence of urban experience which was earlier suggested by the zero-order correlations (in table 11-3) evidently came about mainly because of the interrelation of work experience and years of urban residence.[33] When matching controlled for the amount of factory work a man had, not much predictive power remained in the measure of years of urban experience.

The larger cosmopolitan centers, moreover, may be particularly counterproductive so far as concerns the inculcation of participant citizenship. Thus, the match pitting the capital, Santiago, against the provincial city of Valdivia, produced a strong negative correlation of −.36, significant at above the .01 level. The mean score on the citizenship scale was 57 to 47 in favor of Valdivia. A comparable gap separated the Nigerian group in Lagos from those residing in Ibadan and other lesser cities and towns. Although Buenos Aires nosed out provincial Cordoba with mean scores of 45 to 41, respectively, the difference was not significant. Despite what we were tempted to conclude earlier, the city does *not* seem the place to learn participant citizenship, the *big* city least of all.[34]

If urbanism is not making the factory workers more active citizens, it presumably should not be having much impact on the urban nonindustrials either. Since the UNI does not enjoy the experience of factory work as a school, he should have lower scores than the industrial worker of the same level of education. Cross-tabulations did not support this conclusion.[35] The matches permit a more precise check on this point.

Comparing lines 2 and 6 of table 11-5 we see that factory work turns cultivators into good citizens more powerfully and more consistently than does work as a nonindustrial. Nevertheless, we observe that nonindustrial work does have the apparent capacity to change the cultivator into a more modern citizen. Indeed, in two of five countries the correlation reaches significant levels. When we pit the UNIs directly against the industrial workers, the latter do better in four of six countries, but not even at the .05 level of significance in any; and they do less well in Argentina and Chile, significantly so in the latter (line 7, table 11-5).

To explain these facts in any depth would require a complex and detailed exposition, including an examination of the peculiarities of the urban nonindustrial sample, which was infortunately extremely variable from country to country. Such an exploration is not possible in this context. We therefore confine ourselves to acknowledging that in some countries, with some sets of urban nonindustrials, either the peculiarities of their social or cultural origins or the conditions of their employment stimulate them to participant citizenship in degree equal to or greater than that of workers in industrial organizations. Of these factors, we believe it is mainly the UNIs extensive contact with the public, and their economic activity as petty entrepreneurs, which generate the heightened citizenship qualities of the taxi drivers, barbers, waiters, kiosk operators, and others who make up these subsamples. Industry is a fine school for citizenship, but it is apparently not the only form of employment which may act in this way.

Although the matches knocked out urbanism as an independent determinant of participant citizenship, the mass media survive this severe test. Even with education, factory experience, and other powerful variables controlled, the mass media matches in *all* countries yield correlations with the citizenship scale significant at the .05 level and above (line 5, table 11-5). The match does not, of course, resolve the ambiguity as to whether exposure to the mass media inculcates citizenship values, or whether those with an interest in politics more often look into the press and radio. No doubt the two tendencies act to reinforce each other.

SUMMARY

Our analysis of political orientations in the "common man" stratum of six developing countries yielded results which, on the whole, exceeded our expectations. There was reason to believe that purely local factors would loom so large as to make the pattern of attitudes in each country distinctive. We did, indeed, find that the evaluative component of political attitudes— as measured by our scales of anomie, group hostility, and alienation (or judgment of government effectiveness)—could not be fit to any pattern comparable for all six countries. We discovered, however, that another set of attitudes and behavioral tendencies, designated as the active or participant citizenship syndrome, cohered as a unified entity in much the same way in all the countries. This syndrome includes identification with or allegiance to supralocal and nonparochial public authority; interest in civic affairs; information about political figures; participation in public organizations; and adherence to rational organizational rules as a basis for running government affairs.

The syndrome is apparently inculcated as a result of certain life experiences. Of the early socialization influences, the amount of education a person enjoys seems the most powerful. Indeed, it emerges as one of the most important factors in stimulating active citizenship in competition with any other source of influence. From the distinctive point of view of our research project, however, it is notable that the experience of industrial work has considerable ability to inculcate the values and modes of behaving which go with active citizenship. Both of these determinants survived the very stringent test posed by our analysis with matched groups, although education comes through more powerfully and consistently than does factory experience. The results leave little doubt that these are both truly independent influences. Use of the mass media also qualifies as an independent force, although in this case it remains more ambiguous how far newspaper reading and radio listening are the "cause" and how far the "effect" of active citizenship. We also noted that a decent standard of living seems a necessary precondition to be met before a man will expend the extra energy required for full participation in civic life. Finally, it appears that certain personal qualities, perhaps appropriately defined as personality traits, such as intelligence and a subjectively high estimate of one's skill and social standing, are also characteristic of those who manifest the syndrome of active citizenship. Unfortunately, using matches did not enable us to test how far either economic well-being or the tendency to see the world as benign are truly independent variables in their influence.

Education had previously been identified by many studies as a force making for fuller participation in the citizen role. That we confirm this finding in six developing countries, without exception, is gratifying but not startling. Our distinctive contribution, therefore, lies in establishing occupational experience, especially work in factories, as an independent source of influence. Since the general theory guiding our larger investigation into the sources of individual modernization gives special emphasis to the role of the factory as a "school for modernization,"[36] it is particularly gratifying to discover that industrial employment seems so effective in preparing men for more active participation in their role as citizens.

One might well have begun with the opposite prediction. The factory is organized hierarchically, and authority in it runs strictly along formal lines. Decisions are made not on the basis of consultation and vote, but on grounds of technical efficiency and position in the power hierarchy. Although the worker is expected to do his job as well as he can, it is a rare factory in which he is encouraged to feel himself a cooperative member of a larger community in whose affairs he takes an interest and in whose total efforts he is an active participant. The factory might, therefore, be seen as more likely to reinforce traditional habits and expectations in dealing with authority, rather than to stimulate a man to play a more modern citizenship role. But this conclusion assumes that the man entering the factory comes from an environment in which he already has experienced a good deal of centralized control, one in which the leader's power rests not merely on kinship or some related principle, but rather derives more formally by deputation from some higher, and presumably technically competent, authority. This expectation will not be satisfied if the man comes from the typical village.

There may be a rough democracy in the traditional village, but it often is also atomistically organized around more or less autonomous family units and does not produce a sense of community focused around a central authority. The factory might well, therefore, be an important way of schooling men in the acceptance of a central political authority not resting solely on the diffuse basis of kinship. The traditional small community has no general overarching goals, other than perhaps that of maintaining the peace which permits the family units to go about in pursuit of their own goals. The modern state, as a rule, has more definite collective goals and it asserts a national purpose. Here again the factory could well be a training ground in new values, since it has obvious goals of production, in the attainment of which every worker may see himself as a substantial contributor.

To carry this line of reasoning a step further, we may see the factory as a school in rationality. A factory runs largely according to formal rules guided by impersonal technical norms. Its system of authority and rewards is intimately geared to a more or less objective and precisely graded hierarchy of technical skill which, in turn, rests on formal education. Such an environment might well, therefore, encourage men to carry over to the political realm the expectation that high position should rest on education and skill, and that people should be treated not according to their unique personal qualities or their intimate relation with authority, but rather by rule and according to their formal rights.

Beyond the influence of the factory we observed, but could not adequately explain, the fact that urban but nonindustrial workers are also often surprisingly high on the citizenship scale. This might be thought to result from the effect of urban life. But one of our most striking findings is precisely that urbanism, despite its high zero-order correlation, fails to meet the test of being an independent school for citizenship. Neither urban origins, nor the number of years of urban experience after age 15, produce significant increases in active citizenship when other variables are controlled. This is confirmed by many special matches.[37] Indeed, it appears that the larger and more cosmopolitan the city, the less the frequency of active citizenship in the common-man stratum of society. These findings invite a host of speculations we cannot pursue in any detail here.[38] Urban centers in developing countries are very often poorly organized, and may be chaotic. The rate of population growth exceeds, often swamps, the capacity of the local authorities to provide essential services, let alone any of the amenities of urban living. Housing, in particular, is scarce, and shanty-towns arise everywhere with their odd structures arranged in a disorderly jumble expressing none of the rationality of urban planning. Social control often breaks down in communities of unrelated, often totally heterogeneous, populations drawn to the city from distant corners. These and related features of rapidly growing urban centers in developing countries put them at a marked disadvantage in competition with the factory as schools in modernization. Order, rationality, firm organization, effective technical competence, justice in the distribution of rewards and punishment, even intimate personal relatedness, are often much more common in the factory than in the urban milieu which houses it in many developing countries.

Finally, we may note that when a number of the more effective determinants of active citizenship combine their influence, the result is a very sharp increase in the proportion who manifest that characteristic in "high" degree.[39] That is, the impact of the determinants is apparently *cumulative*, even if not strictly additive. In a group which is engaged in agriculture, has enjoyed few of the benefits of education, and is little exposed to the mass media, the proportion who score high on citizenship participation may be practically zero. In a more favored group, better educated, working in industry, and in regular contact with the mass media, the proportion showing a high level of active citizenship may rise to the point where it is the norm for the group. In Chile, for example, only 3 percent of the cultivators with low education scored high on active citizenship, but among the better educated and more experienced industrial workers the proportion rose to 72 percent. In Nigeria the spread was from 9 percent to 82 percent, and in the other countries the results were strictly comparable.

The implications of these findings for the political future of these developing nations are substantial. Many students of politics have expressed grave concern as to whether a modern political system can ever hope to function effectively in these countries, given their lack of a cultural tradition which can spontaneously inculcate in young people the qualities essential to active and effective citizenship in a modern polity. Our research indicates that what is lacking in the traditional culture may be provided by the institutions of modern society—by the school, the factory, the newspaper, and the radio. These sources of influence evidently have an independent power to effect political socialization, training men to know more about polities, stimulating them to take an interest in political events and to participate in civic affairs, and fostering a shift in allegiance from tribal and local leaders to those representing a wider community of interest.

A nation's political development will be balanced to the extent that the institution of modern political forms does not outrun the growth of schools, industry, mass communications, and other social forces which act to inculcate the necessary attributes of active citizenship in the population.

The balance is, however, inherently delicate. The same forces which train men to active citizenship may act to increase the demands made on the government for effectiveness, efficiency, innovation, and change. The political system may then become overloaded, or for other reasons fail to meet expectations. Alienation, anomie, and radical and extremist forms of political action may result. Then follow those perennial stalemates, coups, revolts, riots, and repressions we have come to know as endemic in so many newly developing nations.

CHAPTER 12

Personal Adjustment
and Modernization

Few ideas have had wider currency among prominent commentators on social life than the belief that the city and its attendant industrial civilization are alien to "natural" man and inevitably breed social disorganization and personal confusion (see White and White 1962). Thomas Jefferson could see some good even in yellow fever since, as he said, "It will discourage the growth of great cities in our nation, and I view great cities as pestilential to the morals, the health, and the liberties of man" (White and White 1962, p. 19). A century later Henry Adams saw New York City as a cylinder which had exploded to throw great masses of stone and steam against the sky, creating an air of "movement and hysteria" in which "prosperity never before imagined, power never yet wielded by men, speed never reached by anything but a meteor, had made the world *irritable, nervous, querulous, unreasonable,* and *afraid*" (p. 72, italics added).

Such images of urban life and industrial civilization were also held by leaders of the burgeoning social sciences in the twentieth century. Pitirim Sorokin was profoundly convinced that the modern sensate culture was everywhere generating a great upsurge in mental illness (Sorokin 1957). Robert Park, leader of the dominant Chicago school of sociology, felt that the city, in the very process of its growth, "creates diseases and vices which tend to destroy the community." The peasant who comes to work in the city, Park held, is the prototypical case for observing the threat to

This chapter was originally published as Alex Inkeles and David H. Smith, "Personal Adjustment and Modernization," in George A. DeVos, ed., *Responses to Change* (New York: D. Van Nostrand, 1976), pp. 214–33. That article itself was based on an earlier publication by Alex Inkeles and David H. Smith, "The Fate of Personal Adjustment in the Process of Modernization," *International Journal of Comparative Sociology* 11 (1970): 81–114. The last section of the chapter, under the heading "Interpretations," is taken from this original source.

individual integrity inherent in urban life. "Man, translated to the city," he remarked, "has become a problem to himself and society in a way and to an extent he never was before" (White and White 1962, pp. 162–66).

If Park's observation were true within the framework of already industrialized Western society, how much greater would be the impact on men in more traditional and isolated cultures whom life and circumstance had lifted from the quiet and security of their villages and cast into the maelstrom of urban industrial life? J.S. Slotkin spoke for many anthropologists when he asserted that no matter how compatible industrialism may *seem* to be, "its ramifications tend to produce cultural disorganization" (Slotkin 1960, p. 31).

Not all anthropologists and sociologists accept the inevitability of the deleterious effects of migration, urban residence, and industrial labor which Slotkin seemed to assume. Some, like Oscar Lewis, have emphasized the relative transferability of sociocultural patterns from the village to the city, patterns which protect the individual from exposure to excessive disorganization and consequent personal disorder. In his study of the migration of Tepoztecan peasants to Mexico City, he found "little evidence of disorganization and breakdown, or culture conflict, or of irreconcilable differences between generations." So far as the individual is concerned, Lewis reported, the Tepoztecan peasants "adapt to city life with far greater ease than do American farm families" (Lewis 1952, pp. 39–40).

Other analysts have stressed the need to differentiate adjustment according to the stages in a migrant's career and the quality and forms of his integration with his new urban environment. Deshmukh (1956), in his study of a floating population in Delhi, distinguished three stages in the life path of the migrant. In the earliest stage, according to Deshmukh, the migrant still enjoys a certain insulation from the impact of his new status. At the second stage, however, "he painfully learns about the difference in his own ways and ways of the town; he is perplexed about everything in the town." According to Deshmukh this period is "the stage of crises for each immigrant." In the third stage, however, some men acquire new skills and new ways, settle down comfortably in the town, and overcome their marginality. These are then presumably out of the crisis condition, and have achieved a new adjustment.

To resolve the controversy whether migration and subsequent modernizing experiences in developing countries are or are not deleterious to mental health, and to determine under what conditions such harmful influences as may result can or cannot be counteracted, required data in a form and on a scale not previously available. The materials collected by our Project on the

Social and Cultural Aspects of Development permit a substantial advance in the assessment of the effects of migration, industrialization, and urbanization on psychic adjustment. As part of our standard questionnaire, we included in every interview a Psychosomatic Symptoms Test (PT). In addition we asked more than fifty questions, in interviews of up to four hours each, which in various ways permit us to assess the validity of the test and to make independent evaluations of the psychic adjustment of migrant industrial workers in the six developing countries included in our study.

PROBLEMS OF CONCEPTUALIZATION AND MEASUREMENT

The conceptualization and the measurement of "adjustment" pose difficult problems. The concept is defined in so great a variety of ways as to render it almost meaningless unless some particular measure or test is specified. So far as measurement is concerned, the situation is not much improved, because so many different and often unrelated measures have been used. In this study, we use the term "mental health" to refer to the relative success or adequacy of an individual's psychological and social functioning, within the limits of his constitutional capabilities and his environment. We emphasize that the criterion of successful functioning must be *relative* to one's physical body and to one's environment. We also stress that adjustment involves successful functioning in the *social* realm. For us, the concept is not limited to internal psychological processes. Broadly speaking, "adjustment" may be taken as synonymous with "mental health."

The major criteria or indices of "adjustment" or "mental health" have been thoroughly reviewed by William Scott (1958). He found six basic research criteria in common use: (1) exposure to psychiatric treatment; (2) psychiatric diagnosis; (3) social maladaptation; (4) failure of positive adaptation; (5) subjective unhappiness; (6) objective psychological symptoms.

We could not afford to subject our interviewees to psychiatric diagnosis, even if they were willing, and we feared that records of psychiatric treatment in developing countries might have little relevance even if they existed. Failure of positive adaptation, the fourth criterion, was also not suitable, at least given the design of our study. The usual test of successful "adaptation" is a man's ability to sustain a major social role, such as holding a job. Our research design required us to sample men who, at the time of the interview, were by definition successfully "adapted" in that they all were effectively employed. For the other three criteria of adjustment, however, we were able to include items in our test battery. In the report presented here we limit ourselves to analyzing our measure for the sixth criterion, namely objective psychological symptoms. To assess the presence of such symptoms we relied on a set of questions which had been widely used for the purpose in the United States and elsewhere. Sets of such questions are called psychosomatic symptoms tests (or scales). The items we used, in what we designate our PT test, are listed in table 12-1.

Such a test recommended itself on the simple ground of precedent. Items such as those in our PT scale had been used in nearly every major study of the mental health or adjustment of groups (as against individuals) conducted since World War II, including the famous study of American soldiers, the midtown Manhattan study, a national sample reported in *Americans View Their Mental Health,* and others. (See Stouffer et al. 1949; Srole et al. 1962; Gurin, Veroff, and Feld 1960; Kornhauser 1965). Even more important for our purpose was the fact that the test had been used with apparent success in cultures at least as different from the Western European as those included in our research—for example, with the Abeokuta Yoruba in Nigeria and the Zulu in South Africa (Leighton et al. 1963; Scotch and Geiger 1963–64).

A quick glance at table 12-1 will make it clear why these questions are considered measures of psychosomatic symptoms, and why they are judged to be indicators of psychic adjustment. Of course, everyone has a headache or experiences some nervousness sometimes. But we do not expect an individual who is well-adjusted to report that he displays a large array of such symptoms, nor that he has them frequently or regularly. If a man tells us that he has trouble getting to sleep, *and* feels bothered by nervousness, *and* is afflicted by bad dreams, *and* has trembling hands, it seems likely that something is wrong. That "something" may, of course, be physical rather than psychic, but the questions included in the test seem inherently concerned with psychic adjustment as expressed in psychosomatic symptoms. They have "face validity."

The face validity of a test may, of course, be a false face. We note, therefore, that in a number of the cited studies which relied on some form of psychosomatic symptoms test similar to ours, the investigators validated the test against independent criteria of personal adjustment (see Kasl and French 1962). The work of Kornhauser (1965), Bradburn (1965), and

TABLE 12-1

Percent of National Sample Reporting Psychosomatic Symptoms, by Symptom and Country

PT Test Question	Argentina	Chile	East Pakistan	India	Israel	Nigeria	Average Across Countries
1[a] Have trouble sleeping? Yes/No	12	23	20	54	37	21	28
2 Limbs tremble enough to bother you? Yes/No	—[b]	—	23	10	15	4	13
3[a] Bothered by nervousness? Yes/No	33	36	36	27	48	9	32
4 Bothered by heart beating hard when not exerting self? Yes/No	—	24	16	13	13	45	22
5 Bite fingernails? Yes/No	—	—	15	6	14	—	12
6[a] Bothered by shortness of breath when not exercising? Yes/No	8	15	9	6	8	22	13
7 Bothered by palms sweating when not exercising? Yes/No	—	—	—	—	22	22	22
8[a] Often troubled by headaches? Yes/No	21	24	26	21	34	44	28
9[a] Bothered by dreams that frighten or upset you? Yes/No	11	22	31	35	21	48	28
50 Health problems affect work in last 6 months? Freq./ . . . /Never	28	35	—	—	—	—	32
51 Couldn't get going to take care of things in last 6 months? Often/ . . . /Almost never	17	33	—	—	—	—	25

52 Bothered by body pains in last 6 months? Frequently/ . . . /Never	40	53	—	—	—	—	47
53 Difficult to get up in morning to face things you have to do? Almost always/ . . . /Never	15	26	—	—	—	—	21
N51 Ever thought you were being affected by witchcraft? Yes/No	—	—	—	—	—	26	26
Average percent of symptoms per country	21	29	22	22	24	28	25
Total cases per country	(815)	(931)	(1001)	(1300)	(736)	(720)	

[a] Represents a "core" item, present in the scale for all countries. All others are "supplementary."
[b] Dash (—) means not included in country indicated.

Leighton (1963) is particularly relevant. We ran our own independent tests to validate the scale, but before we present those results we should explain our particular method for scoring the adjustment scale.

CONSTRUCTION OF THE PT SCALE

In our basic questionnaire we included a standard set of nine Psychosomatic Symptoms Test items which earlier studies had proved useful. However, each country's field director was left free to omit any question which he felt was clearly inappropriate in the culture setting in which he was working, and to substitute others where necessary. Sweaty palms might signal psychological stress in New England, but have little significance as a diagnostic tool in a very hot and humid country such as East Pakistan (now Bangladesh). Thus the final test was slightly different in each of the countries. We constructed two scales: one which was exactly the same for each country, but was limited to a few items and hence less reliable, and one which sacrificed strict comparability to take advantage of the distinctive items we had found to be especially useful in some particular country. Since the two scales yielded highly similar results, we decided for this analysis to blend them in a composite scale. This composite stresses both comparability—represented by a core set of five items which held together most consistently across all the countries—and national diversity, as represented by the addition for each country of supplemental questions which seemed to cohere with the basic set. Table 12-1 identifies the items as core or supplementary, and indicates which were used in the composite scale for each country.

It will be noted that cultural differences were manifested in the variable "popularity" of particular symptoms in the diverse national groups. Trouble with sleeping, for example, was one of the most popular symptoms in India, reported by over half the respondents, whereas it was cited by only about 10 percent in Pakistan and Argentina. For this report, however, we did not consider the significance of specific questions in particular countries. We were, rather, seeking for an array of symptoms which would distinguish one man from another *within the same culture.* As we added to the set of symptoms, moreover, these cultural differences tended to average out, reflected in the fact that of the symptoms in any national scale the proportion cited was about 25 percent in each of the six countries, although the nature of the prevalent symptoms varied from country to country.

On the basis of his answers to the PT test, each person in our sample received an "adjustment score" which could be as low as zero or as high as one hundred. One hundred was the perfect score—it represented a man who claimed not to have any of the symptoms. Any man who reported having *all* the symptoms presented in the PT test for his country received a score of zero. The actual scores obtained in each country covered the entire possible range from 0 to 100, except for India, where the lowest was 13.

The resulting scales seemed to be of good quality. The item-to-item correlations were in a range which compares reasonably well with results obtained in similar studies in the United States. In addition, a principal components factor analysis found that a strong first factor of "general adjustment" emerged in all six country samples. This predominant first factor consisted of the set of items we had already designated as constituting the composite PT scale for each country.

VALIDITY OF THE PT SCALE

The results of the verbal material we recorded and of our several statistical procedures, reported in full elsewhere, confirmed the impression that the PT test is indeed a valid measure of adjustment (see Inkeles and Smith 1970). We saw quite clearly that frustration, disgruntlement, disappointment, and anguish—as revealed in attitude questions—are reflected in the manifestation of more psychosomatic symptoms by the individuals who express those feelings.

Men who were relatively satisfied with their condition, who felt that they were getting a decent break in life, and who judged that others were treating or had treated them well, less often reported multiple symptoms. Multiple symptoms were manifested by those who felt the chances for a poor man to get ahead were decreasing, who felt their social standing was low, and who were unhappy in their work. In some cases the increase in the proportion with extreme symptomatology doubled, or more than doubled, as we moved from the men most satisfied with conditions to those least satisfied with themselves or people around them. In fifty-two out of sixty comparisons we were able to make, those experiencing less satisfaction showed more symptoms.

It should be recognized, furthermore, that validating the PT scales by the use of single items makes a very stiff test. The more common method is to use a scale. When we used a summary satisfaction scale, we found that in five of the countries the observed association between dissatisfaction and multiple symptoms was significant at the .001 level and in the sixth was significant at the .01 level. These findings based on attitudinal measures argue in favor of accepting the PT test as a valid measure of the psychic adjustment of our subjects. Admittedly, the negative sentiments expressed by those with more symptoms are not the equivalent of hospitalization, nor do they carry the same weight as a clinical diagnosis based on a psychiatric interview. Nevertheless, it seems reasonable to assume that men who more often and more vigorously expressed feelings of powerlessness, anger, hostility, neglect, and deprivation, as described above, would be rated by psychiatrists as more "poorly adjusted."

TESTING THE HYPOTHESIS: THE IMPACT OF MODERNIZING EXPERIENCES

The main modernizing influences measured in our research are education, urbanism, mass communications contact, and experience in factory employment. In addition, we are in a position to test how far geographical and occupational mobility, particularly as expressed in the move from the countryside to the town and from agricultural to industrial pursuits, act to produce psychosomatic symptoms. We sought to determine if migration, education, contact with radio and television, exposure to urban life, and work in modern factories conduce to psychic disturbance in anything like the degree they have been alleged to. To effect this test we relied mainly on the results of "matched" groups of respondents. The matches have the virtue of permitting us to examine the influence of any single variable while the other main variables are simultaneously controlled.

Where relevant, we have also presented correlations between the several modernizing forces and the PT test, so that any marked differences between those results and ones obtained with the matches will be readily apparent. In addition, we have supplemented the rather stringent match procedure by the use of partial correlation and regression analysis.

EDUCATION AND PSYCHOSOMATIC SYMPTOMS

Emile Durkheim identified popular education as a factor contributing to "the weakening of traditional beliefs and the state of moral individualism resulting from this" (Durkheim 1951, p. 168). He linked the widespread diffusion of literacy to higher rates of suicide. Others have linked it, for similar reasons, to the greater incidence of psychic strain. However in our data there is a consistent, and at times substantial, trend for more education to be associated with better adjustment as measured by the PT scale. In all six countries the zero-order correlation between education and adjustment was positive, and in three significantly so at the .01 level. When this relationship was examined separately for cultivators and factory workers matched as high versus low on education, thus controlling a number of other possible confounding influences, the difference persisted. A median correlation of approximately .11 was observed between education and adjustment. This pattern was substantially reversed only in Nigeria, where more education went with less adjustment in the factory worker group. Neither in this case, nor in any of the others, however, did the more stringent match test reach acceptable levels of statistical significance. Detailed figures on the results of the match test as used with large sets of independent variables may be found in Inkeles and Smith (1970). We may tentatively conclude that insofar as educational upgrading is a common component of the experience of modernization, then the effect on the individual's psychic adjustment is positive and favorable, even if quite modest in intensity.

We suggest that education plays two roles: it equips men better to understand and thus deal with their own inner problems, stresses, hopes, and fears, enabling them to turn their energy into more constructive rather than self-destructive channels; and it similarly enables men to deal more effectively with their social and physical environment. This is not to say that there are not many stresses and strains to which the more educated man is subjected, especially since he may be expected to assume more responsibility. Yet, on balance, the better-educated seem to be the more favored by good psychic adjustment.

URBAN EXPERIENCE AND PSYCHOSOMATIC SYMPTOMS

The impact of urbanization on adjustment has been examined by several scholars. Perhaps the two most relevant studies are those of Scotch and Geiger (1963–64), and Leighton et al. (1963), both of which are often cited as proving that the experience of urbanization, in Africa at least, is associated with stress and consequent psychological maladjustment. However, we read the evidence somewhat differently.

In our opinion, neither of these two studies, the best known and most careful of their kind, can be cited as providing striking evidence that cities and towns in developing countries have greater concentrations of young men with many psychosomatic symptoms and other signs of psychic distress (see Inkeles and Smith 1970). In both studies the authors pointed out that it was not urban life *per se* that seemed responsible for maladjustment, but rather the rapid cultural change and especially the "social disintegration" that is presumed to accompany urbanization in developing societies. Urban areas in transition may often be characterized by the disintegration of extended kinship ties, loss of religious values, erosion of traditional economic interrelationships, and the like. Yet this disintegration is not an inevitable accompaniment of urbanization and need not be a permanent quality of urban life.

If we compared cultivators and city workers and found them differing in adjustment, we could not tell how far the difference was due to the factor of residence, and how far due to their contrasting conditions of employment. If, however, we restrict ourselves to men of rural origin now employed as factory and nonindustrial workers, we can compare those who have been long in the city with those whose stay has been short. The zero-order correlations (in line 2 of table 12-2) suggest a negative impact of city life, with three of four countries indicating more symptoms with more years in town, the relationship being statistically significant in two of the four countries. Using the match of all those who originated in the countryside but differed in having "few" as against "many" years of city residence, we can make the comparable match test in five countries.[1] In four of the five there was an appreciable tendency for those longer in the city to have more symptoms. In no case, however, did the correlation coefficient reach

TABLE 12-2

Correlations of PT Adjustment Scores with Selected Variables Measuring "Modernizing" Experience,[a] by Country

Modernizing Experience	Argentina	Chile	East Pakistan	India	Israel	Nigeria
Formal education	.05	.02	.13***	.16***	.09*	.11**
Years of urban residence	−.13*	−.07	−.11**	.02	n.a.	−.04
Months of factory experience	−.13**	−.08*	−.06	.10**	−.14**	.13**
Factory size	.04	.05	−.06	.04	.07	.08
Factory modernity	.09*	.07	−.02	n.a.	.14**	.04
Mass media contact	.02	.00	.05	.10**	.03	.04
Minimum numbers[b]	(663)	(716)	(654)	(700)	(544)	(520)

n.a. = not available in the country indicated

*Indicates correlations significant at the .05 level level; those designated by ** are significant at the .01 level; those designated by *** are significant at the .001 level or better. All others are not significant.

[a]The modernizing experience variables are scored from low to high. Adjustment (PT) is scored so that those with *fewer* symptoms earn *higher* scores. Positive correlations, therefore, indicate that having more of the modernizing experience is associated with better adjustment (or fewer symptoms). Negative correlations indicate more of the modernizing experience goes with poorer adjustment.

[b]N given applies to the subsample of factory workers only, reported on lines 3, 4, 5. The N for lines 1 and 6, based on the total sample, is given in table 12-1. In Argentina, Chile, and Nigeria, the N for line 2 differs from that for lines 3, 4, 5, being, respectively, 239, 305, and 184. The difference is due to the fact that in line 2 the cases are limited to men of rural origin only.

acceptable levels of statistical significance (see table 12-2). On this basis, therefore, one cannot claim absolutely that more years in the city are likely to produce more psychic symptoms, although some suspicion is certainly pointed in that direction.

The "years urban since age 15" match allowed us to judge the effect of a given *quantity* of urban experience. We could also test the effect of differences in the *quality* of the urban environment. If urban life produces psychic stress, the more intensely urban a place was, the greater should have been its negative impact on adjustment. We could test this assumption with the match which pitted the larger, more modern, cosmopolitan urban complexes in each country against smaller and less cosmopolitan cities.

The results of these comparisons of urban *quality* rather strengthened the conclusion we reached on the basis of the measures of *quantity*. Despite the presumably greater social disorganization, impersonality, confusion, and discord in the larger, more cosmopolitan, and more rapidly changing urban conglomerates, they evidently did not produce significantly more personal disorientation, individual stress, or psychic disorganization.

FACTORY EXPERIENCE AND PSYCHOSOMATIC SYMPTOMS

Ever since Dickens wrote his devastating accounts of life in the industrial milieu of nineteenth-century England, the smoke, dust, noise, danger, and intense time pressure in factories have all been identified as likely to generate nervous disorder as well as physical disease. The physical conditions of the nineteenth-century factory are no longer so common, even in developing countries, but the image of the factory as an unnatural place, demanding a pace and a style of work alien to human nature, still lingers on.

If work in a factory makes a man nervous or otherwise distressed, the longer he continues at this trade the worse his condition should become. Other studies of the relations of industrial labor to mental health have, surprisingly, not given much attention to the length of time a man has worked in industry. In our samples from developing countries, factory experience does not have a powerful effect on adjustment as measured by the PT scales and, perhaps more important, the effect is not consistently in the same direction. It is indeed the case that in four of the countries those longer in the factory manifest more symptoms. In two others, however, the reverse is true, with an equally strong association linking few symptoms with more years in industrial employment.

Since such correlations often cover up more complex relationships, we regrouped the industrial workers into three sets consisting of "new workers'' who had been in industry less than seven months, those who had worked in industry between one year and five, and highly experienced workers with six or more years in the factory. In addition, we introduced controls for education and migratory status. Furthermore, following clinical opinion on the diagnostic significance of different PT scores, we considered only those having multiple symptoms.

The results gave almost no support to the assertion that factory employment in developing countries is regularly associated with increased psychic stress. If this claim had been correct the predominant rank order pattern for the percentages should have been 1, 2, 3, with the largest proportion of long-time employees having multiple symptoms. In fact, the pattern appeared in only four of the eighteen instances in which we had complete information. Moreover, these cases were offset by two instances of the opposite pattern, indicating that longer factory employment was associated with fewer symptoms. In the great majority of cases, there was no definite progression as men moved up the factory experience ladder. New workers most often had the smallest proportion claiming multiple symptoms, but beyond that no consistent progression over time was evident. In the relevant comparisons, the long-term workers showed a larger proportion with multiple symptoms about half the time; in the other half the workers of middling experience had the less healthy profile.

We are led to conclude that for the new workers, especially those who are migrants, finding a job may have been such a source of relief and gratification that they scored unusually low on the Psychosomatic Symptoms Test. The rosy glow may wear off in a year or two, but that does not presage a *steady* decline. As our comparison of the middle-experienced and high-experienced workers indicates, the psychic health of the industrial worker in developing countries does not consistently deteriorate year by year.

When we considered the factories in the study in terms of their size and modernity, we found no basis for concluding that the larger, and presumably more formal and bureaucratic, factories induced men to develop more psychosomatic symptoms. If anything, the larger the factory, and the more modern, the less probability there was of finding a high proportion of men with many psychosomatic symptoms.

MASS MEDIA CONTACT

The mass media are often accused of contributing to social disorganization and personal stress: they are said to undermine traditional leisure time activities, encourage wild fantasies and unrealizable hopes in their audience, remind people constantly of the luxury goods they cannot have and the places they can never go. Our data, however, did not confirm this view of the effects of the media.

In five of six zero-order correlations, more exposure to the radio and newspaper went with *fewer* symptoms, significantly so in India. In the stringent match test these trends held up. All six countries showed those with more exposure to the mass media to have fewer symptoms, although in no case were the results statistically significant.

THE EFFECT OF GEOGRAPHICAL AND
OCCUPATIONAL MOBILITY

One theory sees the source of personal stress in modern institutions such as the school, factory, city, and cinema. Another considers the source of psychic disturbance to be the dislocation of the individual's primary ties which comes with the shift from the countryside to the city and from rural to urban occupations.

To test this second theory we compared the PT scores of those still living in their traditional villages with those who had moved to the city for factory work. The most relevant comparison was obviously that between new workers, that is, those who had been working in the city seven months or less, and the men who had continued to live in the villages. Israel was not included in this part of the study because of its very different migration patterns.

The new city worker had a better PT score in four out of five comparisons, although none of the differences were statistically significant. The edge held by the new factory workers seemed to decline as time passed and the euphoria of having found a job diminished, but the old-time workers did not have significantly more symptoms than those who continued in farming. Indeed, in India we found the only instance of a relationship in this set which was somewhat significant at the .05 level, and it showed those who had moved to the town to have fewer symptoms than those who had not.

The picture was not much altered by matching factory workers of rural origin with those of urban origin. The matches showed that the factory workers who had been born and raised in the countryside were not significantly more prone to psychosomatic symptoms than their fellow workers who had been born in town. Much the same impression must be drawn from a systematic comparison of the groups of workers alike in education and length of factory experience, but different in their status as migrants or nonmigrants. Out of twenty-six applicable comparisons, the migrants had more symptoms fourteen times and the nonmigrant had more ten times, the remaining two being ties. This hardly makes a compelling case for the proposition that migration has a consistently negative effect on adjustment.

Taking all the measures into account, moving from village to city itself seems to have no striking effect on psychic health. Perhaps the critical factor is whether the postmigratory status permits one to become integrated into a stable, meaningful, and rewarding role in a new environment. It seems that it is not the fact of moving, but more the kind of reward the migrant wins *after his move*, which determines the presence or absence of psychosomatic symptoms (see French 1963, pp. 39–56).

CONCLUSIONS

Of the modernizing experiences frequently identified as likely to induce distruption of personality, none consistently and significantly brought about increased maladjustment as measured by the Psychosomatic Symptoms Test. In our analysis we did find some instances, in some countries, in which a particular modernizing experience seemed to produce more symptoms, and to do so at statistically significant levels. These instances were almost always offset, however, by other findings going as strongly in the opposite direction. The patterns observed in relation to adjustment were not only weak but were also decidedly lacking in consistency across the six countries. We are not dismissing the occasional evidence in favor of the theory that modernization is inimical to good mental health, but we feel the *general* thrust of our results is quite unmistakable. Keeping in mind our reservations, we may summarize our findings as follows.

Increased education, long ago identified by Durkheim as counterproductive of social integration and as more likely to lead to suicide had instead a fairly consistent, and sometimes significant, *positive* effect on adjustment, both among workers and cultivators. Exposure to the impersonality of urban life, to its plethora of stimuli, to its frenzied pace, and to its crowded conditions did not consistently and unmistakably induce psychosomatic symptoms. The jangling flood of music, desire-arousing advertisements, and distressing world news presented by the mass media also did not seem to injure psychic health. Men born in the urban centers were not significantly less well-adjusted than those born in the countryside; men who had lived in town did not have significantly more symptoms than men with fewer years of exposure; those living in the larger and more cosmopolitan cities such as Lagos, Santiago, Buenos Aires, and Ranchi were not psychically worse off than those living in the smaller and often more traditional cities of Ibadan, Valdivia, Cordoba, and Khalari.

Neither can we say that employment as a factory worker is conducive to psychosomatic complaints. Men who have worked longer in industry do not have consistently more psychosomatic symptoms. Indeed, for the more successful men who have technical skills, and especially for those who have been able to buy more goods, there is a fairly consistent and often significant tendency toward better adjustment. Working in large factories—often supposed to be more impersonal, bureaucratized, and dehumanizing—was not more conducive to psychosomatic symptoms than working in small factories; if anything, the contrary was the case. But in any event, the relations were not statistically significant. Much the same lack of differentiation was evident when the factories were classified as more or less modern in technology and personnel policy.

Whatever may cause psychosomatic symptoms in younger men in developing countries, *it is apparently something other than exposure to modernizing institutions such as the school, the factory, the city, and the mass media.* Finally, we found no evidence that migration itself brings about psychic distress, as measured by the development of a large number of psychosomatic symptoms. Men who had moved and taken industrial jobs in town did not consistently have more symptoms than those who remained in their home villages, nor did they seem significantly less adjusted then their fellow workers who were raised in the town and hence came to work in industry without the necessity to migrate.

CHALLENGES TO OUR CONCLUSION

We made a great effort to salvage the hypothesis that factory work and urban life are detrimental. In the numerous match tests very few of the results reached significance, but a certain number did indicate that modernizing institutions might be sources of personal tension. By studying these influences one at a time it is possible we obscured the fact that their impact was in important degree *cumulative*, producing a significant effect only when one negative experience was piled on another. To test that idea we grouped the respondents in each country according to how much they had been exposed to any or all of the modernizing experiences shown in table 12-2. If the effects of modernizing experiences were indeed cumulative, there should have been a steady increase in the proportion showing multiple symptoms as we moved up the scale from minimum to maximum exposure.

Nothing of the kind occurred. In five of the six countries there was no visible pattern of any kind. India was the only country which showed a statistically significant pattern, but there each step up the scale of increased exposure to modernizing influences brought with it a *decrease* in the number of psychosomatic symptoms. The one clear-cut result, therefore, argued that if exposure to modernizing influences had had any effect, it was to *improve* personal adjustment.

In order to decrease the likelihood that we were overlooking significant relationships because of the small size of our matched groups, a multiple regression analysis was also undertaken, using all of our subjects. If the theory about modernization experiences cumulatively leading to maladjustment was correct, all, or at least most, of the signs in the regression analysis of the PT test should have been *negative*, that is, they should have shown a decline in adjustment associated with more exposure to modernizing experiences. In fact, only one-third were negative, and, quite contrary to theoretical expectation, two-thirds were positive.

Finally, as a last resort, one might argue that even if contact with modern *institutions* does not conduce to more psychosomatic symptoms, *personal* individual modernization does. In other words, it might be argued that what is important about the individual's modernization is not what *made* him modern, but rather just *how* modern he has become. Several of the more popular theories certainly assert quite firmly that the more modern a man is, that is, the further he has come from the traditional cultural roots, the more under stress he should be.

This proposition could easily be tested by correlating each individual's score on the OM Scale, the Project's general measure of individual modernity, with his score as to psychosomatic adjustment. Except for the statistic for Israel, all the correlations were positive, indicating that greater attitudinal modernity went with better adjustment, that is, with fewer symptoms. Although the correlations were very modest in size, four of the six were statistically significant (at the .05 level or better). If, therefore, we were stating our conclusions independent of the theory we had been testing, we would be forced to say: "The more modern the individual, the better his psychic adjustment as measured by the Psychosomatic Symptoms Test." However, we had set out to test the null hypothesis: that there are no significant differences between groups which have been much or little exposed to modern institutions. Since that was our original aim, we here restrict ourselves to saying: "We found no basis for asserting that individuals more exposed to modernizing experiences, or who were more modern in attitudes, values, and behavior, were less well-adjusted than those whose modernizing was less advanced."

INTERPRETATIONS

The meaning and significance which is attached to the findings we have presented depends greatly on the assumptions with which one initially approached the relation of social change and modernizing influences to psychic health and personal adjustment. Those who assert that the experience of extensive social change is inherently profoundly disturbing to the individual, and who believe that the forces of modernization such as urbanization, industrialization, and mass communication are invariably deleterious to individual psychic adjustment, will find little comfort here. On balance, the data simply do not support the assertion that these modernizing influences work consistently and importantly to generate poor personal adjustment as measured by psychosomatic symptoms.

The results obtained should be considered as particularly weighty because the design of our research was rather precisely attuned to the requirements of testing relevant theory, the number of cases involved was quite substantial,[2] and the research was repeated in six developing countries involving a wide range of cultural and structural variability. Our findings are, of course, subject to challenge, and are open to different interpretation. We believe, however, that the upshot of the matter is that the theory which sees the transition from village to city and from farm to factory as inherently deleterious to mental health must be, if not wholly discarded, at least drastically reformulated.

There is the possibility that our results are mainly an artifact of our method, and in particular of the instrument on which we based our diagnosis. Our procedure was to test the null hypothesis, requiring that the subsamples differ by more than a certain amount expected by chance. Failure of the subsamples to so differ was interpreted as casting doubt on the assumption that modernizing experiences generate psychic stress. But if our measuring instrument, the Psychosomatic Symptoms Test, were an inherently unreliable and invalid measure of adjustment, then the probability would be great that the subgroups would not consistently differ in PT score, thus inexorably casting doubt on the theory. While acknowledging that the PT test is not a maximally refined or precise instrument, we affirmed its value on the basis of clinical confirmation from numerous other investigations and the extensive evidence presented in this study that the test has substantial validity. One cannot, therefore, dismiss our findings so easily. They challenge the theory linking modernization and rapid social change to personal disorganization and individual psychic strain.

The second line of defense against our findings is to accept the facts, but to question our particular formulation of the theory we claim to have placed in scientific jeopardy. Everyone in our sample was gainfully employed. This means that even those who were migrants had had the good fortune to find jobs, even if they lived in countries and in times in which very large numbers of their compatriots were without employment and were consequently unable to enjoy the income, security, and good standing in the community which go with having a job. *Everyone* in our sample might, therefore, consider himself fortunate, and this, in turn, could be reflected in a generally low number of symptoms in *all* the subgroups of our research. In addition, whether migrant or not, all the men in our samples were, by the mere fact that they held jobs, defined as successfully *coping* with the requirements of life. And it is precisely this fact of successful coping which the PT test is expected to reflect.

This argument founders on the fact that we found men over the whole range of possible scores on the symptoms test. But even if we were to acknowledge the point, we think that acceptance of this argument nevertheless requires a substantial *reformulation* of the classic version of the theory which charges modernization and rapid social change with responsibility for individual psychic distress. From Jefferson through Dickens to Sorokin and Slotkin the assumption has been that the source of trouble lies in the very institutions of modern life, in industry, in urban life, and in rapid communication. In addition, the frequent transitions from one way of life to another induced by modern conditions have generally been assumed to be disruptive of stable social relations, and hence generative of psychic distress. Indeed, the mere experience of migration in itself, the simple movement from one social setting to another, is widely believed to be highly stressful. We note that these theoretical formulations have not singled out the unemployed in cities as the only ones doomed to psychic distress. They have quite unambiguously condemned the city *as such*, industry *as such*, rapid change *as such*, as the sources of individual maladjustment.

At least when stated in this form the theory cannot stand in the face of our findings. If the modern settings and institutions *in themselves* were more stressful, then on the average urban city workers should show decidedly more symptoms than rural cultivators. And those with *more* contact with the city, the factory, and the mass media should be noticeably less well-adjusted than those with *less* contact. This is *not* true in any consistently significant degree in the several institutional settings we studied in six countries. Nor is it true that those who moved from the countryside to city work consistently and significantly showed more distress than those who escaped this experience, either by remaining on the farm or by being born in the city in the first place.

It may well be that those who move but then fail to find work, and therefore cannot get integrated into the new social setting, do indeed find the process of migration and the experience of modernization deeply disturbing. Our data do not permit us to judge the matter. But our results do require that some of the more popular theories about urbanism, industrialism, modernism, and mental health be reformulated. In themselves urbanization and industrialization *may* breed social disorganization. In turn, social disorganization *may* generate psychic distress. Our data are mute on both of these points. We have measured neither the association of urbanization with social disorganization, nor of social disorganization with individual psychic distress. Our data do, however, decidedly challenge the idea that individuals, *merely because they live in cities and work in industry*, are less well-adjusted than those living in the countryside and working on farms. Our data therefore require that the theory linking the urban transition with psychic distress should—if it is not to be rejected altogether—be reformulated. It can no longer correctly state: "Urbanism and industrialism in developing countries in themselves breed psychic strain."

In the light of our findings the only form of the proposition now acceptable is: "The experience of social disorganization *may* breed individual psychic stress," or, alternatively: "Failure to become integrated in an urban industrial setting *may* generate psychic strain." These revised formulations carry very different policy implications from those arising from the assumption that individual stress is an *inherent* and more or less *universal* accompaniment of industrialization and urbanization. The restated propositions allow for the possibility that there can be industrialization and urbanization without ever-heightened levels of psychic distress in the population. If such forms of industrialization and urbanization can occur, and our results suggest they are occurring, then the jeremiads against industrialization and urbanization must be seen, at least on the issue of mental health, as not resting on any firm foundation of fact.

Finally, we wish to point out that the difficulty with the theory of the urban transition as the cause of psychic stress may lie not so much in an incorrect view of city life as in a mistaken image of what village life is typically like. The theory of the urban transition as extremely psychologically stressful rests on the premise that daily life in the traditional village of almost any non-European culture was *inherently* healthier, from a psychological point of view, than almost anything those village residents might encounter in *any* urban industrial setting elsewhere. The theorists believed the individual in the traditional village to more or less invariably enjoy great economic security (even if at a low standard), willing and helpful cooperation from others, certainty as to his status and rights, dignified treatment in accord with his position, and ample emotional support in times of personal need or crisis.

No doubt such villages exist and have existed. Furthermore, there is no reason to deny that in certain exceptional cultures this idyllic situation prevails even in the average village. But as a description of reality in most peasant villages in the majority of the world's cultures during at least the last several hundred years, the picture sketched above is seriously misleading. This idyll does not describe things as they are. Apart from his ignorance and poverty, the average peasant suffers deep insecurity both in his relation to nature, whence he looks for his sustenance, and in relation to the powerful figures in his village, be they more powerful peasants, rich land owners, or government officials. Under these conditions the villager, more often than not, *cannot* rely on the support of others when he is in need. Family and group quarrels, indeed feuds, are often as much the norm as is harmony. Mistrust is frequently rampant, and fear expressed through belief in witchcraft and sorcery may be endemic. Insult and abuse are as common in the village as elsewhere, and one waits a long while between rounds of respectful and dignified treatment. In short, traditional village life is not necessarily so different from the life of the simple and the poor anywhere else, including those in towns, cities, and industrial centers.

Our purpose in pointing this out is not to paint village life black, but only to highlight the significance of this reality for the theory of the urban transition. However dismal urban life and industrial employment may be, moving to them will not necessarily lead to *greater* psychic distress if the village left behind by the migrant is not as imagined in the idyll, but is rather more ordinarily human in being itself quite a stressful place to live. The fundamental mistake of theorists of the urban transition has been to confuse the ideal forms of the *gemeinschaft* type of social organization with the concrete reality of the individual's situation. If security, calculability, support, trust, respectful treatment, and the like are assumed to make for psychic adjustment, it behooves one to locate these qualities of life where they are and not where one imagines them to be. Our investigation suggests that in developing countries such salubrious experiences are no less enjoyed by those who have moved to the city and have taken up industrial employment than by those who continue to pursue the bucolic life of cultivators in the bosom of their traditional villages.

CHAPTER 13

Modernization, Modernity, and Aging

It has often been suggested that the status of the aged declines with societal modernization. Whether the analysis involves a cross-cultural comparison of several societies differing in level of industrialization or focuses on a single society in various phases of its economic development, it is frequently concluded that the status of the elderly relative to that of other age groups diminishes with a shift from an agricultural to an industrialized economy, or from a "traditional" to a "modern" social system (Cottrell 1960; Cowgill & Holmes 1972; Maxwell 1970; Ogburn & Nimkoff 1940; Palmore 1975; Palmore & Manton 1974; Simmons 1945).

Explanations to account for such decline in prestige usually include reference to changes in social relationships caused by the introduction of new technology. With the development of an industrial economy, for example, and with the accompanying specialization of knowledge and productivity, the aged in a particular society possess fewer marketable skills and current information to use as exchange resources in social interaction. Knowledge and control gained by long experience no longer represent useful barter in economic and social exchange; under such conditions aging may lose whatever value it once represented (Cottrell 1960; Simmons 1945).

Based on such observations Cowgill and Holmes (1972) have presented a formalized theory of aging and modernization generalizable across cultures. Their major postulate—suggested earlier by many writers, but never as adequately formalized nor as extensively documented—stated an inverse

This chapter originally appeared under the authorship of Vern L. Bengston, James J. Dowd, David H. Smith, and Alex Inkeles as "Modernization, Modernity, and Perceptions of Aging: A Cross-Cultural Study," *Journal of Gerontology* 30 (1975): 688–95.

relationship between the status of the aged and the degree of modernization characterizing the social setting (Cowgill & Holmes 1972).

Subsequent data presented by Palmore and Manton (1974) lend considerable independent support for the conventional aging and modernization postulate. Palmore and Manton examined the status of the aged compared to the non-aged by means of an "Equality Index" or "Similarity Index." This method tests the relative position of the elderly with the non-aged population on three separate indicators of social status: occupation, education, and employment, examining the proportion of the two groups' percentage distribution which overlaps on these dimensions (Palmore & Whittington 1971). Their findings, based on comparisons within 31 countries which vary in levels of economic development, indicate that the status of the aged in comparison to other groups within the same society gradually declines from approximate parity in non-Western societies to only one-half of equality in some more "modernized" countries.

Several questions have been raised, however, regarding the adequacy of the traditional aging and modernization hypothesis. The Equality Index of Palmore and associates, for example, has been criticized on methodological grounds, to the effect that it oversimplifies complex relationships and encourages unwarranted interpretations (Johnson 1973; see the rejoinder by Palmore & Whittington 1973). Other more general criticisms are that discussions in this area have often suffered from a romanticized or naive portrayal of eldership in preindustrial societies (Harlan 1964; Slater 1964), and that there is considerable discrepancy between "ritual deference" and actual prestige afforded the aged (Lipman 1970). But perhaps the most serious is the criticism that much previous research testing the modernization and aging hypothesis may be questioned on the basis of the "ecological fallacy" (Robinson 1950). This refers to the error of insufficiently separating various levels of analysis: the societal (or macrosocial) and the individual (microsocial) level of observation. Even if it is true that, at the *societal* level, more modern nations give less status to the aged, it does not automatically follow that, at the *individual* level, persons who have been more modernized hold a negative view of the *elderly*. To assume this connection automatically may be to commit the ecological fallacy.

A clear distinction among concepts and levels of observation must, therefore, be made and then tested empirically. The term *modernization* should be conceived as a societal or macrosocial process, whereas *modernity* here refers to properties of individuals within societies regardless of the degree of modernization of those societies. To assert that there is a high correlation between the modernization of society and the modernity of individuals is not necessarily justified. And to assert an inverse relationship between exposure to modernizing experiences and value attributed to the aged is—in the absence of data clearly indicating such covariation—to run the risk of producing an ecological fallacy.

In this chapter we examine data regarding some perceptions of aging from societies that vary in levels of modernization, and from groups within those societies that differ in exposure to modernizing experiences. It may well be the case, as Cowgill and Holmes, and Palmore and Manton, have suggested, that the status of the aged population within a society varies inversely with the degree of modernization of that society. But the question of association between exposure to modernizing experiences and perception of aged status still remains to be examined. The general hypothesis to be tested in this chapter, then, is that favorable attitudes toward aging and the aged are inversely related to (a) individual modernity (exposure to technology, urbanization, and industrial experience); and (b) societal modernization (gross national product, per capita industrial employment, and degree of Westernization). These hypotheses are examined within the context of "developing" nation-states, in which the rate of social change can be assumed to have been substantial.

METHOD

Data collected as part of the Harvard Project on the Sociocultural Aspects of Development have been utilized in this analysis of modernity and attitudes toward aging. On the basis of gross national product and level of industrialization, the six nations in the study could be arranged in two groups: European-oriented cultures with a moderately high rate of per capita industrial output (Chile, Argentina, Israel) and more traditional, less Westernized societies (Indians from the Bihar State, East Pakistanis, and Yoruba Nigerians) with a lower level of per capita output.

Three items along the numerous questions in the project interview measured attitudes toward aging and the aged. These items were originally included because it was postulated they might be part of an attitudinal configuration of social-psychological modernity (Inkeles and Smith 1974). The questions are:

1. *Perceived instrumental or educational value of the aged.* "Some people say that a boy learns the deepest and most profound truth from old people; others say that a boy learns most from books and in school. What is your opinion?"

2. *Attitude toward own aging.* "Some people look forward to old age with pleasure, while others dread (fear) the coming of old age. How do you personally feel about the coming of old age?"

3. *Norms regarding respect and obligations to the aged.* "What are the obligations (duties) which young people owe to old people? (In Bangladesh, India, Nigeria). Or, "How much obligation does a young man have to obey old people?" and "Do you think that contradicting an old person is incorrect?" (Chile, Argentina, Israel).

While other scales, or differently worded questions, might more adequately characterize orientations to aging, the items included in the Project interview do clearly represent at least part of the total range of attitudes one might use to test the modernity and aging hypothesis. One certainly would expect the attitudinal configuration associated with high prestige of the aged to include the assumption that one learns the most profound truth from the aged, the tendency to look forward to a respected old age with pleasure, and the acceptance of many obligations to the aged. These would be the more "traditional" or less "modern" responses. Taken in conjunction with the Project's special sampling design these items allow an intriguing, if less than exhaustive, cross-cultural test of the modernity and aging hypothesis.

So that we could most directly test for the ecological fallacy, we stated our hypotheses in the form dictated by the discussion above. First, in accord with what the literature had shown it was hypothesized that societal

TABLE 13-1

Distribution of Respondents Within Three Occupational Groups in Six Countries

	Occupational Groups			
Country	*Cultivators* (C)	*Urban Nonindustrials* (UNI)	*Factory Workers* (FW)	*Total*
Bangladesh (Pakistan)	234	112	654	1000
India	350	250	700	1300
Nigeria	100	101	519	720
Chile	109	106	668	883
Argentina	98	55	662	815
Israel	102	92	538	732
Totals	993	716	3741	5450

modernization will be associated with negative perceptions of aging so that individuals in "modern" societies would have less positive evaluations of the aged than those individuals from less "modern" societies. Second, we hypothesized that individual modernity (or exposure to modernizing experiences) would be associated with more negative attitudes toward aging and the aged. According to this hypothesis one would anticipate, for example, that urban factory workers would have less positive evaluations of the aged and aging than would rural cultivators. Our readers should be aware that we were quite dubious about the correctness of this second hypothesis. It was our position, as noted in chapter 2, that we did not follow the dominant opinion that individual modernity necessarily led to less respect for, and less value of, the elders. But we put the hypothesis here in the form in which most analysts would have stated it, leaving open, thus, the chance that the data might contradict it.

The method used to test these hypotheses is based on what has been termed "structural analysis" (Riley 1963). The countries are arrayed by degree of modernization, and the samples within each country are arrayed according to the individuals' degree of exposure to modernizing experience. The proportion of individuals exhibiting the traditional or "non-modern" response is obtained for each segment of the samples thus defined. The data are then analyzed in terms of: (a) six within-country comparisons of the three occupational categories, as a test of the modernity hypothesis; and (b) segmental comparisons of each of the three occupational groups taken separately across the six countries, as a test of the modernization hypothesis. The within-country comparisons control, in effect, for degree of societal modernization. Similarly, comparing each "segment" (or occupational grouping) across the six nations allows for control of the degree of exposure to modernizing experience. This method has been discussed in detail (illustrated with hypothetical data from the Inkeles study design) by Riley and Nelson (1971).

To test our hypotheses we must see whether or not the dependent variable, i.e., positive attitudes toward the aged, is randomly distributed among segments of the sample throughout the six countries and the three occupational groups. A systematic distribution of responses, such that the countries ranking lowest on measures of modernization would also show the greatest proportion of respondents with pro-aging attitudes, would be supportive of the *modernization* hypothesis, which predicts an inverse relationship between degree of societal modernization and positive attitudes toward the aged. Similarly, should the proportion of respondents with positive attitudes toward the aged be differentially distributed among

the occupational groups, such that those with least exposure to modernizing experiences, namely the cultivators, gave a higher proportion of pro-
aging responses, then the *modernity* hypothesis would be supported.
Given the analysis model we are using here it would be possible to find that
both hypotheses were correct, only one, or neither. Let us now see how it
turned out.

RESULTS

Perceived instrumental or educational value of the aged. Table 13-2
presents the distribution of responses to the first item from each nation.
Values in the table refer to the percentage of each subsample which chose
what we treated as the least modern of the three possible responses, namely
"the old," the other two responses being "from books" and "from both
books and the old." In the table, samples from each nation are divided into
groups reflecting differential exposure to modernizing experiences: rural
cultivators, urban nonindustrial workers, and urban factory workers.

Analysis of the differences between the three subsamples in each nation
produces equivocal support of the hypothesis regarding modernity. In only
three of the six countries did the occupational group least exposed to
modernizing experiences—the cultivators—have the greatest proportion of
respondents choosing the "traditional" response.

Only in Argentina and Israel does the hypothesis receive strong
support—cultivators more often chose "old," and factory workers more
often chose "books and school." The hypothesis of a universal inverse
association between individual modernity and a perception of instrumental value of the aged cannot in general be substantiated by this result.

The second hypothesis—predicting an inverse relationship between
societal modernization and positive perceptions of aging and the aged—
received stronger empirical support. With the method of segmental
comparisons suggested by Riley and Nelson (1971), if degree of societal
modernization was indeed unrelated to the dependent variable, the rank
ordering of countries by proportion of pro-aging responses should
approximate a random distribution. This is, however, not the case.
Examining each of the occupational groupings across separate nations
(table 13-2) one observes verification of the modernization hypothesis.
Among the urban factory workers, the three countries with the lowest
proportion of pro-aging responses are the three more modern societies—
Israel, Argentina, and Chile. The same pattern occurs with the urban
nonindustrial workers.

TABLE 13-2

Perceived Instrumental Value of the Aged: Percentage by Occupation and Country Choosing "A Boy Learns Most From the Old"[a]

Occupational Group		Bangladesh	India	Nigeria	Chile	Argentina	Israel
Cultivators		19.8	39.4	66.0	8.83	31.6	30.0
Urban non-industrial workers		30.4	39.6	59.4	7.6	18.2	14.3
Urban factory workers		24.0	34.1	57.8	9.8	9.5	10.0
Totals	N	226	474	425	87	104	90
	%	24.0	36.6	59.3	9.3	12.8	13.6

[a] Cell entries do not add up to 100% because they reflect proportions of respondents choosing only one of three alternative responses. Thus, the table should be read: Of the Bangladesh cultivators, 19.8% (35 of the 177 who responded to this question) chose the more "traditional" response, "A boy learns most from the old."

With the third occupational group, the cultivators, the hypothesis also receives support, with one exception. The proportion of cultivators from Bangladesh who volunteered a pro-aging response was smaller than predicted. The proportions obtained in the five remaining countries are, however, consistent with the modernization hypothesis.

Attitude toward own aging. In examining the hypothesis that a positive attitude toward the aging process is inversely related to individual modernity and societal modernization, it should first be noted how relatively few in this sample of "becoming modern" young men suggest that they dread the coming of old age (18 percent). Over half chose the neutral category, "neither dread nor look forward."

Table 13-3 presents the percentage in each sample responding that they "look forward to old age." Comparing first the differences between occupational groups within each country, the data show that the rural cultivators are not the most likely to choose the traditional, least modern response. In fact, in four of the six nations in this sample they are the least likely of the three groups to respond that they "look forward to old age." Such data do not support the hypothesis of any direct relationship between individual modernity and negative attitudes toward aging.

Societal modernization, on the other hand, does seem directly related to the individual's attitude toward aging. Individuals in the three less modern countries, taken collectively, show a greater frequency of looking forward to old age than do those in the three more modern societies.

TABLE 13-3

*Attitude Toward One's Own Aging: Percentage by Occupation
and Country Choosing "Await or Look Forward to Old Age"*[a]

Occupational Group		Bangladesh	India	Nigeria	Chile	Argentina	Israel
Cultivators		32.8	60.5	59.0	16.5	46.9	33.6
Urban non-industrial workers		37.8	46.1	67.3	24.5	16.4	45.7
Urban factory workers		35.8	44.4	77.2	29.7	29.2	35.4
Totals	N	334	632	527	242	234	239
	%	35.4	49.1	73.3	27.6	28.8	36.5

[a] Cell entries can be read as follows: Of the total sample from Bangladesh, 35.5% (334 of 943) of the respondents chose the "traditional" response: they "look forward to old age."

Analyzing each occupational group separately, it becomes clear that, as with the previous variable, the rank ordering of occupational groups does not approximate a random distribution. Among factory workers, for example, the countries with the higher proportions of pro-aging responses are the three traditional societies—Bangladesh, India, and Nigeria. Among cultivators and urban nonindustrial workers, India and Nigeria are the individual societies with the highest proportion of respondents answering that they look forward to the coming of old age. Bangladesh represents the single anomaly in each of the segmental comparisons of cultivators and urban nonindustrial workers.

TABLE 13-4

*Mean Number of Obligations Which Young People
Owe to Old People, by Occupation and Country*[a]

Country	Occupational Group					
	Cultivator		Urban Nonindustrial		Urban Factory Worker	
	x	S.D.	x	S.D.	x	S.D.
Bangladesh	2.62	0.84	2.52	0.75	2.71	0.88
India	2.15	0.63	2.26	0.73	2.01	0.61
Nigeria	2.17	0.75	2.39	0.83	2.51	0.88

[a] In these less modernized nations the number of different types of obligations mentioned by the respondents was recorded; means are based on the number of obligations mentioned. The higher the mean, the higher the perceived obligation to the old on this open-ended question.

TABLE 13-5

Perceptions of Amount of Duty to Obey
Old People, by Occupation and Country[a]

Country	Occupational Group					
	Cultivator		*Urban Nonindustrial*		*Urban Factory Worker*	
	x	S.D.	x	S.D.	x	S.D.
Chile	3.42	0.66	3.01	0.79	3.48	0.72
Argentina	3.65	0.67	3.45	0.78	3.52	0.70
Israel	3.21	0.75	3.19	0.86	3.17	0.68

[a] Fixed-alternative response scored as "4" (much) to "1" (no obligation). Thus the higher the mean, the higher the perceived obligation to obey the old.

Norms regarding respect and obligations to the aged. With regard to norms requiring deference or obligations to the aged, the general modernity hypothesis suggests that the internalization of such norms is inversely related to individual modernity. That is, individuals with a greater degree of exposure to modernizing experiences should enumerate fewer obligations that youth owe to the aged.

In Bangladesh, India, and Nigeria, the open-ended question was asked, "What are the obligations (duties) which young people owe old people?" The respondent was encouraged to think of as many obligations as he could; these then were coded. The mean number of different types of obligations is presented in table 13-4.

In Chile, Israel, and Argentina, a fixed-alternative question was asked regarding how much obligation a young man has to obey old people. Responses ranged from "no obligation" (transformer score = 1) to "much obligation" (scored 4). Means are presented in table 13-5.

The modernity hypothesis is not supported by the data. In Nigeria and Bangladesh, the mean number of obligations mentioned by experienced factory workers is actually slightly greater than the number mentioned by cultivators. In the three more modern societies (Chile, Argentina, and Israel), only slight differences appear between factory workers and cultivators. In Israel, the differences in means among all three occupational groups totaled only 0.04. It is interesting to note that, in Chile and Argentina, it is the urban nonindustrial workers—the "middle-modernity" occupational category—who perceived the fewest obligations to the aged.

Within each society it appears that the effects of modernization on individual modernity and the consequent effects of modernity on attitudes toward the aged is negligible. Contrary to the frequent assumption of an inverse relationship between modernity and positive attitudes toward the aged, exposure to modernizing experiences does not consistently detract from the internalization of norms prescribing respect for the aged.

DISCUSSION

Results for three questions from the Harvard Project data suggest that positive attitudes toward aging and the aged do appear inversely related to the degree of societal modernization, thus supporting the traditional modernization and aging hypothesis. The data do not support the modernity hypothesis, that the amount of individual exposure to modernizing experiences within the society is inversely related to positive perceptions of aging. In fact some of the data support the alternative hypothesis: the greater the modernity, the more positive the attitudes of individuals toward aging and the aged.

Such results question many previously affirmed expectations and emphasize the necessity of distinguishing between modernity and modernization. the zero-order relationships of exposure to modernizing experiences with the attitudes toward aging variables account for less than 5 percent of the variance, compared with regression analyses explaining from 20 to 50 percent of the variance on items reflecting efficacy, fatalism, and information as combined in an "Overall Modernity" score, as reported in chapters 4 and 5. The present findings, therefore, must be taken seriously as an indication that individual modernizing experiences, although they may have powerful effects on other attitudinal variables associated with modernity, do not have an important and consistent impact on attitudes toward aging and the aged.

By contrast the evidence brought to bear on the hypothesis specifying decreased relative status of the aged with increasing modernization is generally supportive. This is not to suggest that the absolute position of the aged in less-industrialized societies compares favorably with that of the aged in more industrialized societies. Harlan (1964), Lipman (1970), and Slater (1964) are correct in noting that physical survival in contemporary society is much less a day-to-day consideration among the aged than it was earlier. Palmore and Manton (1974) agree, observing that the aged in more modernized societies usually have a higher standard of living than the aged in less modern societies. However, compared with younger age cohorts within the same society, the relative value assigned the aged continues to decline with increasing societal modernization.

While structural changes accompanying modernization certainly may undercut the special position of the aged, it had been the view of the Harvard Project that many analysts had exaggerated the corrosive effects of industrialism on the treatment of the aged. We had, instead, argued that:

> Nothing in urban living *per se* requires a person to show disrespect for the aged, and nothing in industrial experience explicitly teaches a man to abandon the aged. Many old men and women in the villages have been abandoned by their children because the children lacked the means to support them. Steadier wages and generally more stable conditions of life for those gainfully employed in industry could well enable those who enjoyed these benefits to be more exacting in their fulfillment of obligations to old people. And they might well be as respectful of the aged as their more traditional counterparts farming in the villages. (Inkeles, 1973a)

We should also note an additional important caveat with respect to the apparent support for the "modernization" hypothesis which our results seem to offer. In this study the three more "modernized" societies are also the three more Western. Whether societal modernization leads to changed views of the aged can properly be established only by considering the degree of development within a set of countries more or less culturally homogeneous. Otherwise one runs the grave risk of inappropriately assuming that a long-standing cultural value is a new view based on the stimulus of economic development.

Perhaps the most important message of these data, and the greatest criticism of the traditional modernization and aging hypothesis, involves the necessity to differentiate between modernization and modernity. The term modernization refers to various societal processes of urbanization, literacy, social mobility, mass media communications, a mature industrial plant, and a democratic polity (Portes 1973b). Consequently, analyses of societal modernization must be considered apart from evidence collected at a more micro-level as, for example, individual manifestations of upward or downward mobility, urban or rural residence, utilization of the mass media, or participation in the political system of a society. These latter variables are more appropriately considered as evidence reflecting the presence of the attitudinal syndrome identified as individual modernity (Inkeles & Smith 1974). Similarly, the status of the aged in any society refers to the collective position of that particular age cohort (usually defined as 65 years or above) with reference to any of several status attributes, including occupational prestige, income, education, or employment status. Knowing someone's status as elderly does not permit one to conclude automatically that he or she experiences disrespect, neglect, or abandonment. The formal status of the elderly as a social group in a given society may be correlated with the treatment they receive as individuals, but the two sets of attributes are, nevertheless, theoretically and practically distinct.

Thus, to test the hypothesis that the status of the aged generally decreases with modernization it is necessary to have data demonstrating that the average income, education, or occupational prestige of the aged vis-à-vis younger aged cohorts decreases with increased urbanization, industrialization, literacy rates, etc. (see, for example, the analysis of Palmore & Manton 1974). Investigations of the relationship between the possession of "modern" (vs. "traditional") values and perceptions of the aged, while an intriguing area of possible research, pose a different question and reflect a different interest than that addressed by Cowgill and Holmes (1972). Consequently, in specifying the nature of the relationship between one of these two sets of variables, we do not necessarily say anything concerning the relationship between the remaining set.

The lack of a strict synchronization between modernization and modernity, as exhibited in the present study with respect to attitudes toward aging and the aged, can be readily inferred from other recently published research. For example, it is observed that traditional value orientations tend to persist during periods of accelerated economic and social development and, in fact, serve to legitimize the resulting transformations in the social order (Armer & Schnaiberg 1972; Portes 1973a; Singer 1971). Similarly, data derived from empirical studies of various "developed" societies (such as Finland, Japan, Germany, and industrialized Brazil) lead to the conclusion that the extended family system and patterns of family interaction with kin remain relatively stable regardless of the state of societal modernization (Lueschen, Blood, Lewis, Staikof, Stolte-Heiskanne, & Ward 1971; Rosen & LaRaia 1972; Palmore 1975; Palmore and Manton 1974).

SUMMARY

The relationship between modernization and the position of aged persons in society has been discussed by many social scientists in recent years. Most often it has been asserted that the position of elders suffers in the course of dramatic social change: as traditional social structures become "modernized" through technological advances and contact with more industrialized social systems, deference toward elderly individuals declines and attitudes toward aging become less favorable. Some scholars, however, have challenged this hypothesis, noting the great variability within "traditional" societies and the tendency for Western writers to romanticize the virtues of pre-industrial cultures.

The purpose of this chapter was to explore data from a comparative cross-cultural study of 5,450 men, aged 18–32, in six developing nations regarding the association between attitudes toward aging and (a) individual exposure to modernizing experiences and (b) social modernization.

We found that: (a) perception of the instrumental or educational value of old people is not consistently inversely related to degree of individual modernity; (b) positive attitudes toward one's own aging are not inversely related to modernity; (c) obligations toward and perceptions of the aged are not inversely related to modernity. But we also found that societal modernization is inversely related to each of these perceptions.

In short, a simple formula anticipating more negative views of the aged with increasing individual modernity is not consistently supported by the evidence. This outcome was anticipated in the theoretical perspective of the Harvard Project, even though its position ran counter to the predominant view held by most observers. The critical point to be considered in present and future investigations is the possibility that individual modernity and societal modernization each manifest a different pattern of relationship to certain aspects of social life such as aging. The two hypotheses should be tested separately. Thus the Cowgill-Holmes (1972) hypothesis, supported by the data of Palmore and Manton (1974), may be correct, i.e., there is an inverse relationship between modernization and status of the aged. Yet at the same time, as indicated by the data presented here, there may be no such association between individual modernity and attitudes toward the aged.

PART SIX

AT THE FRONTIER

CHAPTER 14

The Modernization of Man
in Communist Countries

One element in the ideology of every social movement is a conception of the character of the people as they are and a vision of what they should be like. In those movements which seek to transform the religious order, concern for such characterological issues often lies at the very heart of the movement.[1] But even in movements oriented mainly toward transforming the economic and political order, ideas about the nature of man and his social relations are always decidedly central concerns. If, therefore, we are to comprehend the processes of social change induced and guided by the revolutionary communist parties in the countries in which they have taken power, it is indispensable that we discover and understand their conception of man's social character as it is and as it should become.

In this chapter we advance the idea that the leaders of the two great communist revolutionary movements of our time—those of Russia and China—sought to bring about a transformation of human character and social relations having much in common with the more spontaneous process of change which has characterized other developing countries.[2] No doubt in the socialist countries the process of modernization has been more self-conscious, the goals more explicitly stated, and the resources employed to attain those goals more massive. Nevertheless, it is our position that, far from being a unique historical process, the struggle to create a new type of "socialist man" has been only a special case of the more pervasive concern to convert people who express traditional values and act in traditional

This chapter was originally published as Alex Inkeles, "The Modernization of Man in Socialist and Nonsocialist Countries," in Mark G. Field, ed., *Social Consequences of Modernization in Communist Societies* (Baltimore: Johns Hopkins Press, 1976), pp. 50–59.

modes into men and women who in attitude, value, and action may be called modern.

TWO MODELS OF MAN IN SOCIAL MOVEMENTS

In radical movements, we may distinguish two main perspectives on the issue of character and human relations. One of these I will designate the populist, and other the elitist perspective. Neither term is to be taken as an evaluation, let alone as pejorative.

The elite of populist movements view themselves and their immediate class associates as embodying qualities which are decadent, corrupt, even evil. These must be extirpated, and a new set of personal characteristics and patterns of human relations must replace them as the social ideal and, indeed, as the daily norm. Generally these new qualities are considered not so much new as lost or atrophied. Followers of the movement assume that the lost virtues can be found still alive and vitally expressed somewhere among "the people"—usually this means in the traditional village or among simple, unsophisticated working folk who, precisely because they have been out of the mainstream, bypassed by history, are seen as having preserved in pristine form sterling qualities of character and noble patterns of human relations which should now become the standard for all. In varying degrees this orientation characterized the Narodniki in Russia, reemerging in a peculiar variant in the Zionist movement; it was the basis of much of American midwestern populism; it was built into Ghandism in India; and it made up a substantial element of the contemporary American youth's counterculture.

In the elitist orientation we turn over the coin. Rather than believing that the masses embody the most valued characteristics, the elitist perspective considers the personal qualities of the rank and file to be precisely the main problem obstructing the progress of the historical movement. The masses are passive when they should be active; they are accommodating when they should be uncompromising; they forgive when they should be unrelenting in the pursuit of vengeance; they diffuse their energies when they should be highly organized under tight discipline; they are carried away by passions about trivial matters when they should concentrate their attention exclusively on the really basic structural issues. In this view the masses cannot hope to fulfill their historic mission unless their character is transformed; that is, until they are made over into a new model of man. And, *mirabile dictu*, the embodiment of this new model is already at hand in the very person of the revolutionary vanguard. That vanguard has only to bestir itself, to expose the masses to the possible, and the masses have only to learn from and emulate the vanguard, to insure that reeducation which is essential to achieving the desired revolutionary transformation of man and society.

No doubt this typology, like all schemes of this kind, is crude and exaggerated. Yet it seems to me that these two very general polarized models define a dimension along which we can, without great distortion, locate any radical political movement, whether of the left or of the right.

In the case of Marxism-Leninism I would argue that although the movement incorporated some elements of populism, it was in general decidedly weighted toward the elitist pole of the dichotomy.

The populist element in Marxism-Leninism is found mainly in the mystique which surrounds the conception of the proletariat. In Marx's view history had assigned this class the unique role of transforming capitalism into communism, bringing man to his highest stage of social development. The proletariat was considered able to fulfill this historic mission because its relation to the means of production had schooled it in the organization and rationality essential to running an industrial civilization. Since postcapitalist *society* was to rest on the principles underlying modern industrial production, the anticipated transformation was inevitable and the role of the proletariat as its guide was a historical necessity.

Yet there was a catch. Apart from the propensity of the outmoded ruling classes to use force to prevent change, there existed an additional impediment to the otherwise inevitable transformation of capitalist society. The obstacle lay in the unhappy fact that large segments of the proletariat did not, in fact, incorporate in their persons the qualities which, theoretically, their class membership should have conferred on them. "False consciousness," especially as embodied in religious belief and practice, diffused throughout the proletariat living in even the most advanced capitalist countries a set of historically inappropriate and politically undesirable values, attitudes, and modes of interpersonal relations.

Marx never resolved the issue of what to do about false consciousness. He seemed to assume either that it would in time erode under the impact of the increasing impoverishment of the proletariat, or that it would not matter when weighed against other historic forces which would engulf the capitalist systems and lead to the institutionalization of socialism. Lenin, however, confronted the issue head-on. Lenin's special contribution to Communist theory lay precisely in his instinct for the jugular in this matter. He broke the impasse into which the element of populism in Marx had led the Communist movement by decisively reorienting it in the direction I have designated as elitist.

Lenin's position first became unmistakably apparent in the pages of *What Is To Be Done?* With great force he argued that the revolution could not be expected to develop spontaneously because the masses lacked a revolutionary consciousness. History therefore required a small, dedicated, tightly organized band of professional revolutionaries to carry the movement forward. Lenin argued that one of the central tasks of this movement was to instill in the masses qualities which were lacking, to teach organization and discipline, to heighten awareness, and to stir consciousness. The model to be emulated was provided by the devoted professional revolutionary, who brought this image to the masses "from outside." This "outside" was, as a gesture to the founding fathers, given sanction by insisting it was actually a part of the proletariat, only that part which was the more conscious, developed "vanguard." Despite Lenin's resort to this rationale, however, I see no way in which we can correctly read Lenin's argument, and his early practice in guiding the Communist Party, other than by recognizing that he had moved Marxism, or at least his branch of it, decisively to the pole which I have labeled elitist.

THE SOVIET APPROACH TO INDIVIDUAL MODERNIZATION

When they came to power in 1917, Lenin and his cohorts faced some problems unique to their situation, and others certainly rather distinctive. Nevertheless, many aspects of the situation they confronted were similar to those which have faced the leaders of any number of less developed countries over the past two or three decades. These problems were not all economic, political, or military, but also included as central elements a set which may be designated psychocultural. They found that the character of the population—in particular its modes of living and interacting with nature, man, and society—was not such as to maximize the people's integration into the new and more dynamic social order the Revolution sought to establish.

Some of the indicators of Soviet Russia's under-development were the obvious ones of low levels of literacy and inadequate development of schools; limited diffusion of the means of mass communication; high birth rates coupled with high mortality rates; overwhelming concentration of the population in village agriculture, and concomitant low levels of industrialization. These objective conditions were, inevitably, linked to subjective factors. One segment of the population in Czarist Russia was already over the threshold of psychological modernity by 1917; but this group constituted a very thin stratum of society, limited to part of the intelligentsia, some segments of the industrial and commercial middle class, and a very modest portion of the small urban industrial labor force. The rest of the society, in varying degree, expressed the prototypical orientations of tradition-bound men.

In our research on individual modernization we have established that there is a set of personal qualities which cohere as a syndrome empirically designating a type of man we may properly call modern.[3] The use of the term modern to characterize this syndrome is justified on two grounds. The first, purely theoretical, justifies this usage on the basis of face validity. That is, the content of the questions used in the scales fits our theoretical concept of individual modernity. In addition, use of the criterion method also justifies designating this syndrome as modern. The men manifesting it are more often found among those with more formal schooling, and among users of the mass media, urban residents, and, most important, persons who work in industry or other parts of the modern sector of the economy.

Each element in this syndrome has its analogue in the agenda that Lenin, Stalin, and the entire Communist Party program developed for transforming the Soviet population into a mobilized, industrialized, centralized, and bureaucratized nation. To make the point clear, we present below the main components of the modernity syndrome as we developed it on the basis of men in six noncommunist developing nations. The description of each element of this model of modern man is accompanied by a brief indication of how the theme is relevant to the official conception of the ideal Soviet citizen.[4]

Before we present these juxtaposed models, however, it is essential to sound several cautionary notes. First, the qualities of the modern man as described below should be recognized as relative rather than absolute. Thus, when we say that modern men have shifted their allegiance to leaders of public as against more primordial associations, we mean that this is true only *by comparison* with more traditional men in the same culture. This definition does not require that to be modern a man must have cut all, or even most, of his ties and allegiances to leaders of primary institutions. Second, one must realize that any general model must be used selectively and with discernment when it is applied to a concrete historical situation. Thus, in the Soviet context an intensified reaffirmation of primordial ties with one's ethnic or religious group may be, in certain exceptional situations, characteristic of the most modern rather than the less modern men. This appears to be the case, for example, among Soviet Jews who have attained scientific eminence. Such special cases should not, however, mislead one as to the applicability of the model in most situations. Third, we should note an important difference in the degree to which the two models juxtaposed below can qualify as empirical reality. The model of modern man has been tested empirically, and extensively so. The model of the ideal Soviet citizen, by contrast, remains a mere construct formulated by students of Soviet affairs through an analysis of programmatic utterances found in official sources.

Element 1: The modern man asserts increasing independence from the authority of traditional figures like parents and priests and shifts allegiance to leaders of government, public affairs, trade unions, cooperatives, and the like.

The continuous and continuing preoccupation of the Soviet regime with shifting individual loyalties from primal groupings to other objects, most notably to the Communist Party and the Soviet state, is of course one of the most extensively documented features of Soviet history. Its most dramatic manifestations were in the early campaigns against the influence of the "bourgeois family" and the Orthodox church. At later stages in Soviet development, increasingly intense efforts were focused on developing strong loyalty to the Soviet state, a campaign which from outside has often seemed, to put it mildly, intensely nationalistic.

Throughout, the idea of devotion to the Communist Party and absolute commitment to the support of its leadership, summed up in the idea of *partiinost*, has been vigorously indoctrinated. Indeed, over the decades from 1930 to 1950 the intensity of this effort, especially in the form of extreme concentration on the theme of loyalty and devotion to the person of Stalin, earned it the Soviets' own designation as "the cult of personality." Since Stalin's death, of course, the situation has been normalized. At the same time, the long-term objective has been attained. In some isolated regions of the Soviet Union loyalty to extended kinship networks, to tribe, or even to local religious leaders may still take precedence over allegiance to the Soviet state. On the whole, however, by the end of World War II, certainly by 1970, it could be said, with regard to this first component of the syndrome of individual modernity, that the overwhelming majority of the Soviet people had almost entirely and rather solidly established themselves on the modern side of the line.

Element 2: The modern man shows a strong interest in and takes an active part in civic and community affairs and in local politics.

Meeting this particular requirement of individual modernity in the

Soviet context has involved some ambiguity, and at times has been fraught with considerable tension. In the Soviet Union active participation in local civic and community affairs does not mean participation in an autonomous role as an individual or as a member of a group organized around self-determined objectives. Rather, it means participation in the tasks of building socialism as those tasks are identified, and the means for attaining them specified, by the Party leadership. Within those limits, however, this element of the syndrome of individual modernity has been decidedly emphasized in the model of the Soviet citizen favored by the system. Actively working in the local party organization, serving as an agitator, participating in the special campaigns of the trade unions and other collective organizations, and writing letters to the editor are some of the activities the Soviet citizen is expected to undertake as an active participant in the larger program for building socialism.

Element 3: The modern man strives energetically to keep up with the news, and within this framework prefers news of national and international import to items dealing with sports, religion, or purely local affairs.

The persistent Soviet concern with achieving the fullest development of the media of mass communication and the fullest involvement of the population in the diffusion of a new world view is so well documented as to need no elaboration. News and information concerning the process of national development and, to a lesser extent, news of foreign affairs have been the almost exclusive ingredients of Soviet mass communications. Religious events are of course not reported at all, and sports news plays a very minor role indeed.

Element 4: The modern man is open to new experience, to new ways of doing things in his orientation to nature, to mechanical things, and to interpersonal relations.

The Soviet system has not, of course, encouraged the notion that one ought to experiment with politics, and has not permitted its people to entertain the idea that any system other than that based on the absolute and exclusive leadership of the Communist party is worth serious consideration. In a great many other respects, however, the Soviet system has a long history of experimentation with new forms of social organization in the family, in the school, in agriculture, and in industry. One of the objectives of the regime has always been to train citizens in the ready acceptance of such innovation, especially as it might apply to technological change—as in the introduction of new machinery, new techniques, or new ways of relating the labor force to its tasks in production.

Element 5: The modern man believes in the efficacy of science and medicine and in general eschews passivity and fatalism in the face of life's difficulties. He believes that men can learn to master their environment. In brief, he expresses a sense of both personal and social efficacy.

The commitment to transform nature and society in order to make them conform to man's conception of the good is at the heart of the communist world view. Its particular Soviet form is manifested in the concept of "building socialism," and its concrete expression is in all the vast works of construction which are so typical of Soviet economic activity. The role of the Dnieper Dam as a kind of shrine of the secular religion of construc- tionism, and the later near-deification of the first Soviet cosmonauts, provide relevant illustrations. Passivity, let alone fatalism, is in the Soviet context treated almost as a cardinal sin. To be a Bolshevik is to be one who can overcome all obstacles. Training in the assertion of "will," especially the will to build and to accomplish, is an essential ingredient in the curriculum at all levels of Soviet education.

Element 6: Closely related to the theme of efficacy is the modern man's concern with the mastery of time, the institution of routines dominated by the clock, which orientation is itself only a special case of a larger concern with planning things in advance as a basic component in both personal and national affairs.

The struggle of the Soviet regime to discipline the sense of time of the Soviet population, and especially of the new recruits to industry who flocked in from the countryside, is by now legendary. The struggle was, of course, greatly complicated by the fact that individuals had great difficulty in securing home conditions sufficiently stable to enable them to respond to the imperatives of the clock at the factory and the office. The problem was further complicated by the unreliability of the system of urban public transportation. By the end of World War II, and certainly by 1970, these issues seemed largely to have been resolved.

So far as planning is concerned, little need be said. The emphasis on planning is perhaps the single most distinctive feature of the Soviet political-economic system, and the efforts to involve the entire population in commitment to plan fulfillment are widely known.

Element 7: The modern man expresses an interest in maximizing his personal opportunities to achieve education, to acquire skill, and to improve his personal condition, and he particularly holds high aspirations for his children's education and occupational attainment.

This element of the syndrome of individual modernity is in some ways an extension of the finding that the modern man is efficacious rather than passive or fatalistic. He does not accept his station or condition in life as given or fixed, but rather strives energetically to improve it. In the modern industrial milieu, acquiring additional education and skill, and excelling in production, are among the main channels for the expression of such ambitions. In the Soviet case the elimination of private enterprise, and the sharp restrictions on the accumulation and use of private property, lead people to concentrate their efforts to improve their condition almost exclusively on acquiring additional education or skill, except for that minority which prefers the path of power within the framework of the Party apparatus.

THE CHINESE CASE

The unfolding of Chinese communism has in certain important respects been distinctly different from Soviet development. Nevertheless, certain broad features of the challenge which Mao and his collaborators faced upon consolidating their power in mainland China were very similar to those confronting Lenin and Stalin in their efforts to modernize Soviet Russia. The qualities the Chinese leadership wishes to inculcate in its citizens are clearly reflected in the guidebooks for teachers, and in the readers prescribed for children in the early grades of school. From an analysis of these readers and guidebooks, which have been summarized in some detail by Ridley, Godwin, and Doolin (1971), it is apparent how thoroughly the concern for qualities we have identified with the modern man permeates the educational process in Communist China.[5]

For example, the teacher is charged with "fostering the child's constructiveness, capacity for planning, and creativity" (p. 46). Instruction under the rubric of "life guidance" has as its prime objective "the cultivation of the child's capacity for self-awareness and autonomy, his revolutionary ideology, and his spirit of patriotism and internationalism" (p. 49). To attain these objectives the teacher is urged to adopt "the methods of competitions and challenges in order to elevate the children's initiative and enterprise" (p. 50). As the basic principle of "communist morality" the child should be taught "to oppose all oppression of man by man; to struggle for the liberation of all workers irrespective of race or nationality from every form of exploitation" (p. 54).

The objectives sketched for educators in their guidebooks are reflected in the main themes of the stories in children's readers. These readers include a heavy component of information, ranging from descriptions of the general social organization of communist and traditional China, the Communist Party, and the People's Liberation Army, through rudiments of scientific knowledge, to matters of simple personal hygiene. These stories of course teach that the old society was virtually all bad, and that the new society is decidedly all good. Of particular importance to us, however, are the beliefs and values about daily life which are taught, the personal orientations fostered, and the individual qualities favored by the materials presented in the readers. Thus, under the heading of "beliefs about work" the analysis of readers shows that they encourage the belief that: "Any goal can be achieved by hard work"; "A scientific approach to problems ensures their solution"; "Nature can be conquered by study of natural laws and hard work."

Moreover, the personal characteristics which the readers treat as especially praiseworthy and deserving of emulation include being a person who is: "industrious in work and study"; "diligent and persistent, especially in the face of hardship"; "achievement and goal oriented, desiring to achieve"; "dedicated to the building of the 'new' society"; "prudent and with foresight" (pp. 191–92).

In this agenda for child socialization one may clearly discern most of the themes we earlier identified as characterizing the modern man: allegiance to national and supralocal organizations; active participation in civic affairs; personal ambition coupled with initiative and autonomy; interest in keeping informed about public affairs; belief in science; a sense of personal and social efficacy; openness to innovation and new experience, and so on.

To point up this broad congruence between the elements of our model of the modern man and the mold in which the Chinese leadership seeks to cast its youth is not to deny that there are important differences in emphasis between the Soviet and Chinese cases, and between each of them and countries that have developed, or are developing, under conditions of capitalism or with mixed economies. For example, the Chinese model places exceptionally heavy emphasis on qualities important to being a good farmer, and on the related theme of frugality, whereas the Soviet ideal citizen tends to be either the highly skilled industrial worker or the scientist-professional. Moreover, both the Soviet and the Chinese models approach the theme of individual expression and personal autonomy quite differently from the way that theme is expressed by modern men in noncommunist countries. The former give much more emphasis to group goals, to collective interests, and to communal rather than to individual progress.

Nevertheless, there is an unmistakable congruence between the model of the modern man as he emerges from the study of the less developed nations in the noncommunist world and as the Soviet and Chinese systems define the qualities of their ideal citizen. This similarity in emphasis, so far transcending the limits of time, geography, and culture, suggests that there are common problems faced by all developing countries in shaping their populations to a new standard of value and conduct meant to suit them for fuller and more effective participation in the emerging urban industrial order of society.

VICISSITUDES OF INDIVIDUAL MODERNIZATION

Our models of the process of individual modernization are, of course, too abstract. We draw a line from traditionalism to modernity, and then place individuals along it as we might move the pieces in a game. A is so far along the continuum on this dimension, and B on that. In so doing we gloss over the conflict, the struggles, the dilemmas, and the costs of individual modernization.

Take, for example, the shift of primal loyalty from the tribe, the sect, and the family to the nation, the state, the party, the commune, or the trade union. In the novels of Achebe we have an exceptionally revealing and sensitive account of the strains men experience as they struggle with the conflict of loyalty to clan and family in a modernizing Nigeria.[6] The grim history of the efforts to break the hold of the Orthodox church on the allegiance of the devout and faithful in the Soviet Union are not soon forgotten. Comparable accounts from China's experience are still largely kept hidden from us; but we can easily imagine the strains that must have been created by the demand of total devotion to the commands of the state and its local commune in a culture in which the Confucian canon defined obligation to family and devotion to parents as the supreme duty.

The contradictions are of course not limited to those between the demands of the traditional and the requirements of the modern. Indeed, many of the most interesting tensions are those between conflicting elements within the definition of the ideal modern man. Thus, the modern industrial order requires a man who takes initiative—is autonomous, self-starting, and self-directing. Yet it also requires him to relate to, and to adjust his activities to, the complex patterns of interdependence which modern large-scale organization fosters and rests upon. The balance between these elements can at best be a delicate one, and at many points one must expect an outright clash of principles and requirements. Moreover, the problem is likely to be particularly acute in systems like the Soviet and the Chinese, which are so strongly oriented toward collective goals that cannot easily be rendered compatible with high degrees of individual initiative.

POSTMODERN MAN

The Soviet Union is no longer a less developed nation. By some point after World War II it had moved decidedly into the category of those societies which qualify as developed. It came, in the process, increasingly to share the problems and concerns we identify more with postindustrial society. In this stage of national development, the modernity of average men is no longer statistically problematic; yet issues relating to individual modernity may be a major problem for the system.

In accord with the principle that for each stage of socioeconomic development there is a characteristic type of man, the postindustrial society must reckon with the postmodern man. We are thus entering on a whole new era in the interrelations of personality and social structure. And again we may expect that in some respects the personal qualities which come to the center of attention will in part be shared across the boundaries which divide socioeconomic systems, and in part will bear the distinctive imprint of one or another of these systems. For example, one may see in both the Soviet Union and the United States an increasing discontent and even revulsion with overbureaucratization, and a profound feeling that individuals must be given more control over their own lives. In both societies there is also a widespread tendency to question the logic of unlimited growth, and to argue vigorously for stemming the attendant destruction of delicately balanced ecological structures.

In other respects, however, the two systems seem to generate emphases in contemporary men and women which are at considerable variance with each other. For example, the postmodern tendencies in the noncommunist countries during the sixties and seventies included: a strong interest in communalism; romantic glorification of poverty and of the life style of the uneducated and economically disadvantaged; patterns of dress and hair style which are archaic, symbolic, or otherwise distinctly expressive; and rejection of logic, and a search for transcendental experience. None of these manifestations was or is particularly evident in the dissident culture manifested in the Soviet Union. That movement has been conservative in its approach to personal dress and morality, is logical and practical rather than glorifying feelings and sensations, and insists on the literal implementation of legal and constitutional guarantees rather than emphasizing an apocalyptic or transcendental vision. Distinctions between the postmodern and dissident modes are discussed in chapter 15.

CHAPTER 15

The Future of
Individual Modernity

Psychological modernity is a complex, multifaceted, and multidimensional syndrome. Although it is found in all societies, and at all levels of those societies, it tends to be much more concentrated in those countries that are economically more developed. This is, in part, a contextual effect, but it results mainly from the fact that in such societies there is a greater concentration of the institutional forces that make individuals more modern, such as schools, factories and cooperatives, mass media, cities, and mass markets. Exposure to those institutions produces individuals who are more modern than their compatriots, whether they are located in more or less developed countries. Thus in our six-nation study our index of exposure to modernizing institutions generally produced 2 to 3 percent of modern men at the lowest decile, rising steadily until at the tenth decile of exposure 80 to 90 percent of the men scored as modern, regardless of which country was under study.

INTERACTION OF INSTITUTIONAL CHANGE
AND INDIVIDUAL MODERNITY

If individual modernity depends mainly on the nature of the sociocultural systems in which people live, and on the distribution of experience within those systems, then to read the future of individual modernity we need to predict the future of society. Alas, no one can do that with precision, and certainly not for the long term. But we can specify a range of scenarios with

This chapter was published as Alex Inkeles, "The Future of Individual Modernity" in J. Milton Yinger and Stephen J. Cutler, eds., *Major Social Issues: A Multidisciplinary View* (New York: The Free Press, 1978), pp. 459-75.

reasonable estimates of the probability of their occurring in the short term. And for each of those scenarios, in turn, we can, with much more confidence, suggest the fate of individual modernity.

IMAGES OF TOTAL CATASTROPHE

In this age we cannot exclude from the set of scenarios having claim to probability several that can only properly be described as cataclysms. Such potential total disasters could come in two forms:

Cataclysm I offers death by suffocation. This is the Club of Rome model—it anticipates a breakdown of the world system as population overtakes food and other resources, which leads to the end of industrial civilization. The result is presumably a Hobbesian war or an Armageddon.

Cataclysm II takes the form of a nuclear holocaust, which produces a quicker, but no less certain, end of civilization as we know it.

Both scenarios promise the end of individual modernity as now constituted. Except for some deviant individuals or subcultures, the extinction of individual moderntiy would probably be almost complete within one or two generations, because the structural forms generating and supporting the type would be destroyed. It is unlikely that mankind would return to the Stone Age or even to a condition equivalent to that of contemporary primitives, but impoverished settled agriculture under sociopolitical conditions similar to those of feudalism seems a not improbable prospect. Attitudes and values would then develop in tune with the system, colored by fear and anxiety persisting from the memory and mythology of the precipitating cataclysm. Passivity, fear of the stranger and the new experience, severe subordination of the individual to group norms linked to survival, the exercise of tyrannical personal power, all would come to prevail.

THE STEADY-STATE OR NO-GROWTH MODEL

This scenario supposes that those calling for, and seeking to install, a no-growth model succeed. The result would be not destruction of the present system, but rather its petrification. Institutions, relational patterns, the relative gap between less and more developed countries would be preserved.

Just as the no-growth steady-state model would freeze the absolute and relative inequalities of the present world system, just so would it act to fix the existing differentials in the distribution of modern qualities in the world population. On the world scale, high levels of individual modernity would be overwhelmingly concentrated in the most developed countries.

The elite strata within the less developed countries would manifest modernity levels similar to those in the advanced countries, so long as these elites had access to modernizing experiences at levels comparable to those enjoyed by their opposite numbers in advanced countries, discounting some for the contextual effects produced by the poverty of their countries. But the great masses of the populations in the poor countries, cut off from increased exposure to modernizing influences, would remain at levels of traditionalism similar to those that now prevail.

However, conversion to no-growth might also produce some major unanticipated deviations from present patterns. Since the currently advanced sector has not lived in a steady state for some 500 years, there is very little precedent to guide us. Frustration over inhibited achievement drives, a gradual constriction of cognitive openness, depression and lassitude replacing instrumental activism, diversion of energy to pleasure-seeking or escape into hallucinatory searches for the absolute, all seem plausible outcomes, at least for significant segments of the population. But we need not pursue this line too assiduously, because it seems to me highly implausible to assume that the world will accept a no-growth steady-state approach within the framework of anything like the present, or any immediately foreseeable, world order.

LONG-TERM DEVELOPMENT MODELS

These also come in several versions. Two of the scenarios express a great dream—one revolutionary the other evolutionary.

In the radical's dream we experience a series of revolutions, or one global breakthrough, which establish socialist countries everywhere. China and Russia settle their differences, and a reborn U.S. and Europe join them in instituting social justice everywhere, redistributing resources, maximizing participation and communalism, rationing produce, eliminating waste, and so on.

The liberal's dream calls for balanced growth that gets the poorer countries out of their desperate plight without seriously impoverishing the most advanced countries or significantly eroding their present political and cultural patterns. The gap between rich and poor is not quite eliminated, but is greatly narrowed. More important, the absolute levels of living in the less developed countries are raised so that by today's standards they live reasonably well—with up to 3,000 calories of food daily, eight to twelve years of education per child, reasonable housing, clean water, adequate health care, and so on. All this is accomplished with due speed, say in twenty years, without violence, based on spontaneous economic forces and political goodwill supplemented by moderate global regulation to control pollution and constrain exploitation. Democratic party systems prevail, free movement of people, and especially ideas, is relatively unimpeded, and so on.

OUTCOMES OF THE DREAM MODELS

The radical and the liberal dreams make many common assumptions about the institutional structure of future societies. On this basis our theory predicts common outcomes at the level of individual psychology regardless of differences in the politico-economic context. Among the institutional developments expected by both models are:

1. Greatly diffused and much longer exposure to formal education for the average person.
2. Substantial expansion of mass media and great growth in popular exposure.
3. Increased industrialization, especially technicalization; miniaturization; materials substitution in the mode of the plastic revolution.
4. Mechanization and industrialization of agriculture and food production.
5. Vast population shifts to urban and suburban centers.
6. Maintenance of high levels in, and probably expansion of, basic and especially applied scientific research.
7. Great growth of public services as implementation of the revolution of rising entitlements progresses.[1]

If these structural shifts occur, they should be reflected in substantial changes in the levels, but not the content, of individual modernity among all the peoples affected, but especially in the population of the now less developed countries. Increased levels of modernity would presumably be manifested over the entire range of dimensions covered by the concept of individual modernity, from active public participation, through openness to new experiences, to women's rights. Moreover, these increases in individual modernity would take similar form and would occur at comparable rates whether either the radical or the liberal dream came to pass.

To many it will seem a curious, and even a profoundly mistaken, belief to assume that the future of individual modernity would be basically the same in a socialist as in a capitalist world. Without extensive testing of our modernity scales in socialist countries we cannot assert this proposition without risk of plausible challenge. The evidence available so far, however, indicates that the clearly more important determinants of psychological

modernity are individual exposure to a set of relatively standard institutional inputs, such as schools, factories, offices, and laboratories,
cooperative farms, the mass media, and modern cities. This is not to say
there are no demonstrated contextual effects at the societal level. We already
have available evidence about one such effect based on differentiating the
six countries in our original study on a scale of relative economic
development. In that test, as we saw in chapter 8, 21 percent of the
explained variance was accounted for by the country factor, a modest but
not inconsequential figure next to the 79 percent accounted for by the set of
individual experiences such as education and occupation.

Evidence aside, we can, of course, speculate about the differences in the
individual modernity syndrome that might result from the conditions
specified by the radical and the liberal dreams.

Let us assume, for this purpose, the Chinese rather than the Russian
version of the radical dream were to prevail. Through an examination of
official manuals for teachers in Communist China designed to guide them
in raising the children, I was able to show (in chapter 14) that many
elements of the modernity syndrome as we define it are also emphasized
there. Teachers are urged to inculcate a sense of social and personal
efficacy, to encourage innovation and openness to new experience, belief in
science, and so on. Nevertheless, there is reason to expect the Chinese model
of the modern person would be different in regard to the following:

Individualism. This quality, although of a particular variety, has been
part of the modernity syndrome in virtually all the countries tested so far.
Individualism as it enters into the modernity syndrome does not mean
rugged individualism in the classic American sense. Rather the scale
measures independence from control by parents, village elders, or other
traditional authority figures, especially as concerns intimate associations,
as in the choice of spouse or job. Nevertheless, it is reasonable to assert that,
in the nonsocialist countries studied so far, increased individualism
emerges as a concomitant of increasing modernity.

It seems likely that in socialist countries of the Chinese type this element
of the syndrome would be either muted or would be quite displaced by a
greater emphasis on collectivism. We have in mind the stories from
journalists and visitors who consistently report that when they ask young
people in China, "What do you want to be when you grow up?" the
children reply with astonishing regularity. "I want to become whatever the
party (or country) wants me to become."

Anti-authoritarianism. One indicator of liberating oneself from traditionalism consists in challenging the right of received authority to command obedience merely by right. Although anti-authoritarianism, in this sense, was not explicitly defined as part of the modernity syndrome, it is a quality that seems to suffuse the modernity scale. Moreover, when standard tests of anti-authoritarianism are correlated with tests of modern attitudes, they regularly show strong positive correlations. My reading of the Chinese model of authority suggests that, under it, anti-authoritarianism would be much more weakly, and perhaps even negatively, correlated with other elements of the modernity syndrome.

Equalitarianism. The syndrome measured by our scale of individual modernity tests one's concern for the dignity of those weaker and less prestigeful, readiness to accord women rights equal to those of men, and insistence that in local rule the opinion and vote of all should count equally. We read this set of responses as indicating a strong equalitarian tendency to be part of the modernity syndrome.

Again, how one predicts the fate of this disposition in the radical dream depends on how one reads the social reality of Communist China. For myself, I see the authority of the Communist party and of its local representatives, and the concept of the leadership role of the "proletarian vanguard," as decidedly nonequalitarian. On the other hand, there is the Chinese espousal of communal principles, their extensive organization of cooperatives, their emphasis on consensus, and the strong leveling tendencies in both Communist ideology and practice. Keeping those facts in mind, one might well be led to anticipate that those more modern in attitude in regard to the other elements of the syndrome would, if the radical dream became reality, be more strongly inclined to equalitarianism than would individuals living in the liberal's preferred dream world.

Even if these adjustments to the special conditions of the Chinese model of Communism were to take place, I believe it would still be true that of all the questions and themes that together measure individual modernity, some 80 to 90 percent would have more or less the same weight in the typical individual profile were *either* the radical or the liberal dream to come to pass. Both would bring in their train a strong sense of personal efficacy; openness to new experience; valuing of technical competence; heightened interest in public affairs; positive attitudes toward limiting family size and practicing birth control; being an active, participant citizen; greater knowledge of national and worldwide places, persons, and events; and other elements of the modernity syndrome as already manifested elsewhere in our historical experience.

MORE REALISTIC MODELS

It seems unlikely that either the radical or the liberal dream will come to pass in the next twenty years or so. Instead, we are likely to witness a scene not profoundly different from that which has filled the world's stage during the last twenty or twenty-five years. Some of the less developed countries will continue frozen in poverty and neglect; some will see some minor degree of improvement in the condition of life; the majority will make slow but steady progress; and some few will experience a great surge of development. The major developed countries of the world will, with intermittent crises, probably continue to grow at modest rates, maintaining the main features of their politico-economic systems as now constituted, although progressing further in the direction of centralization, regulation, public welfare, and other forms for diffusing public entitlements. Possibly one or two new members will be added to the club of the advanced, as Japan won its way in during the era just past, but in general the composition of the club will remain basically the same.

For the set of more developed countries and possibly some of the newcomers to the club of the affluent, we may anticipate three main trends.

First, we expect the progressive incorporation into the modern sector of the currently marginal populations—rural black and white Appalachians in the United States; the Ainu in Japan; the oriental Jews in Israel; some portion of the tribal people and the untouchables in India.

Second, a modest increase in the *average* level of individual modernity as educational levels, exposure to mass media, travel, and other modernizing influences continue to increase, except as they may have reached a saturation point in the most advanced countries.

Third, substantial increases in the frequency and diffusion of the qualities of the postmodern man. This type should not be confused with the individuals involved in the ecological movement, with health foods, organic gardening, bicycle riding, and jogging. All those activities are essentially congruent with the syndrome of individual modernity. Indeed, in their expression of a heightened sense of efficacy, their affirmation of personal autonomy, their experimental openness to new experience, and their desire to adapt and direct science and technology to new goals, they may be said to manifest the qualities of psychological modernity in the highest degree.

Instead, by postmodern we mean being increasingly oriented to passive rather than active roles; ready to surrender personal autonomy to collective control; suspicious or defeatist about most forms of science; seeking mystical experience or release from boredom through drugs or violence; hostile to any sort of fixed schedule; skeptical about the payoff from personal or social planning. So marked are some of these tendencies, and so much at variance with the main elements of the modernity syndrome, that they might more accurately be described as antimodern.

Such qualities were previously found in a U-shaped distribution, strong mainly among the most advantaged youth and yet simultaneously widespread among some of the most disadvantaged segments of the population. But these tendencies also had, and continue to have, considerable fascination for many middle-class youths. The high point may have been reached in the 1960s, and this wave's future is problematic in the extreme. Nevertheless marked resurgence of such tendencies would pose considerable challenge to the modernity syndrome and, indeed, could undermine the psychological base on which modern large-scale society rests.

Analogous developments, albeit specific to their social setting, may be anticipated in the so-called socialist countries. The tendencies I have called antimodern are already sufficiently widepread as to be frequently described and discussed in the Soviet press. The pattern includes avoidance of regular work; pursuit of illegal trading, especially in objects of West European provenance; and exaggerated costume, again with a preference for "exotic" items like blue jeans and printed tee shirts. As in the West, these styles seem to attract, with differentiation in the content and mode of expression, both the young people from the most advantaged and those in the more marginal segments of the society.

However, of much greater importance for the future of the socialist countries will be the extent and the fate of those in the movement for greater freedom and self-expression. This group, often called the dissidents, bears important resemblance to those who make up the ecology movement in the U.S. and Western Europe, but in other respects is distinctive. The critical point, however, is that it is quite inappropriate to classify them as a variant of the postmodern personality. On the contrary, we see these dissidents as quintesssentially modern individuals in conflict with a social system that in many respects has failed to adapt its institutional forms, in particular its political practice, to the level of development that characterizes the society in other respects, such as its technological complexity, its dependence on scientific research, and its pervasive system of popular education. The intellectual opposition in the Soviet Union urges greater freedom of expression, openness to new ideas, innovation and experimentation in institutional forms, more opportunity for individual mobility, fuller actual rather than symbolic participation in the public decision-making process. All this is eminently modern. By contrast, the style of the Soviet regime is traditional. Just as the unevenness of development in the U.S. is reflected in our failure to eliminate poverty and unemployment, so it is part of the uneveness of development of the Soviet Union that it continues relatively unchanged its particular forms of legal and intellectual oppression long after the system has, in other respects, developed modern forms of organization and modes of operation common to other large-scale, advanced, industrial societies.

CONDITIONS SPECIFIC TO THE LESS DEVELOPED COUNTRIES

To deal with the specific conditions manifested in the less developed countries, we again need a differentiated scenario. The fate of individual modernity in a country such as Haiti will obviously be vastly different from that in Cuba. And these are, clearly, not the only models. The problem is further complicated by the prospect that nations will not necessarily remain in the same structural category for a long period, but will shift from one to another, at times with confusing rapidity.

Nevertheless, certain major sets of societies do encompass a considerable number of cases, which permits imposing some order and justifies the expectation of some regularity of outcome. We may distinguish several future conditions for different sets of the less developed countries, along with consequently differentiated prospects for the future of individual modernity.

First, there are the countries frozen or locked into backwardness, isolated, forgotten. Their poverty is expressed in GNP per capita of under $100, and electric consumption per capita of under twenty kilowatts per year. Their desperation is expressed in life expectancies at birth under forty, food consumption under 2,100 calories per day, and a ratio of less than one teacher for every two thousand of population. And their isolation is reflected in a total value of exports and imports of no more than $20 to $30 per person per year. In this set we have had Haiti in the Caribbean; in Africa, Somalia and Chad; in Asia, the Indonesian part of Borneo, Burma, Laos, and Afghanistan; while in Latin America, Bolivia might qualify. Such societies are, fortunately, ever fewer in number, and we may hope the category will disappear. But to expect that outcome by the year 2000 is probably too sanguine.

These are the societies profoundly burdened by the most extreme poverty, the most unpromising physical setting, the most severe paucity of resources, so that they are often chillingly designated the "international basket cases." Education, technical change, mobility, a flow of information, free movement of ideas and people are either infeasible or actively prevented by the authorities. Very little change can be expected, and that affecting only a very thin veneer of those at the interface with the outside world. In these countries today's average scores for individual modernity will be much the same twenty years hence.

Closely related to the lands locked into backwardness are the countries where structural change is extremely slow, but where certain elements— such as the military, or an exporting sector, along with the trading and service groups that support them—have created enclaves of differentiated activity bearing some resemblance to the rationality of modern organization. In Latin America, Ecuador and Honduras might qualify; in Africa, Nigeria, the Ivory Coast, or Morocco; in Asia, Indonesia or Sri Lanka; and in the Middle East, Jordan or Iraq.

In these countries even the nominally "modern" sector will be found suffused with sentiments typical of traditional societies. Their modernity will be severely limited to certain realms of action, most notably technical and administrative, and will in no significant degree carry over to reduce social injustice or personal privilege.

Fortunately, the bulk of the developing nations do not fall in the category of the isolated or the near isolated. The unevenness of their development makes it extremely difficult to treat them as a coherent set. They do, nevertheless, have some features in common. Among these are: moderate rates of economic growth; rapid, almost explosive, expansion of their educational programs; intense urbanization, the product largely of a massive flow of population out of the countryside; burgeoning of mass communication; economic infrastructures of roads, harbors, railroads, air and seaports steadily, often rapidly, expanding; and a reasonably stable and moderately effective central civil service apparatus.

While having much in common, this middle range of countries is still markedly differentiated in regard to the following: *politically*, they vary from relatively stable and effective democracies, through all combinations of fluctuating and ineffective party and military regimes, to relatively stable and effective autocratic and dictatorial rule; *economically*, they range from relatively open, classically capitalist, free-market economies, through all manner of mixture of the state and private sector, to relatively complete socialism or, more accurately, state capitalism; *culturally*, they range from ideologically committed, religiously fanatic, totalistic systems, to relatively open, laissez-faire, even libertarian, orientations; *in strati-*

fication terms, they include societies ranging from the most rigid hierarchies and steep pyramids, to those of relative equality in the distribution of power and income.

While acknowledging the existence of this structural differentiation and its significance in political and economic terms, we believe that such contextual forces will, in themselves, not have great impact on the process of individual modernization. The critical factor in that process, the prime determinant of the rate of individual change, will be the extent to which individuals are exposed to the "schools for modernity" such as formal education; factories, modern offices, and other rationalized work settings; the mass media; domestic and foreign travel; and urban conglomerations. In direct proportion to their contact with such institutions and experiences, individuals will become more efficacious, more open to new experience, more active participants in the political process, more flexible cognitively, and in other ways will manifest the qualities of the individual who is psychosocially modern.

Some allowance should perhaps be made for special situations where greatly accelerated economic and social development may create environments highly stimulating to the growth of individual modernity above and beyond what would be predicted solely on the basis of individual levels of education or occupation. Such conditions may currently exist in Taiwan, Singapore, Hong Kong, Brazil, and the People's Republic of China, and will likely develop in some new settings in the next two decades.

PERSISTENT QUESTIONS AND LINGERING DOUBTS

These main scenarios being duly sketched, there remain several questions of a more general nature about the future of individual modernity that deserve at least brief responses.

IS EVERYBODY TO BECOME MODERN?

Since modernity, as we conceive it, is not an absolute but a relative state, this question cannot be answered exactly as it has been put.[2] But insofar as education, industrial or bureaucratic employment, mass media exposure, and other modernizing experiences spread, to that degree more and more people will become more modern than they are now. This process is pervasive and, barring the two cataclysms sketched earlier, we believe it comes as near to being inexorable as any social process can be.

Actually, it *is* possible to express individual modernity in absolute rather than relative terms. One could, for example, arbitrarily classify as modern everyone who gave the modern answer to half or more of the questions on a modernity measure such as the OM scale.[3] Using our experience with the scale so far, we could effectively calculate the proportion who might be expected to score as modern in future years by basing our calculation on estimates of what the social characteristics of the world's population will be like at various later points in time. These projections might be rather discouraging. In virtually all countries the absolute numbers of individuals going to school, or going to school longer, increase regularly. That produces an *absolute* increase in the number of modern individuals. But in some of the less developed countries huge population growth has meant that the proportion of the total population having attained minimum levels of schooling has failed to rise or has even decreased. The consequence is that there is a *relative* decline in the *proportion* of modern individuals. Unless we can provide education for a large proportion of the global population, therefore, it will be a very long time indeed before everyone is psychologically modern.

CAN ONE SKIP STAGES TO CLOSE THE GAP?

The gap in physical wealth separating the most from the least advantaged nations is much greater than that separating them on measures of individual modernity. Nevertheless, the gap is substantial and, as in the case of wealth, we hope to reduce it and, if possible, close it entirely.

Those who start with less cannot hope to catch up unless those who are ahead gain more slowly than those who are behind. Interestingly enough, this seems to be happening in the economic sphere, since the average growth rate of GNP for the most advanced countries tends to be below that of the less developed. A similar "ceiling effect" seems to operate in the case of individual modernity. Those who start with the lowest levels of individual modernity gain most rapidly, given equal-unit increments of exposure to modernizing institutions.

Still, the regular processes will be very slow and indeed protracted. Many people have the sense that the world's expectant people cannot wait that long. They wonder if there is not some way in which people can skip stages, going directly and immediately from psychological traditionalism to psychological modernity, as they might skip the long-distance telephone wire and go directly to line-of-sight microwave transmission.

Since individual modernity has no apparent stages, but rather is a continuous and seemingly seamless web, the very notion of skipping stages seems hardly applicable. Acceleration, however, is another matter. Many individuals and groups seem to have moved with exceptional speed from the lowest to quite high points on the scale of individual modernity within a generation, within a life span, or even within a decade. Such changes, however, depend on providing the individuals concerned with more extensive exposure to the modernizing experiences provided by education, modern employment, and mass media exposure. Alas, to increase the availability of such experiences obviously requires that we solve very imposing challenges of a politico-economic nature. And even if the general *diffusion* of modernizing experiences can be very much increased, that will only influence how *many* people are modernized and how *far* they are modernized. It seems unlikely that it can affect how *fast* they are individually modernized. To produce a person moderately high on the modernity scale, scored in absolute terms, seems to take at least six to eight years of schooling, or more than double that time through work in a modern productive enterprise, or some appropriate combination of the two. It is evidently a slow process, and we know no obvious way greatly to accelerate it.

DOES THE SPREAD OF MODERNITY MEAN THE END OF THE TRADITIONAL?

Few issues arouse more apprehension and generate more misconceptions. Much confusion could be avoided if we could forgo our propensity to use the terms "traditional" and "modern" as global, undifferentiated concepts that can have almost any meaning. As we have defined individual modernity in our work, it refers to a broad syndrome of qualities, but one finite and specific. Other realms of value and forms of social interaction cannot safely be assumed automatically to follow the patterns observed with our measures. One should, therefore, be extremely cautious about projecting onto the conception of the "modern" popular and casually arrived at notions that have not been systematically tested empirically.

For example, it is regularly and widely assumed that becoming modern automatically carries with it decreasing respect for the aged, and increasing unwillingness to assume the burden of care for the elderly. But the research evidence available indicates this is a mistaken assumption. This is not to say that modernity brings no changes in one's orientation to parents and elders. On the contrary, our data show that increasing modernity does express itself in resistance to having one's elders decide who is the right person to marry or which is the right job to take. But this specific expression of independence from parents cannot safely be generalized to all other forms of relation with elders and kin.[4]

A very wide range of religions, kinship patterns, sexual relations, styles of dress, forms of recreation, types of housing and living arrangement, modes of intimate interpersonal relations, forms of linguistic expression, scheduling of daily activity, preference in diet, and other numerous elements of culture are quite compatible with the industrial order and with other aspects of the modern institutional system. Among these many culture patterns compatible with modernity are some that would commonly be considered traditional. Other patterns mistakenly abandoned or officiously driven out in the first waves of modernization may well make their way back. For example, industrialization and Westernization in Japan drove the Japanese businessman out of his kimono into the Western buisness suit, but not out of the geisha house. Retaining the latter, perhaps otherwise deplorable, evidently did not impede his business acumen. And in the future he may retain the geisha while restoring the kimono without losing his share of the world market.

In the political games of life and society there are always circumstances making for strange bedfellows. Traditonal authorities may use modern individuals to support and even strengthen their traditional controls, and modern individuals may seek to capture the force at the command of traditional authority to advance their modernizing objectives.

ARE THERE NO MASSIVE COUNTERTENDENCIES TO STOP OR AT LEAST OFFSET THE MARCH OF MODERNITY TRIUMPHANT?

Of course there are. Modernity must be recognized as being at least as fragile and vulnerable as any other general historical tendency. Either of the two cataclysms sketched above would very likely bring it to a complete halt, and might well eliminate it. Moreover, if it comes to be seen not as a mere social process, but rather as some sort of social movement, it may become the object of ideological warfare designed to halt or even to eradicate it. Rightest movements are the most obvious sources from which antimodern campaigns might emanate, but modernism seems not less attractive as a target for both orthodox Marxism and the New Left. Finally, there is the possibility that individual modernity, as we have conceived and measured it, may itself become tomorrow's traditionalism, a historical anachronism no longer appropriate to the structural features of some as yet unimagined future society radically different in form and content from any we have yet known.

MODERNITY: GOOD OR EVIL?

Some may consider it morally insensitive to have come so far without saying whether modernity is good or bad. One cannot make that judgment without specifying some personal standard of value. The question is rather like asking whether the Industrial Revolution was good or bad. Most likely those who see the consequences of the Industrial Revolution as, on balance, good will also affirm the goodness of individual modernity.

So far as the specific qualities making up the syndrome of individual modernity are concerned, one would probably find general agreement, at least in liberal circles, that modernity is preferable to traditionalism. This judgment would surely apply to open-mindedness, to cognitive flexibility, and to respect for the feelings of those less powerful than oneself. But when it comes to efficacy, to faith in science, or to interest in technical innovation, many, young and old, will begin to hold back their approbation, seeing in these qualities the seedbed that ultimately came to nourish great engines of destruction, such as hydrogen bombs, breeder reactors, strip mining, pesticides like DDT, and defoliants such as Agent Orange.

It can convincingly be argued that the qualities of the modern man have in their more exaggerated, Faustian, form a potential for producing demonic impulses. We would deny that Hitler or Stalin, Khadafy or Amin, in any significant degree embody or symbolize the qualities of individual modernity. But we all have our own frequent nightmare of the demonic villain who will cement all the river banks, or dam all the wild rivers, or cut down all the virgin forests, or bulldoze all the cherished architectural monuments, or turn all the friendly little family groceries and restaurants into supermarkets or fast-food chains. These tendencies are real. To some they are, moreover, not mixed blessings, but rather genuinely desirable manifestations of modernization and progress. And the impulses just described are surely among the less demonic that we can mention or that others have conceived and pursued in the name of modernity.

Acknowledging all this, one may nevertheless believe that without the modern spirit a much poorer future, indeed, one may say a much worse fate, awaits humanity. Being in the condition we are now in, to opt for a return to the mentality of traditionalism would win us not a hoped-for return to a bucolic idyll, but rather to a Hobbesian state of nature. Indeed, we are beyond the point where such a choice is possible. The real choice is no longer between modernism and traditionalism. It is, rather, between one combination of modernism or another—either a modernism linked to a passion for power and to a bottomless greed, resting on torture and erecting monuments to tyranny, or a modernism restrained by humility and tempered by humanism. We hope that the choice will be ours to make.

Notes

CHAPTER 1. UNDERSTANDING AND MISUNDERSTANDING INDIVIDUAL MODERNITY

1. The economists: for a sophisticated example of such analysis see Adelman and Morris (1971); for one of the most fundamental statements on the subject of economic growth see Kuznets (1966). The political scientists: for a general treatise on modernization and government see Huntington (1968); for systematic analysis of data on the historic development of the state see Eisenstadt and Rokkan (1973). The anthropologists: for a general review of the literature and statement of the anthropological view see Goodenough (1963); for a succinct analysis of peasant communities see Halpern (1967). Population experts: a comprehensive review of the interaction of population and modernization will be found in Goldscheider (1971). The psychologists: the most seminal work has been McClelland's (1961), focused predominantly on the role in economic development of the need for achievement; for a more impressionistic case-study approach sharing many of the same assumptions see Hagen (1962). For a general review see Murphy (1961); for a detailed application in the context of development and modernization see chapter 12.

2. A wide-ranging review of the study of modernization by leading scholars from different disciplines is Weiner (1966). The most systematic integrative effort, also incorporating a historical perspective, is Black (1966). Among the more useful bibliographies, Geiger (1969) focuses on national development while Brode (1969) gives special emphasis to sociocultural themes.

3. One of the major forces in casting the discussion in this mold was the appearance, in 1958, of Daniel Lerner's *The Passing of Traditional Society: Modernizing the Middle East*. For one of many criticisms of this polarity see Gusfield (1967).

4. The classic statement arguing the case for education as a stimulus to growth is found in Harbison and Myers (1964). For a much more cautious and sobering conclusion see Meyer et al. (1973). For an example relating growth to income inequality see Adelman and Morris (1973).

5. The best review extant as of this moment, by Brislin et al. (1973), is more oriented to issues of method rather than substance, but it reflects a rather comprehensive perspective and provides an excellent bibliography. For later and

more substantive surveys: from a sociological perspective see Suzman (1973b) and for a psychological and anthropological perspective see Berry (1980).

6. In selecting these ten questions we tried to minimize overlap with the "issues" and "challenges" dealt with in the concluding chapter of *Becoming Modern* (Inkeles and Smith 1974). That source should be consulted as a supplement to the arguments presented in this chapter.

7. The work of Blau and Duncan (1967) on status attainment has been widely hailed as a milestone in modern sociology, yet the obvious variables measuring the individual's social antecedents used by them explained only 26 percent of the variance in the educational attainment, and 33 percent of the variance in the first jobs, of their American sample. When Sewell and Hauser (1975) restricted their model "to a simple accounting of the inheritance of status positions" in a sample of Wisconsin youths, they found that they could explain no more than 16 percent of the variance in their educational attainment and 12 percent of the variance in occupational status. As an example of the limits on our power to predict the obvious in the context of developing countries, see the evidence in Nelson (1969) that objective social characteristics such as low income and marginal status predict much less about political orientation than is commonly assumed.

8. For the origin and first elaboration of this argument see Inkeles (1960). The position is more fully explicated on pp. 139–43, 154–64, and 302–8 of Inkeles and Smith (1974).

9. Notable exceptions, however, will be found in the works of McClelland (1961) and Hagen (1962, 1975).

10. As, for example, when census data on education indicate school graduates multiplying at a much higher rate than the number of available jobs.

11. See the construction of the basic typology of modern, transitional, and traditional types in Lerner (1958, chap. 2 and especially pp. 69–71). Lerner is not alone in electing to measure individual modernity by a scale which combines objective social characteristics with attitude and value measure. For other examples, see Schnaiberg's (1970) modernity scale and Rogers's (1969) "orientation to change" factor. Insofar as one seeks the most complete *description* of the psychological *and social* attributes of the modern individual, this procedure is quite sensible. But, as we have indicated, it limits our ability to test how far objective and subjective factors interact as cause and effect.

12. For an extension of this perspective to American occupational settings see Kohn and Schooler (1973).

13. Although we use the term "individuals," the reader should be aware that the Harvard-Stanford six-nation study, as reported in Inkeles and Smith (1974), was limited to men. However, a variety of later researches using comparable modernity scales give reason to argue that the concept applies equally to women, and that the modernity syndrome among women has fundamentally the same content as it does in men. For citation of the relevant research see note 20 below.

14. The almost invariant linking of sociological typologies to men is another heritage from the era in which we were all less sensitive to the prevalence of sexism in our professional terminologies.

15. If the authoritarian personality syndrome is acknowledged to represent a "type" in the sense we have used the term, then it almost certainly can claim to be

the most extensively assessed type. For a review of relevant studies see Kirscht and Dillehay (1967).

16. Observed *behavior* may be used as an alternative criterion. Thus, the individual more modern in attitude might be expected to join organizations more often or to adopt new innovations in agricultural practice more quickly. Examples of the validation of scales of modern values through utilizing such behavioral indicators will be found in Inkeles and Smith (1974, chap. 18), and in Rogers (1969).

17. This fact makes it extremely dangerous to offer sweeping generalizations on the basis of studying a single sample. An example of how misleading this propensity may be is found in Armer and Schnaiberg (1972). They sought to cast doubt on the discriminant validity of several different modernity scales, including the OM scale, on the grounds that they found higher correlations between the measures of modernity and a scale to assess anomie. Actually, there are no sound theoretical grounds for refusing to consider nonanomic attitudes to be one element in a modernity scale conceived to be a multidimensional measure. But the available evidence argues against that because, from sample to sample, anomie bears no consistent relation to the other modernity dimensions. Thus Almond and Verba's (1963) five-nation study gave reason to believe that measures of political modernity related differently to anomie in Italy and Mexico than in the U.S. The absence of a consistent relation across countries of a political modernity scale and anomie was later conclusively demonstrated for the Harvard six-nation study as may be seen in chapter 11. Armer and Schnaiberg had data from only one quite unrepresentative sample from one American city. Yet even if the relationship they observed were to hold up in other American samples, it would be ethnocentric to settle the relation of anomie to modernity on the basis of the results from one country. In stating their sweeping conclusions, Armer and Schnaiberg simply ignored the massive contrary evidence from these earlier country-wide studies. Some of that evidence is briefly discussed below as part of the response to question 8.

18. Some will insist on scale reliabilities of .8 or above, others will be content with .6 or even less. Factor loadings of .3 are considered adequate by some, but will be dismissed by others as trivial. For an extensive discussion of the different standards for testing the coherence of scales of modernity see Inkeles and Smith (1974, chap. 7, expecially the technical footnotes). Particular attention is there drawn to the different impression of coherence one may get by using a measure of scale reliability such as the Kuder-Richardson as against a measure of the variance explained by a principal components factor analysis. Portes (1973a) also devotes considerable attention to the factorial structure of modernity, and Armer and Schnaiberg (1972) stress discriminant validity, although they apply that standard in a rigid and mechanical way.

19. For example, the main (OM) modernity scale used by Inkeles and Smith (1974) had a median reliability of .82 across six countries; the Schnaiberg (1970) "average modernism" scale, based on 46 items, yielded a reliability of .81 for a sample of Turkish women; Portes (1973a), working with lower-class respondents in Guatemala, found his first principal components factor, weighing attitudes, values, and knowledge, to explain 19 percent of the total variance. This pattern is matched in many other studies, but some researchers do report less satisfying results. Thus, Klineberg (1973) found his first factor could explain only 11 percent

of the total variance in parents' modernity scores, and concluded that "by these criteria, the evidence for a single dimension underlying the 30 items is mixed, if not negative." But Klineberg did not present a Spearman-Brown or Kuder-Richardson reliability estimate for comparison.

20. Several of the most elaborate studies of modernity were limited to men only, as in Kahl's (1968) Mexican and Brazilian samples, and the six nations of Inkeles and Smith (1974). Therefore, special interest attaches to the question of whether the same approach, and the same measures, are appropriate for studying women. Scales to measure modernity developed explicitly for application to women, or based on the responses of both males and females, were reported by Cunningham (1972), Holsinger (1973), Kahl (1968), Klineberg (1973), Portes (1973a), Schnaiberg (1970), and Stephenson (1968), among others. A separate analysis of the same scale for parallel male and female samples is rare, but an important exception will be found in Suzman (1973a). In general, the same elements enter into the definition of modernity in females as in males, and the internal structure of the scale is similar, although there are important differences in emphasis. Insofar as men may score higher on these scales than women, that fact is almost entirely accounted for by differences in the average education and the occupational experience of the sexes. Thus, Cunningham (1972) reported there were no statistically significant differences in the modernity (OM) scores of those young men and women who were at the same grade level in her Puerto Rican high school.

21. For description and analysis of various subscales measuring dimensions conceived to be part of the general modernity syndrome, in some cases including separate reliability estimates and factor analyses, see Armer and Youtz (1971); Galtung (1971); Kahl (1968); Klineberg (1973); Rogers (1969); Sack (1973); Suzman (1973a); and Williamson (1970); and chapter 4.

22. For example, the 14-question subjective efficacy scale used by Williamson (1970) had a median Spearman-Brown reliability of .69 across the six nations of the Harvard study, whereas the overall modernity scale, also with 14 items, but touching on many different themes at once, had a median reliability of .73, as reported in chapter 4. For other comparable results see the sources cited in footnote 21 above.

23. See Inkeles and Smith (1974, pp. 121–24).

24. Use of the term "modern *man*" in this context is meant literally, since the six-nation study was limited to samples of men between the ages of 18 and 32.

25. For an extremely valuable summary and evaluation of the evidence on the role of early manifestations of temperament in shaping later qualities of personality see Buss and Plomin (1975).

26. For a vigorous exposition of the view that the early experiences of the individual are the predominant factor explaining later individual modernity see Hagen (1975). Hagen's statement is presented in the form of a challenge to the evidence in *Becoming Modern*, which showed that about half of the variance in OM modernity scores is accounted for by socialization experiences coming after adolescence. The defense of that evidence is present in Alex Inkeles, "Remaining Orthodox: A Rejoinder to Everett Hagen's Review-Essay of *Becoming Modern*," *History of Childhood Quarterly* 3 (1976): 422–35.

27. One must, of course, consider the alternative explanation, namely that the modernity of the child shapes the modernity of the parents. This model is most plausible where the children secure much more schooling than their parents did, and then carry into the home the modernizing influence embedded in this advanced education. Although this alternative explanation is plausible, it cannot be the whole story since Holsinger (1973) found the mother's modernity score already made a difference in the third grade, and Klineberg (1973) found the strongest correlation, specifically .42, between parental and adolescent modernity in his sample of male school-leavers.

28. As examples of inconsistency, we may note that for high school students in the top quartile academically in Puerto Rico, the mother-daughter correlation of modernity scores of .35 was strong and highly significant, but for students in the bottom quartile academically the comparable correlation was negative and not significant, as reported in Cunningham (1972). In Tunisia, the modernity of male school-leavers correlated .42 with parental modernity, but was at only .06 for boys who continued in school. Bringing other variables under control by means of a regression analysis did not eliminate the inconsistency. See Klineberg (1973). In his path analysis, Pandey (1971) found no important "direct" casual effects of the subjective aspects of parental modernity on either child socialization or child development variables.

29. The evidence is presented in chapter 17 of Inkeles and Smith (1974). Also see the criticism of this effort by Everett Hagen, *"Becoming Modern*: The Dangers of Research Governed by Preconceptions," *History of Childhood Quarterly* 3(1976): 411–21. For a defense of the evidence, refer to Alex Inkeles, "Remaining Orthodox: A Rejoinder to Everett Hagen's Review-Essay of *Becoming Modern*," *History of Childhood Quarterly* 3(1976): 422–35.

30. See chapter 8 for details concerning these "matches."

31. Whether it still is realistic to speak of these institutions as "Western" when, for example, they have been introduced by Japanese into the societies of Southeast Asia, is clearly moot. The issue is, however, beyond our responsibility here.

32. For a summary of evidence concerning the American Indian see Stewart (1952).

33. For a discussion of relevant evidence also see Murphy (1961).

34. Wallerstein (1976).

35. For relevant evidence and explication, see note 17 above. For further discussion of the role played by variation in local and national community contexts, see Cornelius (1975); Verba, Ahmed, Bhatt (1971).

36. An exception to the tendency to measure modernity and traditionalism as contrasting poles will be found in the work of Dawson (1967; Dawson et al. 1971), who gave each individual a separate score expressing his simultaneous acceptance of both traditional and modern positions bearing on the same issue. Pandey (1971) also develops some complex typologies by factor rotation and the use of canonical correlation.

37. Only a small part of the relevant evidence is so far published in chapter 7 of Inkeles and Smith (1974). Specifically with regard to attitudes toward the aged, see chapter 13 of this book.

38. On the problems of fitting individuals to the new role demands of a society undergoing a revolutionary transformation, see Bauer (1952); Inkeles, Hanfmann, and Beier (1958); and chapter 14 of this book.

39. For an elaboration of this point see Inkeles (1971a).

40. See Inkeles and Smith (1974, chap. 18); Rogers (1969).

CHAPTER 2. A MODEL OF THE MODERN MAN

1. An abbreviated description of our fieldwork was included in chapter 4 of *Becoming Modern*. For a fuller account of our fieldwork, see Alex Inkeles, "Fieldwork Problems in Comparative Research on Modernization," published in A. R. Desai, ed., *Essays on Modernization of Underdeveloped Societies*, vol. 2 (Bombay, India: Thacker, 1971) pp. 20–75.

2. Different specialists in scale construction prescribe different standards for judging whether or not a set of questions or subscales "cohere" well enough to be acknowledged as constituting a general syndrome. Our standard scale OM-500, used throughout the analysis in *Becoming Modern*, achieved a comfortable median reliability of .80 or above in all six countries in our study, as judged by the Kuder-Richardson formula. The coherence of the scale cross-nationally was also confirmed by a factor analysis of the version based on 19 subscales. Further details concerning the construction of this and other scales are given in chapter 4. For information concerning the validation of our OM scale, see David H. Smith and Alex Inkeles, "Individual Modernizing Experiences and Psycho-Social Modernity: Validation of the OM Scales in Six Developing Countries," *International Journal of Comparative Sociology*, 16(1975): 157–73.

3. The stability of the family, and even of more traditional family ties, under conditions of urbanization and industrialization has been noted by, among others, Lewis (1952) for Mexico, Lambert (1963) for India, and Husain (1963) for Pakistan.

4. This idea is in line with the main conclusion of Goode's (1963) world-wide survey of changing family patterns. Goode notes that the ubiquitous accompaniment of industrialization appears to be the weakening of extended kinship ties, a dissolution of lineage patterns, and a strengthening of the nuclear family.

5. We have been told there is a similar prayer in the Islamic tradition, but have not found an authoritative source affirming that as fact.

6. Lucian W. Pye, "Introduction," in Pye and Verba (1965).

CHAPTER 3. FORCES PRODUCING INDIVIDUAL MODERNITY: A THEORY OF EFFECTS

1. OM-1 was a version of the modernity scale limited to the 79 questions, asked in all six countries, which dealt exclusively with attitudes and values. Unlike OM-500, most commonly used in our analysis, it did not include questions to test information, or material likely to be acquired directly from the mass media. Further details about the scale are given in chapter 4.

2. These claims of specific effects were based on the known content of the OM scale, but were substantiated by reference to the cross-country median zero-order correlations of *formal education* with each of the *separate themal subscales* in

OM-519, as follows: active citizenship, .24; change valuation, 20; dignity valuation, .26; economic aspiration, .12; education valuation, .24; efficacy, .25; family size, .19; information, .50; minority opinion valuation, .20; modern family, .22; modern religion, 20; new experience valuation, .25. OM-519 is described in Inkeles and Smith (1974).

3. In most of the current discussions of the effectiveness and ineffectiveness of our schools, this aspect of the school's impact has been generally neglected. For an important exception see Dreeben (1968).

4. Our assumption that we might be severely criticized from an orthodox psychoanalytic perspective proved not unwarranted. See the review of *Becoming Modern* by Everett Hagen (1975).

5. This composite qualitative urban experience variable as well as its component indices are described and discussed more fully in Inkeles and Smith (1974). A quantitative measure of urban experience is built into the occupational type index and the urban versus rural origin measures discussed below.

CHAPTER 4. CREATING AND VALIDATING THE MODERNITY SCALE

1. Items were taken directly or adapted from the questionnaires of the following studies, some of which were still in progress when we devised our measures: Almond and Verba (1963); Tumin and Feldman (1961); Inkeles and Bauer (1959); Cantril (1965); Kahl (1968); Woodward and Roper (1956); Lerner (1958); and Silvert (1961).

2. The actual ranges in years of education were: Argentina, 1–15; Chile, 2–11; India, 0–11; Israel, 2–14; Nigeria, 4–13; and Pakistan, 0–8. We also collected a sample of university students in each country, but since they have such special characteristics they are being studied apart from the main samples. They do not, therefore, figure in this analysis.

3. That is, for our sample, "Pakistan" should be read as "East Pakistan," "India" as "the state of Bihar," and "Nigeria" as "the large Nigerian Yoruba tribal area." For further details, see Inkeles and Smith (1974).

4. In fact we have already applied the main body of our questions to a group of Protestant Americans in the Appalachian region of Kentucky. The men mostly had grade school education. The response to the interview was broadly comparable to its reception in developing countries. It was by no means considered an insult to anyone's intelligence. The structure of *individual* answers (as against the modal pattern or national average) was basically similar to the structure of attitudes encountered in other countries. For a brief report on this research see the unpublished Senior Honors Thesis of William W. Lawrence (1965).

5. Indeed, as noted above, in several countries we administered our questionnaire to groups of university students. With modest adaptation it was completed by them without incident.

6. Most of the analysis reported here was done with the Harvard Data-Text System of Programs, created under the direction of Dr. Arthur Couch, Harvard University.

7. The complete questionnaire is reproduced as an appendix to Inkeles and Smith (1974).

8. Our project did develop a modernity scale based on a set of distinctive specialized subscales. We called it OM 5-19 to reflect the fact that it was based on the separate score for 19 different scales such as for efficacy, openness to new experience, etc. However, we did not use these subscales to create differentiated profiles of individual modernity. Instead the scores on the subscales were added to yield a single summary score in much the same way as when individual questions rather than subscales were the basis of the score. Details are given in Inkeles and Smith (1974).

9. Only in the work of Joseph Kahl (1968) on Brazil and Mexico is there a comparable breadth of coverage. Kahl attempted to test values in 14 different realms, with the scale for each area varying from a modern to a traditional pole. His scale areas included several, such as "activism" and "low integration with relatives," which are similar to ours. Tumin and Feldman (1961) limited themselves to Puerto Rico. Although they used a wide variety of questions, they were mainly concerned with the single dependent variable area of educational and occupational aspirations. They presented an eight-element theoretical model of the modern man (pp. 247-78), but did not systematically attempt to measure the qualities it delineated. Almond and Verba (1963) worked in six countries, of which one, Mexico, qualifies as unambiguously underdeveloped; but they limited themselves to measures of political attitudes and relations. Lerner (1958) dealt with six developing countries, all in the Middle East, but was restricted to attitudes and behavior in the realm of communications, using the individual's empathic ability as the key psychological attribute.

10. Details concerning these correlations are given in the second part of this chapter, and are further reviewed in chapter 7.

11. When an individual had not answered a particular question the item was not considered in calculating his average score. We typically had very few DK/NA answers. For details see Inkeles and Smith (1974).

12. Happily, the chosen designation OM is the same as the Hindu mantra which expresses the triple constitution of the cosmos. In the Project's internal reference system, this Long Form OM is labelled OM-2. Use of that number here would be confusing, since the order in which the short forms are presented in this paper does not agree with the order of the Project's internal reference numbers. We cite these internal reference numbers, however, to facilitate responding to communications from our colleagues, concerning the various scale forms.

13. We use the term "reliability" here in a general sense. In a more technical sense, however, the Long Form used here (OM-2) does have the highest reliability coefficients, on the averge, when compared to all six short forms. This is not to say it could not be improved. For example, hindsight could be used to eliminate, or alter, the assumed "modern" direction of items whose direction we misjudged. The project actually has in its battery another summary measure of modernity, designated OM-1 in our internal reference system, which was based more narrowly on items rated by 5 of 6 judges (Project directors and research associates) as unambiguously related to modernity. This procedure yielded a pool of not 119 but 79 items, and not 5 percent of mistakes in judging direction, but only 2 percent. It has higher reliabilities than OM-2. Further details about the reliability of the several OM scales are given in the second part of this chapter.

14. A different way of selecting the items, which would still follow the logic of the item-analysis method, would be to do a factor analysis of the basic set of 119 items. We felt there was good reason to prefer a different approach. For a fuller discussion of the factor analytic approach to long scales such as ours see Inkeles and Smith (1974).

15. We use formula 17.16, involving the average item to test correlations, from Guilford (1956, p. 454).

16. For example, the average internal consistency of 11 scales from the Minnesota Multiphasic Personality Inventory is .69, and the median .75, with split half-reliability coefficients ranging from −.05 to .96; see Dahlstrom and Welsh (1960, p. 474).

17. Actually, we have not established that there is one and only one dimension underlying this item set, nor that all types of items enter equally, nor that the main underlying dimension is "modernity." But we have established *at least one* pervasive underlying dimension, and on prima facie grounds we can argue from the content of the items that this dimension is psychological modernity as we have conceptualized it. No other explanation, such as response set, will suffice.

18. For identification in documents internal to our project this scale (Short Form 1) is designated OM-6.

19. Table 2, of course, gives only a highly condensed version of each question. The full question wording may be identified by the alphabetical-numerical designation for each question in the full questionnaire reproduced in Inkeles and Smith (1974).

20. The theme list used, as given in chapter 4-1, is an expanded version of the list of code letter designations used in the Project's basic questionnaire. In making the list for chart 4-1 we divided some of the more complex themes, such as *Efficacy* and *Women's Rights*, into subthemes which are treated as separate units for present purposes. There is an inevitable element of arbitrariness in our selection and designation of both theme or subtheme area. We tried to be strictly "objective" about our decisions, but in the end appealed to a consensus of the field directors to settle difficult decisions regarding the final list of attitudinal themes for chart 4-1.

21. The three variables are not completely independent. This is especially true for years of factory experience and years of urban experience, since most factories are located in cities. The average correlation of those two variables is .54. But our sampling procedure insured relatively low Pearsonian correlations between origin and education average (r = .27), between origin and years of factory experience (average r = .13), and between education and factory experience (average r = .10). All these averages are for five countries only, because the data for Israel were lacking here when "the r's" were computed. Even though the variables are related, three such separate tests provide a more stringent and more broadly conceived criterion group test than would a single variable.

22. In the internal reference system of the Project, Short Form 3 is identified as OM-9.

23. Five out of the total of 34 are Efficacy (EF) related items. There are also five items from the New Experience (NE) realm.

24. The maximum of 33 is defined by the number of attitude theme areas mentioned in chart 4-1.

25. The Project's internal designation for this Short Form 4 is OM-8.

26. The internal project reference number of Short Form 5 is OM-11.

27. The coding instructions are included in Appendix B of Inkeles and Smith (1974).

28. The internal project reference number for this Short Form 6 is OM-12.

29. This screening was done on the basis of the item to scale correlations in a pool of 159 items. This is different from the Long Form OM we are using in this paper, which had only 119 items. For internal reference in the project, this longer (159 item) summary measure is designated OM-4. In the item competition, we considered separately all information items as a subset, and all behavioral items as a subset, otherwise information items alone would have captured all the vacancies.

30. These correlations will not be found in table 4-1. As indicated in the preceding note, the screening of behavioral and information items was on the basis of a long form (OM-4) which included them along with the attitude items. Since these information and behavior items were not included in the OM-2 version of the long form used in this report, there are blanks in column 1 of table 4-1 opposite the four relevant questions.

31. The project also collected measures of behavior other than those reported by the subject himself, such as those based on an individual's production record or the report of his foreman about his behavior on the job. These proved difficult to code reliably, and were not used extensively in our analysis.

32. In the internal reference system of the project, Short Form 6 is identified as OM-12.

33. In several of the countries studied there were fundamental ethnic subdivisions represented in our sample: In India, for example, we sampled tribal and often only nominally Hindu vs. well-established Hindu groups of classical Hindu culture. There were comparably important ethnic background distinctions in Israel and Nigeria, and lesser but notable ethnic or subgroup differentiation in Argentina and Pakistan. For further details see chapter 7.

34. For earlier statements of this position and a different type of evidence see Inkeles and Rossi (1956).

CHAPTER 5. RESULTS OF THE FIRST PHASE: A SUMMARY

1. Much of the detailed evidence is presented in Inkeles and Smith (1974).

2. Reference is to the reliabilities of the long form of the scale (OM-2) containing 159 items. Reliabilities for some of the various short forms were sometimes lower but were generally in the same range. See chapter 4.

3. Of course, when one uses a scale score to designate a "type" of man, the number of men who fit one's typology depends entirely on one's decision as to a cutting point for both the items and the scale as a whole. For example, in one form of our modernity scale, namely IM-6, a representative subset of thirty-three items is scored so that only by affirming the most decidedly modern position at the end of the theoretical continuum of alternative answers does a man get a point toward his modernity score. On this strict test, getting as many as half the answers "right" would qualify 37 percent of our Nigerian sample as "modern." If we set a higher standard, and reserve the term modern for men who get two-thirds or more of the

answers "right," then only 6 percent qualify. Raising the standard still higher to require that a man get three-fourths or more of the answers "correct" reduces the pool of modern men to 2 percent of the sample. The comparable proportions qualifying as modern by this standard in our East Pakistan sample are much lower, being 14 percent, 2 percent, and 0 percent, respectively. Changing the scoring standard for the individual questions would, obviously, also affect the proportions classified as modern.

4. These included *all* questions which in our opinion measured attitudes and could be unambiguously scored as having a "modern" and a "traditional" answer. For details see chapter 4 and Inkeles and Smith (1974).

5. The correlation (Pearsonian) between education and the overall measure of modernization used here, namely OM-3, ranged from .34 in East Pakistan to .65 in India. The size of these coefficients is substantially affected by the educational "spread" in each sample. That spread was largest in India, with the cases rather evenly distributed from zero to thirteen years of education. Additional correlations of education and other independent variables with OM-500 scores are given in table 5-6. OM-500 being somewhat more sensitive than OM-3, its correlations with education were higher than those mentioned here.

6. In much of the current discussion of the effectiveness and ineffectiveness of our schools, this aspect of the school's impact has been generally neglected. For an important exception see Dreeben (1968).

7. However, in India it was only .08. We believe this to be not a condition peculiar to India, but to our industrial sample there. Everywhere else we sampled from fifty to more than a hundred factories, including all types and sizes of industry, but in India our sample was limited to eleven factories, mostly large, and two of these were not truly industrial; they processed minerals.

8. Keep in mind that the test has a theoretical range from zero to 100, and an observed range in our samples almost as great. With samples of our size, differences so large are significant at well above the .01 level. This test of significance and many of the other statistics presented in this report require that one meet certain conditions, such as random sampling, which our data do not meet. Nevertheless, we present such statistics in order to provide a rough guide or standard of judgment, in the belief that to do so is preferable to leaving the reader without any criterion by which to evaluate one figure as against another. The reader must be cautioned, however, not to interpret any single statistic too literally. Conclusions should be drawn not from single figures but from the whole array of evidence across the six countries.

9. It will be noted that the pattern manifested in the other five countries is not shown in Israel. There the new workers are as well informed as the experienced. We attribute this not so much to the qualities of Israeli industry as to the nature of Israeli society. In that small, mobile, and urbanized environment, information tends to be rapidly and more or less evenly diffused throughout the nation and to all classes.

10. A discussion of the rationale for selecting these particular variables and grouping them so, as well as details of the linear multiple regression analysis is presented in Inkeles and Smith (1974).

11. The strong performance of the late socialization variables held up when we

used the more sensitive modernization measure OM-500, and more precisely coded independent variables. Under these circumstances the early socialization variables typically accounted for about 31 percent of the variance, while the late socialization variables typically accounted for about 37 percent. For details see especially table 19-5 in Inkeles and Smith (1974).

12. An alternative approach to estimating the relative contribution of the two sets of variables is to consider the decrement in the total variance explained when either set is withdrawn from the total pool of predictors. When this was done, the late socialization variables again emerged as more powerful everywhere except in India. The following set of figures presents, first, the decrement in the total variance explained resulting from withdrawal of the early socialization variables, and second, the decrement resulting from withdrawal of the late socialization variables from the total predictor pool: Argentina .127/.155; Chile .100/.184; India .276/.066; Israel .101/.104; Nigeria .068/.120; East Pakistan .070/.131. The fact that these decrements are so much smaller than the proportion of variance explained by each set alone indicates that to some extent the sets overlap, and when one set is dropped the other "takes over" for it in explaining some part of the variance.

13. In the project identification system this scale is designated OM-1. It includes only seventy-nine items selected from the larger pool by a panel of expert judges on the grounds that (a) they dealt only with attitudes, not information, political orientation, or action, and (b) they clearly were appropriate to test the original theoretical conception of modernity as more or less "officially" defined by the project staff. The relation of OM-1 to the other OM scales and to the independent variables was described in chapter 4.

14. This assertion is supported by consideration of the relevant gamma statistics on the relationship of attitudinal modernity (OM scores) and information tests. For this purpose low and high education groups were tested separately (except in Pakistan), hence the number of gamma statistics obtained is twice the number of items used. The average gamma statistics shown below are based on three-part tables, which included middle as well as low and high OM. Separate results are given for items and for scales, since the scales show the combined effects of groups of items, and hence are not truly "independent" additional tests of the hypothesis under scrutiny.

Tests	Argentina	Chile	India	Israel	Nigeria	Pakistan
Based on items:						
average gamma	.20	.23	.34	.24	.21	.30
number of tests	60	62	58	52	46	29
Based on scales:						
average gamma	.31	.30	.45	.31	.28	.34
number of tests	24	24	24	28	24	10

15. Table 5-4 shows the percentage whose behavior validated their oral "claim" only in the case of those falling at the extremes of the continuum on each "claim." To leave no doubt that the outcome was not a fortuitous result of considering only the extremes, we note the gamma statistics for the full cross-tabulation including all steps in both the oral claim and the behavioral test. The five tests of the relation

between claim and behavior applied in six countries yield a potential thirty tests, but some were inapplicable in certain instances. The procedure was repeated separately for the "low" and "high" educated, divided at the median in each country. For the low educated, where twenty-seven of the tests were applicable, the association of claim and behavior was in the expected direction in all cases, and the gammas ranged from .01 to .88, with a mean of .35 and a median of .33. For the high educated, the hypothesis could be tested in twenty-three full cross tabulations. All but two of the associations were in the expected direction, the gammas ranging from −.12 to .70, and over this range the mean gamma was .31 and the median .28.

16. Variants of the test were used with the Yoruba, as reported by Leighton et al. (1963), and the Zulu, as reported by Scotch and Geiger (1963–64). Details on the form of the test as we used it, and the results of our investigation, are given in chapter 12.

17. These independent variables were defined and described more precisely in the second part of chapter 3.

18. The detailed results, by country, are shown in table 20-1 of Inkeles and Smith (1974).

19. For the justification of this assertion, see the evidence presented on pages 422–23 of Inkeles and Smith (1974).

20. This was most notably so for Argentina and Chile, as judged by the Beta weights of a regression including education, mass media, and years of factory work as predictors. For details see chapter 19 of Inkeles and Smith (1974).

21. A special version of the OM scale was administered by Donald Holsinger (1972) of Stanford University to boys and girls in the third to fifth grades of schools in Brazilia. At each grade level, the modernity scores of the girls were equal to those of the boys, and the girls gained as many points on the OM scale as did the boys during each additional year of schooling. In a study of Black women in Boston, Richard Suzman (1973a) administered a modified version of the OM scale. Basically the same items that had been used with our men in underdeveloped countries combined to yield a reliable OM scale for the Boston women. Moreover, the OM scores for women, using the Boston scale, could, in turn, be explained by much the same influences that explained the modernity of men in our samples from underdeveloped countries. It should also be noted that the Kahl (1968) modernity scale, originally developed for use with men in Brazil and Chile, evidently worked quite well when used to study the responses of women in the United States.

22. In his unpublished contribution to the conference on Alternatives in Development sponsored by the Vienna Institute for Development in June 1971, Dr. Salazar Bondy, a leading intellectual of Peru, wrote as follows: "Underdevelopment is not just a collection of statistical indices which enable a socioeconomic picture to be drawn. It is also a state of mind, a way of expression, a form of outlook and a collective personality marked by chronic infirmities and forms of maladjustment."

CHAPTER 6. INDIAN IMAGES OF MODERNITY IN CROSS-CULTURAL PERSPECTIVE

1. The correlation of each question with Indian Scale 1 is inflated because in such a short scale the element of "autocorrelation" plays a major role. Each item, being in the scale, and being perfectly correlated with itself, has an item-to-scale

correlation incorporating this perfect self-to-self correlation. The item-to-scale correlations in table 6-1 involving the OM Scale reflect no such autocorrelation, since the special Indian questions were not included in the OM Scale. An adjustment of the correlations of the items to the Indian Scale to discount for autocorrelation would bring them much closer to the magnitudes of the item to-OM scale correlations.

CHAPTER 7. INDIVIDUAL MODERNITY IN DIFFERENT ETHNIC AND RELIGIOUS GROUPS

1. Hagen (1962), *On the Theory of Social Change.*

2. Our project did make an estimate of the "productivity" of each industrial worker in our samples. In general, the more "modern" the individual proved to be, as judged by our test of individual modernity, the greater was his productivity. This relationship held with education and skill controlled. The correlations were, however, of modest magnitude, even though statistically significant.

3. Some of my reservations about this work were expressed in Inkeles (1971a).

4. Except where otherwise noted, all the individual modernity (OM) scores reported in this chapter are for OM-3, as described in Inkeles and Smith (1974). In some instances where the appropriate computer run for OM-3 was not available, we substituted OM-500, a virtually identical scale. The figures on the percentage modern for different groups are for OM-500. The samples were divided into thirds in each country, and all those in the upper third on the distribution of OM scores were classified as "modern." Subgroups with less than ten cases were excluded from consideration. If they had not been excluded, the contrast between the percent modern in the different subgroups would have been even greater.

We cannot urge too strongly the importance of not jumping to conclusions about these striking differences. It should especially be remembered that our research design made no provision for insuring that any subset of men entering our sample was in any way representative of a defined "parent population" having the same ethnic or religious identity, affiliation, or origin. People entered our sample because they happened to be in the factories we studied and fit the broad categorical sampling criteria of age, education, and occupation used in the larger study, as fully described in Inkeles and Smith (1974). We have no way of knowing the relation between the characteristics of the 39 people from Turkey included in our samples on the one hand, and, on the other, the set of *all* Jews in Israel who had emigrated from Turkey.

5. Analysis of covariance would have yielded modernity scores for each ethnic group, adjusted for the differences in exposure to modernizing influence. Path analysis would make clearer the degree to which initial cultural orientations work through differential educational and occupational paths to influence eventual modernity. It seems clear from analysis we have done that these methods, while supplementing the information available, will not challenge the main conclusions reached in this chapter.

6. Their numbers were, respectively, 314, 431, 284, and 271.

7. Those classified as "high" caste were Brahmin, Kshatriya (Rajput), Bhumihar, and Vaishya (Bania). All others, such as Kurmi, Kahar, Hazam, etc., were treated as "low" caste.

8. The Indian Constitution, Article 46, grants special privileges to both the "scheduled castes," which we call "low-caste," and the "scheduled tribes." However, the distinction between what we have called "low-caste" Hindu and tribal groups, also known as Adivasi, is also one which can be maintained only very imprecisely. Tribal groups often move up in the status hierarchy, and pass over into the lower rungs of the Hindu caste system.

9. According to *The Census of India* (1961) 4:23, in Bihar, of each 1,000 tribals, 720 were Hindus, 175 Sarna, and 105 Christians. Those who are Hindu, however, often retain many elements of their tribal-religious beliefs, and those who remain Sarna practice a religion much infused with Hinduism. We therefore decided to treat them as a single group under the designation "tribal Hindu." In making these distinctions within the tribal group, we disregarded the fact that they are also divided into four well-recognized tribes: Mundas, Oraon, Ho, and Santal. Widespread intermarriage and cultural diffusion among the members of these groups led Dr. Singh to consider the tribal differentiation less important than the religious.

10. The original figures were given as the number literate per 1,000 males, and ran: low-caste 111, tribals 152, residual 349. These residuals were, presumably, the equivalent of our high-caste Hindus.

11. This was especially true in the range commonly defined as "low" in education. Among the farmers in that range, high-caste Hindus had an average of more than five years of education; tribal Sarnas had only one year; whereas tribal Christians had attained a rather better average of 3.6 years of schooling, presumably because they had had missionary schools to attend. Similarly among workers, the average number of years in school varied markedly as one moved from one to another ethnic-religious group. Under the circumstances, any usual "control" that divided the sample into groups "low" and "high" on education would be prejudicial to the tribals, especially the Sarna. One ethnic group "low" in education might actually have five times as many years in school, on the average, as a second ethnic group also classified as "low" in education.

12. In preparing this section we have drawn on two unpublished documents: Dr. Edward Ryan's unpublished "Field Director's Report for Nigeria," and Dr. Olatunde Oloko's (1970) dissertation.

13. These included, notably, the more north-western Yoruba—Oyo, Ibadan, and Oshun. Also excluded were people from the Okitipupa division; the Owo division on the extreme eastern border of the Yoruba territory; the Eko of Lagos, the far northern Yoruba of Ilorin and Kabba; the Egun, living west of Lagos; and the Aworri.

14. We asked our question about religion in this form: "Which *orisha* do you worship?" The *orisha* is the focus of ritual and the object of veneration in traditional Yoruba religion. Dr. Ryan asked the question in this form because he felt that using the Yoruba word for religion (*esin*) might lead the respondents to answer in terms of more formal religions. Nevertheless, only 6 in some 700 men responded by naming a tribal deity. Virtually everyone countered by saying, "Well, I am Christian (or Moslem)." We do not mean to assert, however, that elements of the traditional religions do not infuse these later acquisitions.

15. The 1952 census of Nigeria's Western Region showed the people of Egba Division to be 55 percent Moslem and 34 percent Christian. In the Ijebu division the proportions were, respectively, 49 and 46 percent. Together, the Egba and Ijebu

made up three-fourths of our sample. It is evident, therefore, that in religious composition our sampled groups were similar to the census population. For details, see Oloko (1970).

16. The match on religion in Nigeria (#18) yielded a correlation of −.03, indicating the Moslems were slightly, but far from significantly, more modern. Using the total sample rather than the match group, we obtained zero-order correlation of religion with OM of .08, significant at .05 in favoring the Christians. But the standard partialing process reduced that figure to −.00. For the comparable Beta weight see table 7-3.

17. These subtribes in our sample numbered: Ijebu 245, Egba 313, Ekiti-Ondo 63, and Ijesha 52. The Ijebu include the Ijebu-Remo, and the Ekiti-Ondo groups include 13 who were classified Akure and Idanre. There were also 37 who defined themselves as Egbado, and 11 who were Ife, Modakeke, or Origbo. The bases for deciding which of the Yoruba subgroups to include were established by Dr. Ryan, as field director. First, he felt it important to include a set which was culturally homogeneous, so that cultural proclivities to enter select occupations would not confound our study of the relative modernity of the incumbents of those occupations. Second, he ruled, on grounds of efficiency in locating cases, not to include groups who were known to contribute very few men, in absolute numbers, to industrial employment.

18. The unpublished doctoral dissertation of Olatunde Oloko (1970) includes numerous citations from historical sources to support these statements.

19. Quoted from an appendix to the official 1952 census of the Western Region of Nigeria in Oloko (1970).

20. The resultant match (19X) produced a comfortable N of 69. The match was of good quality, except that the three groups differed markedly in mass-media exposure. To effect equalization on this variable required reducing the N (in Match 19XM) to only 23 cases. The results with this stricter match were in accord with those from the larger match.

21. In the match with N=69 (19X) the correlation of OM with ethnicity in the match groups was .04, favoring the Ijebu over the Egba. In mean score, the Ijebu earned about one point more on OM than did the Egba. However, none of these differences was statistically significant.

22. In Match 19X, N=69, the correlation in the match "Others-Ijebu" was −.11, and in the match "Others-Egba," −.14, thus both times favoring the "Others," who were ahead by two OM points. In Match 19XM, controlling more strictly for mass-media exposure, but with N=23 only, the respective figures were −.10 and −.09. None of the correlations were statistically significant.

23. For relevant background see Eisenstadt (1967).

24. The countries making up these groups and the size of the respective cohorts were: Near East: Iraq 154, Yemen/Aden 104, Egypt 33, Syria 7, Lebanon 2. North Africa: Morocco 209, Tunisia 49, Algeria 21, Libya 18. Asia: Iran 43, Turkey 39, Afghanistan 5, and India 7. There were 48 cases whose country of origin was not recorded. Of course, these placements are subject to debate. For example, some would challenge including the Turks with the Asian group. Indeed, in table 7-4 they were regrouped with the Near East.

25. The Beta weights from the regression analysis will be found in table 7-3. In

the three-way match 19X, with N=19, we obtained the following pattern of correlations: North Africa/Asia −.12; Asia/Near East .10; Africa/Near East .01. Mean OM scores were: Asia 57, Africa 59, Near East 59. In both the matches and the regression the countries were grouped as described in the preceding footnote.

26. Among the African Jews, for example, the Libyan contingent had 44 percent scoring high on OM, whereas only 16 percent of the Tunisians were so outstanding. In Asia Minor the figures were 23 percent for Iran and 56 percent for Turkey. These differences were manifested on OM 500, trichotomized, in groups not controlled for education or the other variables taken into account in the matches.

27. In this review of the characteristics of the Pentecostal Protestants in Chile, we relied heavily on Emilio Willems (1967). Willems did not, however, take a stand on the probability that they would or would not score as more modern than Catholics. That judgement is our responsibility.

28. Our Chilean sample came predominantly from the province of Santiago, in which Protestants made up 5.2 percent of the industrial labor force. We drew smaller groups of men from Concepcion and Valdivia, in whose industrial labor force Protestants made up more than 9 percent. The average of 6.1 percent in our total sample, therefore, seems very close to the proportion in the parent population.

29. Results reported are for match =18.

30. In the total sample the religion variable, entered in the order Catholic/Protestant, yielded the very small zero-order correlation of .04, favoring the Protestants. When seven other main variables were controlled, the correlation was .06, providing one of those rare instances in which a partial was higher than a zero-order correlation. Even with the aid of the clarification provided by the partial, however, the correlation of religion and OM was far below statistical significance.

Since the Protestants were so small a segment of the total sample, we decided to check this relationship within the factory-worker group alone. We now obtained a zero-order correlation of .02 and a partial of .03. Thus, these results support the conclusion that differences in the modernity of working-class Catholics and Protestants do not persist once one takes account of education, mass-media contact, and occupation.

31. For the total sample the zero-order correlation, favoring the Protestants, was .03, and the partial, .04, neither significant.

32. The N for the match was only 29, which made it less likely that the observed differences would attain statistical significance.

33. This was the result when the analysis was applied to the total sample.

34. A path analysis of the influence of religion/ethnicity on individual modernity has been completed and we should note here the main results. Like father's education, one's ethnicity/religion did not seem to confer *directly* any very great advantage or disadvantage with regard to OM scores. Most of the impact of such ethnic or religious background was *in*direct, mediated through intervening variables. We did find some significant *true* indirect effects of ethnicity/religion upon OM scores, mediated through significant relationships with the intervening variables of education-literacy and occupational type. This suggests that men from the ethnic-religious groupings that we ranked as more modern tend to achieve a higher "education-literacy level" and a higher "occupational-type level" than men from less modern ethnic-religious groups. Thus, it seems that it is not the ethnic-

religious group experience *per se* that is a modernizing experience. Instead, being a member of a given ethnic-religious grouping tends to make more probable a man's exposure to greater or lesser amounts of directly modernizing experiences, such as formal education or experience in factory work. The supply of education and factory experience can, of course, be more readily increased and diffused than could some more distinctive cultural value scheme.

35. The ordering of groups within each variable was determined by the outcome of the more detailed dummy variable analysis presented in table 7-3. Thus, in Argentina, those whose parents were both Argentinian were punched 1, and so on through the category "Argentinian plus Spanish," which was punched 6 because that group had shown itself most modern. It should be recognized that constructing the ethnicity measure in this way, based on the criterion itself, gave the variable a decided advantage in competition with other variables in the regression that had been constructed in more conventional ways.

36. In assessing these results, one must keep in mind that in linear regression analysis the outcome for any variable depends not only on its association with other variables in the set, but also on the initial strength of association with the dependent variable. Ours were special samples limited to the working class, and so the range on many variables, such as own education and father's education, was much more truncated than would have been the case if we had had fuller national samples across the whole available range.

CHAPTER 8. NATIONAL DIFFERENCES IN INDIVIDUAL MODERNITY

1. This was in a regression on OM 500. The range in variance explained was from 32 percent in Israel to 62 percent in India (Inkeles and Smith, 1974, chapter 20).

2. This was true only in the sense that we could not meaningfully compare the OM score of a man in one country with that of a man in any other country. However, we could, and did, show that the structure of relations between the "explanatory" and the dependent variables was basically the same across all six countries (Inkeles and Smith, 1974, *passim*).

3. The goal of attaining truly *equivalent* measures across cultures and countries, rather than striving for literal translation, is generally stressed by comparative researchers (Przeworski and Teune 1970; Manaster and Havighurst 1972; Brislin et al. 1973).

4. To establish its relevance a question had to have an item-to-scale correlation (adjusted for autocorrelation) significant at least at the .05 level in all six countries. The scale used was OM-3, our longest. For details about that scale, see chapter 4 and Inkeles and Smith (1974, chapters 6 and 7).

5. An example of a question rendered comparable by minor recording is EF-14, which asked for an evaluation of scientific research into such things as what makes a child come out as a boy or a girl. In four of the countries only two alternative answers were presented: "good" or "bad." In the two remaining countries, the respondent was asked to select his preference from among four alternatives on a continuum from good to bad. We collapsed the four alternatives into two, thus making it possible to score the question following exactly the same procedure in all six countries.

6. Question CH-3 is an example of a question which could not be rendered strictly comparable by any simple recoding, but which nevertheless could be treated as if it were "more or less alike" in all countries. The question was designed to test the readiness of people to accept technical innovations in agriculture. What obliged us to classify this question as only "more or less comparable" across countries was the fact that the field directors had varied the description of the situation in which the innovation came up for discussion. In one country, for example, the father was talking to a boy of only 12, but in another country the son was described as being 18 years of age. Although we could, in all the countries, code the answers as being simply "for" or "against" the innovation, we could not be sure how far the context in which the innovation had been presented in the question might have influenced people in different countries to be more pro or con.

7. The only departure from exact duplication in constructing IM2A was in the recoding of alternatives so that the number in each country was the same as described in footnote 5, above. Questions considered only "more or less" comparable, as described in footnote 6, above, were excluded. The code letter and number of the 93 questions, listed immediately hereafter, may be used to ascertain their wording by reference to Appendix A of *Becoming Modern*: AC-4; AC-6; AG-2; AS-3; AS-6; AS-8; AS-11; CA-2; CA-3; CA-6, CA-7; CA-8; CA-11; CH-1,2; CH 10, 11; Ch-12, 13; CH-14; CI-2; CI-7; CI-13; CI-14; CO-7; CO-8; DI-6; DI-7; DI-8; DI-11; EF-1; EF-2; EF-3; EF-4; EF-8, EF-9, EF-11, 12; EF-13; EF-14; EF-15; EF-16; FS-1; FS-3; GO-1; GO-2; GO-3; GO-4; GO-5; GO-6; GO-7; IN-7; KO-2; KO-3; KO-4; KO-5; KO-6; MM-6; MM-7; MM-10, 11; NE-1; NE-2; NE-3; NE-7; PL-1; PL-2; PL-3; PL-4; PL-5; PL-9; RE-2; RE-3; RE-4; RE-8; RE-9; RE-11; RE-12; SC-2, SC-8; ST-9; TI-3; TI-4; TI-5; TI-7; TS-14; WC-13, 14; WR-1; WR-3; WR-4; WR-6; WR-7; WR-8; WR-9; WR-11; WR-12; WR-13; WR-14. Entries with two numbers such as CH-1, 2 or MM-10, 11 indicate that the answers to two questions were, in our coding, combined as if they had been in reponse to a single question.

8. The reliability of the IM scale was lower than that of the OM scales in all six countries. Clearly we paid some price for insisting that the IM scale everywhere use exactly the same questions and codings. However, the OM scales had been cleaned by eliminating the items in any country which showed relatively low item to scale correlations. When those items were replaced by others with similar content but of greater reliability, the OM scales remained basically alike across all countries while yet being maximally reliable. Since the IM scale permitted no substitutions, and was scored by an inflexible international rule, it showed lower reliabilities.

9. As reported in *Becoming Modern* (Inkeles and Smith 1974, p. 101) OM-3, from which IM2A was derived, included questions representing 24 of the themes we considered relevant to an overall conception of individual modernity. The questions which qualified for inclusion in IM2A represented 22 of those themes. The two topics which did not qualify were: "understanding production" and "work commitment." As chapter 7 of *Becoming Modern* makes clear, no one element of the modernity syndrome was indispensable for defining the syndrome empirically. But even if there had been either theoretically or empirically indispensable themes, these two would certainly have not been among them.

10. Such effects were observed in the process of our examination of the several variants on the IM scale which we initially constructed. Thus, when we used any

one of four longer versions of the IM scale, the Nigerians obtained a mean score (unadjusted) which put them ahead of the Indians and Chileans. However, on the two short forms of the scale, which had only 12 and 17 items, respectively, Nigeria was behind Chile and India. Inspection of the short scales, item by item, revealed that our Yoruba respondents were especially sensitive to questions which pitted luck against other forces. Evidently, without intending it, we had used a disproportionate number of such questions in the very short scales. By very consistently giving less modern answers to those questions, the Nigerians drove down their overall score, and emerged as a seemingly less modern group than they were when tested on the longer scales. Their few extreme answers had, in a short scale, outweighed the otherwise general propensity of the Nigerians to give answers at least as modern as those usually given by Chileans and Indians.

11. By country the standard deviation of IM2A was, respectively: Argentina 7.3, Chile 7.6, India 10.1, Israel 8.3, Nigeria 7.0, East Pakistan 6.8. We consider these to be very similar. Even the Indian case seemed not an anomaly, but rather stemmed from the fact that the Indian sample had a more U-shaped distribution, containing an extra large number of cases with no schooling and an extra large number with some high school education. This evidence on the standard deviation, along with that on the reliabilities, supported our confidence in the cross-national IM scale as appropriate for use in all six countries.

12. Across our six countries, the median Pearsonian correlation of individual modernity (OM-500) with education-literacy was .52, with mass media exposure .45, and with occupation .41. These three measures accounted for about 80 percent of the variance in OM scores which could be "explained" by our full battery of measures. For detailed evidence concerning the role of these measures as predictors, and presumed causes, of individual modernity see chapter 5 and Inkeles and Smith (1974).

13. One interpretation of convergence theory might lead one to expect that industrial workers from different countries should be more alike than sets of peasants from those same countries would be. An alternative interpretation would deny that prediction. This would be done on the grounds that peasant villages in different countries actually have a great deal in common. Following from the assumption that like organizational milieux produce like personal dispositions one should, therefore, predict that a cross-national comparison of peasants will produce no greater diversity than cross-national comparisons of workers, *at least on a general psychosocial measure such as the modernity scale*. The extensive set of cross-national matches we have developed for each occupational group permits some initial testing of these competing theories.

14. The matches presented in table 8-2 were drawn from a much larger pool. We actually constructed a total of 56 international matches, focused on different combinations of occupation and education, such as "high educated cultivators," or "rural origin urban nonindustrial workers." Some of these combinations were applicable in only two countries. Others yielded matched groups with extremely few cases, and it was our general rule not to use matches with an N of less than 10. The matches in table 8-2 were not selected in advance from the larger pool to make any particular point, but to save space and simplify the presentation. The criteria for inclusion in table 8-2 were that the match have a large N, include as many

countries as possible given the occupational and educational range covered by the match, and be minimally redundant. That the matches thus selected led to conclusions consistent with those drawn using the larger set will be evident from data given in notes 17, 18, and 19.

15. The scoring system for the IM scale, as for the OM scales on which it was modeled, was designed to permit this simple interpretation of score differences. Regardless of the number of questions asked, all OM and IM scores are expressed on a scale from 0 to 100. This results from the fact that all answers are scored 1.00 for traditional responses, 2.00 for modern responses, with the total then averaged by the number of questions the individual answered. On a scale with 100 items, a five point difference means precisely five more questions answered in the modern or traditional direction. For shorter or longer scales, containing less than or more than 100 items, a process of extrapolation is obviously involved in making the sort of statement made in the text.

16. It will be noted that the order in which the countries stand when they are ranked according to the percent modern does not accord perfectly with their relative standing when mean scores are used as the basis for ranking, as in table 8-2. Thus, Argentina had the highest mean scores on Match A-1, but India and not Argentina had the highest proportion qualifying as "modern." Such anomalous findings can arise because the same mean can result from a different assortment of high and low scores. Consequently, the same group mean can yield different proportions labeled modern, depending on the *distribution* of the scores which yielded the mean. For example, with the same overall average you could have a large number of individuals bunched just above *or* just below the cutoff point defining the "modern" man. Other scores could smooth out, or equalize, the average, but would not equalize the percent considered modern in the two cases. Because of the smaller numbers used in the matches, we found the "percent modern" figures to be more volatile than the means, and hence in table 8-2 preferred to use the mean scores.

17. As noted above, for lack of space table 8-2 does not present all the available match comparisons we could make. Using our largest set of matches, we had available a total of 65 comparisons of any pair from the set: Chile, Nigeria, India. Of that total, 83 percent were not significant, even at the .05 level. By contrast, in 41 matches pitting East Pakistan against *either* Chile, Nigeria, or India, 34 percent favored the other country over Bangladesh at .05 or better. Indeed, in not a single match were the East Pakistanis ahead of any one of these three competitors, even at a statistically nonsignificant level.

18. In the thirteen available matches comparing the East Pakistanis and the Argentinians, the latter were ahead in 100 percent of the cases, and 54 percent of those matches gave the Argentinians a statistically significant advantage at .001 or better. Comparisons of the Argentinians with either Chileans, Indians, or Nigerians were made in a total of 100 matches, of which 46 percent favored Argentina, significant at .05 or better. By contrast, in not even a single contest were the Argentinians significantly *behind* the Chileans, the Nigerians, or the Indians.

19. In seventeen matches permitting comparison of the Argentinians with the Israelis, each alternated being ahead pretty much 50/50. Of the total, none of the comparisons was statistically significant at even the .05 level.

20. The regression equation for which IM2A was the dependent variable

contained the following independent variables: years of education, years of factory experience, mass media (a scale measuring radio listening and newspaper reading), age, consumer goods possessed, and urban versus rural origin. In addition, the equation contained five dummy variables for "country." These are variables which take on the value 1 or 0, depending upon whether a man is in a certain country or not, respectively. For the logic of this procedure see Searle (1971). The B weights (unstandardized regression coefficients) of the dummy variables, and of the above listed covariates, enabled us to calculate adjusted means for each country. The B's and Betas for the covariates are given in table 8-3. Note that all these variables were coded so as to be strictly comparable cross-nationally, except for consumer goods possessed. That variable actually is based on possession of different items in different countries, and each individual was coded as falling above or below the mean in his own country.

21. This "nationality" variable was based on the mean modernity score of each country on IM2A. The resulting B and Beta weights for the six additional explanatory variables, given in table 8-3, were the same as when we entered nationality in the form of the five dummy variables as described in the previous note. Incidentally, the same six variables were used as covariates in calculating the adjusted means in table 8-1.

22. It is worth noting that the Beta weights from the regression on the original OM scale *done separately within each country*, were, in the median case, quite close to those obtained using the total sample for a regression on the IM scale. Giving the six-country median Beta for OM first, followed by that for the total 5,500-case IM regression, the results were: education .37/.34; mass media exposure .18/.18; occupation .16/.13. The basic eight variables used in the regression on OM yielded a median R^2 of .47, whereas, in our analysis of IM a set of six variables, including country, yielded an R^2 of .43 for the combined multi-country sample. Any regression of this type may be much affected by problems of multi-colinearity. The available space does not permit dealing in detail with such problems here. They are, however, dealth with extensively in the analysis presented in Inkeles and Smith (1974).

23. Both the Indian and the East Pakistan samples were Bengali in culture, and their respective countries stand moderately close on a scale of national economic development. Yet the Indian and East Pakistani samples manifested significant differences in individual modernity. In eighteen match comparisons which controlled for most important variables, the Indian sample was ahead of the East Pakistani 94 percent of the time, and in 50 percent of those matches the difference was statistically significant.

24. The ethnic and religious composition of each of our six national samples is described in some detail in chapter 7. That chapter also deals with ethnic and religious membership as an influence on individual modernity, but the analysis is limited to comparisons *within* each country separately.

25. The assumption of an effect due to culture or national character, the position taken in our third alternative explanation, is to some extent supported by the fact that in making this substitution of GNP for the country dummy variables we reduced the Beta weight for country from .21 to .16, and the unique variance explained by "country" from the former 4 percent to between 1 and 2 percent. That portion of between country variance not explained by GNP might well be due to

cultural differences. GNP per capita clearly is not sufficient to capture or summarize all the qualities of a country which influence the psychological modernity of its citizens.

CHAPTER 9. CONSTRUCTION AND VALIDATION OF A CROSS-NATIONAL SCALE OF FAMILY MODERNISM

1. The main themes dealt with by our questionnaire are set forth in chapter 2 on chart 2-1. For further details about the themes and subscales readers should consult *Becoming Modern* (Inkeles and Smith, 1974). The main themes are listed there in table 2-1 and are discussed there in chapter 2. The 35 subscales are listed there in table 7-2.

2. Each question in our questionaire was identified by a letter code to indicate the theme or scale it represented, and a number to distinguish it from the other questions dealing with that theme. The wording of all questions used in the questionaire may be found in Appendix A of Inkeles and Smith (1974).

3. In addition to the eight questions used in constructing CFM-1 and listed in chart 11-1, we used some 37 other questions in constructing CFM-2, OFM, and the Maximum K-R family scales. Space limitations preclude our giving the precise wordings and response categories for this fuller pool of items, but those wishing to examine them will find them in Appendix A of Inkeles and Smith (1974). The relevant question code numbers to use are: AG-2; AG-3; AG-50; AG-51; AS-9; AS-10; CH-4; CH-5; CH-6; CH-7; DI-7; DI-50; FS-2; FS-4; FS-5; FS-6; FS-51; GO-3; GO-50; ID-3; KO-1; KO-3; KO-4; KO-6; PL-5; SC-8; WR-1; WR-2; WR-3; WR-4; WR-5; WR-6; WR-8; WR-9; WR-12; WR-14; WR-51.

CHAPTER 10. MODERNITY AND ACCEPTANCE OF FAMILY LIMITATION

1. For a full account of construction and content of OM-500, see Inkeles and Smith (1974).

2. It was our judgment that the negative beta weights were not high enough to justify constructing a scale of negatively relating variables.

3. The item content of the scales can generally be accurately ascertained from their labels. However, the "secularism" scale is least obvious; its item content in abbreviated form was: (a) Whom do you admire more: monk or factory owner? (b) Which of the two men, in your opinion, has done more for his country? (c) Which man has best lived up to his religion?

CHAPTER 11. PARTICIPANT CITIZENSHIP IN SIX DEVELOPING COUNTRIES

1. We do not mean to ignore the substantial body of writing in which it has been argued that Russia, Germany, and Japan, while important examples of a modernizing tendency, have indeed not yet attained a "true" condition of modernity. To engage in that particular dialogue would take us far afield from our

main task here. For further discussion see Robert E. Ward and Dankwart A. Rustow (1964), and Robert Bellah (1965).

2. See T. H. Marshall (1964).

3. In this description we have condensed, and blended, elements of what Almond and Verba (1963) term the "parochial" and "subject" political cultures.

4. Lucian Pye (1962) considers this problem of developing identification with, and allegiance to, the national state as the highest priority task of the developing nations.

5. We are not unaware that pull and influence, and family connections and bribery, are common enough in modern states, including and perhaps even especially, in the more democratic ones. But we believe it correct to assert that *expectation*, and the formal system of *values*, in the modern polity run very much counter to such behavior. Whether or not corruption is in fact less common in modern polities, which we believe it to be, would be difficult to establish beyond peradventure.

6. See Alex Inkeles (1972).

7. McClosky and Schaar (1965); McClosky (1967).

8. We borrow here from the essay of Max Scheler (1961), titled *Ressentiment*, in which he describes a psychopolitical syndrome having the characteristics we have sketched above.

9. The core set initially contained 39 questions, but local circumstances dictated the omission of certain items in some countries—3 in East Pakistan, 2 in Argentina, and 1 in Israel. In Chile, Argentina, and Israel, in which time pressure was less severe, and the field directors felt greater freedom to touch on sensitive political issues, these 39 core questions were supplemented by others of local interest, up to a total of 54. Those additional questions, not being available in all six countries, are not considered in this chapter.

10. The individual's score on each subscale ranged from a minimum of 1 to a maximum of 2. This followed from the fact that each item was dichotomized as closely as possible to the median in each country, with a score of 2 assigned to the "modern" answer, 1 to the "traditional." Averaging by the number of items in the scale kept the range of the several scale scores uniform regardless of the number of items in the scale. To simplify reading the score results, we adopted the convention of treating scores of 1.00 as equal to 0 and 2.00 as equal to 100, enabling us to express individual scores on the common scale of 0–100.

11. See Melvin Seeman (1959). For a discussion of findings, see McClosky and Schaar (1965); Neal and Retting (1963).

12. Almond and Verba (1963, chapter 15, esp. pp. 497–505).

13. This refers only to the questions tapping general orientations towards political participation. Questions about which party they favored, or which candidate they supported, or what specific changes should be made in the government, were considered so delicate that we decided against even asking them in East Pakistan. When they were asked in other countries, such questions did sometimes lead to refusal to answer, and in other ways lessened rapport with the interviewee.

14. Tastes and standards will, of course, vary, as to what strength of relationship between the items is required before one will accept a set of items as constituting a scale. We adopted as a rule of thumb that the average item-to-item correlations

should be significant at least at the .05 level in at least four of the six countries. The most widely accepted standard of the quality of a scale is the measure of its reliability. Using the Spearman-Brown formula for the eight scales in six countries, we obtained a range of reliabilities from .60 to .91, with a mean of .71 and a median of .70.

15. A second alternative would be to construct a summary scale based directly on the items making up the several subscales. This has been done, with results reported in note 19 below. A third alternative would be factor analysis of either the subscales or the original questions. This we did not do.

16. The statistical tests of significance used in table 11-1 and at later points in this chapter assume a random sample. Ours are in fact cluster samples selected according to the dictates of our research design. Within those limits we sometimes have not so much a sample as the entire eligible population. In other cases we have taken our subjects as we found them, and in yet other instances drew them at random from a defined population. Given the nature of our "samples" we consider the test of significance based on the assumption of random sampling to be a conservative one, although this might be challenged in some instances. In any event, no single statistic presented here should be considered as having a major or minor weight on the sole basis of the test of significance attached to it. We have used the tests of significance in order to have some general standard which could be applied as an aid in interpreting the statistics presented. The tests of significance given should not be interpreted too literally. They should rather be taken as a rough criterion which permits only a very proximate estimate of the confidence limits of the statistics presented. Most weight should be given to the pattern of results across a variety of measures, and across the set of six countries.

17. The individual's score on this summary scale was the mean of his score on each of the five subscales. From this it follows that in the summary scale each subscale carries the same weight, i.e., one-fifth, regardless of the number of questions on which the subscale is based. But the fact that only five units are included in computing the summary score also contributes to the high correlations shown in table 11-1 between the summary citizenship and each of the subscales. Those correlations are each, in part, autocorrelations. The correlations of each subscale to the summary scale constructed to exclude the given subscale would be substantially lower.

18. Using the Spearman-Brown formula, the summary scale yielded the following reliabilities: Argentina .69; Chile .72; India .75; Israel .72; Nigeria .72; Pakistan .72.

19. The reliabilities thus obtained ranged from .76 to .79 when computed by the Spearman-Brown formula. Using the Kuder-Richardson formula the reliabilities ranged from .69 to .74. These reliabilities are in the same range as those for scales of comparable length dealing with political attitudes in the United States. Thurstone's Patriotism Scale, for example, yielded reliabilities ranging from .69 to .83. Some others have done better, but generally only with college student populations who are more consistent than our less well-educated respondents can be expected to be. See Shaw and Wright (1967, esp. pp. 193–229, 301–29).

20. This inconsistency is not maintained when we consider only the relation of the evaluative scales to one another. In all six countries the scales of anomie, alienation, and negativism toward government effectiveness correlate quite signif-

icantly, and appear to form a coherent "resentment" syndrome. The relation of this syndrome to the scale of participant citizenship is, however, again different in India and Nigeria from other countries, and, throughout, the relationship is weak.

21. We will, later, see that some things which most everyone assumes to be obviously powerful causes of individual modernization nevertheless prove to be embarrassingly ineffective.

22. Since, as noted above, the five subscales had each been scored from 0 to 100, the theoretical range on the summary scales was also 0 to 100. The range of the actual scores was as follows: Argentina 0–87; Chile 0–95; India 0–88; Israel 0–100; Nigeria 0–100; Pakistan 7–93. The scoring system for the subscales insured that each of them would produce a distribution very nearly approximating the normal curve. In combining these five normal distributions, however, we could well have come out with a new distribution very far from the normal. In fact, the distribution of summary scores in each country was very close to normal. This could only have come about if the scores individuals received on any one subscale were in fact very similar to the scores they received on the other four scales, which further justifies our combining these five in one summary scale.

23. We must acknowledge that not all these tests were truly independent. For example, the measures of total years in school, of performance on our literacy test, and the score on a vocabulary ("opposites") test were all highly intercorrelated and might be considered merely alternate, rather than independent, measures of intellectual capacity. Nevertheless, we feel our conclusion stands.

24. We realize, of course, that in itself a correlation coefficient is not proof of cause, but only of covariation. Yet it also is evident that a man's current political attitudes could not have caused his educational level (except, of course, by affecting his recall of how much education he had had). The same case, although admittedly more vulnerable to challenge, may be made for other "objective" indices such as years of factory experience. It does not seem likely that most men enter and remain in factories because of their political attitudes.

25. This theme is further pursued, with some surprising results, later in this chapter.

26. See Clark Kerr et al. (1960); S. M. Lipset (1960, esp. pp. 248–52).

27. Neither do numerous other studies, particularly those undertaken in the United States and Europe, which consistently show those less advantaged also to participate less in politics. See, for example, Almond and Verba (1963, p. 176).

28. This point should be understood as applying to active citizenship as defined in this study, and not as necessarily applying to the evalutation of the government's performance, nor to the degree of individual commitment to the existing political system.

29. We also lose, however, because the matching process leaves us with very small numbers in the groups compared, and often selects a subset not truly representative of the larger group from which it is drawn. An alternative method would be multivariate regression analysis of the sort we used extensively in *Becoming Modern* and in some chapters of this volume. This method, of course, presents still other difficulties.

30. This fear is, however, hypothetical rather than real. We also carefully matched cultivators with men of the same villages who had recently migrated but had not yet been much exposed to industrial life. The evidence is clear-cut that, at

least in our six countries, the men who migrated were not self-selected on the basis of being more modern in attitude and spirit than those who remained behind.

31. The education match might, for example, place in the "low" group men with 0-3 years and in the "high" group those with 8-10 years of schooling, resulting in a substantial gap of 5 years. Few of the high and low education group would then overlap in attitude, and a high correlation would result. If the factory work match succeeded in placing men in the "high" and "low" experience categories with only a two-year gap, the overlap would be great and a lower correlation might be expected. Under such circumstances this lower correlation would not be correctly interpreted as showing that factory experience is a "weaker" variable than education.

32. For example, in the educational match in Argentina the highly educated set had, on the average, six years more schooling than the low-educated. Their mean scores on the citizenship scale were 60 and 38, respectively. The mean difference of 22 points on the scale, divided by 6 for the difference in years of education, yields a gain of 3.6 points per year.

33. For Argentina we have available a correlation of years of urban residence with years of factory experience for a subsample of factory workers only. The figure is very high: .78. Presumably the situation is much the same in the other countries.

34. This conclusion is supported by an unpublished independent multi-variate analysis done by David Smith using the Overall Modernity Scale as dependent variable. He concludes: "The weakest of the six independent variable clusters we have been examining is urbanity. This is a very great surprise indeed. For all six countries the average regression weight of urbanity is .01; factory experience averages .05, objective skill level .07." Additional details are given in chapters 4 and 5, above.

35. For example, in Nigeria, among men of rural origin and low education, 18 percent of both the UNI and the mid-experienced industrial workers scored "high" on citizenship. In Israel among the low educated, both occupational groups had about 21 percent "high."

36. See Alex Inkeles (1966). Almond and Verba (1963, p. 502) also believed that "the occupational changes that accompany industrialization . . . may increase the channels of (political) socialization." They did not, however, gather any evidence from their research to bear on the question.

37. Only some of which have been presented in this report.

38. The issues are dealt with in the chapter on urbanism in the general report on our project by Alex Inkeles and David H. Smith (1974).

39. We scored individuals as "high" on the scale of active citizenship if they fell in the upper third of the distribution of scale scores in their country. It is thus a highly relative designation. In less relative terms, a man had to select an alternative at the modern end of the continuum in somewhat more than half of the questions in the battery in order to score in the upper third of the distribution.

CHAPTER 12. PERSONAL ADJUSTMENT AND MODERNIZATION

1. In Israel nearly all of the respondents were considered of urban origin; hence, the origin test could not apply.

2. This applies only to the zero-order correlations, based on the total samples.

The matches, of necessity, were generally limited to quite small numbers. Nevertheless, as we explained above, the matches have other outstanding virtues which go far to compensate for the small numbers.

CHAPTER 14. MODERNIZATION OF MAN IN COMMUNIST COUNTRIES

1. In radical religious movements central importance is often also attached to transformations in ritual life. Closer examination will, however, reveal that the focus on ritual itself expresses an underlying concern for how ritual embodies or reflects values and interpersonal relations.

2. My failure to include the other socialist countries, especially those of Eastern Europe, should be understood as a matter of convenience rather than of principle. At the moment when the Communist Party came to power in Russia and China, both were in major degree "undeveloped." Although this was equally true for some of the other communist countries—let us say Albania and Bulgaria—others, such as Czechoslovakia, were among the most industrialized and modernized national states in Europe at the time they came under communist rule. To encompass the whole range of resultant types is beyond what is possible in as brief a paper as this must be.

3. For reports of other efforts to measure individual modernity, see: J. L. M. Dawson (1967); Joseph Kahl (1968).

4. There is, unfortunately, no single source known to me in which one can find a comprehensive discussion of the official conception of the ideal Soviet citizen. Forays in the appropriate direction will be found in: Alex Inkeles (1950); Margaret Mead (1951); Raymond A. Bauer (1952); Jules Monnerot (1953); Carl J. Friedrich (1954); Raymond A. Bauer, Alex Inkeles, and Clyde C. Kluckhohn (1956); H. Cantril (1960); Alex Inkeles (1968); Gayle D. Hollander (1972). Some of the sources cited above supplement their description of the ideal Soviet citizen with discussions of the often contradictory model encouraged by actual official behavior. For a more explicit statement of this model see Nathan Leites (1951). A more contemporary account may be found in numerous publications summarizing the *samizdat* materials appearing clandestinely in the USSR.

5. We are particularly fortunate to have available a detailed and highly competent analysis of Communist China's elementary school readers. These books were prepared under the direction of the People's Education Publishing House in Peking and used in Shanghai and Peking between 1958 and 1964 to instruct children in grades one through five of the Chinese elementary schools. See Charles P. Ridley, Paul H. Godwin, and Dennis J. Doolin (1971).

6. See Chinua Achebe (1961); (1965); (1966).

CHAPTER 15. THE FUTURE OF INDIVIDUAL MODERNITY

1. For an evaluation of the extent and force of the popular expectation of ever-greater entitlement to an ever-increasing range of services and goods from education through health to legal aid, see Inkeles (1977a).

2. For an exchange of views on this theme see Stephenson (1968) and Hagen (1976).

3. To facilitate making comparisons among different national populations we have scored the OM scale on an absolute "right or wrong" basis, rather than in the relative fashion utilized in creating the scales as reported in Inkeles and Smith (1974). In this form we call the scale not OM, but IM to stand for "International Modernity." See chapter 8.

4. For evidence that respect for, and readiness to care for, parents and elders persists in the presence of the greater autonomy characteristic of modern individuals, see chapter 13.

Bibliography

Achebe, C. 1961. *Things Fall Apart*. New York: McDowell, Obolensky.
— 1965. *Arrow of God*. London: Heinemann Educational Books.
— 1966. *A Man of the People*. London: William Heinemann.
Adelman, I. 1963. "An Econometric Analysis of Population Growth." *American Economic Review* 53:314-39.
— and C. T. Morris. 1971. *Society, Politics and Economic Development*. Baltimore: Johns Hopkins University Press.
— 1973. *Economic Growth and Social Equity in Developing Countries*. Stanford: Stanford University Press.
Aldous, J. and R. Hill. 1967. *International Bibliography of Research in Marriage and the Family 1960-1964*. Minneapolis: University of Minnesota Press.
Almond, G. A. and S. Verba. 1963. *The Civic Culture: Political Attitudes and Democracy in Five Nations*. Princeton: Princeton University Press.
Althauser, R. and D. Rubin. 1970. "The Computerized Construction of a Matched Sample." *American Journal of Sociology* 76:325-46.
Apter, D. E. 1965. *The Politics of Modernization*. Chicago: University of Chicago Press.
Armer, M. and A. Schnaiberg. 1972. "Measuring Individual Modernity: A Near Myth." *American Sociological Review* 37:301-16.
Armer, M. and R. Youtz. 1971. "Formal Education and Individual Modernity in an African Society." *American Journal of Sociology* 76:604-26.
Bachi, R. and J. Matras. 1964. "Family Size Preferences of Jewish Maternity Cases in Israel." *Milbank Memorial Fund Quarterly* 2:38-56.
Back, K. W. and P. H. Hass. 1973. "Family Structure and Fertility Control." In J. T. Fawcett, ed., *Psychological Perspectives on Population*. New York: Basic Books.
Bardis, P. D. 1959. "A Familism Scale." *Marriage and Family Living* 21:340-41.
Bauer, R. A. 1952. *The New Man In Soviet Psychology*. Cambridge: Harvard University Press.
Bauer, R. A., A. Inkeles, and C. C. Kluckhohn. 1956. *How the Soviet System Works*. Cambridge: Harvard University Press.
Bellah, R. N. 1968. "Meaning and Modernization." *Religious Studies* 4:37-45.
Bellah, R. N., ed. 1965. *Religion and Progress in Modern Asia*. New York: Free Press.

Bengston, V. L., J. J. Dowd, D. H. Smith, and A. Inkeles. 1975. "Modernization, Modernity, and Perceptions of Aging: A Cross Cultural Study." *Journal of Gerontology* 30: 688-95.

Berelson, B. 1966. "KAP Studies on Fertility." In B. Berelson, ed., *Family Planning and Population Programs: A Review of World Developments.* Chicago: University of Chicago Press.

Bergthold, G. D. and D. C. McClelland. 1968. *The Impact of Peace Corps Teachers on Students in Ethiopia.* Washington, D.C.: Human Development Foundation.

Berry, J. W. 1980. "Social and Cultural Change." In H. C. Triandis and W. W. Lambert, eds., *Social Psychology. Handbook of Cross-Cultural Psychology,* vol. 5. Boston: Allyn & Bacon.

Black, C. E. 1966. *The Dynamics of Modernization: A Study in Comparative History.* New York: Harper & Row.

Blake, J. 1969. "Population Policy for Americans: Is the Government Being Misled?" *Science* 164:522-29.

Blau, P. and O. D. Duncan. 1967. *The American Occupational Structure.* New York: John Wiley.

Bloom, B. S. 1964. *Stability and Change in Human Characteristics.* New York: John Wiley.

Bopegamage, A. and P. V. Veeraraghavan. 1967. *Status Images in Changing India.* Bombay: Manaktalas.

Bradburn, N. and D. Caplovitz. 1965. *Reports on Happiness.* Chicago: Aldine.

Brislin, R. W., W. J. Lonner, and R. M. Thorndike. 1973. *Cross-Cultural Research Methods.* New York: John Wiley.

Brode, J. 1969. *The Process of Modernization: An Annotated Bibliography of the Sociocultural Aspects of Development.* Cambridge: Harvard University Press.

Bumpass, L. and C. F. Westoff. 1970. "The 'Perfect Contraceptive' Population." *Science* 169:1177-82.

Buss, A. H. and R. Plomin. 1975. *Temperament Theory of Personality Development.* New York: John Wiley.

Camilleri, C. 1967. "Modernity and the Family in Tunisia." *Journal of Marriage and Family Living* 29:590-95.

Campbell, A., P. E. Converse, W. E. Miller, and D. E. Stokes. 1965. *The American Voter.* New York: John Wiley.

Cantril, H. 1960. *Soviet Leaders and Mastery Over Man.* New Brunswick, N.J.: Rutgers University Press.

—— 1965. *The Pattern of Human Concerns.* New Brunswick, N.J.: Rutgers University Press.

Christie, R. and M. Jahoda. 1954. *Studies in the Scope and Method of "The Authoritarian Personality."* Glencoe, Ill.: Free Press.

Clifford, W. B., II. 1971. "Modern and Traditional Value Orientations and Fertility Behavior: A Social Demographic Study." *Demography* 8:37-48.

Clinard, M. B. and J. W. Elder. 1965. "Sociology in India: A Study in the Sociology of Knowledge." *American Sociological Review* 30:581-87.

Coleman, J. 1966. *Equality of Educational Opportunity.* Washington, D.C.: U.S. Office of Education.

Cornelius. W. A. 1975. *Politics and the Migrant Poor in Mexico City.* Stanford: Stanford University Press.

Cottrell, F. 1960. "The Technological and Societal Bases of Aging." In C. Tibbitts, ed., *Handbook of Social Gerontology.* Chicago: University of Chicago Press.

Cowgill, D. O. and L. D. Holmes. 1972. *Aging and Modernization.* New York: Appleton-Century-Crofts.

Cunningham, I. 1972. *Modernity and Academic Performance: A Study of Students in a Puerto Rican High School.* Rio Piedras, Puerto Rico: University of Puerto Rico Press.

Dahlstrom, W. G. and G. S. Welsh. 1960. *An MMPI Handbook.* Minneapolis: University of Minnesota Press.

Davis, K. and J. Blake. 1956. "Social Structure and Fertility: An Analytic Framework." *Economic Development and Cultural Change* 4: 211–14.

Dawson, J. L. M. 1967. "Traditional Versus Western Attitudes in West Africa: The Construction, Validation and Application of a Measuring Device." *British Journal of Social and Clinical Psychology* 6:81–96.

Dawson, J. L. M., H. Law, A. Leung, and R. E. Whitney. 1971. "Scaling Chinese Traditional-Modern Attitudes and the GSR Measurement of 'Important' Versus 'Unimportant' Chinese Concepts." *Journal of Cross-Cultural Psychology* 2:1–27.

Deshmukh, M. B. 1956. "Delhi: A Study of a Floating Migration." In *The Social Implications of Industrialization and Urbanization: Five Studies of Urban Populations of Recent Rural Origin in Cities of Southern Asia.* Calcutta: UNESCO Research Center on Social Implications of Industrialization in Southern Asia.

Deutsch, K. W. 1962. *Nationalism and Social Communication: An Inquiry into the Foundations of Nationality.* Cambridge and New York: M.I.T. Press–John Wiley.

Doob, L. W. 1960. *Becoming More Civilized.* New Haven: Yale University Press.

—— 1967. "Scales for Assaying Psychological Modernization in Africa." *Public Opinion Quarterly* 31:414–21.

Dreeben, R. 1968. *On What is Learned in School.* Reading, Mass.: Addison-Wesley.

Dube, S. C. 1965. "Cultural Problems in the Economic Development of India." In R. N. Bellah, ed., *Religion and Progress in Modern Asia.* New York: Free Press.

Duncan, O. D. 1966. "Methodological Issues in the Analysis of Social Mobility." In N. J. Smelser and S. M. Lipset, eds., *Social Structure and Social Mobility in Economic Development.* Chicago: Aldine.

Durkheim, E. 1951. *Suicide.* Translated by J. A. Spaulding and G. Simpson. Glencoe, Ill.: Free Press.

Eisenstadt, S. N. 1964a. "Breakdown of Modernization." *Economic Development and Cultural Change* 12:345–67.

—— 1964b. "Growth and Diversity." *India Quarterly* 20:17–42.

—— 1967. *Israeli Society.* New York: Basic Books.

—— 1973. *Tradition, Change, and Modernity.* New York: John Wiley.

Eisenstadt, S. N., ed. 1968. *The Protestant Ethic and Modernization.* New York: Basic Books.

Eisenstadt, S. N. and S. Rokkan, eds. 1973. *Building States and Nations*. Beverly Hills: Sage Publications.

Fallers, L. 1963. "Equality, Modernity, and Democracy in the New States." In C. Geertz, ed., *Old Societies and New States: The Quest for Modernity in Asia and Africa*. New York: Free Press.

Fawcett, J. T. 1971. "Attitude Measures in KAP Studies: An Overview and Critique." *Proceedings of a Conference on Psychological Measurement in the Study of Population Problems*. Berkeley: University of California.

Fawcett, J. T. and M. H. Bornstein. 1973. "Modernization, Individual Modernity, and Fertility." In J. T. Fawcett, ed., *Psychological Perspectives on Population*. New York: Basic Books.

French, J. R. P., Jr. 1963. "The Social Environment and Mental Health." *Journal of Social Issues* 19:39–56.

Friedlander, S. and M. Silver. 1970. "A Quantitative Study of the Determinants of Fertility Behavior." *Demography* 4:30–70.

Friedrich, C. J., ed. 1954. *Totalitarianism*. Cambridge: Harvard University Press.

Galtung, J. 1971. *Members of Two Worlds*. New York: Columbia University Press.

Geiger, H. K. 1969. *National Development 1776–1966: A Selective and Annotated Guide to the Most Important Articles in English*. Metuchen, N.J.: Scarecrow Press.

Gibaja, R. E. 1967–68. "Actitudes Hacia la Familia Entre Obreros Industriales Argentinos." *Revista Latino-americana de Sociologia* 3:411–32.

Goldscheider, C. 1971. *Population, Modernization and Social Structure*. Boston: Little, Brown.

Goode, W. J. 1963. *World Revolution and Family Patterns*. Glencoe, Ill.: Free Press.

Goodenough, W. H. 1963. *An Anthropological Approach to Community Development*. New York: Russel Sage Foundation.

Guilford, J. P. 1956. *Fundamental Statistics in Psychology and Education*, 3rd ed. New York: McGraw-Hill.

Gurin, G., J. Veroff, and S. Feld. 1960. *Americans View Their Mental Health: A Nationwide Interview Study*. New York: Basic Books.

Gusfield, J. 1967. "Tradition and Modernity: Misplaced Polarities in the Study of Social Change." *American Journal of Sociology* 72:351–62.

Guthrie, G. M. 1970. *The Psychology of Modernization in the Rural Philippines*. Quezon City: Ateneo de Manila University Press.

Hagen, E. E. 1962. *On the Theory of Social Change*. Homewood, Ill.: Dorsey Press.

—— 1976. "Becoming Modern: The Dangers of Research Governed by Preconceptions." *History of Childhood Quarterly* 3:411–21.

Hall, J. W. 1965. "Changing Conceptions of the Modernization of Japan." In M. B. Jansen, ed., *Changing Japanese Attitudes Towards Modernization*. Princeton: Princeton University Press.

Halpern, J. 1967. *The Changing Village Community*. Englewood Cliffs, N.J.: Prentice-Hall.

Harbison, F. and C. A. Myers. 1964. *Education, Manpower and Economic Growth: Strategies of Human Resource Development*. New York: McGraw-Hill.

Harlan, W. H. 1964. "Social Status of the Aged in Three Indian Villages." *Vita Humana* 7:239–52.

Heer, D. M. 1966. "Economic Development and Fertility." *Demography* 3:423-44.

Heer, D. M. and E. Turner. 1965. "Areal Differences in Latin American Fertility." *Population Studies* 18:279-92.

Hill, R., J. M. Stycos, and K. Back. 1959. *The Family and Population Control: A Puerto Rican Experiment in Social Change*. Chapel Hill: University of North Carolina Press.

Hollander, G. D. 1972. *Soviet Political Indoctrination*. New York: Praeger.

Holsinger, D. B. 1972. "The Elementary School as an Early Socializer of Modern Values." Ph.D dissertation, Stanford University. Partially published in Holsinger (1973).

―― 1973. "The Elementary School as a Modernizer: A Brazilian Study." *International Journal of Comparative Sociology* 14: 180-202.

Huntington, S. P. 1966. "Political Modernization: America vs. Europe." *World Politics* 18: 378-415.

―― 1968. *Political Order in Changing Societies*. New Haven: Yale University Press.

Husain, A. F. A. 1956. *Human and Social Impact of Technological Change in Pakistan*. A report on a survey conducted by the University of Dacca and published with the assistance of UNESCO. Dacca: Oxford University Press.

―― 1963. "Dacca: Human and Social Impact of Technological Change in East Pakistan." In *Social Implications of Industrialization and Urbanization: Five Studies of Urban Populations of Recent Rural Origin in Cities of Southern Asia*. Calcutta: UNESCO Research Center on Social Implications of Industrialization in Southern Asia.

Husain, A. F. A. and A. Farouk. 1963. *Social Integration of Industrial Workers in Khulna*. Dacca: Bureau of Economic Research, University of Dacca.

Husen, T. 1972. "Does Time in School Make a Difference?" *Saturday Review* 55:32-35.

Imtiaz, A. 1966. "Note on Sociology of India." *The American Sociologist* 1:244-47.

India. 1961. *The Census of India* 4:23. Bihar.

Inkeles, A. 1950. *Public Opinion in Soviet Russia*. Cambridge: Harvard University Press.

―― 1960. "Industrial Man: The Relation of Status to Experience, Perception, and Value." *American Journal of Sociology* 66:1-31.

―― 1966. "The Modernization of Man." In Myron Weiner, ed., *Modernization: The Dynamics of Growth*. New York: Basic Books.

―― 1968. *Social Change in Soviet Russia*. Cambridge: Harvard University Press.

―― 1969a. "Making Men Modern: On the Causes and Consequences of Individual Change in Six Developing Countries." *American Journal of Sociology* 75:208-25.

―― 1969b. "Participant Citizenship in Six Developing Countries." *American Political Science Review* 63:1120-41.

―― 1969c. "Harvard Project on the Sociocultural Aspects of Development." *Sociological Inquiry* 39:100-112.

―― 1971a. "Continuity and Change in the Interaction of the Personal and the Sociocultural System." In B. Barber and A. Inkeles, eds., *Stability and Social Change*. Boston: Little, Brown.

—— 1971b. "Fieldwork Problems in Comparative Research on Modernization." In A. R. Desai, ed., *Essays on Modernization of Underdeveloped Societies*, vol. 2. Bombay, India: Thacker.

—— 1972. "National Character and Modern Political Systems." In F. L. K. Hsu, ed., *Psychological Anthropology*, new edition. Cambridge: Schenkman.

——1973a. "A Model of the Modern Man: Theoretical and Methodological Issues," In Nancy Hammond, ed., *Social Science and the New Societies: Problems in Cross-Cultural Research and Theory Building*. East Lansing: Social Science Research Bureau, Michigan State University.

—— 1973b. "The Role of Occupational Experience." In C. S. Brembeck and T. J. Thompson, eds., *New Strategies for Educational Development*. Lexington, Mass.: D.C. Heath.

—— 1973c. "The School as Context for Modernization." In *International Journal of Comparative Sociology* 14: 163–78.

—— 1975. "Becoming Modern: Individual Change in Six Developing Countries." *Ethos* 3:323–42.

—— 1976a. "Remaining Orthodox: A Rejoinder to Everett Hagen's Review-Essay of Becoming Modern." *History of Childhood Quarterly* 3:422–37.

—— 1976b. "Social Structure and Individual Change: Evidence from Modernity Research." In G. Chu, S. A. Rahim, and D. L. Kincaid, eds., *Communications for Group Transformation in Development*. Communications Monograph no. 2. Honolulu: East-West Communication Institute, East-West Center.

—— 1976c. "The Modernization of Man in Socialist and Nonsocialist Countries." In M. G. Fields, ed., *Social Consequences of Modernization in Communist Societies*. Baltimore: Johns Hopkins Press.

—— 1976d. "Understanding and Misunderstanding Individual Modernity." In L. A. Coser and O. Larsen, eds., *The Uses of Controversy in Sociology*. New York: Free Press.

—— 1977a. "Rising Expectations: Revolution, Evolution, or Devolution." In H. R. Bowen, ed., *Freedom and Control in a Democratic Society*. New York: American Council of Life Insurance.

—— 1977b. "Individual Modernity in Different Ethnic and Religious Groups: Data from a Six-Nation Study." In L. L. Adler, ed., *Issues in Cross-Cultural Research*. *Annals of the New York Academy of Sciences* 285: 539–64.

—— 1978a. "The Future of Individual Modernity." In J. M. Yinger and S. J. Cutler, eds., *Major Social Issues: A Multidisciplinary View*. New York: Free Press.

—— 1978b. "National Differences in Individual Modernity." In R. F. Tommason, ed., *Comparative Studies in Sociology*. Greenwich, Conn.: JAI Press.

Inkeles, A. and R. A. Bauer. 1959. *The Soviet Citizen*. Cambridge: Harvard University Press.

Inkeles, A., E. Hanfmann, and H. Beier. 1958. "Modal Personality and Adjustment to the Soviet Socio-Political System." *Human Relations* 11:3–22.

Inkeles, A. and D. B. Holsinger. 1973. "Education and Individual Modernity in Developing Countries." *International Journal of Comparative Sociology* 14:157–62.

Inkeles, A. and D. J. Levinson. 1969. "National Character." In G. Lindzey and

E. Aronson, eds., *The Handbook of Social Psychology*, 2d ed., vol. 4. Chicago: Aldine.

Inkeles, A. and K. A. Miller. 1974. "Construction and Validation of a Cross-National Scale of Family Modernism." *International Journal of Sociology of the Family* 4:127–47.

Inkeles, A. and P. Rossi. 1956. "National Comparisons of Occupational Prestige." *American Journal of Sociology* 61:329–39.

Inkeles, A. and A. K. Singh. 1968. "A Cross-Cultural Measure of Modernity and Some Popular Indian Images." *Journal of General and Applied Psychology* (Bihar Psychological Association, Ranchi-Patna, India) 1:33–43.

Inkeles, A. and D. H. Smith. 1970. "The Fate of Personal Adjustment in the Process of Modernization." *International Journal of Comparative Sociology* 11:81–114.

—— 1974. *Becoming Modern: Individual Change in Six Developing Countries*. Cambridge: Harvard University Press.

—— 1976. "Personal Adjustment and Modernization." In G. A. DeVos, ed., *Responses to Change*, pp. 214–33. New York: D. Van Nostrand.

Janowitz, B. S. 1971. "An Empirical Study of the Effects of Socioeconomic Development on Fertility Rates." *Demography* 8:319–34.

Johnson, M. 1973. "A Comment on Palmore and Whittington's Index of Similarity." *Social Forces* 51:490–92.

Johnston, J. 1972. *Econometric Methods*, 2d ed. New York: McGraw-Hill.

Kahl, J. 1968. *The Measurement of Modernism: A Study of Values in Brazil and Mexico*. Austin: University of Texas Press.

Kasl, S. V. and J. P. R., French, Jr. 1962. "The Effects of Occupational Status on Physical and Mental Health." *Journal of Social Issues* 19:67–89.

Keller, A. B., J. H. Sims, W. E. Henry, and T. J. Crawford. 1970. "Psychological sources of 'Resistance' to Family Planning." *Merrill-Palmer Quarterly* 16:286–302.

Kerr, C., J. T. Dunlop, F. H. Harbison, and C. A. Meyers. 1960. *Industrialism and Industrial Man*. Cambridge: Harvard University Press.

Kirk, D. 1966. "Factors Affecting Moslem Natality." In B. Berelson, ed., *Family Planning and Population Programs: A Review of World Developments*, Chicago: University of Chicago Press.

—— 1971a. "A New Demographic Transition?" In *Rapid Population Growth: Consequences and Policy Implications*, vol. 2. National Academy of Sciences. Baltimore: Johns Hopkins University Press.

—— 1971b. "The Effectiveness of Family Planning Programs in Less Developed Countries: The Evidence from Survey Data." *Food Research Institute Studies in Agricultural Economics, Trade, and Development* 10(1).

—— 1971c. "Some Reflections of a Sociologist-Demographer on the Need for Psychological Skills in Family Planning Research." *Proceedings of a Conference on Psychological Measurement in the Study of Population Problems*. Berkeley: University of California.

Kirk, D. and K. S. Srikantan. 1969. "Correlates of Natality in Countries of the Latin American Region." Unpublished manuscript, Stanford University.

Kirscht, J. P. and R. C. Dillehay. 1967. *Dimensions of Authoritarianism: A Review of Research and Theory*. Lexington: University of Kentucky Press.

Klineberg, S. L. 1973. "Parents, Schools, and Modernity: An Exploratory Investigation of Sex Differences in the Attitudinal Development of Tunisian Adolescents." *International Journal of Comparative Sociology* 14:221–44.

Kohn, M. L. and C. Schooler. 1973. "Occupational Experience and Psychological Functioning: An Assessment of Reciprocal Effects." *American Sociological Review* 38:97–118.

Kornhauser, A. 1965. *Mental Health of the Industrial Worker*. New York: John Wiley.

Kuznets, S. 1966. *Modern Economic Growth: Rate, Structure, and Spread*. New Haven: Yale University Press.

Lakra, E. 1963. "A Comparative Study of Occupational Choice of Tribal and non-Tribal College Students." Master's thesis, Patna University, India.

Lambert, R. D. 1963. *Workers, Factories, and Social Changes in India*. Princeton: Princeton University Press.

Landsberger, H. and A. Saavedra. 1967. "Response Set in Developing Countries." *Public Opinion Quarterly* 31:214–29.

Lawrence, W. W. 1965. "Occupations and Attitudes in Hazard, Kentucky." Unpublished Senior Honors thesis. Department of Social Relations, Harvard College.

Leighton, A. T., T. A. Lambo, C. C. Hughes, D. C. Leighton, J. M. Murphy, and D. B. Macklon. 1963. *Psychiatric Disorder among the Yoruba: A Report from the Cornell-Aro Mental Health Project in the Western Region, Nigeria*. Ithaca: Cornell University Press.

Leites, N. 1951. *The Operational Code of the Politburo*. New York: McGraw-Hill.

Lenin, V. I. 1929. *What Is To Be Done? Burning Questions of Our Movement*. New York.: International Publishers.

Lerner, D. 1958. *The Passing of Traditional Society: Modernizing the Middle East*. Glencoe, Ill.: Free Press.

LeVine, R. A. 1966. *Dreams and Deeds: Achievement Motivation in Nigeria*. Chicago: University of Chicago Press.

—— 1973. *Culture, Behavior, and Personality*. Chicago: Aldine.

Levinson, D. J. and P. E. Huffman. 1955. "Traditional Family Ideology and its Relation to Personality." *Journal of Personality* 23:251–73.

Levy, M. J., Jr. 1952. *Modernization and the Structure of Society*, 2 vols. Princeton: Princeton University Press.

Lewis, O. 1952. "Urbanization Without Breakdown: A Case Study." *Scientific Monthly* 75:31–42.

Lipman, A. 1970. "Prestige of the Aged in Portugal: Realistic Appraisal and Ritualistic Deference." *International Journal of Aging and Development* 1:127–36.

Lipset, S. M. 1960. *Political Man*. New York: Doubleday.

Lueschen, G., R. O. Blood, M. Lewis, Z. Staikof, V. Stolte-Heiskanen, and C. Ward. 1971. "Family Organization, Interaction, and Ritual: A Cross Cultural Study in Bulgaria, Finland, Germany, and Ireland." *Journal of Marriage and the Family* 33:228–34.

McClelland, D. 1961. *The Achieving Society*. Princeton: D. Van Nostrand.

McClosky, H. 1967. "Personality and Attitude Correlates of Foreign Policy

Orientation." In J. N. Rosenau, ed., *Domestic Sources of Foreign Policy*. New York: Free Press.

McClosky, H. and J. Schaar. 1965. "Psychological Dimensions of Anomie." *American Sociological Review* 30:14-39.

Manaster, G. J. and R. J. Havighurst. 1972. *Cross-National Research: Social Psychological Methods and Problems*. Boston: Houghton Mifflin.

Marsh, R. M. and A. R. O'Hara. 1961. "Attitudes Toward Marriage and the Family in Taiwan." *American Journal of Sociology* 67:1-8.

Marshall, A. 1946. *Principles of Economics*, 8th ed. London: Macmillan.

Marshall, T. H. 1964. *Class, Citizenship, and Social Development*. New York: Doubleday.

Maxwell, R. J. 1970. "The Changing Status of Elderly in a Polynesian Society." *International Journal of Aging and Human Development* 1:127-46.

Mead, M. 1951. *Soviet Attitudes Toward Authority*. New York: McGraw-Hill.

—— 1956. *New Lives for Old*. New York: William Morrow.

Meyer, J., M. Hannan, and R. Rubinson. 1973. "National Economic Development 1950-1965: Educational and Political Factors." Paper presented at a Southeast Asian Development Advisory Group (Seadag) Seminar on Education and Development, Singapore.

Miller, K. A. and A. Inkeles. 1974. "Modernity and Acceptance of Family Limitation in Four Developing Countries." *Journal of Social Issues* 30:167-88.

Monnerot, J. 1953. *Sociology and Psychology of Communism*. Boston: Beacon Press.

Moore, W. E. 1951. *Industrialization and Labor*. Ithaca: Cornell University Press.

—— 1963. "The Strategy of Fostering Performance and Responsibility." In E. de Vries and J. M. Echavarria, eds., *Social Aspects of Economic Development in Latin America*, vol. 1. Medina: UNESCO.

Murphy, H. B. M. 1961. "Social Change and Mental Health." *Milbank Memorial Fund Quarterly* 39:385-445.

Nash, M. 1968. *Machine Age Maya*. Glencoe, Ill.: Free Press.

Neal, A. G. and S. Retting. 1963. "Dimensions of Alienation Among Manual and Non-Manual Workers." *American Sociological Review* 28:599-608.

Nelson, J. M. 1969. "Migrants, Urban Poverty, and Instability in Developing Nations." *Occasional Papers in International Affairs*, no. 22. Harvard University: Center for International Affairs.

Ogburn, W. F. and M. T. Nimkoff. 1940, 1958. *Sociology*, 3rd ed. Boston: Houghton Mifflin.

Oloko, O. 1970. "Some Social and Psychological Factors Affecting Commitment to Industrial Employment in Nigeria." Ph.D. dissertation, Harvard University.

Palmore, E. B. 1975. "The Status and Integration of the Aged in Japanese Society." *Journal of Gerontology* 30:199-208.

Palmore, E. B. and K. Manton. 1974. "Modernization and Status of the Aged: International Correlations." *Journal of Gerontology* 29:205-10.

Palmore, E. B. and F. Whittington. 1971. "Trends in the Relative Status of the Aged." *Social Forces* 50:84-91.

——1973. "Reply to Johnson." *Social Forces* 51:492-93.

Pandey, R. S. 1971. "Socialization and Social Policy in Modernizing Society." Ph.D dissertation, Florence Heller Graduate School for Advanced Studies in Social Welfare, Brandeis University.

Parrinder, G. 1953. "Religion in Village and Town." In *Proceedings of the Annual Conference, Sociology Section.* Ibadan, Nigeria: West African Institute of Social and Economic Research, University College.

Parsons, T. 1943. "The Kinship System of the Contemporary United States." *American Anthropologist* 45.

—— 1951. *The Social System.* New York: Free Press.

Pool, I. D. 1963. "The Role of Communication in the Process of Modernization and Technological Change." In B. F. Hoselitz and W. E. Moore, eds., *Industrialization and Society.* Paris: UNESCO.

Population Council. 1970. *A Manual for Surveys of Fertility and Family Planning: Knowledge, Attitudes, and Practice.* New York: Population Council.

Portes, A. 1973a. "The Factorial Structure of Modernity: Empirical Replication and a Critique." *American Journal of Sociology* 79:15-36.

—— 1973b. "Modernity and Development: A Critique." *Studies in Comparative International Development* 8:247-79.

Przeworski, A. and H. Teune. 1970. *The Logic of Comparative Social Inquiry.* New York: John Wiley.

Pye, L. W. 1962. *Politics, Personality and Nation Building.* New Haven: Yale University Press.

Pye, L. W. and S. Verba eds. 1965. *Political Culture and Political Development.* Princeton: Princeton University Press.

Ridley, C. P., P. H. Godwin, and D. J. Doolin. 1971. *The Making of a Model Citizen in Communist China.* Stanford: Hoover Institution Press.

Riesman, D., in collaboration with R. Denney and N. Glazer. 1950. *The Lonely Crowd: A Study of the Changing American Character.* New Haven: Yale University Press.

Riley, M. W. 1963. *Sociological Research: I, A Case Approach.* New York: Harcourt, Brace & World.

Riley, M. W. and E. E. Nelson. 1971. "Research on Stability and Change in Social Systems." In B. Barber and A. Inkeles, eds., *Stability and Social Change.* Boston: Little, Brown.

Robinson, W. S. 1950. "Ecological Correlations and the Behavior of Individuals." *American Sociological Review* 15:351-57.

Rogers, E., in association with L. Svennig. 1969. *Modernization Among Peasants.* New York: Holt, Rinehart & Winston.

Rosen, B. C. and A. L. la Raia. 1972. "Modernity in Women: An Index of Social Change in Brazil." *Journal of Marriage and the Family* 34:353-60.

Rosen, B. C. and A. B. Simmons. 1971. "Industrialization, Family, and Fertility: A Structural-Psychological Analysis of the Brazilian Case." *Demography* 8:49-69.

Roy, P., F. B. Waisanen, and E. M. Rogers. 1969. *The Impact of Communication on Rural Development; an Investigation in Costa Rica and India.* Hyderabad: UNESCO (Paris) and National Institute of Community Development.

Rudolph, L. I. and S. H. Rudolph. 1967. *The Modernity of Tradition.* Chicago: University of Chicago Press.

Russet, B. M., H. R. Alker, K. W. Deutsch, and H. D. Lasswell. 1964. *World Handbook of Political and Social Indicators*. New Haven: Yale University Press.

Ryan, E. [n.d.] "Field Director's Report for Nigeria." Unpublished report for the Harvard Project on Social and Cultural Aspects of Economic Development, Department of Social Relations, Harvard University.

Ryder, N. B. and C. F. Westoff. 1969. "Fertility Planning Status: United States, 1965." *Demography* 6:435-44.

Sack, R. 1973. "The Impact of Education on Individual Modernity in Tunisia." *International Journal of Comparative Sociology* 14:245-72.

Safilios-Rothschild, C. 1970. "Toward a Cross-Cultural Conceptualization of Family Modernity." *Journal of Comparative Family Studies* 1:17-25.

Samuelsson, K. 1961. *Religion and Economic Action: A Critique of Max Weber*. New York: Basic Books.

Scheler, M. 1961. *Ressentiment*. New York: Free Press.

Schnaiberg, A. 1970. "Measuring Modernism: Theoretical and Empirical Exploration." *American Journal of Sociology* 76:399-425.

—— 1971. "The Modernizing Impact of Urbanization: A Causal Analysis." *Economic Development and Cultural Change* 20:80-104.

Schuman, H. 1966a. "The Random Probe: A Technique for Evaluating the Validity of Closed Questions." *American Sociological Review* 31:218-23.

—— 1966b. "Social Change and the Validity of Regional Stereotypes in East Pakistan." *Sociometry* 29: 428-40.

—— 1967. "Economic Development and Individual Change: A Social Psychological Study of the Comilla Experiment in Pakistan." *Occasional Papers in International Affairs*, no. 15. Harvard University: Center for International Affairs.

Schuman, H., A. Inkeles, and D. H. Smith. 1967. Some Social Psychological Effects and Noneffects of Literacy in a New Nation." *Economic Development and Cultural Change* 16:1-14.

Scotch, N. A. and H. J. Geiger. 1963-64. "An Index of Symptom and Disease in Zulu Culture." *Human Organization* 22:304-11.

Scott, W. A. 1958. "Research Definitions of Mental Health and Mental Illness." *Psychological Bulletin* 55:29-45.

Searle, S. R. 1971. *Linear Models*. New York: John Wiley.

Seeman, M. 1959. "On the Meaning of Alineation." *American Sociological Review* 24:783-91.

Sen, L. K. and P. Roy, 1966. *Awareness of Community Development in Village India*. Preliminary Report. Hyderabad: National Institute of Community Development.

Sewell, W. H. and R. M. Hauser. 1975. *Education, Occupation and Earnings: Achievement in the Early Career*. New York: Academic Press.

Shaw, M. E. and J. M. Wright. 1967. *Scales for Measurement of Attitudes*. New York: McGraw-Hill.

Silvert, K. H. 1961. *Reaction and Revolution in Latin America*. New Orleans: Hauser Press.

Simmons, L. W. 1945. *The Role of the Aged in Primitive Society*. New Haven: Yale University Press.

Singer, M. 1966a. "The Modernization of Religious Beliefs." In M. Weiner, ed., *Modernization: The Dynamics of Growth*. New York: Basic Books.

—— 1966b. "Religion and Social Change in India: The Max Weber Thesis, Phase Three." *Economic Development and Cultural Change* 15:497-505.

—— 1971. "Beyond Tradition and Modernity in Madras." *Comparative Studies in Society and History* 13:160-95.

Singh, A. K. 1963. *Indian Students in Britain*. Bombay, India: Asia Publishing House.

—— 1967. "Hindu Culture and Economical Development in India." *Conspectus* (Quarterly Journal of the India International Centre), March, pp. 9-32.

—— [n.d.] *"Industrialization, Modernization, and Economic Development in India."* Unpublished manuscript. Mimeographed.

Singh, A.K., ed. [n.d.] *"Modernization of India: Studies on Sociocultural Aspects."* Unpublished manuscript. Mimeographed.

Slater, P. E. 1964. "Cross-Cultural Views of the Aged." In R. Kastenbaum, ed., *New Thoughts on Old Age*. New York: Springer.

Slotkin, J. S. 1960. *From Field to Factory: The New Industrial Employees*. Glencoe, Ill.: Free Press.

Smith, D. H. 1967. "Correcting for Social Desirability Response Sets in Opinion-Attitude Survey Research." *Public Opinion Quarterly* 31:87-94.

—— 1969. "Factory Experience and the Sense of Efficacy: Results from a Six-Nation Survey." *Proceedings of the 77th Annual Convention of the American Psychological Association* 4:589-90. Washington, D.C.: American Psychological Association.

Smith, D. H. and A. Inkeles. 1966. "The OM Scale: A Comparative Socio-Psychological Measure of Individual Modernity." *Sociometry* 29:353-77.

—— 1975. "Individual Modernizing Experiences and Psycho-Social Modernity: Validation of the OM Scacles in Six Developing Countries." *International Journal of Comparative Sociology* 16:157-73.

Sorokin, P. A. 1957. *The Crisis of Our Age: The Social and Cultural Outlook*. New York: E. P. Dutton.

Srole, L. et al. 1962. *Mental Health in the Metropolis*. New York: McGraw-Hill.

Stephenson, J. B. 1968. "Is Everyone Going Modern? A Critique and a Suggestion for Measuring Modernism." *American Journal of Sociology* 74:265-75.

Stewart, O. C. 1952. "Southern Ute Adjustment to Modern Living." In S. Tax, ed., *Acculturation in the Americas*, vol. 2. *Proceedings, Twenty-Ninth International Congress of Americanists*. Chicago: University of Chicago Press.

Stouffer, S. A. et al. 1949. *The American Soldier: Adjustment During Army Life: Studies in Social Psychology in World War II*, vol. 1. Princeton: Princeton University Press.

Stycos, J. M. 1968. *Human Fertility in Latin America: Sociological Perspectives*. Ithaca: Cornell University Press.

Stycos, J. M. and K. W. Back. 1964. *The Control of Human Fertility in Jamaica*. Ithaca: Cornell University Press.

Sussman, M. B. 1965. "Relationship of Adult Children With Their Parents in the United States." In E. Shanas and G. Streip, eds., *Social Structure and the Family: Generational Relations*. Englewood Cliffs, N.J.: Prentice-Hall.

Sussman, M. B. and M. Brooks. 1972. "Comparative Family Research: A Nine-Nation Study." Paper presented at the Conference on "Methodological and Theoretical Issues in Comparative Family and Fertility Research" by the Institute for Comparative Sociology, Colombus, Ohio.

Suzman, R. 1973a. "The Modernization of Personality." Ph.D. dissertation, Harvard University. Partially published in Suzman (1973b).

—— 1973b. "Psychological Modernity." *International Journal of Comparative Sociology* 14:273–87.

Tumin, M. and A. S. Feldman. 1961. *Social Class and Social Change in Puerto Rico.* Princeton: Princeton University Press.

United Nations. 1964. *Statistical Yearbook.* 16th issue. New York.

Verba, S., B. Ahmed, and A. Bhatt. 1971. *Caste, Race, and Politics.* Beverly Hills: Sage Publications.

Verba, S., B. Ahmed, A. Bhatt, N. H. Nie, and J. Kim. 1971. *The Modes of Democratic Participation: A Cross-National Comparison.* Beverly Hills: Sage Publications.

Wallerstein, I. 1976. "Modernization: Requiescat in Pace." In L. A. Coser and O. N. Larsen, eds., New York: Free Press.

Ward, R. E. and D. A. Rustow, eds. 1964. *Political Modernization in Japan and Turkey.* Princeton: Princeton University Press.

Weber, M. 1947. *The Theory of Social and Economic Organization.* New York: Oxford University Press.

—— 1963. *The Sociology of Religion.* Translated by E. Fischoff. Boston: Beacon Press.

—— 1969. *Protestantism and the Rise of Capitalism.* Translated by T. Parsons. New York: Charles Scribner's Sons.

Weiner, M., ed. 1966. *Modernization: The Dynamics of Growth.* New York: Basic Books.

Weintraub, R. 1962. "The Birthrate and Economic Development." *Econometrica* 40:812–17.

Westoff, C. F., R. G. Potter, and P. C. Sagi, 1963. *The Third Child.* Princeton: Princeton University Press.

White, M. and L. White. 1962. *The Intellectual Versus the City: From Thomas Jefferson to Frank Lloyd Wright.* Cambridge: Harvard University Press.

Willems, E. 1967. *Followers of the New Faith.* Nashville: Vanderbilt University Press.

Williamson, J. B. 1969. "Subjective Efficacy as an Aspect of Modernization in Six Developing Nations." Ph.D. dissertation, Harvard University.

—— 1970. "Subjective Efficacy and Ideal Family Size as Predictors of Favorability Toward Birth Control." *Demography* 7:329–39.

Woodward, J. L. and E. Roper. 1956. "Political Activity of American Citizens." In H. Eulau, S. J. Eldersveld, and M. Janowitz, eds., *Political Behavior.* Glencoe, Ill.: Free Press.

Yaukey, D. 1961. *Fertility Differences in a Modernizing Country: A Survey of Lebanese Couples.* Princeton: Princeton University Press.

Index

Abeokuta Yoruba in Nigeria, 261
Achebe, Chinua, 305
Achieving Society, The, 26
Active citizenship, *see* Participant Citizenship
Adams, Henry, 258
Adaptation, 260-61
Adelman, Irma, 207
Adjustment, *see* Mental health; Psychic adjustment
Adult socialization, *see* Late socialization
Advanced industrial societies, and individual modernity, 124
Africa: religion in, 43; tribal, 229; psychic adjustment, 267; and modern organization in, 317; *see also* Nigeria; Yoruba people
Aged persons, 44; attitudes toward, 191; status of, 279, 280-81; and individual modernity, 320
Agriculture: in Communist China, 304; and economy, 114
Agricultural cooperatives, 19; and family planning, 212
Agricultural life: and psychic adjustment, 21; and factory compared, 67, 104; and change, 117
Ainu of Japan, 314
Aldous, J., 188
Alienation, 8, 9, 22, 23; and politics, 231-32, 237; *see also* Anomie
Allegiance, political, 233, 238
Allport and Vernon Test of Values, 60
Almond, Gabriel A., 21, 22, 230, 232 (quoted), 236-37, 244 (quoted)
America, *see* United States
American citizen, 230-31

Americans View Their Mental Health, 261
Amin, Idi, 322
Analytical model of modern man, 227; *see also* Modern man
Anomie, 236, 238, 241, 253, 257, 325n; *see also* Alienation
Anti-authoritarianism, 312-13
Antimodern tendencies, 315
Antioquenos of Columbia, 18
Appalachians in United States, 314
Argentina, 8, 15, 18, 32, 77, 174-75; and political ideology, 22; and mass media, 68; and urbanization, 69; sample in, 83; ethnicity and religion in, 140, 155-57, 163; traditionalism in, 161; International Modernity Scale in, 171; and nationality, 178; schooling in, 179; and Westernization, 179; and nationalism, 181; and family research, 195-96, 200; and birth control, 214; Allegiance Scale in, 238; migration in, 245; and radicalism, 246; and participant citizenship, 251; and Psychosomatic Symptoms Test, 264; and the aged, 281-82, 284, 287
Armer Michael, 7, 14, 22, 290
Asia, 317; religions in, 43; emigration from, 140, 150, 152
Aspiration, 191
Athens, family study in, 190
Attitudes, 330n; and education, 103; and microstructural influences, 115; and behavior, 124; Indian, 131; in family realm, 196-98; and birth control, 208-12; in political realm, 233, and social system, 309; *see also* separate entries such as Efficacy, Modernity